Catholic police officers in Northern Ireland

MANCHESTER
1824

Manchester University Press

Catholic police officers in Northern Ireland

Voices out of silence

MARY GETHINS

Manchester
University Press
Manchester and New York

distributed in the United States exclusively
by PALGRAVE MACMILLAN

Copyright © Mary Gethins 2011

The right of Mary Gethins to be identified as the author of this work has been
asserted by her in accordance with the Copyright, Designs and Patents Act 1988.

Published by Manchester University Press
Oxford Road, Manchester M13 9NR, UK
and Room 400, 175 Fifth Avenue, New York, NY 10010, USA
www.manchesteruniversitypress.co.uk

Distributed in the United States exclusively by
Palgrave Macmillan, 175 Fifth Avenue,
New York, NY 10010, USA

Distributed in Canada exclusively by
UBC Press, University of British Columbia, 2029 West Mall,
Vancouver, BC, Canada V6T 1Z2

British Library Cataloguing-in-Publication Data is available

Library of Congress Cataloging-in-Publication Data is available

ISBN 978 0 7190 8743 1 paperback

First published by Manchester University Press in hardback 2011

This paperback edition first published 2013

The publisher has no responsibility for the persistence or accuracy of URLs for any external or
third-party internet websites referred to in this book, and does not guarantee that any content
on such websites is, or will remain, accurate or appropriate.

Printed by Lightning Source

Dedication

In memory of my parents, Elizabeth and William,
who brought me up – in Northern Ireland – to respect
the sincerely held religious and political principles
of people from all traditions,
while maintaining developmental fidelity
to my own.

Contents

List of tables   ix
Preface   xi
List of abbreviations   xv

Introduction   1

1   Historical overview   9
2   Digging for treasure   37
3   Speaking from experience: retired officers   54
4   Veterans but still serving officers   84
5   More of the same? PSNI trainees   137
6   The verdict on Patten   155
7   Looking back and looking forward   183

Appendices
1   Questionnaire and quantitative analysis: tables   221
2   Interview guide   240
3   Confidentiality agreement and the terms and conditions of access to
    the RUC for research purposes   243

Bibliography   246

List of tables

1	Summary characteristics of the survey sample	48
2	Typology categories applied to serving officers and trainees	233
3	Religion of respondents, partners and parents	233
4	Certainty of belief in God: Catholic police officers and the general Catholic population of NI	233
5	Patterns of church attendance comparing Catholic officers and the Catholic population	234
6	Types of schools attended by officers and their children	234
7	Highest education qualifications compared	235
8	Perceived social-class profiles of officers' neighbourhoods	235
9	Percentage of Catholic officers' neighbours perceived to be Catholic	235
10	Catholic officers' employment experience before joining the RUC	236
11	Catholic officers' distribution of ranks	236
12	Most important reasons for officers joining the RUC	236
13	Level of encouragement from Catholics to a close relative wishing to join the police	237
14	Self-reported political ideology and extent to which it was shared with their family	237
15	(a) Sources of opposition; (b) Strength of opposition	237
16	Officers' descriptions of police cultures	238
17	Views on Patten's recommendations related to length of service	238
18	Officers' perception of PSNI success in Catholic recruitment	238
19	Catholic officers' perceptions of community commonality	239
20	Respondents' constitutional preferences compared with those of NI Catholics	239
21	Police treatment of civilians: comparison	239

Preface

I owe warm thanks to a number of people who have helped me along the road towards completion of this book. First, let me thank my colleagues from the past, Don Cooper, Open University, and the late Val Rice, Trinity College Dublin, for convincing me that my topic was worth researching. My sincere gratitude goes to John Brewer, the main supervisor of my doctoral research on which this book is based, for his support throughout the process and to Karen McElrath, Tony Glendenning, Ciaran Acton, Patricia Devine, Dirk Schubotz and Ronnie Rainey for their advice at various points along the academic way.

Without the ready permission of the last Chief Constable of the RUC, Sir Ronnie Flanagan during his final days in office, this research might well have been delayed. I thank, in particular, Christine Marks for expediting administrative arrangements on behalf of the senior RUC team and, very importantly, my referee, Sam McBrien, for convincing the decision-makers that granting me access was a risk worth taking. The energetic cooperation and professionalism shown in the early stages by successive liaison officers Joe Crawford, John McCaughan and Wendy Middleton, I thank and admire. The unfailing support of the librarian at the Police College, David Linton, was unstinting. Whenever I approached him – and that was often – he cheerfully accepted a challenge as an opportunity to demonstrate skilful service. To staff of the Police Service of Northern Ireland (PSNI) – police officers and civilians – Joe Stewart, Roy Fleming, Karen Porter, Alan McConnell, Ursula Merrick, Jim McCrudden, Paul McIlwaine, Tony Matheson and Steven Reid I record my thanks for smoothing my path in myriad ways.

Initially Rosemary Cavill, then Michelle McGaughey through no fault of their own, are more knowledgeable than they might have chosen to be, about policing in Northern Ireland. Their expertise has ensured that presentation is of professional standard. To both I offer my since appreciation, especially for their patience. I give my affectionate thanks to Betty and to Dodo (since sadly deceased), who have encouraged, supported and cajoled as necessary throughout this odyssey. I thank also Peter Sheridan, Chief Executive of Cooperation Ireland for reading this book in draft form and for making helpful comment.

Unfortunately, for security reasons, I cannot name the 138 respondents who completed my questionnaire or the seventy brave souls who agreed to be interviewed.

Their contributions have been crucial to the success of my study. I thank them, more than I can say, for their time, their trust and the insights they provided. Their commitment to serving all the people of Northern Ireland made a lasting impression, which guarantees that the PSNI success story will be a subject of enduring interest to me as it unfolds.

This book examines recruitment of the minority Catholic population to the former Royal Ulster Constabulary (RUC) and to the PSNI. This is one of several issues central to the problem of policing the divided society of Northern Ireland in the past and which are central to improvements in police–public relations in the future. Police reform in Northern Ireland was made part of a broader process of political change as a result of the 1998 Belfast Agreement's decision to appoint a Commission, under Chris Patten, former Governor of Hong Kong, to fashion a new police force for a new society and for the first time offered the possibility of root-and-branch reform rather than the piecemeal reform that began with the 1969 Hunt Report. The problematic relationship between the police and Catholic community was seen as part of the difficulty; improved recruitment of Catholics became part of the solution. Several burdens from the past make this no easy solution. The RUC's history and tradition as a colonial police force, the long experience by Catholics of partisan policing, and the high levels of civil unrest that made the police a special focus of attack all complicate the issue of Catholic recruitment. In theoretical terms I try to assess how policing can be transformed from a neo-colonial model into a liberal model by police reform alone, and how far success is contingent upon further social and political change that assists in demilitarising policing.

The seed which produced this book began to germinate when the Patten Report was published in 1999, a follow-up, in policing terms, to the Belfast Agreement of 1998. (An alternative name, favoured by Nationalists, is the Good Friday Agreement.) The British government realised that the RUC presented a huge problem to Catholics in Northern Ireland and, therefore, to the potential success of the power-sharing accord. One of Patten's core recommendations was to increase representation by Catholics in what promised to be a new and vastly different policing organisation.

My thoughts in the aftermath of Patten strayed back to a day when I was about 10 years old. I was enjoying one of many conversations I had with an intelligent and well-schooled elderly woman who talked to me about her life and about modern Irish history. She was obviously very proud to tell me that her father, two brothers and her husband had all served in the Royal Irish Constabulary (RIC), which preceded the RUC and was disbanded when Ireland was partitioned. 'Police provide a very important service', she stressed. 'They're needed in order to keep good people safe from rogues'. She explained that in Irish villages the police were key members of the community, on a par with the priest, the doctor, the vet and the district nurse. She did, however, clarify little for me by alluding to the sad end of the RIC and how 'their own people turned against them and shot them, but it wasn't their [the RIC's] fault that it happened'.

As a schoolgirl and undergraduate in Northern Ireland I acquired some understanding of that lady's words, but was intrigued and saddened that among my Nationalist and Republican-minded peers there was strong anti-police feeling. I was an exile for twenty-five years of the Troubles, unhappily familiar with the media portrayal of atrocities and counter-atrocities and the central role which the RUC played in trying to keep the situation contained. Patten's contention that police reform and social and political change are inextricably linked in Northern Ireland appealed to me as an idea to be pursued. I wanted to set off on an exploratory expedition to find out how far Patten's optimistic suggestions could be realised. Two clear questions formulated in my mind: (a) why was Catholic participation in policing historically so low and (b) would Patten solve the problem?

I see the PSNI as a powerful catalyst for a better Northern Ireland and I want to make a contribution to that future. Catholic police have never before been surveyed as a discrete group (at least, not by independent researchers). This book fills that gap by directly accessing the subjective lives of Catholic policemen and women – past and present.

List of abbreviations

AOH	Ancient Order of Hibernians
CAJ	Committee on the Administration of Justice
CID	Criminal Investigation Department
CIRA	Continuity IRA
DK	'Don't know' [questionnaire response]
DPP	Director of Public Prosecutions; District Policing Partnership
DPPB	District Policing Partnership Board
DUP	Democratic Unionist Party
EC	European Community
FTR	full-time reserve
ICPNI	Independent Commission on Policing for Northern Ireland
IMC	International Monitoring Commission
IRA	Irish Republican Army
MLA	Member of Local Assembly
MSU	mobile support unit
NI	Northern Ireland; Northern Irish
NICRA	Northern Ireland Civil Rights Association
NILT	Northern Ireland Life and Times
NIO	Northern Ireland Office
NIPB	Northern Ireland Policing Board
NISA	Northern Ireland Social Attitudes Survey
PANI	Police Authority of Northern Ireland
PC	politically correct
PSNI	Police Service of Northern Ireland
RIC	Royal Irish Constabulary
RIR	Royal Irish Regiment
RIRA	Real IRA
RUC	Royal Ulster Constabulary
SB	Special Branch
SDLP	Social Democratic and Labour Party
SPSS	Statistical Package for the Social Sciences
TUV	Traditional Ulster Voice

UDA   Ulster Defence Association
UDR   Ulster Defence Regiment
USC   Ulster Special Constabulary
UUP   Ulster Unionist Party

Introduction

I locate this study historically and comparatively by tracing the history of the RIC and RUC in their political and social contexts over a period of 180 years since 1822, in order to establish reasons for Catholic under-representation. Commentators and politicians have given their explanations, but I wanted to correct any misunderstandings and to provide an authoritative analysis.

From my survey I am able to make broad comparisons, using research carried out by others, to compare Catholics who became police officers with the cultural group from which they came. The main findings from the in-depth interviews are presented as a trilogy which traces the experiences, views and attitudes of males and females aged between 22 and 75 years in policing, past and present. Broadly similar questions are addressed in the case of each sample – retired, serving and trainees. First, I explore biographical aspects, motivation for joining and the attitudes of family and peers to their career choice. A second section focuses on life in a work context internal to the organisation as well as relations with the Catholic community, including clergy and Republican activists. Of central interest are the ways in which the role of the Royal Ulster Constabulary (RUC), a pillar of the Unionist Protestant establishment, impacted on the lives of Catholic members and their families. A third theme explores respondents' views of the Patten reforms. A variety of perspectives is provided by Catholic officers who have never served in the Police Service of Northern Ireland (PSNI), by those who have transferred from the RUC to the PSNI, and by those who answered the call to join addressed to Catholics very shortly before I carried out my research.

For me, one of the joys of this book – and I hope there are more than one – is the infinite variety of quotations from the conversations which I conducted with seventy generous men and women, representing three generations, who agreed to talk about sensitive issues and to share some of their pains and their pleasures with a complete stranger. Their contributions, sometimes angry, sometimes amusing, mostly serious and reflective, paint a picture on a huge canvas of their difficult but rewarding collective and individual lives. Using another metaphor, the respondents open up a treasure chest which has, until now, remained locked, its content being only guessed at, anticipated inaccurately, or dismissed by opponents and apologists.

From the content of my interviews with seventy Northern Irish Catholics who have joined the police, I have been able to identify ways in which they are similar to and different from the Catholic community in general. I come to a conclusion that those who join are self-selecting individuals. I find that they tend to come from traditional Catholic homes, family backgrounds and education, but they interpret their Catholicity in divergent ways and have an apparently natural propensity to cross the community divide with ease. The move away from their community inevitably throws up problems which they have to manage.

The ways in which they responded to manage two of their dominant identities, as police officers and Catholics, lead me to consider how my work reported here contributes to sociology. I present a typology inspired by earlier researchers, as another attempt to find clusters within fragmented and fluid identities. These identities I have named flaunters, chameleons, deserters and victims, depending on respondents' descriptions and motivations presented to me. It covers a spectrum from those who enact or react, from those who prosper, to those who merely survive among the challenge they face in their careers. I hope that my typology is plausible and that I have located my work successfully in relating it to current sociological debate in an area where culture and identity meet. It is, I believe, important to engage theoretically with the powerful forces to be found in police culture, challenged by equally powerful constraints and interests supplied by the multiple identities of Catholic police officers.

Finally, one comes full circle to the current, still early, stage in its development which the PSNI has reached and relate it to my practical and theoretical conclusions. Progress made in police reform by the PSNI and its potential to continue and to keep up momentum is measured against the demanding criteria of the liberal model. In particular the question is posed whether the PSNI by its own efforts is capable of embedding a fully developed liberal model, or if progress is contingent upon parallel progress in the social and political domains.

Parameters of the research

The broad topic which I chose to research was police reform in Northern Ireland. There were two related aspects (a) the reasons for under-representation of Catholics in the RUC and (b) the likely success of a 50:50, Catholic:non-Catholic recruitment policy by the PSNI as recommended by the Patten Commission in 1999 in order to redress the balance, thereby testing the viability of the liberal-democratic model of policing in the province. In researching relevant literature to inform my search I adopted an eclectic approach, dictated by the nature and scope of my topic. My purpose was to draw upon several relevant bodies of literature so as to provide a logical framework for my research, which would highlight gaps in extant knowledge and assist me in focusing on specific research questions to be pursued, using appropriate methodology.

It was not until the 1960s that sociologists identified policing as a rich vein to mine. Early American studies (Skolnick, 1966; Westley, 1970) and the pioneering work of Banton (1964) into police culture in Britain were added to by Bittner (1970), Cain (1973, 1979), Manning (1972), Punch (1979, 1985), Reiner (1978). Valuable impetus was given by Banton's biannual seminars at Bristol in the 1970s, where senior police officers and police sociologists came together for the first time in Britain, acting on a dawning realisation that if research – especially of an ethnographic nature – were to be carried out, cooperation, initially in the form of access, was necessary.

Beginning in the 1980s British sociologists identified a clear contrast from post-Second World War consensual policing to confrontational policing caused by change in value systems and assertive expression of hostility to policing tactics by increasing numbers of ethnic minorities. The Home Office and the Metropolitan police establishment were keen to find inspiration from any source – including sociologists – to deal with this growing threat to public order. A prolific team emerged with different or overlapping interests, writing from a variety of ideological perspectives and working backgrounds, including police officers who had become academics. These include: Brogden (1982, 1989, 1995); Brogden and Shearing (1993); Fielding (1988); Holdaway (1983, 1991, 1996); Reiner (1985); Waddington (1991, 1999); Weitzer (1985, 1986).

Other groups of academics providing relevant insights were political scientists (Guelke, 1994; Hillyard, 1997; Hillyard and Tomlinson, 2000; Horowitz, 1994; Lijphart, 1975; McGarry, 2000; McGarry and O'Leary, 1995, 1999; Rose, 1971) who offered alternative explanations for enduring societal division in Northern Ireland and also lawyers and criminologists (Boyle and Hadden, 1994; Committee on the Administration of Justice, 1996; Law Society of England and Wales, 1995).

Though the authors might be described as 'insiders', theses and dissertations by serving and retired RUC officers (Maguire, 1994; McGuigan, 1995; Wiggins, 1998) have provided additional food for thought. Similarly, in relation to the Royal Irish Constabulary (RIC), some of the commentators were retired members of the RUC, the Royal Irish Constabulary (RIC), or of the Garda Síochána, the force which succeeded the RIC in the Republic of Ireland (Brady, 1974; Breathnach, 1974; Fennell, 2003; Garrow-Green, 1905; Herlihy, 1997; Hermon, 1997; Latham, 2001). Social historians have provided a contextual backdrop, though their perspectives have varied, of the society which the RIC and the RUC were obliged to police (Arthur, 1984; Darby, 1976; Farrell, 1980, 1983; Griffin, 1991; Harkness, 1983; Laffan, 1983; McLysaght, 1950; Ó Dochartaigh, 1997; Phoenix, 1994; Ruane and Todd, 1996; Shea, 1981; Strauss, 1951; Townshend, 1975, 1983). Brewer's oral history (1990) provides an illuminating presentation of the subjective lives of the last surviving members of the RIC.

Some sociologists carried out illuminating comparative studies, but a fairly limited number chose Northern Ireland as a major focus of attention. The most directly relevant work on which I have drawn successfully has been that of Ellison and Smyth, 2000; Mapstone, 1994; Ryder, 2000, 2004 (a journalist with a particular interest in the RUC) and especially Brewer who, building on a body of experience acquired abroad (especially South Africa), applied his insight to Northern Ireland (1988, 1990, 1992, 1993a, 1993b, 1993c, 1993d).

Cast in a wide historical and political context Ellison and Smyth (2000) focus on the period from the outbreak of civil unrest in 1969 and the difficulties encountered when police are used as a counter insurgency force in a divided society. Ryder (2000) relates sympathetically the story of the RUC in great detail from the vantage point of a well-informed and highly respected journalist. In his more recent book (2004) he looks through wide lenses at the unhappy relationship between the Catholic community and the RUC since the force was formed in 1922 but which reached unprecedented depths after 1969 when 'there developed the fateful split' (Government of Northern Ireland 1972 – the Scarman Report).

Mulcahy (2006) chooses to examine police legitimacy – a critical and elusive dimension of the liberal policing model – against a pre- and post-Patten background and within the wider context of the Belfast Agreement (1998). The work of Brewer and Magee (1991) comes closest to mine in origin and purpose. It is the result of postgraduate ethnographic research, albeit into routine policing in one Belfast station while 'the Troubles' were at their height.

Apart from inevitable overlap in reference to historical and social context, my study is complementary to but different from the titles to which I have referred. It is original in that no one else has produced a tightly focused in-depth examination of the role of Catholics in the police which contains rich interview and ethnographic data. The seventy life histories and the Catholic police officers' own subjective narratives of their working lives in the RUC/PSNI were shared with me when I was fortunately afforded privileged access to an organisation traditionally perceived to be suspicious of and closed to inquisitive civilians. Using a combination of methods I have, in my opinion, produced a thorough piece of empirical research and found a treasure trove of primary material which, I hope, may be of use to other researchers in the field.

Models of policing

I have outlined briefly the scope of the literature which places my research within a context of related academic studies and other sources. But my historical survey needs touchstones against which to be measured. The two contrasting models of policing are the colonial and the liberal-democratic in their ideal forms. Uglow (1988) favours placing them at either end of a continuum stretching from imposition (colonial model) to integration (liberal model), referring to the relationship between police and civilians in a society. While one would agree that the two models do not represent discretely different sets of functions, structures and styles

(Uglow's headings) when applied in real-life contexts, for analytical purposes it is better to treat them as if they did.

Colonial model

Since colonial societies were, certainly in the early stages at least, rather unstable, the policing function constituted prevention and detection of crime as defined by the metropolitan governments and consisted mostly in suppressing any signs of resistance and exercising heavy surveillance of perceived restive elements. Although colonial police were supposedly implementing the Westminster model abroad, they inevitably came into conflict with native populations. Their behaviour served only to alienate the communities they were supposed to serve and protect. To the natives their presence symbolised conquest and they applied repressive measures to quell plentiful dissent. The political and economic interests of the ruling élite had to be served, even if this meant consistent repression of the indigenous population. The 'new order' was imposed in a thorough and systematic way: 'British institutions, from medicine to law enforcement, were transplanted to the Empire: to delegitimise indigenous customs; to impose centralised social control, and to incorporate local society as a branch of imperial society' (Brogden *et al.*, 1988: 10).

Colonial police enjoyed arbitrary powers and little restriction was placed on their use of weapons. Keeping the peace at all costs was the end product which the imperial government wanted. Their Director General was accountable to the Crown's representative in the territory but colonial police forces were in no way responsible to the local population. A bureaucratic dimension was included in their policing role as an attempt to legitimise the colonial state (Anderson and Killingray, 1991). While officers recorded information for ostensibly plausible reasons as they carried out administrative duties, they were allegedly building up a comprehensive database which they used to suppress potential or real dissent.

Colonial police lived in barracks, dressed in military-style uniform, bore arms, carried military rank and were under the command of British ex-Army officers (Jeffries, 1952). They were physically apart from the natives and unaccountable to anyone except the dominant colonial élite, ensuring, it would seem, that there was no possibility of consent, compliance or partnership. Even in countries where natives were recruited, they were treated as inferior, denied promotion, often kept in separate units, and frequently had their loyalty severely tested in harsh policing of their own people. They were also closely linked to the military (Bayley and Mendelsohn, 1969) on whom they called when the level of civil disorder required a united effort to suppress it.

It would be an understatement to say that colonial police were unrepresentative of the local population. The main features of the colonial model clearly show that these police forces lacked legitimacy, accountability, impartiality and their dual role – 'ordinary' policing as well as civil order policing – inevitably brought them into conflict with the native population whose trust and support they could not hope to win. The main reason for failure was the absence of moral justification for British presence and control in the colonial territories. This general conceptualisation of colonial policing was not applied uniformly in all colonial police forces – more so in parts of Africa and Palestine, for example, but less so in Canada, Australia and New Zealand. However, all police forces which started during the colonial period have tended to end up having to face problems similar to those in Northern Ireland.

Liberal–democratic model

The liberal-democratic (sometimes referred to as the 'traditional' or 'Westminster') model is seen as British policing at its best. As the nineteenth century progressed and the violent suppression of social and economic divisions subsided, the 'Peeler' (earlier used as a pejorative term derived from the name of Sir Robert Peel) became accepted as the citizen in uniform and 'personification of the true-born Englishman' (Uglow, 1988: 30). The symbolic significance of the police officer shifted from being a heavy-handed government agent to being the visible 'rule of law' to which police, as well as other citizens, were subject.

This neat linkage between government, law and citizen gave the police the most fundamental characteristic of the liberal model – legitimacy. In Britain, a country where there is as yet no written constitution delineating the rights of the individual it is very important that accountability should be to local representatives rather than the government of the day. It must be conceded though that popular control could develop only over a long period as the franchise was extended to more and more categories of citizens. Decentralisation thereby became a feature of the liberal model to ensure that local needs are met and that the police are held to account by the communities they serve.

If the police enjoy legitimacy, then consent follows logically, in principle at least, from all but the 'criminal classes' who do not share the moral values of the vast majority. Consensus about the policing role and who should carry it out is implicit in the term 'policing by consent' and it is carried out in partnership with the community it serves. If a police service is legitimate, decentralised, locally accountable and enjoys consent (which subsumes compliance), then those officers need resort to the use of weapons only on rare occasions and in exceptional circumstances, when no other solution is adequate. In practice only the British police have a history of being unarmed. Most others in the world are and always have been routinely armed.

When applying the law, accompanied by the use of weapons or not, officers must do so in demonstrably neutral fashion, favouring no class or ethnic group at the expense of any other. A potentially serious problem for the liberal model arises when the principle of supposed neutrality is translated into practice by a body of officers who are not representative of the entire community or communities they serve and are perceived to be partisan in their application of legal constraints on the rights of the individual.

The liberal model in its purest form, therefore, requires a modern, democratic state in which to operate, where police act as a buffer between state power and the freedom of the individual and embody the law which imposes clear boundaries around the exercise of power. If proper democratic institutions and practices do not operate effectively, then in that society the liberal model cannot be applied. The liberal model requires flexible, sensitive and responsive political and social conditions in which to flourish. The liberal model presupposes a particular kind of society – stable, politically democratic, with value consensus – and this exists rarely, if at all. It was thought to have existed in Britain, evoked by the image of Dixon of Dock Green, but social and political change threatened it.

The ideal liberal model of policing would work only in an ideal society. Doubts are raised in the literature that it was ever a reality in British policing: Brewer (1988) and Fielding (1991) all cite plentiful examples of ways in which it was departed from. Further reference to such departures in the context of Northern Ireland and attempts to reform it will be made in the section on the RUC.

Having outlined the main features of the two contrasting models of policing I shall examine in Chapter 1 how the RIC provides an excellent illustration of the colonial model in practice, bequeathing a legacy which still affects policing in Northern Ireland nearly ninety years after that force's demise. The story provides an explanatory backdrop to the problems which the RUC inherited and failed to solve in relation to policing Catholics.

Outline of the book

Chapter 1 traces the history of policing in Ireland over 180 years between 1822 and 2002 showing the inadequacy of the neo-colonial model, through the lifetimes of the RIC and the RUC, in winning the support of the Catholic population.

Chapter 2 describes the research samples, the design and data collection procedures. Related political, logistical and personal issues are discussed. Findings from a computer-generated random sample of 300 Catholic PSNI members who transferred from the RUC are summarised. [Tables are to be found in Appendix 1.] The survey was carried out in November-December 2002, one year after the PSNI replaced the RUC. From a response rate of 46 per cent, results are compared on a variety of biographical and attitudinal variables with data on the wider Catholic community provided by Northern Ireland Life and Times (NILT) surveys. From the quantitative data, analysed with the assistance of SPSS (Statistical Package for the Social Sciences), questions to guide in-depth interviews were generated.

Chapter 3 presents data from one-to-one interviews with a snowball sample of ten retired Catholic officers who served in the RUC between 1945 and 2001. Their testimonies provide a historical perspective on policing in Northern Ireland before and during the Troubles. Topics include respondents' family background and education, motivation for joining, their subjective experiences as police officers in a predominantly Unionist organisation and their relations with the Catholic community. Though they spoke as retirees, their views of the Patten reforms are included in the data.

Chapter 4 records interview data from fifty serving officers who transferred from the RUC to the PSNI and whose policing experience was restricted to the post-1969 period. They were a volunteer subset of the survey respondents. The topics covered at interview were broadly the same as those discussed by the retired sample. A typology of categories is developed to explain the various ways in which officers managed their Catholic identity as a small minority in the RUC.

Chapter 5 focuses on a snowball sample of ten trainees and provides qualitative data from in-depth interviews. The emphasis is, of necessity, different in some aspects from that applied to the other samples, as the trainees had little or no experience of operational policing. Instead, their personal and family backgrounds, pre-PSNI work experience, their motivation for joining and their aspirations are analysed.

Chapter 6 examines similar and contrasting opinions of the Patten recommendations in action. Serving officers had practical, though brief experience of sudden and profound change in their working lives and were positioned to offer verdicts on both positive and negative aspects of the relatively new PSNI. The trainees, however, were the personification of one major Patten reform incorporated in legislation – 50:50 recruitment. Though short on experience they had clear views, some of which were already influenced by the values to be found in traditional police culture.

Chapter 7 reviews the data gleaned to assess longitudinal change in policing Northern Ireland. Contemporary sociological theory on the concepts of culture and identity are discussed in order to explain findings and to position this piece of research as a contribution to modern discourse on the developmental and fluid nature of Catholic identity in particular. Research questions are revisited and reflective speculation proffered regarding the viability of the liberal model of policing being embedded without full implementation of the Belfast Agreement.

1

Historical overview

The Royal Irish Constabulary – rise and fall

The first point to note is an early association of the policing function with the state and the ascendancy of Protestantism, setting up an antagonistic relationship with the native Irish Catholic population which was to be of lasting significance. When Sir Robert Peel arrived in Dublin Castle to begin his term as Chief Secretary of Ireland (1812–18) he had major modernisation of the police system in mind. For the previous quarter-century, responsibility for law and order in Ireland rested principally with baronial constables who had to be Protestant. They were mainly pensioners appointed by magistrates and, while they were capable of carrying out courthouse-based duties and serving writs, public order and attendant violence had to be dealt with by the military. Peel's Peace Preservation Force was formed, following the passing of appropriate legislation in 1814, for two reasons. First, the Napoleonic Wars were placing an undue strain on military resources and so soldiers could not be available to support the constabulary. Second, Peel objected in principle to the notion of soldiers enforcing the public peace, as their use in that capacity would make people look upon them as their enemies rather than their protectors.

However, Army intervention was called upon frequently, on some occasions when there were threats of serious widespread disorder and more usually when local violence occurred. Britain's answer to the failed rebellion of 1798, led by the United Irishmen imbued by the revolutionary spirit of the American colonists and of the French, was to pass an Act of Union (1801), denying Ireland a separate parliament, having had one for a mere eighteen years. This serious source of political grievance was accompanied by equally serious social and economic injustices which together ensured that the Irish Constabulary faced a challenging nineteenth century of confrontation, mainly with Irish Catholics. Demands for urgent repeal of the Penal Code in the form of Catholic Emancipation, achieved by 1829, was aggravated by burgeoning agitation against paying tithes to the Established (Anglican) Church, not disestablished until 1869. An abortive Fenian Rising in 1867 was dutifully quelled, earning for the force the prefix 'Royal' from Queen Victoria.

One mistake made by the British government was to have lasting consequences. No effort was made to enlist the support of the Catholic gentry and the potential influence which they might have had on their poorer co-religionists, who were increasingly moved to action by the liberation movements in mainland Europe as the century advanced. By 1822 it was optimistically agreed by Westminster that Ireland was to have a unified, non-military Irish Constabulary as soon as was practicable. It was an unfortunate coincidence of history that the predominantly Protestant County Constabulary was identified with the Anglo-Irish landowning classes and, in times of need, had to draw support from the military – perceived to be their armed wing. In these circumstances it is not surprising that the Irish Constabulary failed to gain the consent of the native Catholic population.

Successful progression by Catholics to senior ranks, accompanied by commensurate influence, might conceivably have made the force more acceptable to Catholics in general. However, though Catholics came to dominate the ranks, promotion to positions of power and influence were very restricted. It should be remembered that, prior to Catholic Emancipation being granted in 1829, Catholics could not be admitted into any police force in the British Isles. A minority who were Catholic were registered as Protestant. It was only after 1836 that the door was opened to Catholic recruits:

> the new [amalgamated] Force consisted of seven thousand men, five thousand of whom were Orangemen; the five Inspectors General and the County Inspectors were Protestants. Drummond [Under-Secretary of Ireland] insisted on the admission of Catholics to the police. 'If you do not admit Catholics,' he said prophetically, 'you do not gain the confidence of the people'. (Fennell, 2003: 6)

Though Catholics were theoretically encouraged to set their sights on reaching commissioned rank, in practice promotion to very senior ranks was almost exclusively reserved for Protestants. Although from 1895 onwards about half of those reaching commission level had risen through the ranks, the other half of posts were filled by those who short-circuited the system via the Cadet Scheme, entering (after training) at District Inspector level. There had been gradual improvement in the proportions because before the 1860s only one in six was chosen from the ranks; by the 1870s, it was one in four. The RIC retained the rigid distinction between officers and men (cadets and others) right up until the Force was disbanded in 1921 – in contrast to English forces – reflecting the imperial power's supremacy over the native population and the absence of equal treatment for Irish Catholics.

RIC historians tend to be critical of these cadet officers, explaining that they were generally drawn from 'the landless or less fortunate sons of the gentry', adding that the Phoenix Park cadet school in Dublin, where senior officers for all the colonial forces were trained from 1840 'was regarded as a very suitable finishing school for the less promising sons of Eton or Harrow who did not make it to Sandhurst and who were therefore destined for a career in the constabulary' (Brady, 1974: 13). Unlike the lower ranks, the officer cadets appear to have emerged from the depot ill-fitted for professional police work. Relying on their Head Constables (usually the most senior rank which Catholics attained) to do the real work, men of the Garrow-Green (1905) cadet cadre enjoyed a lifestyle which 'reflected their privileged Anglo-Irish Protestant and military background' (Brewer, 1990: 5).

After the mid century the religious composition of the RIC altered dramatically at rank-and-file level, from 51 per cent Catholic in 1871 to almost 81 per cent in 1914, outstripping the proportion of Catholics in the general population of approximately 74 per cent in 1911 (Griffin, 1991: 314). Even by 1914 Protestants still occupied a disproportionately high number of officer positions. It was only when the RIC reached its final period of existence after the Rising of 1916, when the numbers of resignations increased dramatically and the Black and Tan mainly ex-Army English auxiliaries were drafted into Ireland, that Catholic promotions to senior positions rose as the political situation and the British government's response to it became more desperate. The ethnic and social gap between officers and men made the RIC typical of colonial forces where the natives, while numerically indispensable, were generally kept in subordinate positions relative to those representing the dominant élite.

It was inevitable that policing of Catholics by Catholic members of the RIC was likely to present great difficulties. Absence of legitimacy and consequential absence of consent from the population at large made the RIC a paramilitary force responsible for public order policing as well as civilian policing – a demanding brief which seriously impacted on police-Catholic relations. The Army influence on the RIC, who were viewed as a kind of cavalry regiment and commanded by an ex-Army colonel, was strongly reflected in design of uniform and in the curriculum followed by recruits during initial training in the Phoenix Park depot – weapon handling and infantry and cavalry drill occupying a disproportionate amount of time and energy, along with learning large chunks of law by rote. Those commentators who give sympathetic treatment to the RIC, for example Brewer (1990) and Ryder (2000) rejoice in the reputation which RIC standards of discipline and integrity earned its members. The contradiction between their reputation and their treatment is not missed, though: 'Ironically, while a background in a police force such as the RIC was considered suitable for other forces, the RIC itself tended to be placed in the charge of ex-Army officers' (Brewer, 1990: 3). All the more puzzling when he records that at one point eleven out of twenty-four chief constables in English forces were ex-RIC personnel.

The enormity of the RIC's dual policing role was reflected in police staffing levels relative to civilian population numbers: 'In 1836, the number of police officers per head of population was three times that of England and Wales and still twice the level of the United Kingdom in 1897' (Ellison and Smyth, 2000: 15). One can only conclude that in accordance with the colonial model the main role of the RIC was the suppression of dissent, a crusade in which it was unfortunately partnered by the Army. In the native Catholic mind, memories of atrocities against their forbears, committed by the yeomanry, lived on and proved an enduring obstacle for the RIC.

The Tithe War of the 1830s, the Young Ireland Rebellion of 1848, the Fenian Rebellion of 1867, the Land War of the 1880s and the murders of Cavendish and Burke, Chief Secretary and Under Secretary respectively, summarise the ongoing agitation and violence, reflected in movements and events which relentlessly absorbed the energies of the RIC and cast them in a paramilitary role, as the enemies of Catholics translating legitimate grievances into actions which broke the law.

The impression of a German traveller to Ireland in 1836 of the RIC's function and style encapsulates the image the constabulary presented:

> these men with dark green uniforms are fully armed, well educated and disciplined force, and stationed as they are throughout the country (mostly in towns and villages but often in remote places as well) might be considered a military garrison. Their main duty is to detect and prevent crime, protect property and suppress disorder. They patrol the roads, protect landlords and their agents, put down faction fights and break up seditious meetings. Being Irish themselves, they know the country and the people well and are able to deal with local problems. (Herlihy, 1997: 46)

While the comments were, no doubt, intended to be laudatory, they contain observations which underline the hostility which these men experienced from many of their fellow countrymen, for example protecting landlords and their agents by attending evictions of poor families for non-payment of rents. Victims of repressive legislation, who were largely Irish Catholics, saw the RIC as their enemies because the Constabulary, by the nature of their job, were obliged to uphold the law, however unfair and repressive it might have been.

The end approaches

Two of the three major issues against which the Catholic Irish fought won gradual resolution as the nineteenth century progressed. By 1870 problems associated with the Anglican Church had been resolved and by 1903 Wyndham's Land Act had finally dealt with the land question. The basic political problems around colonial occupation brought a thrust towards national self-determination, which was to gather momentum as the twentieth century progressed and was to sound the death knell for the RIC. Gladstone's acceptance of the justice of Home Rule for Ireland brought a certain inevitability to the fate of the RIC. Violent opposition to Home Rule from Ulster Unionists was matched by equally violent determination by Irish Republicans that nothing less than complete separation from England would satisfy their aspirations.

One could argue plausibly that the RIC successfully integrated into the local community in times of peace, but that such successful civil policing was negatively affected by the public order role in times of conflict. It was as individuals that the RIC membership succeeded in transcending the Force's colonial 'policing by strangers' image, a practice which the London Metropolitan police retained in modified form until the 1960s. In addition to being welcome guests at weddings and christenings, and perceived as desirable and reliable sons-in-law, in the course of their official duties they assisted the community in reading and writing letters, in completing official forms. The areas of responsibility which their work as administrative agents of government covered reads like an endless list, including such diverse activities as saving life and property in areas where there was no fire brigade, compiling agricultural statistics, Weights and Measures inspection, likewise for Food and Drugs, arresting vagrants, accompanying patients to mental hospitals, noting content of political speeches lest they be deemed seditious and overseeing election polls (Brewer, 1990: 6). The bureaucratic role of colonial forces masquerading as a form of 'normal' policing is seen by some as having menacing overtones of state surveillance (Finnane, 1990), though the charge is robustly challenged by others (Fennell, 2003).

Although RIC members may have carried out their civil policing duties in a way which won the passive gratitude of the population, historians are in no doubt as to their ultimate purpose. One states that they:

> were usually respected and even popular. They were the pick of the countryside's youth, athletic, intelligent and – relative to their neighbours – well educated . . . [however] . . . on the other, more basic level, they knew and the people knew that when a crisis would come the Peeler's first loyalty would be to the Crown. (Brady, 1974: 11–12)

Another, while agreeing that the RIC enjoyed relatively good relations with the general Irish Catholic population in times of peace, succinctly sums up the RIC's purpose unequivocally: 'The RIC was a native Irish police force, loyal to the Government and enforcing the law of the land' (McNiffe, 1997: 5).

Even within the civilian policing role, sinister intentions are detected in some quarters. According to this perspective, even completing forms for local people in English can be seen as part of a concerted plan to modernise and Anglicanise Irish society, consolidating the use of the English language and trying to eradicate the native Gaelic tongue. The rationale for the use of bureaucratic policing as part of the civilian role is interpreted to have arisen 'from the lack of legitimacy of the colonial order, and the inability of informal methods of social control to master the situation' (Ellison and Smyth, 2000: 9). Periods of civil policing, though they tended to lengthen as the nineteenth century advanced, were, in fact, interludes which were preceded and followed by bursts of civil unrest which required typical colonial methods of suppression. As the British presence became more and more untenable, it is unsurprising that the RIC asked to be disbanded when the colonial model could no longer be applied in practice. The Force had no option as the reality of Partition approached.

Ineptitude on the part of the British government and inability to deal with the Republican threat brought negative repercussions for the RIC in the forms of hatred and violence. In 1914, a confidential intelligence report sent by the RIC Inspector General to the Chief Secretary in June stressed, in an ominously accurate way, the gravity of the security situation: 'Each County will soon have a trained Army, far outnumbering the police, and those in control of the Volunteers will be in a position to dictate to what extent the law of the land may be carried into effect' (O'Sullivan, 1999: 225). This report was ignored. Perhaps the most damning indictment was the decision by Lieutenant-Colonel Sir John Maxwell to make examples of the 1916 leaders, mainly poets and philosophers, by executing them; by his actions he converted them into martyrs. His ill-considered directive brought a huge swell of sympathy and anger from a hitherto indifferent general public – and queues of young men and women, hungry for excitement and revenge, joined Sinn Féin and Cumann na mBan respectively.

Increasing numbers of Catholics joined the RIC as the twentieth century progressed until an abnormal situation made it not only a very difficult but also a very dangerous job to do. Abandoned by the British government, they were alienated as a Force by large sections of the population, and, at worst, considered legitimate targets for violence by the incoming political regime and their supporters. Intimidated into resigning, subjected to boycott by shopkeepers and other service providers, the RIC acknowledged that it did not have the resources necessary to defeat the Republican guerrilla campaign. In the closing years, 1920–22, one RIC member in twenty paid the ultimate price of violent death at the hands of the IRA, while many others had to flee the country with utmost haste in order to survive the death squads.

In this section I have tried to demonstrate that the RIC was doomed from the beginning when its early link with the state and the Protestant ascendancy inevitably established an antagonistic relationship with the native Catholic population. Members were expected to carry out both paramilitary and civil policing roles, but their wider political role sacrificed the civil policing to the public order role in times of conflict, which recurred at closer intervals during the first half century of their existence when grievances were most strongly felt. Ill-conceived judgements by the British government at times of crisis hastened their demise and finally abandoned them to their inevitable fate. Commendable efforts to integrate with the people could only be temporary and partial because partnership was impossible. The Irish Catholic community, from whom increasing numbers joined but never enjoyed their fair share of promotions, had, at best, an ambivalent attitude towards them. They were perceived to be agents of a foreign power by the bulk of the population, despised by many and barely tolerated by others.

The basic reason for the unhappy relationship between the RIC and those they policed must be attributed to the imposition of a colonial model, so effective from the British government's point of view that other colonial police forces were trained by its senior officers. It lacked legitimacy, it was accountable to no one but the Crown and the Ascendancy élite, who also controlled the courts. Neutrality was impossible since their duty was to uphold the Establishment cause. There was neither consent nor compliance from the people, nor was there any community orientation. Its *raison d'être* was the maintenance of public order at all costs in the interest of ongoing colonial domination, beyond a point where such had become an anachronism in twentieth-century Europe.

The epitaph of this rather enigmatic body of men, whose membership became increasingly native Irish as time passed, is modestly spoken by one of Ireland's most famous literary sons, Seán Ó'Faoláin, whose father, Denis Whelan, served with the RIC in Cork City. Of the tragic 1921–22 period he states: 'Men like my father were dragged out in those years and shot – so be it. Shot to inspire terror – so be it. But they were not traitors – they had their loyalties and they stuck to them' (Herlihy, 1997: 103). Further light is cast on RIC men's interpretation of loyalty by Fennell (2003: 154) who explains that it was 'to themselves and those depending on them'.

Perhaps this brief statement neatly explains how these Catholic Irishmen negotiated their identity as paid servants of the Crown. Whether or not this kind of accommodation between personal and official lives was also true of their successors in the RUC I shall address later.

Northern Ireland and the RUC

In the next section of this chapter I shall consider the problems experienced by the RUC because the model of policing which they inherited in the political conditions of Northern Ireland in 1922 precluded the possibility of winning consent from the Catholic population. I shall show that the RUC repeated the failures of the RIC. Indeed, I shall argue that it left a more challenging legacy to the PSNI, namely a highly problematical relationship with the Catholic population that impacts negatively on Catholic recruitment to the police.

Like the RIC, the RUC was early identified with the ascendancy of Protestant Unionism. Whatever the ideological approach adopted, commentators do not deny the important role which the RUC carried out in support of the Northern Ireland state and its government since 1922. This role constituted the RUC's basic problem of failing to establish moral authority with the whole population. The RUC represented and symbolised the Northern Irish state's legitimacy problem. Identified by the majority Unionist and Protestant population as 'our police', the RUC was used as a formidable bulwark against the perceived threat from Irish nationalism. The police established and maintained the new state's existence and security against imagined irredentist threats from the Irish Republic, expressed through the minority Catholic Nationalist population, who refused, either actively or passively, to recognise the legitimacy of Northern Ireland.

One can argue convincingly that, in a divided society such as Northern Ireland, that overt approval of citizens is not necessary for the stability of the state, but only the approval and support of dominant groups such as powerful state institutions 'charged with cultural control and more concrete forms of repression and exclusion' (Smyth, 2002: 110). These criteria were met during the first fifty years of the state's existence and only after the emergence of the civil rights movement did the edifice crack in the late 1960s. In Northern Ireland a paradoxical situation existed whereby in Protestant communities there was 'normal' liberal model policing, while many Catholic communities were subjected to paramilitary colonial model policing. This identification of one section of the population with the RUC as 'our police' suggests 'clientelism' characteristic of colonial policing.

The identification of the RUC with Protestant Unionism was much more marked than in the case of the RIC with the Anglo-Irish ascendancy. RIC members were forbidden to exercise their franchise or to join political or religious organisations except the Free Masons, in order to maintain their reputation for theoretical impartiality (Fennell, 2003: 69). In contrast, an Orange Lodge for police officers was established within three months of the RUC's birth. Estimates of recent membership range from 11–15 per cent (Farrell, 1983; Ellison, 1997). Until the mid-1990s processions were protected by the presence of the RUC in strength, as Orangemen marched accompanied by bands playing sectarian tunes, while expressions of Nationalist identity were suppressed by legislation under the Public Order Act 1951 and Flags and Emblems Act 1954. Routine police practice was underpinned by this legislation, starting at a period when intelligence warned of an impending period of IRA activity which failed to attract popular support.

The Flags and Emblems Act, 1954 which denied cultural expression of Nationalist identity, can be seen as a continuation of RIC policy. The colonial model principles include the systematic erosion of local culture. It is alleged that the RIC practised surveillance of traditional Irish cultural events such as festivals and fairs, putting them under suspicion so as to promote Anglicisation, especially of Gaelic speakers (Ellison, 2000: 15). The Stormont government made the display of an Irish tricolour in public a crime and the RUC had to police observance of the law. The greatest burden for the RUC was arguably the Special Powers Act 1922 which was renewed and applied consistently up until 1993. This legislation empowered the executive at the expense of the judiciary and enabled the Stormont Minister of Home Affairs to 'take all such steps and issue all such orders as may be necessary for the preserving of the peace' (Ellison and Smyth, 2000: 31). Crucially, these powers he could delegate to individual officers, making the RUC one of the most powerful and partisan institutions in the province. One enduring piece of legislation, therefore, alone denied the possibility of a liberal model of policing being implemented for seventy years, since accountability, partnership, consent, neutrality and impartiality were logically excluded by its retention on the statute books, having changed in name only in 1974.

The policing function can clearly be seen to have set up an antagonistic relationship with the minority Catholic population who have felt no loyalty to the dominant Unionist regime. It is not surprising that, given the circumstances described above, Catholic membership of the RUC never reached a one-third quota recommended by Sir Dawson Bates' Committee in 1922. Officers were to have been drawn one-third from the largely Protestant ex-RIC, one-third from the heavily Protestant dominated Ulster Special Constabulary (USC), who came to be known as the sectarian 'Specials' by Catholics, and one-third from open competition to Catholics. Prominent Unionists in the nascent Stormont government feared that 'the RIC was riddled with Catholics and Republican sympathisers and was not to be trusted' (Ryder, 2004: 30). The quota for Catholic membership was not met. It peaked at under 22 per cent in 1923 and declined to below 8 per cent by the year 2000.

Under-representation by Catholics could not be attributed directly to the RUC, in that recruitment was open to all who met the requirements, but resulted mainly from the partisan use made of the force by the Stormont government. The Nationalist population considered the 'Specials' to be the Orange Order in uniform, the modern equivalent of the notorious yeomanry in previous centuries, and poorly trained and ill-disciplined. They built up an unenviable reputation for harassment of Catholics, particularly in border areas. Prior to disbandment in August 1969, their strength was 425 full-time; 8,481 part-time, none of whom was Catholic (Arthur, 1984: 28).

However alienated the Catholic population felt from the Unionist Establishment because of its lack of legitimacy, the main problem for the RUC, its armed agents, lay in the conflicting functions which the RUC were obliged to carry out. Both the RIC and the RUC failed to execute successfully the dual role thrust upon them of policing public order as well as civil policing duties. Both Constabularies enjoyed a reasonable degree of success in civil policing during often extended periods of superficial 'normality', but each was destroyed by a crucial test which challenged their ability to deal with serious public unrest. In the case of the RIC it was the War of Independence; for the RUC, it was the events of 1968–69.

Fifty years of Unionist hegemony was characterised by discrimination on sectarian grounds in employment and public housing allocation, together with gerrymandering in order to ensure political dominance in areas where numbers failed to justify it, most famously in the city of Derry/Londonderry. Just as events in mainland Europe during the nineteenth century fuelled the flames of rebellion in Ireland, culminating in unsuccessful bids to obtain Home Rule, the civil rights movement in the USA and student movements across Europe struck a chord with receptive elements in Northern Ireland – initially mainly students. The expansion of higher education and increased access of those qualified but economically disadvantaged brought a groundswell of discontent, expressed by the People's Democracy movement. This development ushered in an era of Nationalist confidence in their demands for human rights, which is still being worked through. Infiltration by the IRA, however, complicated the scenario and changed a human rights movement, which crossed both religious and class divisions, into an overtly political and violent challenge to the Stormont government and inevitably to the RUC.

Although the British government in the nineteenth century had slowly enacted legislation which eased pressure for basic reforms such as Catholic Emancipation, granted in 1829, and the Disestablishment of the Anglican Church in Ireland which came in 1869, no comparable progress can be recorded in the case of Northern Ireland during the first fifty years of the Stormont government's existence. The role of the RUC in supporting the political status quo was even more challenging because the British government conveniently ignored the internal affairs of Northern Ireland and brought no discernible pressure on Stormont for evolutionary change in a supposedly liberal democracy. Even the introduction of European post-war Keynesian economics and social democratic welfare legislation in the 1940s, establishing the National Health Service and providing free secondary education for all, was delayed – possibly because it was feared to be the beginnings of rampant socialism which would benefit Catholics.

The troubled years

It was the formation of the Northern Ireland Civil Rights Association (NICRA) in 1967 and the policing of its peaceful marches, as well as threatening counter-marches led by Reverend Ian Paisley, that marked the beginning of the end for both Unionist dominance in Northern Ireland's politics and for the RUC in its traditionally unchallenged form. The irony is noteworthy – that extreme Loyalism began the process of dismantling the RUC, as it did Stormont too. That phase in the history of both stretched over thirty years. Queen's University, an institution noted for its support at the highest level for the Stormont government, sired a monster in the form of a non-violent protest movement. Its significance is summed up thus: 'The brilliant and strategic choice of a civil rights movement . . . undermined the Stormont regime in British and international public opinion' (McGarry and O'Leary, 1995: 261, cited in Ellison and Smyth, 2000: 50). The response of the RUC and especially of the USC was found wanting by two eminent lawyers, who reported on police behaviour at widely publicised violent events during 1968 and 1969. Lords Cameron and Scarman, who reported in 1969 and 1972 respectively, made injurious criticisms of police behaviour and credibility tending, however, to point a finger at individual senior RUC officers, rather than the entire force, though the USC received stronger general criticism.

The British Home Secretary, James Callaghan, acknowledging that the RUC was incapable of dealing with the security situation, took decisive action on two fronts: by putting the Army in charge and by initiating the first serious investigation of the RUC and its operations. Control of policing was effectively removed from Stormont to Westminster. Reluctantly, the Stormont government agreed that a Commission should be set up to 'Examine the recruitment, organisation, structure and composition of the Royal Ulster Constabulary and the Ulster Special Constabulary and their respective functions and to recommend as necessary what changes are required to provide for the efficient enforcement of law and order in Northern Ireland' (Northern Ireland Parliament, 1969: 7).

Recognising that policing was part of the problem, the Home Secretary called upon Sir John Hunt, knighted for his climbing achievements on Mount Everest in 1953, who found himself with a less familiar but equally formidable mountain to climb – police reform in Northern Ireland. His brief, however, was to find a way of reducing violence and of making the RUC more acceptable to Catholics, whose moderate representatives had been alienated by recent police performance. One detects a clear change of policy by the British government, reflected in the stance taken by Callaghan who briefed Hunt on the outcome he wanted – a paramilitary force along the border with the Republic and a police force recruited from both Catholics and Protestants which would 'result in the Northern Ireland province not having to depend for its security on an armed citizenry' – referring to the 'B' Specials (Ryder, 2004: 140).

Callaghan's actions and words heralded a total departure from the British government's traditional attitude towards Northern Ireland's internal affairs and acquiescence in Stormont's requests for more armed citizenry when they considered the safety of the state to be at risk from Republican violence. After nearly half a century of apparent indifference, the British government took control of policing and of day-to-day security in the province. Very significantly, it began relegating the colonial model of policing to history and introducing the liberal-democratic model. Within an incredibly short period of six weeks, Lord Hunt and his two businessmen colleagues produced a report (October 1969) which was to signal a watershed in Northern Irish policing history, recognising the dilemma of policing this divided society.

The Hunt Report
Based on the 1964 Police Act in England and Wales, the Hunt Report tried to impose a liberal model of policing on a divided society, without the socio-political structure on which the liberal model needs to be based. The RUC at that stage still met the major criteria of the colonial model inherited from the RIC. The RUC and USC had become demoralised, exhausted and demonstrated inability to cope with peaceful civil unrest, which under civil rights leadership used tactics other than those which the RUC had learned to deal with over the years. Peaceful protest and concerted demand for civil rights imported from the USA successfully challenged the RUC at both leadership and rank-and-file levels. Hunt partially met one of the civil rights movement's demands – disbandment of the RUC – by abolishing the discredited and wholly Protestant 'B' Specials (USC) and by replacing them with the RUC Reserve and new part-time military reserve, the Ulster Defence Regiment (UDR).

He recommended that the RUC should be disarmed, thereby separating the community policing role from counter-insurgency. He gave the RUC greater autonomy by establishing a Police Authority of Northern Ireland (PANI), thereby ending direct Stormont control of the RUC and establishing the principle of police accountability. A complaints procedure was included – a step towards transparency as well as accountability. The Hunt Report also sought repeal of substantial parts of the Special Powers legislation. It thereby set out to treat Northern Ireland as a 'normal' part of the UK, in which the presence of Special Powers legislation indicated absence of policing by consent and resort to coercive measures in order to control the Nationalist population who, on the whole, had denied legitimacy to the Stormont regime and, consequently, to the RUC.

Hunt clearly wanted the RUC to become similar to the British police forces and to embrace the liberal model as far as possible by disarming, changing the colour of their uniform from green to blue, civilianising it to make it more 'user-friendly' to Nationalists from whose numbers, he stressed, greater representation should be invited. He wanted to change the military character of the RUC further by demilitarisation of the rank structure and its terminology, and to have the use of force and of firearms tightly controlled. Hunt was also sensitive to the importance of ethos and recommended the establishment of a Community Relations branch which would initiate direct contacts with the communities served, in order to enhance mutual understanding and to promote cooperation.

Focusing on two broad principles of the liberal-democratic model, autonomy and professionalism, the Hunt Committee bravely but perhaps naively attempted to superimpose a Westminster model in a Northern Irish context not yet, if ever, ready for it. With the benefits of hindsight, one might argue that the Hunt Report erred fundamentally in trying to isolate policing from the political, legal, economic and social context in which the RUC operated and that they merely tinkered with the structure and style of a seriously flawed institution. One must remember, however, the tight brief they were given, the outcome expected and the urgency with which they were required to come up with an effective solution to a serious and pressing security problem. The British government at this stage still did not realise, it would seem, that street violence, now seriously infiltrated by the IRA, was a visibly expressed symptom of serious malaise in a deeply divided society.

Hunt's forty-seven recommendations tackled problems such as lack of legitimacy and policing by consent; he also took cognisance of pressing operational matters and of unfavourable image and partisan identity. His overall strategy might be seen to have been civilianisation of the RUC. In this endeavour he was doomed to fail. Violent Loyalist reaction to the appointment of Sir Arthur Young as the first Chief Constable of the RUC in 1969 followed the forced resignation of the last Inspector General Peacocke, deemed by Prime Minister Callaghan's advisers to be inadequate. This response signified Protestant extremists' opposition to the Hunt package, which forced an Ulsterman to give way to an Englishman as their most senior police officer.

Unfortunately for the RUC the security situation deteriorated, ruling out the possibility of establishing themselves as an unarmed, civilian force who, as such, might have been able to establish gradually and carefully better relations with the Catholic population. Instead, they were forced back into the dual role as the British government, mindful of damaging media coverage of key events, such as the 'Battle of the Bogside' in 1969, revisited in Lord Scarman's report (Government of Northern Ireland, 1972), tried to lower the Army's profile by a policy of 'police primacy' or 'normalisation'. By January 1971 the security situation had deteriorated so seriously, while the Stormont Minister of Home Affairs, Major Chichester-Clark, still struggled with Whitehall to retain control, the British government reluctantly realised that internment and Direct Rule were inevitable, according to the official, unreconstructed colonial mindset.

Commentators representing different perspectives agree that the RUC treatment of the essentially peaceful civil rights movement created a chasm between the police and Catholics in the community. Lord Scarman referred to 'the fateful split', while an ex-RUC sergeant explained: 'It totally destroyed the RUC's relationship with the Catholic community – it was never the same after that' (cited by Ellison, 1997: 155). The images portrayed on television were retained in Catholic memory banks and influenced that community's attitudes towards the RUC ever since: 'the police punched, batoned and pursued civil rights demonstrators in a brutal display of concerted violence' (Ó Dochartaigh, 1997: 5).

In spite of partial implementation of the Hunt recommendations in the post-1970 period, poor relations between the Catholic population and the RUC were exacerbated by the unfortunate acquisition of a reputation for police deviance. The institution was seen to engage in large-scale counter-terrorism activities (particularly Special Branch), alleged collusion with death squads, interrogation with 'white heat'-type torture at holding centres, supported by emergency legislation and partisan treatment by the judiciary – demonstrated by absence of convictions against its members (Amnesty International, 1994; Bennett, 1979; Murray, 1990; Stalker, 1988).

Outside observers from the legal profession clearly made the point that the judiciary contributed significantly to the RUC's poor reputation by the partial way in which its members interpreted legislation. Investigating the lethal use of firearms by the security forces in Northern Ireland, serious conclusions are reached and recommendations made:

> The law governing the use of deadly force by the police and Army in Northern Ireland is inadequate. We find that judges in Northern Ireland and in the British House of Lords have interpreted the law in a manner which allows too much scope for members of the security forces. The attitude of some judges amounts virtually to endorsement of martial law. Internal Army and police instructions on the use of firearms are kept secret from the public and breaches of those instructions go unpublicised . . . Several senior judges, particularly Lord Diplock, Lord Justice Gibson and Mr Justice McDermott have made statements from the bench that . . . are fatal to public confidence in judicial impartiality, especially when they are considered against the background of an acquittal rate approaching 100 per cent for members of the security forces charged with the

unlawful use of firearms. We believe that these judges should not continue to adjudicate on cases arising under the emergency legislation. (Asmal, 1985: 125–7)

The report of this prestigious group of international lawyers who obviously distanced themselves from their Northern Irish counterparts in order to criticise their performance with unequivocal clarity, invites serious reflection. At the highest levels in the British state assent was given to the security forces to treat British citizens as though in a nineteenth-century colonial context and the guardians of the law protected those applying it from its rigours.

Civil unrest, politics and policing
It would be simplistic to assume that the serious security situation which spanned almost thirty years after 1970 neutralised the efforts of Hunt and that police reform was put on hold. Reform was, however, attempted in very inauspicious circumstances which were, ironically, often accompanied by or resulted from political change intended to improve the context in which policing took place. The most important political developments of those years might be summarised as Direct Rule (1972), the Power-Sharing Executive (1974), the Anglo-Irish Agreement (1985) and the Belfast Agreement (1998). These political advances can be seen to have gradually persuaded the minority community that the British government had, at last, determined to introduce proper functioning British democracy into a long ignored corner of the United Kingdom. Direct Rule from Westminster administered by British ministers and civil servants located in Northern Ireland was quickly followed by an attempt to bring the Nationalist community into a working Executive of Unionists, Alliance Party (with a middle-class cross-community base) and largely middle-class Catholic Social Democratic and Labour Party (SDLP).

The Secretary of State, William Whitelaw, recognising the need for input from the Irish Republic's government, invited its representatives to take part in negotiations intended to establish, among other things, cross-border cooperation in policing as a means of reducing political violence. An all-Party committee was to investigate the way forward in achieving effective and acceptable policing so that the RUC would receive universal approval. An independently refereed complaints procedure was to be part of the package. Unfortunately, the plan was stillborn for the executive was brought down within five months by a workers' strike of hugely effective proportions organised by the Ulster Workers Council, a powerful group of Loyalists who feared that accepting a Council of Ireland to oversee progress would lead to reunification of the island.

The next significant political event was the Anglo-Irish Agreement (1985) which again provoked angry and violent reaction from some Unionist quarters which, like the workers' strike, brought the RUC into direct conflict with Protestants from whom they had traditionally drawn support. At this stage RUC members saw themselves as 'a third force' and indeed, their Chief Constable John Hermon was renowned for having reminded recruits at their passing-out parade, that in Northern Ireland there were three religions – those of Catholics, Protestants and police officers.

Brewer is keen to point out that while implementation of the Hunt recommendations could, at best, have been only partially successful, they left a valuable legacy grasped and tenaciously retained by successive chief constables. These two principles of autonomy from local political pressure and professionalism are keystones of the liberal-democratic model guaranteed ever since Direct Rule. Brewer equally draws attention to the main disadvantage accruing to the RUC from the removal of Stormont. Media coverage of events in 1969 kept international interest in Northern Ireland alive and the British government sacrificed the RUC's chances of developing a civilianised image, in order to gain approval from powerful allies, particularly the USA administration. The policy decision forced the RUC back into its dual role of counterinsurgency as well as normal policing (Brewer, 1993a: 188–9).

So, as the British government attempted to move forward implementing a policy of parity of esteem for all citizens in Northern Ireland, the RUC found itself isolated from the Catholic population in general and also from extreme elements within Loyalism. There had emerged a clear division as parliamentary Unionism split into the Ulster Unionist Party and the Paisley-led Democratic Unionist Party (DUP). Further difficulties for the RUC were presented by the paramilitary role which they were expected to carry out with the Army as their partners; indeed until 1976 the Army was in charge. For the RUC this arrangement brought significant ongoing disadvantage: the goodwill which the RUC had built up, particularly with middle-class Catholics from their ordinary policing work, completely disappeared because the police were seen as part of the security forces, whose judgement and tactics were frequently a subject of justifiable criticism.

Superior knowledge of their local areas and greater insight into the minds of local people were allegedly ignored. For example, newspaper coverage of the death of Frank Lagan, (in June 2005) the senior RUC officer in Derry on 'Bloody Sunday' (31 January 1971), has raised awareness and confirmed that his advice was ignored by the Army Commander, who refused him permission to talk to the leaders of the demonstration with whom he had carefully built up a relationship of mutual respect. The result, thirteen unarmed civilians shot when the Parachute Regiment went into the Bogside, has resonated ever since, and been a repeated subject of judicial enquiries. From the RUC perspective 'the Army took over and for eight years thereafter [until 1976] the police did what the Army asked them to do' (Ryder, 2000: 114).

The role which the Army played in Northern Ireland during 'the Troubles' suggests that the province had not yet been decolonised. The traditional role of the British Army is to 'defend the realm', while that of British police is to uphold the rule of law as representatives of the community which they serve, being subject to the laws of parliament through redress to the judiciary. British police forces, for a century before large-scale civil unrest broke out in Northern Ireland, developed into unarmed officers in positions of social control. The RUC's difficulties were further compounded by the unwillingness of their colleagues in mainland Britain's police forces to be seconded in order to assist them, a partial solution to the security problem which was mooted by the British government but quickly dropped because of its unpopularity.

The British government, by intervening too late in the internal affairs of the province, played into the hands of the provisional IRA, who employed consistently the strategies and methodologies of terrorism, militarising the political situation. By the policy of 'police primacy' the government theoretically denied the IRA recognition as an Army, but could not avoid introducing and practising repressive measures which assisted the IRA in winning the political support of the victims of those measures. By maximising the propaganda potential of counter-insurgency policy and techniques, the IRA legitimised, in the eyes of the RUC's critics, a relentless programme of shootings, bombing, killing and maiming police personnel (Baxter, 1999). The legacy for the RUC was deaths and injuries, alienation from elements of both communities, and a reputation for deviance, as energy was sapped and morale lowered.

In spite of the unflattering reputation which the RUC built up in the 1970s and 1980s, fairly disposed commentators record progress in police reform promoted from within. Chief Constables Newman (1976–79) and Hermon (1980–89) are given credit for having, in essence, progressed from implementing a modified colonial model of policing to taking a proactive role in grasping and institutionalising some of the basic principles from the liberal-democratic model which Hunt had identified. The result is sometimes referred to as the 'rational-legal' or 'professional' model.

Sir Kenneth Newman, recruited from the Metropolitan Police and with experience as a detective fighting terrorism in Palestine, was appointed Chief Constable in 1976. His Assistant was John Hermon, who was to succeed him in 1980. Two important previous events influenced Newman's approach. First in importance was the Ulster workers' strike of 1977, when the entire population was deprived of electricity and, more importantly, RUC members were seen to have been less than united in their policing of it. Second was the publication of the Gardiner Report of 1975, which recommended abolition of Special Category Status for political prisoners and a policy of criminalisation instead. Intended to separate prisoners held on terrorist charges from their supporters, the new philosophy was to be actioned using 'police primacy' security strategy favoured by the Black Committee (1976).

From January 1977 the Army was relegated to provide 'military aid to the civil power'. Newman set out to 'professionalise' the RUC by 'the persistent, impartial and professional application of the law' as well as increased cooperation between the RUC and the local community – not least the Catholic community (Newman, cited in Ryder, 2000: 158). He was, in fact, drawing upon basic principles of the liberal-democratic model – impartiality and policing by consent.

However, professionalisation took the form of high-level technical and technological efficiency, which increased intelligence gathering and surveillance, culminating in a crack Special Branch unit E4A established in 1980. In effect the RUC
returned to being a counter-insurgency force which enjoyed the support of the
British and Irish governments in conducting an undercover war against the Irish
Republican Army (IRA). Policing by consent certainly made no progress as proactive surveillance, both covert and overt, targeted undifferentiated groups of people,
often considered suspect simply because of their religious affiliation or their residential location. Professionalisation meant a return to militarisation under a policy
of 'police primacy', even though the higher echelons of the Army had little respect
for the quality of police intelligence and suspected that some police officers had
close links with Loyalist extremists (Urban, 1992).

Internment, juryless Diplock courts and the use of supergrasses brought nothing
but discredit to the RUC and did little to impair the vigour of the IRA campaign.
Tested by an opinion poll (*Belfast Telegraph*, 6 February 1985) the Catholic population was undoubtedly alienated by RUC policy, tactics and lack of accountability.
On the positive side, 'police primacy' earned for the RUC international admiration
for effectively combating terrorism, though paying a high price, as the most dangerous police force in the world for the personnel serving in it. Although Newman
set out to give Northern Ireland a professionally skilled, impartial police force, the
high visibility of the technological efficiency and related accusations of suspect ill-
treatment were counter-productive in terms of the powerful negative image which
they projected.

It was perhaps for their impartial approach in policing contentious public demonstrations and the strong lead which they gave in separating policing from politics
that Newman and Hermon will best be remembered in a positive light. Hermon, an
Ulsterman, sensitive to the significance of religion as a divisive factor in Northern
Irish society, became for many officers an iconic figure. He offered them a welcome
neutral identity in attributing to them membership of 'a third religion', whatever
their community origins. In May 1977 a Paisley-inspired protest in the form of
a 'constitutional stoppage' against government security policy brought a robust
response which demonstrated neutrality from riot police in predominantly Loyalist
Portadown. The behaviour showed marked progress in impartial policing from the
more ambivalent response to the Ulster workers' strike. However, ongoing criticism (Amnesty International, 1978; Bennett, 1979; Stalker, 1988; Taylor, 1980) of
identification and treatment of suspects built up a bulging dossier pointing to widespread police deviance, some suggesting a 'rotten apples' explanation, others opting
for a 'rotten barrel'. The Stalker enquiry, in particular, and the hasty removal of
Stalker among accusations of cover-up by the RUC and MI5 (Military Intelligence
– relative to state security), sullied further the reputation of the police and highlighted the absence of transparency, a lasting reminder of the colonial model.

Sir John Hermon's leadership of the RUC in dealing decisively and professionally with violent forms of orchestrated Unionist opposition to the Anglo-Irish Agreement (1985) demonstrated undoubted progress in police reform. The historic Agreement between the British and Irish governments, eased by their common membership of the European Community (EC), committed the two signatories to work towards a consociational form of devolved government for Northern Ireland. The Agreement recognised parity of esteem for Unionism and Nationalism. British acknowledgement that the Republic of Ireland, another sovereign state, should exercise legitimate influence in future political and constitutional arrangements, predictably angered some Unionist politicians and a sector of the Unionist community. Street violence was met with non-partisan policing, typical of the liberal model and a far cry from the earlier days when the RUC would have received their instructions from a Unionist Minister of Home Affairs. Protestant opposition was visited upon police officers from 'Ulster Says No' campaigners and they had to withdraw with their families into police 'ghettos' for their personal security, now alienated from large sections of both Protestant and Catholic communities.

A very significant nettle which Hermon began to grasp was the annual show of sectarian hostility during the marching season, celebrating the victory of the Protestant King William of Orange over his father-in-law, the Catholic Stuart King James at the Battle of the Boyne in 1690. Annually, the triumphalism of the Orange Order marches through Nationalist areas stirred up violent clashes. Partially motivated by a desire to conserve resources – human and financial – but also hoping to move towards community reconciliation, Hermon advocated the appointment of an independent public body which would decide on the route to be taken by marchers, relieving the RUC of the onerous burden. Such a development would bolster the RUC's image of impartiality. He chose as his focus probably one of the most consistently contested locations, the Catholic 'Tunnel' area of Portadown.

It was unfortunate for Northern Ireland that Hermon's successor, Hugh Annesley, failed to capitalise on the progress made by his predecessors. A Dubliner who had achieved Assistant Commissioner rank in the Metropolitan police, he failed to follow through on a number of timely issues (Ryder, 2004: 254–66). Changing the internal culture of the RUC could have been attempted using the Fair Employment Act of 1989 to increase the numbers of Catholics recruited. He failed in this regard, as well as by making disastrously indecisive judgements about subsequent Orange marches at Portadown, and by failing to create a 'neutral working environment', also demanded by the Fair Employment legislation. Progress on these issues could have contributed significantly to convincing Catholics that the RUC was genuinely striving, at least at establishment level, to make the force more acceptable. His contribution, therefore, to developing the liberal model's characteristics of impartiality, partnership, representativeness and neutrality was negative.

Brewer (1993a) reviewing police reform over the two intervening decades since the Hunt Report of 1970 reminds his readers of noteworthy achievements which he can list as advances towards the liberal model, in spite of all the problems which have been identified above. Progress includes formation of the civilian police authority PANI, in order to provide autonomy from Unionist politicians; formation of an independent complaints procedure and appointment of lay visitors to police stations in order to enhance public accountability; the establishment of a Community Relations branch within the RUC to increase dialogue between Catholics and the police; the introduction of liaison committees to discuss local policing needs, a gesture towards partnership; the beginnings of community policing, another tentative step towards partnership; the adoption of a code of ethics and strict disciplinary standards to discourage deviance; clearly defined boundaries restricting the use of force while suspects or prisoners are in police custody and also in relation to discharge of firearms, though further progress needed to be made in crowd control techniques. He modifies his checklist of successful developments, however, by his reference to remaining 'under-representation of Catholics in the force, wholly as a result of negative opinions of the police among Catholics rather than any resistance on the part of the police in employing Catholics' (Brewer, 1993a: 190).

Brewer places modern academic literature on the RUC in three categories, in accordance with the writers' perceptions of the level of reform achieved. At one extreme there are those whose view is strongly influenced by how the police have carried out their counter-insurgency role and how their visible behaviour witnessed or photographed in ghetto areas sometimes shows them using excessive force. Reforms within the organisation at policy level tend to be played down or ignored (McArdle, 1984; Walsh, 1988). At the other extreme are those who, while acknowledging the negative impression given by carrying out the paramilitary role, would see police deviance as unrepresentative behaviour, outweighed by successful routine policing. They would stress the reforms achieved, particularly under Newman and Hermon, in moving the RUC much closer to the fully professional and liberal model, falling short only in its relationship with the Catholic community, particularly by lack of progress in recruiting Catholics to the RUC (Enloe, 1980; Kennedy, 1967; McCullagh, 1981; Newman, 1978; Ryder, 2000). The third group of academics, within which Brewer places himself, take a middle-of-the-road approach. Recognising reforms achieved, they see further progress severely inhibited by constraints both internal and external to the organisation, particularly public order policing which forms a huge obstacle to further demilitarisation (Boyce, 1979; Weitzer, 1985, 1986, 1987, 1995).

By the mid-1980s there was a marked reduction in the number of fatalities and injuries of both security personnel and civilians in Northern Ireland. The Republican Party, Sinn Féin under the leadership of Gerry Adams, showed signs of moving towards political accommodation by favouring democratic constitutional Nationalism. The Party gradually published documents to this effect in 1987 and 1992, each containing the word 'Peace' in the title and in November 1993 a statement appeared in the Party's newspaper, *An Phoblacht*, which read: 'All across the world, direct and indirect dialogue is used as a means to end seemingly intractable conflicts . . .'. Progress had been made from their standpoint, in that they had not been defeated by the might of the British Army, and the eyes of the world were on the British and Irish governments' handling of political change in Northern Ireland to suit the whole community.

Peace and police reform

When, after eighteen years of Conservative government, Tony Blair and 'New Labour' swept into office in 1997, they put police reform in Northern Ireland at the top of their agenda. The broken IRA ceasefire of 1994 was reinstated and the organisation committed to exclusively peaceful means of resolving conflict. Mo Mowlam, the new, feisty and keen Secretary of State was determined that legislation for police reform would go before the House as soon as possible. The Police Act (Northern Ireland) 1998 moved policing closer to the liberal model in a number of ways.

The oath of allegiance to the monarch, traditionally taken by trained recruits, was replaced by a much shorter declaration promising faithful discharge of duties. This departure obviously removed from officers (Catholics or otherwise) a need to identify with the British state, but instead focused on promising to carry out a neutral policing role as citizens policing fellow citizens. Another feature of the liberal model was added by providing for the appointment of a Police Ombudsman to investigate complaints and to replace an unsatisfactory system whereby the RUC policed itself. The Act tackled the problem of police costs which had escalated in attempts to contain violence, especially at flashpoints during the marching season. The chief constable, in agreement with PANI, was made responsible for the budget and according to given criteria he had from this point on to justify expenditure.

While the reforms contained in the Police Act were commendable, they failed to tackle the more elusive aspect of moral responsibility. The separation of policing from state control was not advanced as the respective roles of Secretary of State, PANI and the chief constable were not delineated clearly. Indeed, by the terms of the Act, the Secretary of State could interfere in the chief constable's exercise of his professional duties without reference to PANI.

In the period of almost thirty years which elapsed between 1969 and the signing of the cross-party Belfast Agreement, police reform can clearly be seen to have been made, slowly and often painfully. The chances of successful implementation of the Hunt Report were thwarted by protracted political and civil unrest. Over this period police reform rocketed to the top of the political agenda and remained there as a focus of attention perceived by the British, Irish and US governments as a necessary, but not sufficient condition of success in bringing stability to Northern Ireland. Successive Conservative governments, in spite of huge propaganda blunders, such as Margaret Thatcher's intransigence over the hunger strikes of IRA prisoners in the early 1980s, attempted to move the peace process forward by reaching accommodation with the Irish government, and indirectly with northern Catholics, via the Sunningdale and Anglo-Irish Agreements in particular.

A prohibitively strong obstacle in the form of paramilitary violence postponed the likelihood of significant internal political change and any commensurate significant reform in policing. The British government appeared to draw upon the Westminster model on occasions, but to retreat to invocation of the colonial model of counter-insurgency – bolstered albeit with modern technological techniques and tactics – when it seemed that the security situation was getting out of control. How aware politicians and civil servants were of the need for a political break-through is not clear, but the fact that secret talks with the IRA and Sinn Féin had begun in the time of William Whitelaw's stewardship in the 1970s suggests a dawning realisation by the British government that lasting stability was conditional upon political progress towards power sharing.

The RUC was only part of the entire state apparatus whose activities rendered community policing virtually impossible over much of the province. They were the victims, too, of inter-agency jealousies and struggles for control and, indeed, of intra-RUC antipathy between the Criminal Investigation Department (CID) and Special Branch, who refused to share intelligence with their colleagues. It would not be inaccurate to describe the RUC as a political football, even after the fall of the Stormont government, though the evidence suggests that this was certainly not their wish. In the post-1970 years, at least, the RUC was the unwilling victim of hostile working conditions dictated by a divided society in which who the police are, and what they symbolise, is always of great political significance. Attempts to reform the RUC by some chief constables, notably Newman and Hermon, and latterly by Flanagan in the mid-1990s, enjoyed mixed success. However, these efforts serve to remind even the strongest critic that there was an internal will at the highest levels to reform the RUC in terms of its function, structure and style, in ways which would make it independent of political control over operational matters and even-handed in its application of the law, thereby more likely to win the support of the Catholic community and to draw more Catholics into the force.

The Patten Report

In this section I shall briefly draw attention to the context in which the Patten Report was produced, some responses to it by stakeholders and commentators, the most significant recommendations intended to establish a liberal model of policing in Northern Ireland, and some recommendations which went further than that classic model required.

Rationale

The Report of the Independent Commission on Policing for Northern Ireland (ICPNI) published in 1999 provided a blueprint for the implementation of a liberal policing model. After others had made several attempts to improve policing in various ways, which could only be partially successful at best, the Patten

Commission provided a well written reflective analysis of the best from world policing in divided societies to guide ambitious plans for police reform. The political context was, crucially, different from that in which the Hunt recommendations were made – as was the time frame given to report. The cross-party peace talks encouraged by paramilitary ceasefires and international support finally brought the Belfast Agreement on Good Friday 1998. The participants believed that 'the agreement provides the opportunity for a new beginning to policing in Northern Ireland with a police service capable of attracting and sustaining support from the community as a whole' (Northern Ireland Office, 1998: 22). Logic demanded nothing less, if the power-sharing Agreement between the Nationalist and Unionist traditions was to lead to a new political era when cooperation rather than conflict between communities was to begin to develop.

The Belfast Agreement promised to offer for the first time in Northern Ireland a political framework engineered by the British and Irish governments with input from the USA – a local, devolved Assembly which established the principle of equality and power sharing. This consociational political framework, operating in presupposed favourable social conditions of shared values and stability, would facilitate embedding the liberal model of policing. The commissioners set about designing a new institutional framework to replace the RUC without disbanding that organisation. An enhanced liberal model was their desired outcome which met the classic criteria: legitimacy, decentralisation, local accountability, policing with consent, representativeness.

However, as I explained earlier, policing was an even more contentious issue in the RUC era than it had been in the previous century. Tinkering with 'their' police was viewed with nervous, sometimes aggressive suspicion by Unionists, while Nationalists wanted nothing less than reformed policing as part of a new political deal, whereby they genuinely enjoyed parity of esteem. The British government quickly grasped the opportunity by appointing Chris Patten, last Governor of Hong Kong, to head a commission and to make recommendations for 'future policing structures and arrangements'. Membership reflected international experience and insights and included three from the USA and two from Canada, in addition to four from Britain and Northern Ireland. Appointed in July 1998, they reported in September 1999, having consulted widely using public focus-group meetings throughout the province from autumn 1998 until spring 1999. This was a positive move away from the attitude surveys of previous years and the contentious interpretations of results which abounded (Ellison and Smyth, 2000). Their qualitative approach brought data from 10,000 people attending forty meetings, reflecting the polarised views of the divided society.

Since disbandment was not an option, Patten developed Hunt's idea of a 'civil police force' into that of a police service. He sought to address the difficulties faced by the RUC, particularly the effects of being 'identified by one section of the population not primarily as the upholders of the law, but as defenders of the state' (ICPNI,

1999: para. 1.3). Ignoring the contentious history of the RUC and international condemnation of many aspects of its practices, Patten focused on the future and did not engage in recrimination. A fundamental component of the liberal–democratic rhetoric is 'policing by consent for community safety' (ICPNI, 1999: para. 1.16), a principle which forms the basis of Patten's thinking and from which all the recommendations stem.

Patten implemented

One significant component identified by both Hunt and Patten (Sinclair, 2000: v) is police accountability. Patten found that PANI, established after Hunt, fell short of providing democratic accountability. Patten recommended a new Northern Ireland Policing Board (NIPB), comprising ten political representatives from the local Assembly and nine independent members nominated by the Secretary of State. They would work alongside a variety of other public agencies – one aspect of a partnership approach. The NIPB holds the chief constable to account for the police service in action, giving him operational responsibility for security, rather than operational independence. He can be held to account for operations retrospectively. Financial accountability was demanded in the form of annual audits and policing plans prepared by the chief constable, in consultation with the Board and endorsed by the Secretary of State.

Another thorny aspect of accountability, in its legal sense, has received much attention in the literature on the RUC (Brogden, 1995; Ellison and Smyth, 2000; McGarry and O'Leary, 1999; Ryder 2000). Even after Hunt and repeal of the Special Powers Act of 1973, an Emergency Provisions Act followed in the same year, giving wider powers of arrest to the security forces. It was followed by the Prevention of Terrorism Act 1979. Critics' observations on apparently unquestioned autonomy, evidenced by reluctance on the part of the judiciary to prosecute police or soldiers for over-enthusiasm in applying their extraordinary powers, the use of supergrasses to provide evidence, and prosecution of an alleged shoot-to-kill police in the 1980s, focused Patten's attention on a need for drastic reform in this area. One extension of the liberal model took the form of a police Ombudsman who would investigate all complaints and initiate enquiries even if complaints had not been made, the Commission decided. Internal accountability was also included. Each officer would be obliged to observe a code of ethical and professional standards which, if not observed, could lead to dismissal. Patten's recommendations were much more stringent than Hunt's, in keeping with a worldwide trend in policing.

Provision for and involvement by the entire community brought recommendations for relevant new structures which combined partnership and decentralisation. Each District Council was to have a District Policing Partnership (DPP) with a majority of elected members selected by the local Council on a party proportional basis. In practice, these partnerships involve four activities aimed at bringing the police and the community closer. The police consult, using focus meetings, discussions with local community groups and residents' associations to find out what issues relating to crime cause greatest concern in each council district. These issues are used by the local police commander in drawing up priorities for the local policing plan. Six times per year public meetings are organised by each DPP at which the district commander presents a report and responds to questions from elected representatives and members of the public, so that policing is publicly monitored. In addition, the police engage with the community 'to gain the cooperation of the public with the police in preventing crime' (NIPB, 2004–05: 06). A website provides further detailed information. While the four-part strategy – consultation, prioritisation, monitoring and engaging – is theoretically sound, consent across the entire community cannot be fully achieved in practice, since infiltration by paramilitaries would be seen by many to be counter-productive, while further progress on the political front is awaited. The success of DPPBs in practice depends very much on individual officers within the PSNI, in the local team, and the support given and input made by the civilian members who may, or may not, choose to play out the traditional political game in miniature.

Decentralisation, another prominent feature of the liberal model, was the main recommendation made in relation to structure. It is another strand of the partnership theme and a move away from 'policing by strangers', characteristic of the colonial model. Administratively, the focus was to establish district units of 50,000–60,000 people, with District Commanders having devolved responsibility for human and financial resources. Officers would serve in one area for three to five years, do foot patrols and adopt a problem-solving approach with locally determined objectives, arrived at by consultation with local representatives of DPPs as explained already.

The use of firearms and the military appearance of police concerned Hunt. He felt that disarmament would make the force more acceptable to Catholics. Deterioration in the security situation, however, forced an early termination of this reform in 1970. While Patten considered that 'the rule of law, not the rule of the gun and the baseball bat, should prevail within the community' (ICPNI, 1999: para. 1.18), the Commission realistically recommended that disarmament would be impractical until the peace process had been completed. In the meantime, he suggested that an alternative to plastic bullets should be used in riot control. Patten had obviously learned from the previous thirty years history that a good idea in principle and in a vacuum is not necessarily a good idea in practice, that contextual factors are of crucial importance when trying to instate a liberal model of policing.

The most contentious recommendations, arguably, made by Patten proved to be the change in name from the RUC to the PSNI. While Hunt advocated a mere change in colour of uniform from green to blue, Patten decided that a change in name and badge were required, in a province where political symbols are of mystical significance and are seen to represent invaluable cultural currency. Patten's decision was based on the realisation that Nationalists and Republicans generally viewed the RUC as being alien to their sympathies, and their appearance conveyed their Britishness and loyalty to Unionism, with the crown dominating the harp on their insignia. A new neutral name was to be matched by a badge devoid of political connotation and expressive of altruistic values and noble aspirations to inspire the new PSNI. In order to support this visual expression of neutrality, the display of the Union flag and portrait of the Queen at police stations was to be discontinued, to avoid association with the Crown and the Union, and to gain acceptance by both communities. This would reflect the 'parity of esteem' between the two traditions, a pillar of the Belfast Agreement. These recommendations for change in image and appearance contributed towards meeting the thorny, elusive and very fundamental liberal criterion of legitimacy.

In relation to the very important and controversial issue of force composition, Hunt recommended that 'vigorous efforts should be made to increase the number of Roman Catholic entrants into the force' (Northern Ireland Parliament, 1969: 45). Patten provided much more detailed thinking. Over the following ten years he suggested that the size of the force should be reduced to approximately 7,500 officers; the Police Reserve (mainly Protestant in composition) should be phased out and recruitment should reflect a 50:50 Catholic:non-Catholic ratio. The Report recommended that police recruitment should be contracted out to an independent agency and that there should be community involvement in the process of selecting trainees on a 50:50 Catholic:non-Catholic basis, thereby redressing the balance in community representation and going beyond the scope of the generic liberal model.

A timely coincidence gave the Patten recommendations a firm philosophical and ethical basis in that the new PSNI had to comply with the provisions of the Human Rights Act of 1998. This requirement provoked the publication of a code of ethics drawn from the European Convention on Human Rights and other instruments. Since March 2003 its provisions apply to all members of the PSNI, regardless of rank. The application of human rights legislation prompted Patten to make recommendations obviously intended to curtail the autonomy of Special Branch by amalgamating it with the CID. Furthermore, covert operations were to be monitored by a commissioner and a special complaints tribunal. The application of human rights legislation and philosophy was to form the core element in all training and development. The Commission's heavy focus on human rights is well summed up in the final sentence of the appropriate section of the Report:

> Behaviourally, [police officers] should perceive their jobs in terms of the protection of human rights. Respect for the human rights of all, including suspects, should be an instinct rather than a procedural point to be remembered. (ICPNI, 1999: para 4.13)

The Patten Report unsurprisingly received a mixed reception, robust criticism from local vested interests and more considered critique from academic commentators. While the leader of the Unionist Party, David Trimble, described the Report as 'a shoddy document', it was welcomed as a significant step forward by the SDLP, calling for full implementation, who clearly separated themselves from the other party representing Catholic voters, Sinn Féin, by nominating members to sit on the Policing Board and on DPPBs. Republicans wanted bolder and faster change, including disbandment of the RUC, with human rights vetting for officers entering a replacement service. They complained that Special Branch had not been reformed. They alleged that senior figures, including some under investigation by the Stevens Enquiry, transferred from the RUC and occupied senior positions in the PSNI. At least one of the Sinn Féin leadership, Martin McGuinness, however, saw a need for continuity in the form of personnel transferring from the old to the new replacement service (Ryder, 2000: 476).

In addition to opposition from Republicans and from Unionists who, wishing to retain a central authoritarian model, disapproved of the idea of accountability at local level for fear of infiltrations by present or past IRA members, there were the police representatives on the PANI. The police, via this body, used opinion polls to show a comfortable level of satisfaction with policing from the two communities and saw demand for reform as a measure of ingratitude to the RUC for the sacrifices which they had made (Hillyard and Tomlinson, 2000; Mulcahy, 2000). The proposal to recruit on a 50:50 Catholic:non-Catholic basis was opposed by Unionists. They argued that Protestant applicants rejected on the grounds that they did not have a Catholic 'partner' could justly feel that they had suffered from discrimination, in spite of fair employment legislation. This recommendation was not, however, new as a Unionist politician, Ken (now Lord) Magennis had earlier advocated it over a ten-year period, calculating that Catholic representation would rise to 25 per cent.

Patten failed to take into account the sizeable and growing number of civilians in the police service, reckoned to be 85 per cent Protestant (McGarry and O'Leary, 1999: 46). Another omission in relation to the force composition was any reference to the gender ratio. These commentators saw greater representation by women as a partial solution since women, on demographic evidence, make up just over 50 per cent of the population. According to their calculations, if officers were recruited on a basis of 50:50 men:women and if female recruits were drawn proportionally from cultural Catholics and cultural Protestants, the proportion of Catholics would rise from 8 to 24 per cent. They stress the political advantage resulting from such reform: it would benefit women from both traditions and would draw attention away from what some consider 'positive discrimination' of choosing on an overall 50:50 Catholic:non-Catholic basis. Official RUC projections showed that a 40 per cent rate of Catholics will be reached in 2030 (Northern Ireland Affairs Committee, 1998, Appendix B: 14). More recent figures project 30 per cent by 2010 (NIPB, 2004–05: 13).

Though the Patten recommendations have been widely recognised as a blueprint for effective modern policing beyond the confines of Northern Ireland, such reform in a divided society is likely to succeed only if it is part of a wider discourse to include significant political reform acceptable to both communities. The two most important conditions of its success are political will and community support. In the course of its relatively short life, the Local Assembly has been suspended twice but was reinstated in May 2007. Some commentators would not place the entire blame on intransigent positions taken by local political parties to explain lack of progress. They would point a finger at the Westminster government for grasping at suspension too readily, and 'retreating to the colonial comfort zone of direct rule' (Hillyard and Tomlinson, 2000: 398) whenever stalemate reigns.

However strident and diverse the criticisms levied at Patten, and however short the Police Act of 2001 fell of Patten's vision fully implemented, he provided a persuasive, carefully argued and detailed explication of an enhanced liberal model of policing in place in Northern Ireland. Its success presupposes, however, that the political arrangements will deal with the causes of conflict in Northern Irish society, in short that the Belfast Agreement will be fully implemented as the Peace Process develops to achieve agreed ends. Elections, for Westminster and for local councils, held in May 2005 brought results which did not augur well for this aspiration, as the results brought significant increases in representation for the extreme parties, the DUP and Sinn Féin, squeezing the moderate parties into a much reduced centre space.

Conclusion

I have drawn upon the work of others in my historical survey of policing in Ireland since 1822, focusing on the problematical relationship between the RIC – then the RUC – and the Catholic population. Using the contrasting colonial and liberal models, I have shown that while Ireland was wholly colonised until 1921, and after Partition, when Northern Ireland retained many of its colonial features, fundamental policing reform was impossible in the political and social context which obtained.

It was only when far-reaching political change was agreed in the form of the Belfast Agreement (1998) intended to end division and to establish parity of esteem for the two major religious traditions, coupled with a comprehensive blueprint for radical change in policing, that aspirations towards establishing a liberal police service became even theoretically possible. The Patten Report is replete with liberal rhetoric and the recommendations, if implemented, would instate the liberal model for the first time since Ireland came under British rule. Experience of policing diversity in other countries such as the USA, Canada, South Africa and Australia, as well as in England, clearly informed and influenced the Patten Commission's thinking.

Research aims and objectives
My literature search indicated that Catholic police officers in Northern Ireland have not been a subject of in-depth research. No one appears to have investigated a representative sample during the life of the RUC to find out the reasons for such

a consistently small minority from their community background having pursued careers in the RUC. I wanted to plug that gap, since third-party anecdotal evidence from sources with frequently strong political bias was the only discourse in existence on this topic. My aim was to couple my questions about reasons for absence of numerical representation with testing the capability of the PSNI, using the Patten template, to transform policing in Northern Ireland from largely satisfying the colonial model to meeting liberal model criteria. The test of viability of that latter model I chose to apply was enhanced Catholic recruitment on a 50:50 basis.

In order to achieve this aim I set out to focus via interviews on (a) the experiences of Catholic officers in the RUC, as they recounted them, that might have hindered a more socially representative force; (b) the factors within the force and in the communities whence they came which might explain low recruitment figures; (c) any discernible positive change within the PSNI or within their communities which might increase recruitment; (d) differences in experiences, views and attitudes of three constituencies – retired RUC, currently serving officers who transferred from the RUC to the PSNI, and those newly recruited to the PSNI. The attitudes, motivations and aspirations of the trainees might be different from those of their predecessors, since they represent the post-Patten generation who possibly have a different mindset. The chapter which follows gives details of how my aims and objectives outlined above were operationalised and the context in which the research was carried out.

2

Digging for treasure

I set out to seek privileged access to a sample of grossly under-represented Catholic officers to test the viability of increased recruitment in a new political context after the Belfast Agreement (1998). In this chapter I shall describe the research sample, the design and the data collection procedures which I followed.

Although the population census of 2001 showed approximately 44 per cent of the population of Northern Ireland to be Catholics, only 7.72 per cent of police officers were perceived to be Catholic when the RUC ceased to exist (3 October 2001). However small the numbers, there have always been *some* Catholics who chose policing as a career. It was my intention to research the experiences and the attitudes of a sample of these to allow some comparison to be made to the Catholic community in general, as revealed in the NILT survey. The research design would include qualitative and quantitative methods.

Using a sample made up of three discrete groups of officers (a) currently serving who were experienced in the RUC and had transferred to the PSNI; (b) those within their first two years of service; and (c) retired officers, I wanted to learn if there were any discernible differences in attitudes to Patten relating to variables such as age, length of service, reasons for recent recruits being attracted to the PSNI which suggested that their aspirations might be shared by increasing numbers of Catholics. The historical perspective afforded by the testimonies of retired officers seemed a valuable source of supplemental data. Older respondents were able to discuss recent developments, subsequent to the Belfast Agreement, as civilians, yet advantaged by the experience and insight gained as police officers, some even before 1969 and the outbreak of sustained conflict. (I was unable to find any female retired officers willing to be interviewed.)

I selected (a) survey research (b) focus groups and (c) one-to-one in-depth interviews as the three features of my enquiry. The survey was conducted to provide a descriptive profile of Catholic police officers in Northern Ireland in order to give an informed background to my in-depth interviews. Survey findings obviously helped in formulating an interview guide for use in addressing the broad research questions discussed earlier. The qualitative data generated by the interviews was to form the major focus of my research – in mathematical terms probably approximating 90 per cent weighting.

1. The postal survey was administered to a computer-selected random sample of 300 currently serving officers from a total population of 700–800. A total of 138 individuals responded to the survey, which represented a 46 per cent response rate.
2. Follow-up in-depth interviews were conducted with 50 of the survey respondents who volunteered to participate further in this way.
3. In-depth interviews were conducted with 10 officers who had a maximum of two years of service in the PSNI. They were identified as a non-probabilistic sample using the snowball technique, whereby each interviewee names another to be interviewed. Additional interviews were conducted with 10 retired officers. Together, these three subgroups furnished a historical dimension to the qualitative data produced. In total, the data for this study were derived from 138 questionnaires and 70 in-depth, one-to-one interviews.

The primary purpose of my postal survey was to provide a means of contacting and identifying a sample of Catholic officers who would be willing to participate in in-depth interviews. The survey findings were used qualitatively for the purposes of description and, additionally, the survey allowed for some key comparisons to be made with other descriptive profiles obtained from previous small-scale surveys of police officers, and also, large-scale population surveys carried out in Northern Ireland. Attention was paid, however, to ensure the reliability and validity of the postal questionnaire. The questions were piloted on a random sample of twenty and non-responders were followed up. Both sample size and response rate were authoritative – 300 from a total universe estimated to be 700–800, bringing a response rate of 46 per cent.

A further advantage of the survey method very relevant in this case was confidentiality and anonymity. The RUC was keen to show willingness to cooperate by affording me access. However, it stressed that access was conditional upon protecting their officers' confidentiality and anonymity, that respondents had to volunteer to be involved and that no pressure from inside would be brought to bear on them. These points were clearly made in a covering letter which accompanied my questionnaire sent out by the liaison officer. The postal survey (see Appendix 1) posed intrusive questions which sought data on very sensitive issues, so recipients needed protected space in which to decide whether or not they were willing to participate. The survey served the dual purpose of satisfying the organisation's requirements and respecting the rights of the potential respondents.

Sampling proved to be a rather difficult problem. Before Patten and the 50:50 recruitment ratio of Catholics:non Catholics was introduced, applicants were not asked their religious denomination, so the only indicator of religious affiliation was the name or type of primary (or junior) school attended. This assumption can lead to errors in measurement of the concept of religious background. For example, Catholic officers who attended (state)-controlled or integrated schools or preparatory departments of Protestant grammar schools would not be picked up in a random sample of perceived Catholics. Equally likely, a non-Catholic who attended a primary or preparatory school with a saint's name would be wrongly categorised as Catholic. An additional difficulty emerged in the form of a ruling by a 'remote' gatekeeper, PSNI's equal opportunities officer. According to his interpretation of the relevant legislation, the questionnaire, designed specifically and exclusively for perceived Catholics, had to be sent to an equal number of perceived non-Catholic officers even though I had no intention of using their data. I was not afforded an opportunity to meet the civilian who made the decision in order to receive a plausible explanation, much less to negotiate its application.

Questionnaire

The questionnaire was in five sections and consisted of a total of twenty-one multiple choice questions, fifteen of which had several sub-questions. Some questions were taken from the NILT survey to facilitate comparison with Catholic responses in the community as a whole and some from a survey by Mapstone (1994) researching attitudes of part-time RUC officers towards policing and a number of social and political issues of continuing interest to researchers and others. A copy of the questionnaire is reproduced in Appendix 1.

Multiple methods

Some of the weaknesses of the questionnaire method in accessing complex and sensitive material were overcome in my research design by the use of multiple methods. Specifically the qualitative nature of in-depth interviews provided more detail on the nature and experiences of Catholic officers. Further, this approach allowed me to invite respondents to raise any other issues they considered relevant but which were omitted in the questionnaire. These issues included the role of the media in portraying the police, officers' experiences with the Catholic Church as well as with individual clergy, and officers' perceptions of the RUC's public relations work.

The original research design included the collection of data through a survey, focus groups and in-depth interviews with three groups of retired, current experienced and recent recruits. However, the plan to conduct focus groups was abandoned. The liaison officer, when she attempted to form ten such groups consisting of six officers of mixed ranks, gender, service duration and stations, found negative reaction to the idea. It was felt by a sample of potential participants with whom she discussed the matter that a focus-group environment would have an inhibiting effect on the generation of open in-depth data in response to searching, sensitive questions. Negative factors included the presence of officers holding different ranks and concern about possible breaches in confidentiality. Logistical problems arising from shift work, absence through illness, last-minute changes in work schedules and emergency duties were also cited as causes for the necessary change in plan. In hindsight, the sensitive nature of the research topic might have created problems in a focus-group setting, for example many people are not willing to contribute in a group setting with the same degree of honesty which they would in a one-to-one interview. Equally, some participants might modify the tenor of their contributions in order to be on the 'winning' side, or not to be seen to counter another with position power, knowledge power, personal power or influence. Moreover, confidentiality might also be compromised in a group setting.

The purpose of the in-depth interviews was to penetrate the subjective reality of officers' lives past and present. Interviews focused on finding answers to my broad research questions about Catholic representation in policing assisted by ideas generated in survey data analysis (see Interview guide, Appendix 2). Developmental trends, reactions to Patten's recommendations and their (partial) implementation, actual and planned change within PSNI were also targeted by questions. Interviews were conducted without gatekeepers either in officers' homes, the researcher's home or at a neutral location. The choice of interview site was decided by respondents which shifted the balance of power from the interviewer to the respondent. Having described my research sample and design, I now turn to the subject of data collection.

Getting in and getting on
Interviews averaged 1.75 hours, but ranged from 1.5 to 4.0 hours. The total time commitment was in excess of 120 contact hours which required more than 3,000 miles of driving throughout Northern Ireland. Organising the interviews fell to me. I was provided with station telephone numbers linked to names of volunteers who had ticked the appropriate box on the anonymous questionnaire. I planned to carry out two interviews per day – allowing me time to complete my records immediately after each interview and to make notes on demeanour, location, impressions of personality and plausibility of response to me in gender, class, age terms. I did not systematically cover all these criteria, but simply commented on any feature which seemed worthy of note.

The interviews were carried out nine to twelve months after the survey was conducted. It was necessary, therefore, when I eventually reached the officer by telephone, to remind him/her of who I was, what I was doing, achieve agreement to meet, arrange a date, time and place. Some were able to settle these issues during the initial contact; others had to seek approval from a senior officer. The liaison officer had assured me that permission was given in principle that individual officers would be released, subject to the exigencies of duty. In a significant number of cases, however, the shift system made it very difficult to arrange two interviewees in reasonably close locations within a normal working day. I had to be flexible in my scheduling of interviews going, for example, on a round trip of about 90 miles to meet two officers on night duty, beginning at 7 p.m.

A small minority opted to meet me away from base at a local hotel and a very small number (mainly retired) opted for their own homes and one came to mine. The usual location was a pre-booked interview room in a station where the officer was serving, or one close by, if he/she preferred to be interviewed off duty at a station convenient to home. In a small minority of cases I conducted the interview in the (senior) officer's own office, or in the custody suite, especially if the officer was a member of the crime squad. One of my priorities was to establish rapport as quickly as possible by reinforcing what I had said on the telephone about confidentiality and security, explaining what I was trying to do, assuring that the only 'right' answers were their honest ones – both facts and opinions. I tried to remove pressure and stress the element of choice by suggesting they said 'pass' if they did not choose to answer a particular question. No one, in the course of seventy interviews, said 'pass', though the choice offered did not preclude the possibility of receiving non-committal or incomplete answers. No one baulked when I told them that the interview would take one and a half hours.

In order to protect confidentiality of subjects I was very discreet when telephoning police stations. If the individual were not available, I was generally told when he/she would next be on duty. In addition, however, and in accordance with good public relations practice by office staff, I was invited to accept help from someone else. I had to decline the offer without revealing the reason for wishing to contact a specific officer. In order not to raise curiosity levels, I invariably advised that I wished to make an appointment to discuss 'a private matter'. I felt I could not be honest about the focus of my research as I might be revealing an officer's religious affiliation to someone who did not know it already and who might use the information in a damaging way. (My approach did not avoid some amusing speculation: in one case the officer was asked by the message-taker if he was in financial trouble, another if he was having an illicit romantic affair.)

Arranging interviews and dealing with necessary changes absorbed a surprising amount of time. On average, four telephone calls were made before an interview resulted. I have already alluded to the change in research design from focus groups to in-depth one-to-one interviews. The other major change came in the form of a directive, presented as strong 'advice' that interviews could not be taped. The liaison officer, again on advice, reported to me that officers did not favour this admittedly usual practice, because taped interviews with suspects are a normal part of police work with attendant overtones of criminality, evidence that might be used in court and a general confrontational atmosphere.

A procedure which subjects considered threatening would not permit 'a conversation with a purpose', the description of the interview which I wanted to sell in order to maximise my chances of obtaining valuable, rich data. So I would have to (a) ask questions from my interview schedule; (b) maintain eye contact as much as possible to establish and maintain trust and to interpret body language; (c) write as quickly as possible using a personal form of shorthand, and leaving space at the end of words to be completed later; (d) process what I was hearing; (e) decide on follow-up questions in order to probe or delve; (f) sift the wheat from the chaff in terms of insightful comments and revelations, questions which neatly encapsulated ideas, or contradicted expected responses or previously held assumptions.

In the field, I found that the liaison officer's advice in regard to taping interviews proved to be accurate. Some said that they would not have taken part or, more frequently, that they would not have refused but 'I certainly would not have told you as much'. In contrast, one senior officer decided that it would save me 'a lot of bother', if he were to put a tape in a readily available recorder. This tape was replaced by a second when necessary. Giving me both to take away, he assured me: 'Everyone knows my views anyhow'.

I believe that my introductory 'spiel' helped to smooth initial concerns or uncertainty on the part of the interviewee. I pointed out the researcher's code of ethical conduct, stressing I intended to keep their identity anonymous and the data secure. Complete privacy was provided in police stations; in hotels, we had to be careful about our location relative to other guests and about our voice levels. In retired officers' houses, after presenting refreshments, spouses discreetly withdrew while the interview took place.

During interviews at police stations, interruptions were at a minimum and only of momentary length, usually caused by fellow officers who did not realise that the room was in use. On one occasion an officer from the drug squad needed to keep his mobile phone switched on because plans were in place for an imminent swoop on dealers while they took delivery of a large consignment of hard drugs. His team of uniformed colleagues sat around a table, a suitable distance away, waiting for their signal to pounce. Another amazed me by keeping his radio on while he 'monitored' calls to and from police cars throughout the entire interview. He answered my questions thoughtfully and coherently at the same time, with only brief pauses.

At all stations I visited, except four, I was given prearranged permission to use the police car park. In one instance lack of space was an obviously legitimate reason for polite refusal. In another case, I was offered space in the grounds of a church nearby. While this arrangement proved convenient, I felt that it associated the police with one (Protestant) community in that town. The other two locations were in Belfast east and west, serving areas with high levels of paramilitary activity, where I sensed a siege mentality towards civilians in general at the entrance, and a reluctance to treat any visitor without suspicion. At all locations, save one, I was offered coffee and, despite the generally spartan conditions prevailing, was given a chair and a table in a room heated to a comfortable temperature.

Having discussed my research design and data collection, I shall now consider relevant political and personal issues.

Political and personal issues

Researching police officers presented me with challenges of a political nature. These challenges I found to be ongoing, though not surprising, because my research was on a sensitive topic. Being an institution of the criminal justice system, a police service is one of the 'dark corners of society which tend to be closed and circumspect towards intruders' (Lee, 1993: 2). In my case, centralisation of power in the RUC/PSNI is one source of difficulty. Legal justification for secrecy through laws protecting the activities and identities of Special Branch and MI5 personnel is another. Absence of clarity regarding the decision-making structure within the PSNI and the respective roles of the Secretary of State, the chief constable and the Policing Board is a third source. The contract which I had to agree with the chief constable (Appendix 3) imposed stringent rules on monitoring and publication of the content of my research findings. These conditions illustrate the power exercised by the PSNI.

Although keen to appear open to scrutiny in pursuit of a positive public relations image, the PSNI is by its very nature a closed institution, being an important part of the criminal justice system of Northern Ireland which can modify its openness at will on 'public interest' grounds. For example, in 2004 access to researchers was officially – though temporarily – withdrawn by the PSNI. The PSNI establishment, in affording me access, may have been attempting to match the relatively high level of enforced transparency which resulted from the Pattern recommendations with a measure of voluntary transparency within carefully controlled limits.

Moving on from the macro-political context of policing within which permission to gain closed access had initially to be negotiated, I shall consider the ongoing exercise of power and control during the research process. Gatekeepers are the carefully selected individuals within an organisation who are entrusted to ensure, on behalf of the organisation, that the conditions contained in the contract drawn up by the dominant party are met. Those selected are required to exercise cautious vigilance in supporting the research process unilaterally – some strategically, some operationally. These gatekeepers included the senior director of human resources, the equal opportunities officer, the police librarian (all civilians). The coordinating gatekeeper was, however, a police liaison officer, staff officer to that senior director. Reference has already been made to changes in my research design resulting from gatekeeper control, in particular dropping a focus-group element and conducting in-depth interviews without tape-recording them. While these modifications were made for plausible reasons, I had no choice but to comply.

Closely related, I suspect, is the fact that I was afforded only 'closed' access to the RUC, and subsequently to the PSNI. I soon realised that control over access was exercised by individuals, literally and even physically throughout the interview stage of my research. At every police station I attempted to convince the person on duty that I had permission to park inside the grounds. Furthermore, he or she had to be persuaded that the named colleague had agreed to see me. Officers in a security role, therefore, acted as gatekeepers to both property and individuals. The dilemma of the researcher in relation to access is well summed up by Mason: 'You must continue to use your critical judgement and to assess what kind of access you have – for example, it might be full, partial, conditional, intermittent – and to which regions or interactions' (Mason, 2002b: 91).

The role of liaison officer was a difficult one for the officers who mediated between respondents and me. They had to follow instructions and sometimes to impose restrictions while at the same time try to use the opportunity to make the research exercise a public relations success for the PSNI. I had to establish and maintain the liaison officers' trust which had to be re-established each time a new liaison officer was appointed, while pushing them beyond their comfort zone. The liaison officer's role included that of buffer between the organisation and individual officers. One incumbent had to deal with negative feedback, for example, irate phone calls and letters from self-styled 'targets' of the survey who, at least temporarily, felt that their employer was not protecting their privacy or their security.

On reflection, one must admit that the response from subjects which I have just described was not unreasonable. The problem arose from the absence of informed consent from officers who felt aggrieved that they received a questionnaire by post without prior knowledge. Recipients were not afforded an opportunity to give their consent, informed or otherwise, since they constituted a computerised random sample. The 300 recipients perceived to be Catholic according to official police records and, as a result, were given a label that identified them as 'belonging' to the Catholic community. Such an approach is very sensitive in the Northern Ireland context. It is undoubtedly true that, in spite of letters from the liaison officer and from me explaining the nature and purpose of the research, that individuals were not given an opportunity to be omitted from the sampling frame.

When volunteers identified themselves for one-to-one interviews, I informed them of the purpose of my research by telephone and at the beginning of the interview sessions. I also discussed with them issues pertaining to confidentiality and invited questions before proceeding to my interview schedule, in order to obtain their consent. Judging by their response, it would seem that they were comfortable to trust me, especially on those aspects which appeared most important to them – confidentiality and security of identity and of data.

The caution with which police officers view requests from sociologists to participate in research is easily explained by a dominant feature of police culture. The point is made by Manning in relation to the secrecy which surrounds police work and the suspicion with which they regard outsiders who ask questions and pry into their private professional world. 'Secrecy means that policemen must not talk about police work to those outside the department' (Westley, 1970: 774). I considered it prudent, therefore, to take great pains to ensure the confidentiality of my business with volunteer interviewees. Though not talking to me directly about police work, they might have been perceived by hostile or nervous colleagues to have been betraying professional practice and so endangering their own and others' safety.

Wishing to establish confidence and to allay possible fear of bias, I asked about 10 per cent if they would like to know my religion. They hastily said that they would not, possibly because members of a police service wishing to present a neutral image could not suggest that they needed to know my religion. I am inclined to the view that, if questioned afterwards, they would have been able to say that they did not know, thereby avoiding any possible suggestion of collusion in producing data biased religiously or politically against either the RUC or the PSNI. One exception was a retired senior officer, more than 70 years old, who asked the question directly at the beginning of the interview in his own home, exercising the territorial imperative.

I settled for the 'acceptable incompetent' label (Lofland, 1971: 100). I felt there would be a beneficial measure of reciprocity between my need for data which they could help create and a feel-good factor on their part, arising from a realisation that I valued what they had to say. I sensed that I was accorded respect as someone doing academic research and coming from a well-known and respected institution.

Even if one succeeds in penetrating the protective armour of secrecy which traditionally surrounds police officers and their work, one has to confront a consequential danger – 'going native'. Maintaining detachment of judgement in order to avoid bias while being faithful to the multiple moral demands of the 'ethnographic self' made this research project an ongoing and ever-changing challenge, continuously demanding the exercise of multiple mental and social skills. For example, one serving officer, after reminding me that 'police officers trust nobody' went on to give an apparently open and cooperative interview, though he was free, as every other interviewee was, to 'give me the party line'.

The circumstances surrounding my research seemed to make it impossible for me to build up a good reputation for myself as an interviewer, thereby easing my path. Let me explain what I mean. With each interviewee, I had to establish rapport; I could not benefit from building up a cumulative merit bank resulting from individuals passing on positive comments on their interview experience of me. The possibility of such was denied by the fact that subjects were as eager to keep their identities anonymous after the interview as they were before – with notably few exceptions.

As I reflect on the whole interview process I am conscious that I paid perhaps a justifiable price when I asked sensitive questions. The presence of relative trust in the transaction between my informants and me did not rule out the possibility of officers being untruthful when I tried to penetrate their psychic selves. Whenever I touched on sensitive topics such as possible police collusion with paramilitaries, the hitherto unaccountability of Special Branch or reported ill-treatment of suspects at holding centres, I found almost palpable a huge sense of regret and of helplessness in many. At least within themselves, they had to admit that morally reprehensible behaviour might have been enacted in their name. Complex mental activity involved balancing many elements including loyalty to their organisation, to individuals within it, to themselves. Such activity was likely to generate feelings of guilt, embarrassment, regret, even anger over events and processes which they had consigned to history.

By asking sensitive questions I felt on many occasions that I was asking them to confront painful issues on which they had not pronounced before. My questions were likely to produce mental and emotional turmoil in those who had to reconcile loyalty to the organisation which they had served over many years, yet not to every subgroup within it. Moreover, they had been socialised to present a united front to me, an 'intruder'. There may, understandably, have been temptation to lie or embellish or distort the truth when discussing probably the *most* sensitive area: how they fared as members of a small religious minority group within the RUC. Did they, I asked myself frequently, want to appear clever, macho, resourceful, resilient when they described how they handled (invariably rare) reported incidents of sectarianism, 'giving as good as I got', or enjoying the support of a predominantly Protestant group of colleagues against an errant Protestant colleague?

The reflexive ethnographer must visit and revisit with a critical eye her research design, data-creating process and results, against a yardstick of quality. In practice, I believe that quality is the ultimate goal towards which one strives, but a qualitative researcher can never be completely confident about how closely her data approximate quality. A brave attempt can, however, be made by assessing the relative balance within a project in terms of its strengths and shortcomings, though such evaluation must, of necessity, be subjective.

The traditional criteria for evaluating research in the social sciences have been reliability and validity and ethnographers have sought to find terms which distance them from positivists (Altheide and Johnson, 1998; Atkinson, 1990; Brewer, 2000; Hammersley, 1990). The term 'reliability' cannot be even considered in the case of ethnographic studies, since by the very nature of the data-gathering process and the importance of the researcher in its creation, a study cannot be replicated though questions can. Other terms can, however, be substituted. Lincoln and Guba (1985) suggest 'generalisability' or 'transferability' but warn that these cannot claim to provide external validity (as positivists would require).

A study's 'generalisability' can be strengthened by triangulation of data sources. In my study I attempted triangulation at design stage, though the sources were reduced in number when a focus-group element had to be omitted. There remain, however, survey data which fed into the interview schedule. I compensated though by including three categories of police officers (experienced, new and retired) with different life 'realities', giving a historical perspective on similar social phenomena.

I did not feel obliged to link closely all survey questions with interview questions. Instead, I selected according to the emerging picture built up from an 'outsider's' knowledge and experiences of policing in Northern Ireland in its social, historical and comparative contexts and the confirming or contrasting data from the survey, which invited further research. Data from the survey provided an additional 'ideas pool' to be used in structuring an interview schedule. To that survey I now turn.

Survey findings

My survey was conducted with a computer-generated random sample of 300 PSNI police officers in November–December 2002. These officers were perceived to be from the Catholic community and drawn from a total population of 700–800 Catholics who were employed by the PSNI and who had transferred from the RUC when the latter was replaced by the former in 2001. If, in completing a form, an applicant showed that he had attended a Catholic primary school, for example, Our Lady's or St. John's, that person was perceived to be culturally Catholic. The purpose of the survey was to establish a general profile of Catholic officers serving in Northern Ireland – since none such existed in terms of personal biographies, their career experiences in a socio-political context and their attitudes towards issues which might affect their personal or professional lives. An internal survey of religious and political harassment and discrimination in the RUC carried out five years previously brought a response rate of only 34 per cent, though it was a census of all officers (N = 12,814) (RUC, Personnel 'B' Department, 1997).

The data from my study were coded using SPSS, cleaned and frequencies for variables were generated. Cross-tabulations following recoding were used in some instances. The survey findings were used qualitatively for descriptive purposes. I did not set out to seek explanations or causal relationships from survey data, as my study was predominantly qualitative. The outcome of my research was intended to be the presentation and analysis of Catholic officers' subjectively experienced lives, part of a quest towards identifying ways in which Catholic recruitment might be enhanced. I did not feel that complex quantitative analysis of survey results would serve my purpose further.

Where possible, data from this survey will be compared with similar data from Catholics in the general population of Northern Ireland. The most frequently quoted source of this comparative data will be the attitudinal surveys covering religion, politics and social issues carried out annually by the NILT survey which succeeded the Northern Ireland Social Attitudes survey (NISA) in 1998. The NILT survey is an annual collaborative venture carried out by staff from the two universities – Queen's University Belfast and the University of Ulster. Reference will also be made to a study of the attitudes of part-time police officers in the RUC (Mapstone, 1994). This data was generated by a survey of all part-time RUC on the establishment at 1990, which brought a 57 per cent response rate. The main objective was 'to identify the nature of the explanations members of the RUC reserve provide for their membership of the police and their behaviour within it' (Mapstone, 1994:1). Caution should be exercised in comparing Mapstone's data with mine, since the religious composition of the part-time force was only 3 per cent

Catholic in 1992 (Mapstone, 1994: 29). By 2002 Catholic full-time officers in the PSNI were estimated to constitute 7–8 per cent of the total from a general Catholic population of 44 per cent (Northern Ireland Census 2001: Key Statistics, 2003: 22, table KSO76).

In this section I examine my survey data divided under three headings. Respondents' personal biographies reveal Catholic officers' attitudes and practice regarding religious belief and worship, moral issues, education, family background and neighbourhood. These topics were chosen because they address the main cluster of features which characterise cultural Catholicism in Northern Ireland. A second area dealt with is these officers' career biographies. It focuses on their reasons for choosing the RUC and the attitudes of family and peers to their choice, as well as their experiences, positive or negative in a predominantly Protestant police culture. Third, the Patten reform programme is addressed – particularly the 50:50 Catholic:non-Catholic recommendation which had begun to be implemented at the time the survey was conducted – and the socio-political context in which this blueprint for a liberal model of policing was set. Findings discussed in this chapter are presented in tabular form in Appendix 1.

Personal biographies

First, I present a summary profile to introduce my sample.

Table 1   Summary characteristics of the survey sample (N = 138)

Gender	Male 82%	Female 18%
Age	Average 39 years	Range: 25–54 years
Marital status	Married 65%	Co-habiting 12%
	Divorced/separated/widowed 14%	Never married 8%
Length of service	Average 15 years	Range 3–32 years
Place of birth	N. Ireland 88%	England 7%
	Republic of Ireland 3%	Other/DK ['Don't Know'] 6%
Current religion	Catholic 76%	Protestant 3%
	No religion 15%	Other/DK 6%
Religion of partner	Catholic 28%	Protestant 49%
	No religion 3%	Other/DK 17%
Religion of father	Catholic 92%	Protestant 8%
Religion of mother	Catholic 98%	Protestant 2%
Respondents with fathers who were/are police officers	18%	
Respondents with mothers who were/are police officers	3%	

The information given above shows basic biographical data which were pertinent to the research topic – the low recruitment of Catholics into the RUC and the
reforms planned to redress the balance. In the course of this section I shall refer to
their significance at various points.

From the data on personal biographies it appeared that an overwhelming majority of officers had been brought up in traditional Catholic families, having two
Catholic parents and attending Catholic primary and second-level schools. Their
formal educational achievements were higher than those of Catholics in general
in all response categories. In spite of a general trend towards an increased level of
mixed marriages in Northern Ireland, respondents emerged as being exceptional
in that they were much more likely to have a Protestant than Catholic partner.
This accelerated trend away from traditional marriage practice was matched by the
numbers of their children who were attending schools not exclusively Catholic.
Choice of schools might have been determined on ideological grounds but might
also denote a compromise on the part of Catholic officers accommodating to the
wishes of their children's non-Catholic mothers.

While 76 per cent of officers identified themselves as Catholic, about one in seven
stated that they had no religion, though they qualified for the description of 'cultural
Catholic' in that they had been brought up Catholic, but no longer accepted the tenets
or observed the practices of the Catholic Church. They were more likely to be non-
believers than Catholics in general tended to be. Poor levels of attendance at worship
by Catholic police reinforced the separation. On moral issues, respondents emerged as
comparably conservative to the Catholic population on sex outside marriage, but different in their divided attitudes to same-sex relations. Questions on officers' residential
environments brought clear data that a large majority lived in predominantly middle-
class areas, or those which were well mixed in class terms. Equally, a vast majority lived
in predominantly non-Catholic areas. On a variety of significant criteria respondents
had identified themselves as a group apart from their co-religionists. Their low levels of
cultural Catholicism provided a fruitful vein to mine at interview stage.

A pattern of high percentages of missing data began in answer to a question on
previous employment. Responses showed though that a large majority of officers
had experienced paid employment outside the RUC, so they had been exposed to
other work cultures which might, however, not all have been civilian. Their possible
influence on or contrast with police cultures seemed worthy of pursuit at interview
stage, in order to assess the strength of police cultures on officers' subjective experiences of them. Almost one-fifth would not give their rank, but the proportions not
willing to give detail of the sources and strength of opposition which they faced
from significant others on joining the RUC reached 55 per cent and 50 per cent
respectively. It seemed reasonable to assume that fear of being identified was being
expressed, but perhaps the higher figures indicated ongoing pain aggravated by
direct questions which focused on the personal price they had to pay for becoming
Catholic members of the RUC.

Nearly six out of ten said they were constables. Of the ranks above inspector level there was very low representation, though the 19 per cent who failed to respond may have included higher ranks who, precisely because of their seniority, reckoned that they might be more easily identified. (I tried to redress the balance by seeking over-representation of senior ranks in the snowball sample of retired officers who agreed to be interviewed.) The range of service spanned three to thirty-two years, the average being fifteen years. Officers had served mainly in large stations in urban areas of Northern Ireland.

Almost two-thirds joined for noble reasons – challenge and service, whereas almost one-quarter did so for material reasons. When the Catholic officers' responses to a question about the level of support they would give to a friend interested in joining was compared with a similar question put to the general population by NILT shortly before, there was perhaps surprising agreement from the Catholic population. The youngest group of working age, those under 30, and the oldest, those aged 46 and above, provided data which could be read as heralding optimistic outcomes to 50:50 recruitment drives by the PSNI.

There was almost total response to questions which required self-reporting on political ideology espoused prior to joining. Almost nine out of ten reported themselves to have held neutral or mildly nationalist views substantially shared by close family in 50 per cent of cases. This area was identified as one worthy of exploration during interviews since the picture was strongly at variance with the political affiliations of the Catholic population. Catholic police and their families emerged as a very unrepresentative subset.

The difficulties endured by Catholic police officers caused by the negative attitudes of significant others to their choice of career must inevitably be considered as a potential source of isolation from the Catholic community in general. Responses to a survey question showed that approximately two-thirds had to position themselves apart from their community. More than four in ten officers reported that they had to do so to a large extent or almost totally, though almost one-quarter refused to answer. Their choice of career presented a surprisingly large percentage of Catholic officers with no choice but to separate themselves from family and community. For almost one-quarter of respondents their families' opposition presented problems to them, though the strength of opposition was equally divided between being strong and being mild. For almost half, the difficulties lasted only a short time, but for three in ten it continued.

Police culture is a research topic which has generated an enormous literature over the past forty years (Banton, 1964; Brewer and Magee, 1991; Cain, 1973; Fielding, 1994; Reiner, 1992; Reuss-Ianni, 1983; Skolnick, 1966 – to name a few). A distinction is generally drawn between the official and the unofficial cultures, though they are not discrete entities in practice. Data were sought on Catholic officers' perceptions of the dominant types of culture in their organisation.

Considering official and unofficial cultures together, they were perceived to be markedly British, neutral and welcoming to Catholics. 'Negative' criteria, Unionist and Protestant, scored at middle range, though the unofficial culture scored more highly than the official. Approximately four officers in ten reported never having experienced discomfort from colleagues in the RUC because of their religious identity. Sectarianism took the form of hostile jokes for 24 per cent. Twenty 'open' comments were made on the cultures, a majority on the unofficial culture. These included explanations for unjustifiable behaviour, assurances that over time sectarianism had become less common. Some offered ways of dealing with it, such as letting others take care of the offenders or going down the legal complaints route. Bullying, labelling, Masonic influence and pathological bigotry were all cited as aspects mostly of the unofficial culture. The response figures identified personal experience of police culture to be a topic worthy of inclusion at interview stage.

The Patten Report and police reform

The Patten Report of 1999 which followed shortly after the Belfast Agreement of 1998 brought far-reaching recommendations. The most significant resulted in the RUC ceasing to exist by April 2002. The Catholic officers whom I surveyed were asked for their views on the implementation of recommendations while they were all involved in and affected by this first huge exercise in police reform since Northern Ireland was established eighty years previously.

A clear majority, whatever their length of service, felt that there had been too much police reform in accordance with Patten's recommendations. Whether they referred to pace or scope of reform, or both, was a question to be pursued later. One of the key recommendations, that recruitment to the PSNI should be on a 50:50 basis, was deemed by more than six out of ten officers to be a successful strategy for making the PSNI more representative of the entire population than has ever been the case in the course of the RUC's history. The reasons for one officer in seven adopting an opposing stance was also worthy of further investigation.

There were thirteen 'open' comments on recent police reform, some of which placed the implementation of Patten in a socio-political context. Regret was expressed that religion had been made an issue. Disparity in numbers between Catholic and non-Catholic police officers in Northern Ireland was explained as intimidation by Republican activists. There was strong feeling that too much emphasis on civil rights had dictated a Republican agenda, causing some areas to be run by extremists from either end of the political spectrum. Negative comment was relieved by approval of reform in principle, but accompanied by criticism of the scale and pace. The role of the Catholic Church as an institution and of individual clergy in officers' work and private lives was identified as another worthy topic for the interview schedule.

A comfortable majority of respondents agreed that the two major communities in Northern Ireland enjoyed community commonality, though a significantly higher score was recorded by Mapstone a decade earlier, before a consociational political arrangement was tested for viability with disappointing results since 1998. Nearly nine officers in ten in the current study felt that religion will always be a divisive factor in Northern Irish society, an increase on Mapstone's figure.

Asked about their constitutional preferences and compared with those expressed by the Catholic population, a majority of officers opted for the province remaining part of the United Kingdom. Just under half of the Catholic population chose reunification, marking a clear difference in aspirations or predictions with those of the police officers. When this finding was compared with a large majority of respondents' declaration earlier, that they held either neutral or mildly Nationalist views on joining, one speculated as to the reason for this marked transformation for so many into unionist Catholics. On the basis of the NISA (later renamed NILT) research since 1989, the gap between Catholic police and the Catholic population in their constitutional preferences was widening, placing these officers closer to the general Protestant population than to Catholics. Did this change denote considered judgement of recent political events, or have dominant police cultures been powerfully influential, or have both affected officers' views in varying degrees?

The response to the final multi-choice question on police officers' perceived treatment of civilians in Northern Ireland showed almost identical scores for Catholic officers and for the Protestant population when asked a similar question (NILT, 1998). The Catholic population figure was exactly half of both. This close identity between Catholic police and the Protestant population was consistent in all response categories and consistently different from the figures for the Catholic population. This gulf between Catholic police and their co-religionists might be construed as a potential obstacle to recruitment. It has, however, to be considered alongside the evidence cited earlier on the high level of agreement between Catholic officers and some sections of the Catholic working population on the support they might give to friends interested in choosing a policing career in Northern Ireland.

Final 'open' comments referring to this section of the survey reiterated resentment that the Belfast Agreement had favoured paramilitaries in particular. Advice was given that officers' judgments about community relations, Catholic recruitment possibilities, the Belfast Agreement and police treatment of civilians were likely to be strongly coloured by the geographical area that they had served in most recently. It was suggested that officers' location of upbringing might have been influential in their choice of the RUC as a career. They had probably spent their formative years in northerly towns, in mixed communities where cross-community friendships were the norm.

Conclusion

The data showed Catholics who joined the RUC to be atypical on a cluster of criteria normally characteristic of Catholics in Northern Ireland. These officers were products of traditional Catholic parentage and upbringing, yet their cultural Catholicism appeared to be very weak. One wondered if they had found themselves obliged to denude their Catholicism in order to function in the RUC, an organisation perceived by a majority of their co-religionists as a bastion of Protestant Unionist hegemony that has, historically, policed the Catholic community in accordance with a modified version of the colonial model. The officers' motivation for joining and remaining in policing and their views of the Patten reforms were of particular interest since my underlying questions sought to find out why so few Catholics had joined in the past and what the chances were of Patten's solution to under-representation – 50:50 recruitment of Catholics and non-Catholics – being achieved in the foreseeable future. Management of their Catholic identity within a strongly Protestant police culture and of their identified dissimilarities in perceptions and aspirations from the Catholic community promised to be revealed as constant challenges which they faced.

The survey findings guided the interviews in that the descriptive profile drew attention to features which needed richer, qualitative data before analysis and explanation could be attempted. Survey results were very helpful in identifying the questions which respondents found most sensitive and potentially most rewarding to pursue. High levels of missing data assisted this process. If respondents were clearly divided in their experiences or attitudes, the reasons for such disparity prompted follow-up. The 'open' comments gave rich clues to the topics and perspectives which interviewees were keen to expand on in a relaxed, one-to-one context. The survey findings contributed greatly to the efficiency of the interview process.

In the following four chapters I shall discuss qualitative data generated by seventy in-depth interviews with three samples of respondents – my next stage in testing the viability of police reform in Northern Ireland, in accordance with the liberal-democratic model.

3

Speaking from experience:
retired officers

Introduction

The chapters which follow form – in addition to functioning as an oral history – a trilogy of stories which resulted from in-depth interviews with a total of seventy Catholic retired, serving and trainee officers. The interviews were conducted during the period September 2003-January 2004. My data were analysed without redress to a qualitative computer package. I preferred to code, using themes and categories, then describe and explain my observations using supporting quotations.

The trilogy seeks to answer my basic questions: why have Catholics been underrepresented in policing and are the Patten reforms likely to redress the balance? Evidence from the three groups of respondents shows selected aspects of policing in Northern Ireland over time, during which the political and social context altered dramatically, and how these impacted on the private and professional lives of Catholics who chose policing as a career. All three groups provided data which can be categorised (similar to the survey) as referring to personal background, career experience and attitude to the Patten model as a vehicle for embedding liberal policing in Northern Ireland.

1 Retired officers: managing Catholic identity

Sample profile

This first of four chapters offers rich evidence from four officers whose career started between 1970 and 1972 and from six officers who could compare the relatively calm years before 1969 with the turbulent years that followed. The oldest, aged 75, joined in 1945 and the youngest, aged 51, joined in 1970. All were born in Northern Ireland, seven in predominantly Protestant towns, two from towns with fairly balanced Catholic–Protestant populations and one was born and spent his childhood in west Belfast. Six chose to be interviewed in their homes, two in hotels, one in a police station where he had served and one, a neighbour, came to my home. Their profile showed them to be strong cultural Catholics of whom eight practised their religion regularly and frequently. Eight of the ten were educated in Catholic grammar schools and two at (mixed) technical colleges. There were two graduates among the four who had reached chief superintendent rank or above. All ten had married Catholic women; one was widowed and one had divorced and remarried, describing his second wife as 'broadly Christian'. The retirees' average age was 64 years and length of service was thirty years. Only one emerged as having sent his child to a state grammar school; all the other children attended Catholic schools. One stressed the importance he put on his children being educated at Catholic schools in order to make them 'good Catholics and good Christians' while three enthused about the merits of integrated education, which was not available in their areas when their children were of school-going age.

The third feature on the escutcheon of the traditional Northern Irish Catholic after religious membership and education is political affiliation. Although born into Catholic families, Catholic educated and exposed to Nationalist culture, the retirees stated that their parents all held mild or moderate Nationalist political identities, though two said that their parents did not vote. One officer said that he was a consistent non-voter, explaining: 'I have no faith in politicians. They do nothing about domestic issues such as water rates'. Three said that they always voted Alliance, one having been chairman of his local branch; three voted SDLP; two made up their minds whether to vote Alliance or SDLP depending on their judgement of the candidates' worthiness and one described himself as 'neutral'.

None voiced strong political preferences for the future of Northern Ireland. One felt that 'Direct Rule will be with us for a long time'; another envisaged 'a united Ireland about 100 years down the road'; while one-third contended that 'a federal arrangement seems the best idea'. It was not surprising that these men were rather indifferent to the political scene since they all criticised Unionist dominance of the RUC as well as of the province for fifty years. They were equally critical of Nationalist political parties, although individual politicians from both parties were praised. These included Lord Fitt, Brian Faulkner, 'the last real politician the Unionists had', John Hume, 'He saved this city [Derry] from anarchy', and Mark Durkan, 'a decent lad', though not Lord Alderdice, described as 'hell-bent on his own promotion'.

Reasons for joining

Bearing in mind their atypicality in terms of political affiliation, I was keen to find out their reasons for joining the RUC, during a period when Catholic membership was very low, and for giving an average thirty years of service.

Financial security, a sense of purpose, camaraderie and solidarity were the reasons given for joining the RUC. Nearly all the officers joined for security, but several placed it second to providing a service. Typical comments were: 'You felt you could do something for the community' and 'It's an honourable calling'. For one of the younger high-flyers it was his third career and won his wife's approval only when he promised that he would reach superintendent rank at least. He kept his promise, though on joining he took a 50 per cent drop in salary. One came from a three-generation police family on his mother's side, and he was an officer's son, so for him joining 'was the natural thing to do'. One was influenced by the appearance of police officers he saw regularly in the border village where he was brought up: 'They were always well turned-out in their uniform'. With three uncles in police services outside Northern Ireland, he succumbed when the local sergeant asked his father: 'Would some of your boys not like to join?'.

Another, a younger senior, had, as a teenager, been hit on the head by 'a B man's baton' near his father's business, when accidentally caught up in a minor riot. In spite of his experience, he accepted an indirect invitation from the station sergeant when he accompanied a friend seeking an application form to join: 'You're a brave big fella and you look bright. Why don't you take a form too?'. One, however, admitted to being reluctant to join the RUC, though keen to become a police officer. Initially he was interested in joining his cousin as a member of the Garda Síochána in the Republic, but found the entry-level requirement in the Irish language excluded him.

Serendipity seemed to play a role for at least some of the officers in choosing a career, though for a majority, wherever the initial idea or invitation came from, their decision to join was for more than one reason. They presented laudable explanations, only two hinting that the machismo dimension played a part, even though they were all, with one exception, aged 18 to 20 when they joined. One illustrated the importance of drama in his career. He spent his earliest years serving in a Republican town, 'the hottest place in Northern Ireland where waitresses were tarred and had their hair cut off for serving police' and lived in a station frequently attacked by the IRA. He found promotion and transfer to a middle-class Unionist village 'boring. I didn't even need to wear a flak jacket'.

Whatever their reasons for joining, it was unlikely that they were able to anticipate at that stage the difficulties they would have to encounter in managing two of their identities, namely being Catholic and being police officers. Even their children suffered.

Children's problems

Police officers' children have not, to my knowledge, received any research attention, yet their stories could cast much light on the private cost which officers have paid in addition to the well-documented professionally and socially based problems which they encountered. In the case of Catholic officers' children, there is a sad, silent story, as many respondents' remarks showed. Five, without prompting, mentioned problems faced by their children because their fathers were Catholics in the RUC. One in the older group made the sacrifice of not seeking promotion so that his children's education would not be interrupted, but more importantly, because they lived in a town and went to a Catholic school where they experienced no hostility. He knew that promotion would bring transfer and exposure to risk.

Harassment of less fortunate children took the form of physical violence on sports fields and in playgrounds. In one instance, it took a more sinister form, having bullets placed in their schoolbags, with a map of Ireland showing no border. Another officer's daughters were verbally abused in the street. Hostile graffiti in the toilets of his sons' school were particularly offensive for children whose father had three attempts made on his life by the IRA. The message read: 'Missed, but you won't get away next time [adding his surname]'. In the interests of his family's safety he always secreted his personal weapon in his home, though no other member of the family knew where he kept it.

Apart from active harassment expressed in the ways I have outlined, a couple of other officers referred to the fear in which their children lived, having routinely and consistently to exercise vigilance in answering doorbells, telephone calls and carefully examining cars before getting inside. Sons seemed to have been more common targets of harassment than daughters, though one officer reported harassment and ostracism directed at both his teacher wife and pupil daughter in a Catholic grammar school for girls.

In spite of having a reduced level of enjoyment of their childhood, even those who suffered most were reported to have been academically successful. Five referred to their children's careers. Collectively, they pursued studies in medicine, dentistry, nursing, social work, economics and criminology. A total of at least six children went outside Northern Ireland for higher education. The caring professions were clearly favoured, perhaps reflecting their fathers' wish to serve the public. One explained why his children went to an English university: 'They'd put up with enough. They could be more relaxed in [name of city]'. A son who suffered harsh physical abuse from fellow pupils was one of two pursuing successful careers as detectives in the London Metropolitan Police. Another had a daughter whose first application to the PSNI was rejected, but she planned to apply again. Two other officers, who did not mention their children, reported that when approached by Catholics for advice, they counselled a career in the Met 'for the right person'.

Children from Catholic police families consistently suffered, it would appear, but managed to be academically successful and some did not rule out policing as a career. Though participation in sport was often quoted as being a site where the children suffered physical abuse, some of their fathers found in sport a means of combining successfully an aspect of their Catholic culture with their RUC membership.

Sport

Participation in sport figured largely in the lives of more than half of these men and obviously brought pleasure as well as success. Two played rugby for the RUC as well as for teams in towns where they were stationed. Another in the 1950s played Gaelic football for a border-town team, but converted to playing rugby when transferred to a Unionist town. 'Sport opens many doors' said one all-round sportsman, who in retirement worked voluntarily to strengthen cross-community links by encouraging children to develop sporting interests, particularly football.

Three of these men were educated by the Christian Brothers, noted for strict discipline. None voiced a criticism stronger than 'It was tough but good to me. There was a strong Nationalist ethos. The Irish language was pushed. You were obliged to do it to Senior-Certificate level'. (Senior Certificate was a group certificate examination pre-dating 'O' and 'A' levels.) Although Gaelic football was part of the cultural package, football was played 'unofficially' and swimming achievements were reported as notable. Although the Gaelic Athletic Association banned police officers from joining their teams, these men used Gaelic training and skills acquired at school as a passport into a new sports arena. Rugby, in Northern Ireland, is seen as a middle-class game which, unlike football, does not attract sectarian supporters. So these rugby-playing Catholic officers used their transferable skills to gain mainstream acceptance and popularity, while enjoying the process and demonstrating their flexibility. The perceived effectiveness of playing rugby was reflected by one younger senior officer who said that one of the great regrets of his career was not transferring from Gaelic to rugby. Those who did used one of their identities creatively – as Catholic sportsmen – to negotiate their paths as Catholics and police officers. Perhaps their physical flexibility was a product of mental flexibility which enabled them to enact rather than react to their work environment generally.

Flaunters and deserters

Participation in sport may have served as a form of 'easing' or as a means of reassurance that Catholic officers could feel and act as though fully integrated into the RUC 'family'. The retired respondents drew attention to contrasting ways in which their fellow Catholics managed their two dominant identities in a Protestant culture. Chief among those censored were colleagues who were accused of 'playing the Green card'. Brewer and Magee (1991: 143) define this term as describing 'a Catholic who does not disguise his or her religion but flaunts it, presumably either to annoy Protestant colleagues or to gain advantage'. Comments made on this phenomenon suggested that it did not emerge until after 1970, coincidentally after Hunt and when Catholics began to receive more promotions.

One of the senior officers from the younger group, having acknowledged 'the odd smart remark' from Protestant colleagues, took much more serious offence at the behaviour of the 'Green mafia': 'Any bigotry came from Catholic officers ... The Green mafia ... We'll play the downtrodden for our own ends. We'll stick together ... This group persisted till pre-Patten'. An older junior officer, describing himself as 'an ordinary guy', who never sought promotion and who came to specialise in community policing in a very testing location, was the most critical of those he saw as 'Green card players'. Of all ten interviewees he was most consistently acerbic in his comments, reflecting a career which included much sadness. He exemplified unacceptable behaviour in his opinion by narrating as follows:

Catholic police came out of the woodwork in the 1970s. They masqueraded as Catholics. They went to the annual police retreat at Portglenone [Monastery], made open confessions to Father Martin. They went to be seen by McAtamney and Lagan [command-level Catholics]. Thought that would do them good. Not at Mass for fourteen years was [name of colleague]. Playing the Green card . . . The senior officers were all at it. What a sacrifice . . . Those men had nothing to offer.

A mid-ranking officer regretted that instead of 'playing the Green card' – which he did not advocate either – a majority of his co-religionists would not even acknowledge their cultural background: 'Even when Catholic membership was 8 per cent, only about 25 per cent of those attended the annual retreat. Only 1 or 2 per cent would stand up and be counted'.

Reference here was to an annual two-day retreat organised by a Catholic officer for nearly twenty years but which ended in 1990 when the organiser had died and only three officers turned up. According to a recent rector of the monastery, policing demands made by the Troubles rendered the event no longer viable. He commented: 'A pity, because it was always very successful'. The idea has not been revived in more peaceful times. The RUC facilitated attendance at the retreat by Catholic officers as far as the exigencies of duty allowed. This acknowledgement of Catholic identity dates back to policy from early RIC times:

> The officers and men are at all times, when practicable, to attend divine service in their respective places of worship; and are to show an example of due respect for, and observance of, the Sabbath day, and a strict attention to their religious duties. Any man who is negligent of these highest obligations cannot be trustworthy in other respects. (RIC Standing Rules and Regulations, 1837, paras 377–8)

There was obviously a difference of opinion on why colleagues went to the retreat. Either they were promotion-seeking but not spiritually hungry, or they were not promotion-seeking but were spiritually hungry. One might suggest that some were motivated by a little of both reasons advanced. Absence might have indicated a wish to appear a member of the 'third religion' or to keep one's religious affiliation a private matter. Fissures within cultural Catholicism have been well documented and they were to be expected among police officers. Antipathy between Catholics voiced even in this small sample about how they played out or managed their Catholicism in the RUC was just as strong as criticisms levelled at the behaviour of non-Catholic colleagues against them as Catholics. Another mid-ranking officer questioned the idea that by flaunting their Catholicism some colleagues achieved promotion. His view was:

> Catholic police were promoted on merit. There *was* discrimination of a kind when Catholic officers got to the top in greater numbers because they were placed more carefully so that they could be representative. There was never a divisional commander and his deputy who were both Catholics. It was just common sense in distribution of resources.

An older senior colleague drew attention to an alternative strategy to flaunting their culture adopted by some Catholics in the RUC – protesting their loyalty and trustworthiness in the service of the Unionist establishment. With experience dating back to 1950 he referred to 'traitor' colleagues who denied their cultural legacy, thinking such behaviour would enhance their promotion chances. He cited one such colleague who in front of influential non-Catholic colleagues in the officers' mess referred to a complimentary copy of the Nationalist daily newspaper, the *Irish News*, as 'that rag' and adding rhetorically: 'Who would want to read it anyhow?'.

Managing identity as Catholics and police officers

A pertinent question behind the overt questions which I asked these retired officers was: how did they manage to be police officers and Catholics? The message coming through pointed towards their approach to the difficult career which they had chosen and also to the way they demonstrated their religious beliefs in carrying out their duties. Building upon two dichotomous classifications, enactors–reactors and extended–restricted Catholics, I developed a typology which is explained and exemplified in Chapter 4. At this stage I was of the opinion, after speaking to only ten, that the enactors had found their own perspectives and strategies to remain in control of their lives – even though these were under permanent threat. They were more likely, therefore, to be fulfilled, whereas the reactors stressed the problems and the lack of control over what their colleagues and members of the community 'did to them'.

I decided that these officers generally had been heavily and permanently influenced by the teachings of their Church, particularly on matters of social justice. It seemed, though, that they were atypical of the archetypal Northern Irish Catholic whose identifying label implies certain predictable political and social characteristics. Their testimonies pointed towards these men having gone beyond a restricted code of Catholicism, displaying an empathy and facility in dealing with people from different cultural backgrounds. Perhaps the notion of 'extended' Catholicism and 'extended' Protestantism was what Sir John Hermon frequently described as 'the third religion'. This sample of retired officers emerged as Catholics who happened to become police officers and Christians who happened to be Catholic.

2 Policing in the past

In this second part of Chapter 3 I shall consider my retired interviewees' perceptions of serving in the RUC and problems which they encountered in carrying out their duties. Internally, they identified in particular the influence of Freemasonry, the Orange Order and the Unionist Party, as well as the behaviour of Special Branch and 'B' Special colleagues. Externally, they found difficulty in relating to the Catholic Church and some members of the Catholic community from whom the IRA and Sinn Féin had sprung.

Sectarianism in the RUC

Asked if they had experienced hostility on religious grounds and, if so, when it had happened, they gave a variety of responses. Those who served before 1969 in both Protestant and Catholic areas agreed that there was no bigotry in the early days – identified as being the 1950s and 1960s – though one exception, who served long term in a border county, stated that it began during the 1956–62 IRA campaign when police stations situated along the border were favourite targets for bombs. He explained:

> You felt you weren't trusted as others were [by non-Catholic colleagues]. It was just a feeling. The conversation would stop if you came into a room, as if a stranger had come in. The attitude to the Catholic community changed dramatically too after 1956, though there was only the odd incident and it was relatively quiet till 1969.

This statement seemed to suggest that attitudes hardened and Catholic officers were seen by their Protestant colleagues as part of the lumpen Catholic population when Republican violence showed itself. All Catholics were suspect as possible Republican sympathisers and Protestant officers felt threatened by all Catholics, even their colleagues. The words quoted hint at the officer's disappointment that he was treated as an outsider, denying him the comfort of solidarity which he might have expected as being traditional in police forces, especially when faced with a common threat.

Five of the six older retired officers thoroughly enjoyed their training period in the depot. One 'had a ball', another 'loved every minute of it' and another 'found his calling' there. It was noticeable that those who praised their period of training were good at sport, which possibly helped them to find favour with their fellow recruits and also attracted the positive attention of their instructors. The oldest retired officer, who had been a detective constable, shared the sentiments I have quoted about the depot, but was able to claim that, though he worked for over thirty years in a variety of non-border towns, some Nationalist, some Unionist, retiring in the mid-1970s, he did not encounter 'sectarian banter' from colleagues. Another officer who retired at command rank in the 1990s, had a different story to tell:

> When I was in the depot [training college] we paraded to different churches for Sunday services. A Protestant colleague who came to Mass with me was ridiculed . . . I was serving in [name of town] in the late 1980s. A typical sectarian joke doing the rounds [within the station]was about a Protestant being on holiday in Rome, going into a Catholic church and mistaking a confessional box for a latrine.

He obviously found evidence of sectarianism at the beginning of his career and also thirty years later. He made the point that hostility towards Catholicism was always in the background, though in his experience he had not suffered it consistently. His career, very successful in promotional terms, may also have protected him, though his general comment was 'You always felt you were in the club – but you were in the foyer'.

Among the younger group of four there was an interesting breakdown according to rank. The three who occupied senior and mid-rank positions testified to very different experiences from those of a constable. The words of the two most senior officers almost echoed each other in conveying an impression that sectarianism was not widespread in the RUC. They may have described what they genuinely believed to be true – though it sounded close to official rhetoric. One assured me:

> There was the odd smart remark. Only once was there real malice. He was quickly chastised by the senior constable closely allied to Ian Paisley. 'You'll not be travelling any further with us', he said. We left him standing in the Short Strand [an area well known for communal conflict].

This experience suggested that the senior constable was able to separate his private religious affiliation with extreme Protestantism from his duty to ensure that Catholic colleagues did not suffer because of their different cultural background.

His colleague's experience was:

> I could not have been treated better by my colleagues. Police are no different from society here. Some guys have some views about some things. They're not aimed at you personally. . . I was disappointed in some colleagues, but not the force. You couldn't work with a greater bunch of guys.

A third admitted he had had difficult moments, but readily offered a solution:

> There was banter but you gave as much as you got. The recipient's response determines the outcome. I remember a whispering campaign against me. 'Don't tell him because he's a Catholic'. My boss was transferred because he didn't deal with the situation.

In each of these three cases the presence of sectarianism was admitted either directly or indirectly. Each sought to show that they had the resources available, either from within themselves, or the RUC official policy was implemented to deal with it. A 'bad apples' explanation provided an opportunity to write off any personal insult implied. The third man quoted trivialised the significance of banter, seeing it as an opportunity to engage in riposte and to win.

Another type of problem in the case of a junior officer showed that apparent sectarian behaviour demonstrated instead, or in addition, a misunderstanding of cultural symbols:

> I was accused on a night out that I had deliberately gone to the toilet while the national anthem was played. I hadn't. I didn't know that it was going to be all over while I was away.

Another Catholic constable cited a story, this time about a Catholic symbol:

> At the time of the Enniskillen bombing I had to search a Catholic church with a Protestant colleague who asked me what I thought the sanctuary lamp meant. When I tried to explain he said 'How could you have anything to do with anyone who believes that?' . . .. He didn't know what I was.

There seemed to be an underlying assumption by both a Catholic and a Protestant officer that each should have a detailed understanding of the other's cultural background. Both stories can also be understood as examples of sectarianism. In the first case, the Catholic officer's colleagues probably knew his cultural background and that was their reason for implying that as a Nationalist he would not stand while the national anthem was being played. In the second case, the Protestant officer in his remark showed disrespect for a Catholic symbol of religious belief and in doing so, demonstrated a sectarian attitude to all Catholics. The Catholic officer who explained that the incident upset him did not reveal his cultural background at that point. He chose to conceal his identity as a means, one assumes, of avoiding further discomfort.

Sectarianism could be found in the types of duty which Catholic officers were given to carry out. A junior officer, retired about twenty years, cited occasions when Catholics had to police Loyalist bands, taking verbal abuse, because in the small town where he was serving, the religion of each police officer was known to all. However, according to him there was a no-win situation because:

> Every Easter Monday [the anniversary to the 1916 Easter Rising against British rule in Ireland] three Catholics had to take abuse from the lorries [on which platforms were erected], from the speeches. The attitude of the authorities was 'Good enough for them'.

This constable's evidence suggested that some RUC officers who prepared duty rosters showed no sensitivity to the problems which Catholic officers had to face when policing both Loyalist and Republican parades – perhaps even taking pleasure instead. He added 'Catholic officers are of a much higher calibre than their Protestant counterparts, but they were abused by the authorities'. This remark suggested a level of sectarianism underscored by earlier comments which I made. Reference to 'calibre' was reinforced by another Catholic officer who referred to abolition of the 'B' Specials by Hunt. Many of them, after their disbandment, applied to enter the regular force and were accepted, thereby diluting the quality of personnel. The oldest retiree I interviewed countered the experience of the constable quoted above by citing an acceptable division of labour in one of the Catholic towns where he served in the 1950s: 'Protestants went with the Orange bands and vice versa. We did the job fairly and they [the organisers] might have thrown you a "tenner" for a meal to say thanks'.

It must be remembered that parades by the Orange Order might have been less contentious in the 1950s, since Catholic opposition to routes taken was not mobilised as it was after 1969. To this apparent indifference by Catholics towards expression of Protestant triumphalism must be added the Unionist government's concern, approaching paranoia, of expressions of Irish culture – which were forbidden, for example, by the Flags and Emblems Act of 1954. The RUC as the Unionist government's armed branch was obliged to suppress any Nationalist aspirations, even of a peaceful nature, showing that the security of the statelet of Northern Ireland was the paramount policing priority. Sectarianism by the police establishment in their treatment of the Ancient Order of Hibernians (AOH), a Nationalist Catholic organisation, caused understandable embarrassment for Catholic officers. One of the older senior officers explained how detailed continual surveillance worked:

> The AOH was seen as disloyal. In the 1950s you'd be asked how many Easter lilies were worn, how many went to Irish dancing classes. A fellow was under suspicion because he was seen sitting on a wall outside the local AOH hall.

The socio-political context, therefore, lent credence to the Catholic officers' stories of sectarianism and lack of trust displayed towards them, since they had been recruited from a cultural group who did not enjoy parity of esteem with the Protestant community. They were obliged, in effect, to police Catholics according to a benign form of the colonial model of policing, in contrast with the liberal policing which Protestants enjoyed. Such conditions provide a persuasive reason for Catholics joining in low numbers, fearing harassment and alienation from 'the armed wing' of the Unionist Party. Probably the major obstacle to recruitment was identified by one of the older senior retired officers, who explained the RUC's treatment of the AOH above. He conveyed the general attitude of the RUC to Catholics as far back as the 1950s, reflected as the main criterion for selection:

> The big question about Catholic officers was 'Is he loyal?' You see, you had to be seen as a loyal member of society, the recruiting sergeant had to sign this undertaking. It meant in practice loyalty to the Unionist government, to the Orange Order.

These retired officers focused heavy criticism in a united way in proclaiming the Masonic Order and to a lesser extent the Orange Order as malevolent influences on the ethos of their work environment. To this was added Unionist government dominance. An officer who resigned after fewer than four years service offered an explanation:

> The Unionist government used the RUC disgracefully. That's why the Catholic community turned against them. The Unionist Party was the downfall of the RUC. They were at the government's beck and call. The Orange Order have done the most harm but the Masonic influence was very, very strong. There should be a register of loyal orders.

He explained the problem for Catholic officers as being the inextricable link and overlapping identities of government ministers who were almost entirely Orangemen. This link continued through Protestant members of the RUC determining the ethos and the interpretation put on the policing role and function.

Unionist, Protestant hegemony in Northern Ireland was reflected in the RUC by the significant role which the Masonic Order played in influencing, if not controlling, some purely police affairs such as promotion, my interviewees asserted. The oldest officer, who retired in 1975, demonstrated how the Masons invited Protestant officers to join so that they could benefit professionally from membership:

> I'd seen all these 'bay window' envelopes in the letter rack in the guardroom. I was curious because none ever came for me. This day I found one in the canteen. It had been opened. I looked inside and it was an invitation to the [name] Lodge. I asked a Protestant colleague 'Why the [name] Lodge?'. He told me 'The Buck Cat in – [a village near his station] looks after the promotions.

The story shows how a Catholic officer's curiosity led to a discovery that invitations to join the Masonic Order were given to Protestant officers but not to Catholics. 'The Buck Cat' refers to the senior Mason in the local Lodge who, it would seem, was widely recognised within the RUC community as being an influential figure in deciding which officers were promoted.

Judging from the remarks made by most retired officers on the subject, it would appear that there was a policy change in the early 1970s, in that selected Catholics were invited to join the Masonic Order. Invitations were extended to Catholics in later years, perhaps to identified high-flyers at a time when positive steps were taken to promote a higher number of Catholics to senior ranks, in keeping with internal reforms and civil rights demands. Such an extension of invitations does not justify the Order's interference in the internal affairs of a police force, whose promotion system should have been transparently fair, but simply underlines the absence of accountability in this still neo-colonial period of policing.

Four said they had been invited to join the Masons (three of senior rank and one who had held middle rank), but all said they had declined. One who had achieved very senior rank claimed that there had been Catholics who became Masons even earlier than the 1970s:

> Before 1972 there was an old boys' network. They had strong influence on promotions. Some used it for their own ends, including Catholics. I was invited many times to become a Mason. Instead I got involved in Catholic parish work . . . We all knew about Waring Street Lodge [a Masonic lodge with large police membership].

One senior ranker surprisingly did not mention the Masonic influence. I wondered if he had joined the Masons, as his story was almost totally positive. He had found it easy to identify with the Protestant community, influenced probably by bitter experience in a Republican-dominated small town early in his career. He identified himself as being a non-practising Catholic who had his child educated at state schools and spoke of his 'closeness with the Protestant community' in the predominantly Protestant town in which he retired. His words identified him as a Catholic 'deserter' which was, conceivably, the status which might be accorded other Catholics who became Free Masons.

A junior retiree, one of eight who criticised Masonic influence in the RUC, corroborated the views expressed by others in vitriolic terms, citing personal experience:

> The Masonic Order ruined, destroyed, was the curse of the RUC . . . One colleague commented to me when he was promoted 'My mother and – [mentioning a Stormont cabinet minister's name] are first cousins' . . . But I had personal experience of the power of the Masons. I had a girlfriend whose father was a prominent professional in the town and a high-up Mason. He sent word to the sergeant that I wasn't suitable for her, being a Catholic, and he wanted the relationship to finish. I was told to back off. Just imagine, the power of the Masons dictating to the RUC . . .

The data suggested that there was undoubted Masonic influence, indeed power, operating within the RUC élite whose members could benefit professionally from multiple identities as police officers, Orangemen and Masons, all of which made them members of the Unionist 'family'. It would seem that after 1970 and the impact of civil rights agitation the RUC considered it prudent to promote larger numbers of Catholics. The muscle of the Masons was not reduced, however, but some Catholics were invited into the favoured circle. I had no conclusive evidence from my small sample that any of them accepted, but I am inclined to infer that those who did were considered to be loyal to the Unionist establishment and were deserters from cultural Catholicism.

The insidious influences of Unionism, Free Masonry and Orangeism were not the only sources of sectarianism with which Catholic officers had to deal in the course of their work. They identified three categories of colleagues in this regard. One was the 'B' Special Constabulary. Hunt's disbandment of the 'B' Special Constabulary was approved by the older retired who had served with them before 1970. Although I did not mention the 'B' Specials specifically, four out of six commented seeing them as a group apart from regular officers. They voiced criticism of how these men did their jobs, but their main complaint was against their symbolic importance as part of the Unionist structure, engaged principally to keep Catholics under surveillance in border areas. It should not be forgotten that many of the 'B' Specials became members of the Reserve, some full-time, after 1970. This fact cannot be detached from the widely agreed view by the Catholic retired that standards of recruit deteriorated after the outbreak of violence and the government was obliged to increase police manpower resources.

A very long-serving officer whose career began in the 1950s and ended in the early 1990s was well positioned to comment. Of his border experience working with 'B' Specials he said:

> I am a Catholic who became a police officer. I'm not bigoted, in fact sometimes I thought I was too tolerant. In your presence those lower standard Protestants who came in after 1969 would make you feel bad. There was no condemnation of Protestant paramilitaries, but 'F – the IRA'. They might try to annoy you by saying it 100 times in your presence. I never responded . . . Some of those with that kind of thinking are still in the force.

My oldest interviewee concurred:

> I had very little respect for the 'B' men. They were all Protestants who sang party tunes in the [police] car.

Two retired officers provided evidence showing members of the 'B' Specials to have intimidated their children in full knowledge of who the boys' fathers were. In one case his son was stopped by them four times over a couple of days; on each occasion he was asked to show his dog licence. Another was repeatedly stopped and questioned about his whereabouts. After the discussion one 'B' Special put a stick between the spokes of that boy's bicycle, so that he was prevented from riding off until he was 'released'.

The only positive comment made was 'there was the odd decent fellow among them'. The 'B' Specials had a reputation for harassing Catholics particularly in border areas, where this auxiliary force was most numerous. It would appear from the evidence cited that they took an undifferentiated approach to Catholics, whether colleagues or not. A change in name after 1970 did not guarantee a change in attitude on the part of the Reserve force. A new thrust towards professional, impartial policing probably resulted in sectarianism taking a less overt form than hitherto, as official policy clearly did not condone it.

Sectarianism on the part of the predominantly Protestant 'B' Specials and later Reserve forces was likely to have had an adverse effect on the possibility of the RUC recruiting Catholics into its ranks. Another group of police officers who earned a notorious reputation among the Catholic public was Special Branch. Indeed, no department of the RUC was accorded greater odium during the protracted period of counter-terrorist activity than Special Branch. Their lack of even internal accountability was legendary. It was not surprising then, that the officers I interviewed had strong feelings about their colleagues' interpretation of their role, their rather élitist view of themselves, and the accusations which were made against them of colluding with Loyalist paramilitaries, although they were not without apologists.

One of the most senior retirees highly placed outside Special Branch, was clear that:

> Special Branch had an overriding influence on what operational police were doing. You'd upset their applecart if you knew. We had a saying, 'The Special Branch clock doesn't tell you the time' . . . They had far too much control . . . The ammunition was picked up afterwards . . . There were Catholics in Special Branch.

These words hint at the displeasure which this retiree felt about the activities and style of Special Branch. Described as 'a force within a force', they did not share intelligence even with very senior officers outside their functional area. Reference to ammunition reinforces civilian accusations that they were often found to have been at the scene of stake-outs, having discharged arms, but had disappeared by the time CID were notified. Their presence could be identified by the type of weapons and ammunition which they used. Reference to 'their apple cart' means that they ran informers whom they sometimes protected, even though the informers were committing crimes for which CID would have wanted to prosecute them. This officer seemed to have difficulty in reconciling this kind of behaviour with Catholic values.

Another senior officer, though of the younger generation, expressed very different sentiments. He described Special Branch as 'the only thing that protected us from anarchy. The IRA demonised it'. Having voiced ritualistic approval as 'an organisation man' he went on, however, to reveal his true feelings. He served a matter of months in Special Branch, but asked to leave. He seemed to find the reputation which the security forces had earned to be something from which he had to disassociate himself:

> It was very brutal in the early 1970s. I remember Girdwood Barracks behind Crumlin Road prison, a holding centre. The white noise torture was basic and brutal. Prisoners were roughly treated. They were handed over to the police by the Army. It was an unjust regime. . . I tried to make things as easy as I could . . . for both sides . . . 16-year-olds crying for their mothers . . . I asked out. It was a necessary evil at the time. I don't know that they achieved a lot . . . only a recruiting ground.

He was clearly trying to be as honest as he could about harsh reality while soothing his conscience, by reminding himself that even within this barbaric context he was able to show his humanity, though he was an agent of the perpetrators. Service in Special Branch would have been in direct conflict with his active membership of the Saint Vincent de Paul Society – a charity which raises funds and ministers in various ways to the poor and needy. He was able to distance himself sufficiently to cast serious doubt on the value of the ends, irrespective of the means used, concluding that it was a counter-productive operation, as police violence simply attracted more members to join the IRA. It seemed that he could rationalise at institutional level, speaking as a senior officer, but had to reject the whole practice on personal and humanitarian grounds.

A contemporary of the last contributor, and of similar senior rank, had never served in Special Branch. He adopted a more uniformly defensive stance:

> Special Branch was absolutely necessary. If it didn't exist, you'd have to invent it. We would not have survived without it. Many Republicans would not have survived. . . It was a dirty game . . . It's easy to blame them when things go wrong . . . Information often was wrong . . . I have nothing but the highest regard for them.

He voiced the rhetoric of a senior officer who felt he had to justify the existence of Special Branch, of its methods and of its shortcomings. He pointed to the fact that some Republicans targeted by Loyalists were pre-warned of the danger by members of Special Branch, but admitted that mistakes made had serious implications while these officers conducted an intelligence war. Another senior officer with twenty years' experience in Special Branch, though defensive too, admitted more in cryptic terms, but would not be drawn to make further comment.

Special Branch should not condone or run murderers. We did *not* deal with known murderers . . . You cannot legislate for 'bad apples' . . . Some things might have happened but they were not condoned. Special Branch and MI5 (NI) would protect informants who would otherwise lose their lives. An angel was no good to us. Collusion was possible but it didn't happen.

He implied that some Special Branch officers and MI5 might have colluded with Loyalist paramilitaries in planning the deaths of Republicans, or by allowing murders to take place, because the targets were not warned.

Two others from the older generation, one junior and one middle ranking, reported having been invited to join Special Branch, but they refused. One said: 'I'd seen enough of them at work. They were rotten to the core'. (He'd served in the CID.) The other officer acknowledged: 'They're necessary in some form in every country, but in Northern Ireland they were so bigoted. A band of evil men. Information gathering is OK, but it has to be fair'. The latter's reference to bigotry and evil might be construed as referring in coded form to collusion with Loyalist paramilitaries.

The general picture which emerged from the retired interviewees' perceptions and experience of Special Branch was negative. It is important to remember that whether working inside or outside of Special Branch, these men collectively represented a very substantial period of service. During that time this special unit was at the forefront, with British Intelligence, of fighting a 'war' against the IRA. The British government interpreted it as a 'war' to be won using military means. It was only after prosecuting the 'war' for thirty years and for some of that time against military advice that British ministers, especially the prime minister, pursued a vigorous and concentrated campaign to achieve cessation of violence by political and diplomatic means. So far as Special Branch was concerned, the end justified the means they used to extract evidence from suspects and their reputation was vulnerable to negative comment by commentators and by the media. It was also conceivable that the image which Special Branch projected was used as a propaganda tool by the IRA and proved to be a strong factor deterring some Catholics from joining the RUC.

I did not ask these retired officers for their views on the role of the Army in supporting the RUC or what their personal experiences were of interacting with soldiers. Four, however, volunteered opinions. I shall include these because they may have presented problems to some Catholic police, since in the eyes of many civilians the RUC and the Army together constituted 'the security forces'. The Army received more criticism than praise and at best were seen as a mixed blessing. One officer singled out Bloody Sunday and put the blame for the disastrous outcome firmly on the Army:

The Army thought they could take control. The police did not want what happened . . . The Army weren't the answer to the problem. If the police had had sufficient numbers, they'd have been better without them.

Yet he conceded: 'Drumcree could not have been policed without them. They can fly in hundreds of men at short notice'. However, he advised that while they helped solve some problems in the short term, they created others by harassing the people in Catholic areas.

Two others said that the Army presented problems; one placed the blame on the British government, believing that instead of depending on the Army to defeat the IRA, it should have been recognised that political change was necessary. He recalled, disparagingly, an anecdote to make his point:

> I remember a lieutenant calling at [name] police station asking if he was going the right way to Omagh. He said 'In six months we'll have all this sorted' . . . A naive young man just out of Sandhurst . . . No preparation for the task.

His junior colleague stressed the unsuitability of Army personnel to carry out policing duties:

> Some could not be let out – only under supervision . . . Briefings were done in England at 'orange-and-green' level. They came here with preconceived ideas and perpetuated a 'Brits out' attitude . . . There was the problem of joyriding [referring to youths stealing and driving vehicles without tax or insurance] . . . The Army believed in the way they were trained. Soldiers are trained to kill. Protect life, uphold the law – that's what police officers are taught to do . . . Poles apart.

Catholic officers' reservations about the professionalism and training standards of the Army personnel were probably shared with similar thinking non-Catholic police colleagues. However, there seemed to be an additional problem presented to Catholic police. The association in the Catholic public mind of the RUC with the Army served to increase the distance further between the Catholic police and the Nationalist population.

I have examined and reflected on the human context in which my snowball sample of retired Catholic officers experienced their professional service and have identified evidence of sectarianism against them. Perhaps the greatest psychic problems for many of them arose from the distance which existed between themselves and their fellow cultural Catholics, the community from which they came.

The Catholic community and the Catholic Church

These officers' relations with the Catholic community including the Catholic Church must inevitably include their comments on the IRA, an organisation which drew active support from a tiny minority and passive support or tolerance of numbers which varied, depending on the socio-political profile of a particular area in which an officer served.

Since four of the interviewees served in Derry for long periods, they tended to use the city as the locale for their illustrations. Derry was a constant centre of civil unrest and media attention during the Troubles, being associated with civil rights marches, IRA atrocities and Bloody Sunday, to name but a sample. Their comments suggested a certain empathy with the Catholic people there and respect for them. Though a small minority of cultural Catholics became IRA activists, Catholic officers saw many Catholic civilians as victims of the IRA movement and its actions. Fear of the power of the IRA and the punishment that it inflicted was mentioned by officers who asserted, however, that the Catholic population generally supported the police, but not overtly, for obvious reasons. This hidden base of support has been a perennial theme in claims by Unionist politicians, the PANI and in research carried out by NILT. One senior officer judged that:

> The large majority of Catholic people want peace and respect the police. They were confused by the civil rights; then the IRA came along. The ruffian took over supposedly to guard the street . . . The Derry people are articulate and intelligent . . . I never met anybody who objected to being treated fairly.

A middle-ranking officer endorsed this approval. Describing the people in the 92 per cent Catholic area where he worked in the city, he said: 'The community supported all police – Catholic and Protestant. They supported law and order'. The junior officer mentioned earlier with extensive experience in community work blamed Sinn Féin for causing social problems in Derry which alienated young people in particular from the police:

> Sinn Féin wanted radical religion, radical politics, radical lifestyle. Young people were attracted to this and turned against the police. That suited Sinn Féin. The young people who were SDLP-orientated were isolated. To go with Sinn Féin was the sexy, trendy thing to do. Of the 14–30-year olds in Derry, 70–80 per cent are Sinn Féin.

Sinn Féin was not the only political party to warrant criticism, though. He blamed both Nationalist and Unionist politicians for failing to do their duty to their communities in the period prior to 1969, accusing them of 'courting votes' to prevent the growth of trade unionism and Labour: 'If Labour had been allowed to develop, polarisation would have gone away. Eddie McAteer saw BSR [Birmingham Sound Recorders] collapse and he did precisely nothing'. This statement refers to the unfortunate fate of employees in a large factory who, the officer alleged, received no support from the local Nationalist MP – unlike Unionists who repeatedly fought successfully for government funding to keep the shipbuilding firm Harland & Wolf in business in east Belfast. This officer spoke at length about the community work carried out by himself and his non-Catholic colleague working as a team. The colleague was shot dead and this officer was targeted by the IRA. He had to escape to a relative's home in a Protestant town a long distance away, where the house had twenty-four-hour Army protection. He painted a more detailed picture than others of the problems which confronted police officers in the communities they served. Though from a moderately Nationalist background, he was an Alliance Party member and one-time officer. As I have indicated above, he saw the people as being duped by their politicians for political ends. He criticised the misguided energy of Sinn Féin, but equally so the lack of energy shown by the long-term Nationalist MP for Derry, Eddie McAteer, for ignoring the economic interests of his constituents and continuing to tolerate and benefit from a divided society.

All reported that trying to do their jobs in a professional, neutral way was their *modus operandi*. One senior illustrated by a story how he changed the hostile attitude of at least one family towards the police:

> At 3 a.m. a girl from a Provo family was in custody. She stated repeatedly that her baby was very ill and needed a doctor. Colleagues thought this was just a story. I phoned a doctor who went to the house and found the baby had meningitis. That changed her family's outlook completely.

Another, who occupied junior rank, explained his approach thus:

> People are people to me. So long as they are not brutal with their politics. I look for the good in people rather than the bad. That way you keep out of the lion's mouth. Where possible, I tried to help people. Many responded.

While junior officers could not empathise with the IRA's motives or activities, some of the seniors were able to distance themselves and make balanced comment. An officer who had been in Special Branch for nearly twenty years reflected ironically:

> I have great admiration for the IRA/Sinn Féin leadership. They've got rid of the RUC, of Special Branch, of the operational thrust that the old police service had. They've brought an end to the Troubles they started. They were so dedicated . . . The Loyalists are money-oriented. The Republicans have an ideology. They attracted a more thinking person because of the dedication that was needed.

This was the same officer who had slept in a bed off which bullets had ricocheted in a Republican town. He rationalised thus: 'I was accepted, welcomed by the whole community . . . People were horrible to the uniform but not to me'. This conclusion seemed to contradict in part a statement he made previously that he could not attend Mass in this town, because having done it once, he was 'surrounded by a hostile circle in thirty seconds' as he came out. In addition one could reasonably assume that the bullets targeted at his bedroom were fired by members of that 'whole community'.

The officers negotiated their individual paths from day to day by believing that they were serving the two communities in a worthy, impartial way while identifying the main source of problems – the IRA – as being rooted in their own community. Two expressed their sadness at the lack of overt support from Nationalist (as opposed to Republican) Catholics, many of whom quietly supported the police in their community role while not allowing officers to call at their homes, for fear of repercussions from the IRA. The officers also castigated in this regard the SDLP politicians whose public utterances contradicted the good relations police had with individuals from the party. These respondents did not like being criticised for their policing by members of their own community. They felt the sting of politicians' criticisms and expected more tolerant understanding from the SDLP.

A majority could afford, from the luxury of retirement, to take a cerebral approach because the memories of their unpleasant, even dangerous experiences had begun to fade as they applied themselves to civilian activities. These took the form of Catholic charity work for five, while another carried out the traditional role, common from RIC times, of assisting members of the public in filling in forms and supporting applications for pensions, passports and gun licences.

If this sample of retired officers felt the sting of disapproval from lay Catholics, they arguably felt it more sharply from their church and/or individual clergy. Religious belief being at the very core of cultural Catholicism, it is easy to appreciate Catholics officers' bitterness and disillusionment if they felt that their clergy did not empathise with them as they tried to be Catholics and police officers. There was general reflective disappointment at, or condemnation of, the Catholic Church, seen as a potentially powerful and influential organisation that shirked its responsibility in giving leadership and guidance to its members over the thirty years of the 'Troubles'. In more specific terms they regretted lack of political leadership and the tolerance which they perceived as support for IRA, or fear of repercussions – for example in affording 'normal' burial rites to dead IRA activists. They also noted differences in attitudes between individual clergy towards Catholic police officers, some sympathetic, some hostile – depending on their political views.

One older senior officer explained how the status of the parish priest impacted on his police work. He took the view that 'a police officer must immerse himself in the culture of the area he serves. I had to get used to the fact that in County [name] Catholics always consulted their parish priest before going to the police'. He was referring to the days when clergy played a strong role in people's lives before the arrival of social liberalisation and decline in Mass attendance in the 1960s. He remarked on Bishop Filbin's relaxation of the requirement to attend Mass on Sunday, aware of police officers' fear of assassination if their movements followed a set pattern. He advised them that attendance on any day of the week would suffice. Regular attendance at Sunday Mass was something on which all of the older group placed a great deal of emphasis, though one admitted that for a time he went only when he was on holiday, for security reasons.

Two other older officers referred back to the pre-Troubles period when the church catered to the spiritual needs of Catholic ex-service personnel. They diplomatically did not refer specifically to the church as an organisation, but simply pointed to absence of support in the last thirty years as compared to the 1950s and 1960s. One from west Belfast with close family who had served in the World Wars recalled that:

Friends from [a Nationalist area of Belfast] joined the RAF and the Army in the 1950s and 1960s. The Paras . . . There was a Catholic ex-service club till the late 1960s in Ardoyne. The Church supported this. There was Mass for the members. Then fear set in . . .

Yet, from his own experience as a police officer, he regretted that:

The Catholic Church as an organisation gave me no support . . . We had no chaplain . . . Bishops should have been unequivocal. They were weak. When there were Republican parades in west Belfast [demonstrating their paramilitary strength], priests were afraid of Sinn Féin.

The passive stance adopted by the church was the main source of grievance expressed, two believing that a fear of 'upsetting the flock' was the reason, while another cited an example of a priest in the Republican town where he served, as having been threatened by the local IRA precisely because of his outspoken condemnation of atrocities. One officer with very short service contrasted the church hierarchy's words and actions in relation to the IRA campaign: 'There was no leadership given. But, of course, you could always be sure the bishop would say plausible things in front of the TV cameras'.

The funerals of Republicans were a source of great annoyance to three of the retired officers. Two objected that activists who blew themselves up planting bombs or were shot by security forces were given normal funeral rites, though one conceded that this criticism applied equally to Protestant clergy and Loyalist paramilitaries. One older irate officer generalised from his experience of attending a funeral of a well-known Republican 'godfather' who had died of natural causes. He accused the priest conducting the Requiem Mass as being 'steeped in Republicanism' because he did not make reference to the deceased man's Republican identity. He continued:

'Canonising' Republicans sickened me. I remember Father [name] speaking at the funeral of [name] about him being a respected local businessman. The truth was that he brainwashed youngsters. I remember well he left one young man bleeding in pain on Dr [name]'s doorstep when weapon training went wrong . . . That lad had injuries for life.

This officer was supported by the testimony of three other retirees in objecting to the police identity of Catholic colleagues being ignored in their funeral eulogies. They explained that they were diligent attendees at the funerals of former colleagues but routinely witnessed their service in the RUC being ignored by the clergy conducting the Mass. I wondered about possible reasons for this omission when I experienced this happen as I attended the funeral in 2005 of the oldest officer in this snowball sample. I decided that the relatively young priest would not have known of the deceased's police service if his family did not advise him of it. The business which the retiree owned for twenty years was mentioned, but his RUC career, which spanned a previous thirty years, was ignored. Perhaps the omission was deliberate on the part of his widow, whose family had strong Republican sympathies. She may not have wished to reopen wounds which had been successfully healed over her husband's long retirement years. There was an echo in this story of Catholic officers' difficulties in joining the police in Northern Ireland, being accepted by a Catholic spouse's family and coping with hostility from the Catholic community generally.

In spite of objections to the way funerals were carried out, some of the retired officers showed that the church was protective behind the scenes. A long-serving older officer who had much to say about his days in a Republican city contrasted the attitude of a Catholic parish priest with that of the cardinal. When his fiancée announced her forthcoming marriage, her parish priest's response was 'I'd rather see you in the cemetery than marry that man'. (The objection was towards his occupation). However, when life became close to insufferable, because his wife and children were being harassed and he was under permanent threat from the IRA, he asked his bishop for guidance. A message came from Cardinal Conway which said: 'Under no circumstances resign. We need Catholic police like you'. (It has been reported, though I cannot confirm, that the cardinal's father served in the RIC; at anecdotal level it has also been suggested that it was not unusual for RIC officers' sons to become priests.)

The oldest interviewee had an assassination attempt made on him by the IRA. This event had forced him to leave his home in a middle-class Catholic neighbourhood. He recalled an incident later, when a priest protected him against a likely second attempt on his life:

> My father-in-law had died and I was determined that I wouldn't let 'the boys' [IRA] keep me away from his funeral. I was in the cortège behind the coffin. Then suddenly Father [name] stepped into line beside me. A Catholic colleague in Special Branch had probably organised it.

The source of agreed criticism of their clergy centred on lack of appreciation of Catholic officers' service to and in the Catholic community, as well as generally. The other locus of criticism was that as leaders of a flock from whom IRA perpetrators of atrocities were recruited, the clergy had been non-committal, carried out burial rites for IRA dead as if they were 'ordinary' faithful and failed as leaders clearly denouncing murder. The retirees were divided in identifying possible reasons for this behaviour, including having Republican sympathies, or – more likely – fear of IRA censure if they spoke out critically. In spite of the difficulties with which they had to cope over a lifetime of service, their memories of time spent in the RUC were surprisingly positive on the whole.

Good memories and bad

For a variety of reasons, which I have discussed, it would appear that the price paid by these officers pursuing careers in the RUC and by their families was uncomfortably high. Their remarks, however, indicated that they found policing, per se, a rewarding career but likely to be less problematical outside Northern Ireland. Nine out of ten in my sample served at least thirty years, so in spite of the high price they paid, they seemed to find that the rewards outweighed the cost. Despite the problems encountered, I was left with a distinct impression that all these officers, with varying degrees of confidence and conviction, believed they had achieved something worthwhile for society. Even though three from the later period referred to an aspect common in police culture, the almost messianic mission of the RUC in saving the province from anarchy, they all tended to stress less dramatic features of their experience.

The features mentioned by almost all of the interviewees were camaraderie and solidarity (already well researched) in the face of a common enemy. A sentiment frequently expressed was 'In a tight corner you were totally dependent on your mates'. Another acknowledged its importance thus: 'You're in your own wee world. You're institutionalised, but the camaraderie makes it all worthwhile. Camaraderie is so very important. I'm still in touch and close to colleagues who served with me in [name]'. The Republican town which he named was his first station. He stressed the enduring nature of camaraderie, though I wondered if it would survive far into retirement. He had retired less than two years prior to interview. On balance it seemed that he probably would keep up these friendships, because three officers made statements to the effect that after retirement their best friends were Protestant, perhaps partially explained by retiring in 'safe' areas. After retirement the camaraderie may be extended on a one-to-one level rather than as broadly based continuity with the past. I noticed, for example, that a couple of the older seniors had ceased being part of the police scene, declining invitations: 'I get about twenty invitations a year to police dinners, but I don't accept. That era in my life is past. I'm a civilian now'. For these, at least, the camaraderie was bounded in time and was deemed to be no longer relevant except for faithful attendance at the funerals of former colleagues.

When one considers that all of these retired men had some service since 1969 and for more than half, all of their service was during that violent period, it must be assumed that camaraderie and solidarity were of crucial importance in trying to stay alive. Their stories testified to the daily danger they were in. It was noticeable that the younger retired accepted policing the Troubles as normal work, as they had no earlier experience with which to compare. Eight out of ten, including all of the younger, were targeted by the IRA for assassination precisely because they were Catholics and perceived by Republican activists as 'traitors' to their cultural heritage. One reported having been shot; one had to be transferred to a distant location; one escaped death three times, and one of the two not targeted specifically said he 'expected to be shot, like everybody else'.

The double disadvantage of being a Catholic police officer in an armed force is well summed up by one of the retirees as follows:

The downside, well you were always aware of danger, often scared going out in an operational area, for example a family row. But it was your duty. The police officer's first duty is to preserve life. I never fired a weapon. Glad I never had to. I carried a personal weapon when I was visiting along the border. Your nerves could crack and your life might not really be in danger. Better to be without it in general.

3   Forward to Patten and the PSNI

I shall move on to consider the retired officers' evaluation of the Patten reforms and the establishment of the PSNI to replace the RUC. I asked interviewees to comment in particular on three recommendations, namely the change in name and uniform, increased police accountability and 50:50 recruitment. The broader question I tried to address was whether or not they felt that the PSNI will be capable of delivering liberal policing. Predictably, they commented on the process of police reform, as well as specific changes. Before commenting on recommendations which have been incorporated into the PSNI, some of the retired officers began by giving their views on the political context in which the Patten Commission worked and reported.

One senior, older officer summed up its significance as follows:

The Good Friday Agreement contains the answer to Northern Ireland's problem. It's not about good policing. It's essentially a political problem. Patten goes to the very core. The government has a right to tell you what to do but not how to do it. Operational independence . . . It needed a strong overhaul . . . Get them out from the grip of politicians.

A long-serving junior rejoiced: 'There's a new dawn. Never again will Unionist politicians be accepted at Westminster. The USA is overlooking the process'. Yet he acknowledged: 'Patten had to balance old and new. He had to be careful about a reaction that would be detrimental to society . . . PSNI is on the move'.

These short quotations suggested a clear appreciation of the politically sensitive circumstances which surrounded the introduction of radical police reform in the shape of a liberal model to replace a neo-colonial one whose day had passed even in the eyes of some stalwart supporters in the Unionist Party. A need for internal reform, as well as a clear separation of police accountability from operational independence based on professional judgement and a new relationship with political representatives, received approval from these officers. Three identified a variety of early signals of minor political success, including a drop in violence levels, a more stable society, though with modifications flagged by one as 'within hard-line areas things aren't much better'. A long-retired officer with the shortest service saw in the establishment of the PSNI an opportunity to clear an otherwise honourable force of 'bad apples'.

The British government's decision to bring in a team from outside the province to reform policing was heavily resented by the retirees. In the younger group those most senior and, therefore, most likely to know what was happening at the top of the RUC, gave generous credit for reform to the last chief constable. One summed up:

> Ronnie Flanagan and his team gave the blueprint to Patten . . . The recommendations of Ronnie would have been enough, but they wouldn't have made the same political impact . . . Getting rid of the RUC was a sop to Republicans. Patten came with a mission from the British government, a platform to negotiate with the IRA. Patten talked at you rather than to you. No 'What changes are needed?'.

This was the same officer who described Sir John Stevens as a 'complete and utter idiot . . . led a bunch of English detectives out for glory'. He resented the Stevens Enquiry into accusations of RUC collusion. He ridiculed their methods, including searching UDR men's houses and describing members of that part-time Army regiment as 'these terrorists . . . Arresting those with 4–5 rounds of ammunition . . .'. The idea that any individual or group had to come to Northern Ireland to tell the RUC how to conduct an enquiry or to introduce reform was anathema to him. In addition, he resented the RUC being used as a bargaining chip in negotiations between the British government and Sinn Féin.

His contemporary, equally senior in rank, corroborated his colleague's admiration for the publicly unrecognised work spearheaded by the last chief constable, for which Patten was credited. He took the opportunity presented by the interview to record a series of reforms which had been initiated by the RUC ahead of Patten's invited intervention:

> A need for reform was recognised in Ronnie Flanagan's Structural Review (1995). New plans for Special Branch, CID, new boundaries, new structures . . . Trying to make police more accountable . . . He was behind Unit Beat [a form of community policing]. He introduced the community safety concept – now it's an NIO [Northern Ireland Office] theme. There was a pilot scheme in Ballymena. The people were given a say in how they were policed. It involved other agencies. The emphasis was on social issues, not symptoms. It's still part of the discourse . . . We had Irish language classes in 1986. The community relations aspect got attention from John Hermon . . . Civil liberties in the curriculum since 1986 . . . Patten was not properly thought through. Too many senior police officers were got rid of. That left nobody with experience to carry out the enlightened ideas . . . Coming up to thirty years? – They got severance to encourage them to go. Too many, too quick. Talent was sent away. Then we were bombarded with changes. It was to the credit of the former RUC officers who made it work – not the PSNI. The steadfast RUC made it work.

This officer's agenda was clear. He obviously wanted to believe and to convey the idea that Patten had brought no new thinking and that, left to themselves, the RUC would have transformed itself into a PSNI-type of organisation without changing the name.

He was obviously reluctant to give credit to the new PSNI members for successful implementation of any of the recent reforms. He had to believe that although their organisation had been made a hostage to fortune, ex-RUC personnel had, in practice, brought the 'new dawn' in policing which was the brainchild of Sir Ronnie Flanagan and his top team. However, he made a valid point in relation to the zeal with which experienced officers were encouraged to retire with very attractive severance packages. This was a point brought up by two others, that highly educated young men and women in the PSNI found themselves having to lead patrols in the knowledge that no one in the group had relevant experience on which to draw in a challenging or emergency situation where 'book knowledge' was insufficient.

Having acknowledged strongly the reform measures either implemented or planned by the last chief constable of the RUC and his team, the retired officers commented on specific Patten reforms, often with mixed views. While no officer rejoiced that the name of the RUC had gone, eight out of ten acknowledged a need for change, mainly to make it more acceptable to Nationalists. One said that it was unnecessary and disapproved of 'the NYPD-style uniform', while a senior younger officer saw the change in name and insignia as being 'not important to the Nationalist or Unionist communities. It was all about political expediency. We kept our RUC stuff . . .'. It seemed that officers were willing to make an undoubted emotional sacrifice in accepting a change of name and appearance (even though they retained RUC uniform and regalia as mementos), if they could be satisfied that the result would be of political benefit. 'It's time for change, if not change in name. It's a price worth paying', said one.

A typical example of ambivalence in retired officers' attitudes is demonstrated below, where the principle of accountability is acceptable, but not the Patten version. All officers agreed that accountability was desirable in any police force. Two were especially critical of accountability according to the Patten model, one older junior and one younger senior – agreement between experience and seniority. Both focused on the Ombudsman. The younger officer declared:

> There is too much accountability now. The Ombudsman came in with all the grace of the Gestapo, with a view that everything was bad in the RUC. She was going to sort it out. Guilty till proven innocent. She would never recruit ex-RUC. Now she has four or five in it . . . The police, the Catholic Church, the legal profession should have the full rigour of the law applied to them.

His colleague was critical of [now Baroness] Nuala O'Loan, the first incumbent in the role, in her dealings with Sir Ronnie Flanagan, though he blamed Special Branch for 'letting him down'. 'They've gone from not enough to too much. We've gone overboard. They're not investigating impartially, though it's getting better.' These officers were much more critical of Nuala O'Loan's performance than of the introduction of her role, per se. Her manner and her first unfortunate public encounter with the chief constable in which she censured him for his investigation of the Omagh bombings seemed to make them rush to the defence of Sir Ronnie, one of their own. There was resentment expressed by the officer quoted above, at the police being singled out as though in need of accountability in radical form to account for their actions, while two revered institutions, not noted for transparency, neither practised nor were being forced to practise similar innovation.

This aggressive defensive stance contrasted with that of a third officer, another of the senior ranking younger group, who sought to downplay a need for greater accountability while admitting that all was not entirely satisfactory: 'It's hard to find the truth, to define the truth . . . The system certainly wasn't perfect. The Army and Intelligence were involved in wrongdoing, possibly SB [Special Branch] to some extent'. (This was the officer who, earlier, had defended Special Branch against accusations of collusion.) The consensus suggested that a system was needed to deal with a small minority of less worthy colleagues, there being five references to 'bad apples'. A transformation from no external intervention in their disciplinary system to the Patten approach of almost total transparency seemed to present a challenging mental leap for a majority. Subtle, gradual change was recognised to be necessary, but not the version favoured by the Patten Commission.

On another radical recommendation there was wide variety of comment, although general approval in principle. Four officers voiced unqualified approval of the 50:50 recruitment system; three qualified their approval; three veered towards a negative approach, doubting its success in the short to medium term, though approving the principle of better numerical representation of the Catholic population. One of the latter felt that a 40:60 Catholic:Protestant ratio would satisfy him and be more realistically attainable, while another believed that 20:80 would be an achievement in the foreseeable future. He added: 'There's no point in golden handshakes if you get more of the same . . . If they kept at it, it might work in time. There's plenty of lads out there but they're still wary'. The eldest interviewee, seemingly influenced by low Catholic recruitment in the past and seeing Northern Irish society as being slow to change, was confident that: '50:50 is not working. Falls Road people will not join. Fifteen dropped out from the first intake'. The short-term service officer could not see any figure approaching 50:50 being realised without accepting ex-Republicans, against which he was firmly set. Perhaps they were unable to engage mentally with the possibility of vast increase in numbers and more so with the thought of ex-IRA being accepted, since they had constituted 'the enemy' for so long.

The two younger, senior officers made thoughtful comment about what they considered quite a complex issue. They obviously disliked the crude religious tag given to the policy, suggesting a preference for discretion. One said:

> They should anonymise the recruitment system. There are three religions as we all know in Northern Ireland . . . Don't come forward just because you're a Catholic. It's a demanding career. You've got to be good at it. You depend on your colleagues for your life . . . Take the best possible people. The system should be cleansed of background. It would make it clear that you're being taken for your moral standing, intelligence, self-esteem.

He illustrated a point by recalling an example of an applicant who had been turned away by her local RUC sergeant in a Republican town because her brother was a known IRA activist. His point was this: a mathematical formula ignores the personal dimension which, in this case, he summed up in the words: 'She gave up a helluva lot to even present herself at the station'. An assumption was made about her values, based simply on those known to have been espoused by her brother. He wanted the best of two systems to work together.

His colleague did not see 50:50 alone to be a solution to the problem of Catholic under-representation in policing. On the one hand he wanted the service to be numerically representative, yet not making religious background the principal selection criterion. He felt that a more robust recruitment campaign, with a greater concentration on Northern Ireland, assuring applicants that Catholics are promoted on merit, was likely to be a successful strategy. Evidence of success in targeted recruitment was offered by a third colleague, also a young senior. He had served as a county recruitment officer and spoke confidently of his successful experience going into Catholic secondary schools, having been given permission by 'strong principals'. They were located in Protestant towns mostly, so the principals, in contrast to those in Republican areas, had little reason to fear repercussions from the local IRA. However, this situation he thought was likely to continue. If, in the recent past, Catholic representation did not top 8 per cent and modestly fruitful recruiting grounds were Protestant towns such as Larne, Carrickfergus, Ballymena and Bangor, then new sources of supply will need to be found. Further success would require new political and social attitudes, if the PSNI were to become truly representative. One of the older senior officers voiced a warning against recruiting from 'police families': 'Police families took their fathers' values with them. They didn't enter the RUC with fresh enquiring minds. They were half-reared policemen already . . . Get new, untainted blood into the PSNI'.

In addition to commenting on the political context surrounding the Patten data collection exercise and specific recommendations, views were expressed on the PSNI in action, albeit necessarily over a very short period. Though only one retired officer had served in the PSNI and he for one year, six officers made direct comment on the PSNI. Two from the older group viewed the new force positively and one of the younger group opined: 'Given the resources, the PSNI will do a good job'. Three others were critical of aspects of PSNI policy and practice, to which they had paid some attention. One was critical that police in Northern Ireland had lost their distinctiveness: 'We're going the way of the English police who were never as good as us. It's not the policy to get out into the streets any more'. Another based his criticism on the PSNI's perceived imprudent choice of priorities: 'The PSNI is concentrating on nothing but speeders. They're getting the backs up of the people who would support them. For the local commanders it's another tick in a box'. This quotation refers to the record-keeping dimension of accountability and the temptation to focus on catching and prosecuting speeding motorists, since it is a relatively uncontentious form of duty and results are easily quantified.

Scarcity of resources was recognised as a genuine reason for inadequate service, for example, scarcity of patrol cars. The oldest retired officer had tested the efficiency of the new force against his experience as a civilian victim. Wishing to stress the contrast in service to the community in the 'old days', he voiced disappointment at the lack of reporting back from his local station. Immediately he was aware it was happening, he notified an attempted breaking and entering at his home, which he foiled, in the middle of the night. His ongoing correspondence with the district commander regarding absence of follow-up he described gleefully as 'rattling the PSNI cage'. He added: 'They'll work hard at community policing to get Nationalists on board. It'll not happen over night, history tells us'.

Another older, junior retiree saw joint involvement of the British and Irish governments as capable of bringing the elusive, yet most fundamental features of the liberal model – legitimacy and consent. He predicted confidently:

> Over time, a long time, more Catholics will join and slowly the PSNI will win the consent they never had. The Southern government's heavily involved now. We've power sharing. It was a different kettle of fish when the Unionists were in control. We [the RUC] hadn't a hope.

A third man, who had reached the highest rank of the group on retirement, was cautiously optimistic, adding an extra ingredient to the mix:

> Increase in 'ordinary' crime [non-political] will make the 'good majority' want to support the police. They'll know it's in their interest. The problem lies with the politicians. Will they be able to work together? Will Sinn Féin support the PSNI and when? Community policing sounds good and right, but it won't work without community support. It'll be a slow, hard road.

Their comments on politics and politicians sounded collectively cynical about the progress of the political process, though they held out some hope 'if Sinn Féin came onto the Policing Board'. One said: 'I don't see the Assembly up and running', but counselled: 'We must look to the future, not wallow in the past'. Two strongly disagreed with the idea of ex-paramilitary prisoners being even considered for acceptance into the PSNI, yet one of the older seniors implied that he foresaw a more positive approach in ex-terrorists being allowed the option of a career change: 'Let's just reflect on Makarios, Mandela and their stories. One of the problems in Ireland, in Northern Ireland, is that we drag our past around behind us'. He reminded us that in other divided parts of the world, Cyprus and South Africa, former terrorist leaders Archbishop Makarios and Nelson Mandela became influential and respected democratic leaders, after a significant political settlement had been reached.

While admitting the logical need for a new policing regime, they saw their contribution as RUC officers being diminished as a consequence. The demise of the RUC was clearly a very sad event for these men, of whom nine out of ten had served thirty to forty-two years. Some feared that their contributions would be forgotten or trivialised, while others focused on precisely what Patten was trying to do – to introduce the Westminster model of policing into Northern Ireland.

Reluctant though they appeared to be to praise the PSNI, lest it should imply that the new service was more professional than the RUC had been, some retirees were willing to admit that in the future, policing might approach the liberal model. There was obvious conflict between head and heart in the case of three retired officers, exemplified by one who began thus: 'The RUC held Northern Ireland together. The George Cross Award recognised it'. But added: 'Given the resources, the PSNI will do a good job'. Three viewed the PSNI as being capable of reform along liberal lines but returned to the crucial importance of the political and social context in which it was being attempted. One who had recently retired at senior rank said:

> Of course, the PSNI will do all that is required. They're professional police – and the very best you'll get. They'll moan about change, but they'll get on with the job. They'll do what Patten asked of them.

Conclusion

Over a time span of fifty-seven years which the service of these ten officers covered, from 1945 until 2002, the RUC seemed clearly to have moved away from a neo-colonial model towards a more professional version, when overt sectarianism was no longer acceptable and Catholics were given their fair share of promotional opportunities. Problems which remained – such as poor image reflected by interrogation methods, allegations of collusion – were shared by non-Catholic colleagues, though they caused great difficulties for Catholic officers because the vast majority of victims were from the Republican community. The Catholic officers, therefore, suffered contamination by association in the minds of less discriminating non-Catholic colleagues.

With the exception of one or two, there was cautious optimism expressed about the likelihood of the PSNI being accepted across the board if accompanied by appropriate political change, especially agreement from Sinn Féin to join the Policing Board. There was overwhelming confidence expressed in the current top team of the PSNI to establish an impartial police service, in spite of substantial challenges – such as greater accountability than any comparable service – given enough resources to meet demanding public expectations.

Taken as a whole, the views of these ten retired officers suggested that police culture and Catholic identity were two major areas to concentrate on in a later chapter, with reference to the work of other researchers. In Chapter 4, I discuss my main sample of fifty currently serving Catholic officers, the numbers allowing generalisation, impossible with a sample of ten.

4 Veterans but still serving officers

Introduction

The experiences and perceptions of retired Catholics were a significant element in a longitudinal study of policing Northern Ireland when the Catholic population withheld its consent from the RUC. The sample provided valuable material on how they managed as cultural Catholics in spite of enduring problems arising externally from the Catholic community, as well as from internal sources. Distance, however, may have lent enchantment to the view as they looked back at the 'golden days' of the best years of their lives. Since their experiences were in the past, they may have mellowed and their judgement may have lost its sharp edge.

Chapters 4, 5 and 6 provide continuity with Chapter 3 as well as direct contrast. The crucial test of the RUC came with the outbreak of paramilitary violence in 1968–69, which found the RUC wanting, and heralded an era of counter-terrorist policing which continued for thirty years. All the Catholic officers discussed in this chapter began their service in 1970 or later. IRA violence exacerbated the difficulties with which Catholic RUC officers had to cope and made their choice of career even more problematical than in the case of their predecessors. With their Protestant colleagues they had to participate in dual forms of policing – 'normal' and paramilitary. Their political masters were Westminster politicians who, beginning with the Hunt Report in 1970, set out for them a long and difficult road towards reforming policing as part of a general attempt to bring justice and parity of esteem to all the province's citizens.

Structurally Chapter 4 is slightly different from Chapter 3. It comprises two parts which address in turn the questions:

- How did Catholic officers manage their cultural identity as Catholics and police officers? (Part 1)
- What problems, internal and external to the RUC, presented them with difficulties and had these changed since the earlier years of the RUC which were recounted by retired Catholic officers? (Part 2)

Since both serving officers and trainees have experience (though brief in the case of the latter) of the Patten recommendations translated into practice, I shall compare their views on recent police reform in Chapter 6.

1　Private lives

The first part of Chapter 4 will focus on data which describe and analyse the cultural backgrounds of fifty serving Catholic officers and the transition which they experienced in becoming and remaining RUC officers. The unifying theme will be the strategies which they used to manage being Catholics and police officers in a bitterly divided society. First I shall provide a summary profile of my sample.

Sample profile

The average age of the serving Catholic officers was 40 years. They had completed seventeen years, on average, of service in the RUC and had very recently transferred into the PSNI. Service ranged between four and thirty-four years. Forty-one (82 per cent) were male and nine (18 per cent) were female. They included twenty nine (58 per cent) constables, eight (16 per cent) sergeants, ten (20 per cent) inspectors/chief inspectors and three (6 per cent) superintendents/chief superintendents. They represented a range of functional areas: twenty (40 per cent) in beat and patrol/community, twelve (24 per cent) in CID, 9 (18 per cent) in training, nine (18 per cent) in eight various specialist roles which I have decided not to name in case identification of individuals might be facilitated. Four (8 per cent) held a Master's degree, sixteen (32 per cent) a primary degree or equivalent, thirteen (26 per cent) had passed A-levels, thirteen (26 per cent) had passed O-levels/CSE and four (8 per cent) registered no formal qualifications. The sample represented a reasonably good spread across gender, ranks and functions. Their educational qualifications, with a figure of 40 per cent graduates, were significantly higher than 15 per cent of the survey respondents and 11 per cent in the general Catholic population (NILT, 2003).

Forty-five officers (90 per cent) said they were married (for a first time); five (10 per cent) were separated or divorced, of whom two (4 per cent) were with second partners. Three (6 per cent) were with new Catholic partners having been remarried by a renegade priest. Twenty-eight (56 per cent) reported that they were regularly practising Catholics; seven (14 per cent) practised irregularly; eight (16 per cent) had ceased to practise but attended christenings, weddings and funerals as social events. These figures approached survey responses showing 76 per cent who considered themselves Catholics. Two (4 per cent) practised in other Christian churches, though not members; one (2 per cent) had converted to the Church of Ireland; one (2 per cent) described himself as Christian, having become a member of a sect; three (6 per cent) said they were atheist/agnostic. The reported religious affiliation of these Catholic officers' partners was much less differentiated: twenty-two (44 per cent) were said to be Catholic; twenty-five (50 per cent) were Protestant and one (2 per cent) was described as Christian and intended to mean 'neither Catholic nor Protestant'. (Two did not have partners.) All fifty (100 per cent) of the officers had Catholic mothers and forty-six (92 per cent) had Catholic fathers.

Numbers of parents who were Catholic were very similar to survey findings. In the case of Protestant partners, figures were almost exactly the same as in the survey, while the 44 per cent given for partners of interviewees being Catholic was considerably higher than the corresponding figure for the partners of survey respondents, which was 28 per cent. However, the difference was accounted for by the 'Other/ DK' category of 17 per cent – a less likely response in an interview situation.

The officers' political sympathies were wide ranging and were measured by expressed voting preferences. One (2 per cent) said he was 'unionist with a small u'; eight (16 per cent) declared to be Nationalist; three (6 per cent) voted for the cross-community Alliance Party; ten (20 per cent) claimed to be non-voters; twenty-two (44 per cent) chose to ignore party politics; four (8 per cent) indicated that they made up their minds at each election, their choice depending on the merits of the candidate; two (4 per cent) remained non-committal. Lack of political commitment was a strong feature of the sample profile – similar to the survey profile of 66 per cent neutral. A vast majority had been brought up in Northern Ireland, twenty-three (46 per cent) in predominantly Protestant areas, nine (18 per cent) in predominantly Catholic areas, nine (18 per cent) in mixed areas. Only six (12 per cent) were from outside: three (6 per cent) from the Republic of Ireland, two (4 per cent) from England and one (2 per cent) from Scotland. (Eighteen per cent had a police officer parent, close to 21 per cent in the survey.) These figures, though low, marked a departure from the retired officers who had all been born in Northern Ireland. It is noteworthy that, though not the products of mixed marriages, most had been brought up outside Catholic areas.

Typology
The data provided by the sample of fifty established clearly that there was enormous variety among people who were all cultural Catholics. Within their working lives in an environment hostile to them in many ways, they had to manage being Catholics and being police officers. In answering the question of how they managed these two identities, I analysed the data with a view to developing a typology which would go some distance towards categorising the broad strategies which Catholic officers used. The categories I have named are chameleons, flaunters, deserters and victims.

These are not mutually exclusive categories; for example, some flaunters may also possess some of the characteristics of victims because by drawing attention to their cultural identity they may invite a sectarian response from Protestant officers who associate Catholicism with Republicanism. I shall, however, give a brief sketch of each ideal type.

Chameleon refers to those who are staunch in their traditional beliefs but who live out their Catholicism in unconventional or unpredictable ways. They do not see their cultural Catholicism as being a readily recognisable cluster of behaviours such as socialising with co-religionists, participating in Gaelic cultural activities or of steering clear of contexts of activities usually associated with being Protestant.

They perceive themselves as police officers who see their vocations as the path along which they travel and live out their Catholicism, not flaunting it but not denying it. They are flexible and adapt according to the demands of a situation. The idea of two mutually exclusive tribes with completely distinct profiles who must consistently oppose one another is not their perception of reality. Vignette A below exemplifies a chameleon type of Catholic officer.

Middle ranking, approaching retirement, born in west Belfast, stationed in a Unionist town, Officer A had a British Army, Church of England father who converted to the Catholic Church of which his Northern Irish mother was a member. He was married to a former RUC officer, a colleague of his in the depot, who converted to Catholicism from the Church of Ireland, where her brother was a clergyman who conducted their wedding ceremony. In spite of his grandmother's strong Republican family, he had been a boy soldier in Hong Kong, Belize, Cyprus and the UK for five years since the age of 16. This unconventional, regularly practising Catholic explained:

> I learned Irish and Gaelic football; then I transferred to Rugby in the Army . . . A Dominican nun and a Maynooth priest were godparents to our younger son . . . I'm a Mason. I joined in 1995. They do wonderful charity work. I believe in a supreme being. That's all that was required of me. The Board of BP will not report on what it talked about. Why should Masons be obliged to? Our older son [a student] is a barman in his spare time at the Masonic Club.

While believing that 'the Catholic Church could have been more supportive', he claimed to have an excellent relationship with the Catholic clergy where he was serving and was made welcome in Catholic schools. When in Republican towns the clergy protected him, one priest having passed on information that a 500lb bomb was hidden by the IRA in a parked white van.

He socialised 'with all kinds of safe people'. He believed that political control should stay in Westminster because 'Our present crop of politicians are not mature enough to make an Assembly work. They're only interested in points scoring'.

Flaunters readily identify themselves as Catholics because they are combative or feel it would be denial of their heritage if they did not consistently remind others of their distinctive identity. I include those brought up in a Nationalist or Republican environment who simply see no reason to present themselves in a modified or conciliatory way. Some have not been used to living in a divided town and tended to be conscious of only one culture from experience. They are often those who were visible as Catholics or, more likely, as Nationalists while they were in training. Sometimes the unwittingly high profile which they gave themselves ensured that the spotlight continued to be on them. The fact that they flaunted their cultural background, which they felt to be a strong part of their identity, did not mean they were static in their views. Quite the contrary, in company with other Catholic officers, experience in policing, particularly through interaction with the public, caused them to modify their attitudes. An experienced male officer from a Nationalist town features in Vignette B.

Officer B, about two-thirds of the way up the promotion ladder, already beyond 40 years old and looking to a second career in higher education, was born into a 'comfortable middle-class Catholic family'. From 'a politicised generation' he saw no reason to stop presenting himself as 'as Irishman, a Catholic, a Nationalist'. With both Christian and surnames which clearly declared his cultural background, he had spurned the idea of altering his first name to make him less culturally identifiable. He despised others who had allegedly done this, allowing themselves to be 'assimilated not integrated' into the RUC.

Having stumbled at A-level stage and failing to obtain a university place in law, he boasted that he had not lost out financially, since his salary was equivalent to that of a general medical practitioner. He and his police officer wife were regularly practising Catholics.

Officer B felt that his 'outspokenness as a Catholic' was the reason for being turned down for a Special Branch post. 'I wasn't supported by the organisation, but they're quick to use me on radio'. His criticism was levelled at the PSNI, which he compared unfairly with its predecessor: 'The RUC was loyal to its workers; it rewarded people who put their heads above the parapet'. Knowledgeable about police reforms in a world context, he was critical of the way the Patten recommendations were implemented in Northern Ireland.

Deserters are those who have left their cultural background behind. They do not deny it – in fact they praise parts of it, for example, the benefits of Catholic education, but they tend to desert because they have rejected Catholicism as conscientious objectors (a very small number) or as a matter of convenience. For example, two find it more comfortable to worship in a non-Catholic church or nearly half of them marry non-Catholics whose culture is too strong to resist in relation to children's upbringing and education. Those who married Presbyterians who were unwilling to convert, tended to do so in a Church of Ireland ceremony, which they saw as a 'halfway house', intermediate in theological terms between Catholicism and Protestantism, often with a Catholic priest participating in the ceremony. Deserters typically found the behaviour of the Catholic hierarchy unacceptable in their unwillingness to condemn the IRA and their atrocities and their willingness to afford IRA members the courtesy of a Christian burial. They felt let down by their church and by their community, who did not support them, leaving them easy targets of criticism from sectarian Protestant colleagues. One wondered at times if desertion were a permanent state and if it would end with the officer's retirement. One victim accused deserters he had known of having denied their identity, even lied about the schools they attended. Vignette C below outlines the story of a high-ranking deserter, beyond mid-service, who looked back as well as forward in a reflective way.

Officer C was one of the three most senior ranking that I interviewed. Born to Catholic parents and with a father from a Republican background, he was brought up in predominantly Protestant towns and experienced no sense of severance from his community when he joined the RUC. He attended a state grammar school where he completed A-levels. On the subject of identity he said: 'In the early days I submerged myself in police culture, leaving aside Catholic culture'. He did not attend family celebrations of his father's (Republican) relatives, but took seriously his middle-class mother's condition when she agreed to his joining the RUC: 'OK, but don't remain a constable'.

'I became a chameleon. Married a Presbyterian in her Church in the country. I'm a practising Presbyterian, but "Protestant" would stick in my throat'. His Presbyterian Orangeman father-in-law expected that his grandchildren would be brought up Presbyterian. Officer C's response was 'I've no big issue with that'. However, he added, 'Inside me it *has* become a big issue. I've become friendly with a Church of Ireland minister in [name of town]. It's a manifestation of what's going on inside me. I still take Communion and I've a strong individual spirituality. I've an eclectic title now. I'm a Christian and a cultural Catholic'.

Victims are those who have a consistently negative view of how they have been treated as Catholic police officers. Most often, they blame their Protestant colleagues, the authorities, but also the society they serve, either Protestant or Catholic, or both. They tend to be reactors who assume that they cannot change a situation by their intervention in order to achieve a better outcome for themselves. They do not see their work as a successful, enjoyable career, but 'live' outside of work and, in spite of the difficulties, they strive to be conscientious professional officers. In the life story of some of the victims in my sample there was a consistently negative narrative which began in their childhood, particularly if they were from among the 18 per cent who were police children. Another kind of victim was brought up in a Nationalist town which presented no problems. A typical example was catapulted into challenging locations as a police officer, with poor coping skills. He was quickly labelled 'a paranoid Catholic' and in spite of one promotion retained that reputation. Having no belief in the disciplinary system or even the political correctness of the PSNI, he bore his cross, seeing no way out.

The young female whom I have chosen as Vignette D presented as disadvantaged for being Catholic, but also for being female.

Officer D was from a middle-class family, had a retired police officer father who had not spoken to her about life in the RUC and had not influenced her choice of career. Shocked by the police culture, she admitted she had probably made a mistake and should have chosen to work with animals. She had experienced sexual harassment in the depot, to be followed by sectarian bigotry when she was appointed to her first station where she felt she was not trusted and her first insult was couched in racist terms. 'A black man is better than a Fenian.' She perceived herself to have been the 'token Taig' in her section. Her name clearly indicated that she was Catholic, so she was given an Irish nickname and told by the IRA on a peace line: 'You're top of our list' [of possible targets].

Having applied for CID work she was offered an appointment which she would have found it impossible to take up for family reasons. The authorities, instead of offering an alternative location, gave her a post in a typically female dominated function, investigating rape and child abuse. Disillusioned by her experience, she said 'This is not a job for a woman. Single women are just shunted off to the back of beyond at a whim'.

With about ten years' experience but no promotion [which appeared not to interest her] she presented as timid in her relationship with her colleagues, fearful that our conversation might be overhead by her superiors. She was the only female appointed in ten years to the station where I interviewed her, in a hard-line, predominantly Protestant area. With a Protestant partner she then 'lived' outside her work and outside a specific community.

Trouble from family and friends

'Tell me about your home background. Did your choice of career give anyone a problem when you joined the RUC?'

In answering this question the serving interviewees provided data on parentage and ancestry, family politics and the responses of family, friends and neighbours when they joined. A very large majority said that their parents were devout Catholics with mild Nationalist views. Eight per cent had non-Catholic fathers, while all the mothers were Catholic, including one who had converted on marriage. About 10 per cent mentioned the strong influence which their mothers had on their religious thinking and practice, for example 'My mother taught me the value of prayer. She would not allow us to criticise other people – not even Paisley'. However, one senior officer, a deserter, found that his mother's piety had had a negative effect, concluding 'Perhaps I got too much of it'. Two officers had fathers who were local councillors, one SDLP and one Alliance. The latter explained the family environment in religious and political terms thus: 'My parents were devout Catholics and free thinking. Dad was an Alliance councillor. We went to the Orange Parades in [name of small town in South Armagh]'. The breadth of tolerance implied in this statement by an officer looking back beyond his twenty years' service proved to be the rule, rather than the exception. Officers born in the 1950s and early 1960s, especially those with fathers in the RUC, were brought up in those pre-civil rights times to see Orange processions as attractive spectacles, rather than demonstrations of Protestant Unionist ascendancy – denial as a means of managing their cultural identity. Their family backgrounds beyond parentage were diverse in terms of political affiliation and almost 30 per cent had family links with the Republic of Ireland or England and with the cultures of those countries, usually through holidaying with relatives.

It was especially noticeable and probably made them atypical of Northern Irish

Catholics in general, there having been no conscription in the province during the World Wars, that a relatively high proportion of just over one-quarter had ancestors, some going back over three generations, who had made careers in the British armed services. The 8 per cent who had relatives in the IRA one or two generations before them seemed to have belonged to families who reviewed their loyalties as political events unfolded. One officer quoted his grandfather, an active Republican in his youth, to have remarked to this grandson, pointing towards an RUC officer on duty in a Republican town, 'See, that's the job you should go into when you leave school'. Perhaps he could see potential benefits of a secure career compared with ephemeral rewards from Republican idealism.

The generally flexible approach, which about 50 per cent of serving officers reported, contrasted with the stories of those who experienced family opposition. Those who had relatives who were still staunch Republicans had, predictably, greater and more sustained difficulties than those who had parentage or recent ancestry of Protestant, even Orangemen stock, who were almost entirely on the paternal side. A female drop-out from university, now at mid-rank, born in the Republic, explained her difficulties:

> My mother came from a large family, mainly Nationalist, but with a strong Republican element. I have two uncles priests and my great-grandfather was in the IRA. My parents put every obstacle in my way and asked others to do so. I was seen to be fraternising with the enemy. My IRA uncle died at 90 last year without knowing that I was an RUC officer and have been for twenty-four years.

In contrast, a seasoned male officer whose father served in the RAF – although he had been in the IRA in the 1940s – explained how his potential fate was no secret: 'My mother's relations in the south left me in no doubt about my fate. They told me "If you come down here, we'll arrange to have you shot"'. In the case of a junior officer in mid-career, born in a predominantly Nationalist city, he was not threatened but was immediately rejected by his relatives. He found his choice of career to be completely unacceptable in a 1980s context; rejection was total: 'The family's attitude to joining? They threw me out. It was too dangerous for the rest of the family. The big problem went away in time, but they're still worried if I visit'. There was a marked contrast, as illustrated by the quotations above, that objections from people living in the south of Ireland towards Catholics joining the RUC were based on loyalty to Republicanism, whereas Catholic families in Northern Ireland were more likely to be concerned about the potential physical threat ensuing for the whole family, if a member became an RUC recruit.

About one-half of Catholic officers referred to isolation from some or all school friends as a price they had to pay for joining the RUC. In addition, those school friends who remained in their shared neighbourhood could make lasting difficulties for the officers and their families. The complexity was explained by a junior officer with twenty years' experience who was born in a border area, attended a Catholic boarding school and had, surprisingly, joined the police cadets before sitting his O-levels. He admitted:

> I'm not in touch with any of my school friends. I couldn't attend my brother's wedding because the bridesmaid and best man would have recognised me. I couldn't turn up because I'd have put my brother's safety at risk. My [Protestant] wife went instead.

Catholic officers from strongly Republican areas such as west Belfast, obviously identifiable as cultural Catholics in a close-knit community, seemed to feel at greater risk from co-religionists whose disapproval of their career choice might take a violent form. Officers in this danger used various strategies to protect themselves, their parents or siblings. One junior officer with relatively short service explained how he protected his mother and himself. 'My mother lives in [name of street] in west Belfast. She doesn't know where I'm stationed. That's for her protection in case she might be "used" by others'. An interesting example of a Catholic who decided to join the RUC and presented as a chameleon, was very conscious of the physical dangers which threatened. He planned accordingly:

> I laid my plan four years in advance. I was from west Belfast. I got a flat away from my mum and I visited her regularly. Then I got a job in England and I visited her – less often, of course. Now I'm in the PSNI and I can still visit her. When the neighbours see me they say 'I see [his name] is home on holidays'.

The long-term adverse effects of joining the RUC were most poignantly felt when parents or other close relatives died in Republican areas. They appear to have had a clear choice to make among three options – not to attend; to attend with RUC protection, thereby raising their visibility; or to take a calculated risk by visiting the home of the dead person unprotected. 'It was very hard when you couldn't attend your father's funeral' was a remark typical of the three-quarters who commented on this ongoing disadvantage to being a Catholic police officer. One, largely a victim type, born in a Nationalist town explained how he had used a mixed strategy when his mother died:

> While I was in my mother's bedroom standing over her coffin, I looked up and saw two Republicans looking at me. I left the room immediately, got out through a bathroom window, shinned down a drainpipe at the back of the house, into my car and sped away.

Defiantly, he returned to her funeral the following day with discreet police protection, as he did when his sister died some time later. This kind of situation was one in which the RUC facilitated Catholic officers to retain family links at times of bereavement.

Forty-two per cent of the survey sample refused to identify sources of opposition to joining the RUC and 50 per cent to state the strength of opposition. Those fifty who volunteered to be interviewed, however, appeared to have no problem in talking about family opposition to their joining the RUC, or to the duration or strength of the opposition.

It was clear that for a substantial number of these officers their difficulties began before they had an opportunity to sample life in the RUC, making their reasons for joining of compelling interest. Those who experienced opposition from family, friends or neighbours were most likely to develop a chameleon profile, though two were hybrids, showing flaunter characteristics in part.

Reasons for joining

Since Catholics have traditionally been grossly under-represented in the RUC, it was important to establish the reasons which this sample of cultural Catholics gave for bucking an established trend. The implications of making such a career choice were likely to be far-reaching and long-term answers to the two-part question: 'Why did you decide to join the RUC? What was your main reason?' elicited two broad categories of reasons – vocation and financial security. Vocation was expressed in a variety of ways such as 'making a contribution towards stopping the Troubles', 'I wanted to make a difference' and 'It will never change if more Catholics don't join. Change from within rather than gripe from without'. About 70 per cent gave a vocational reason alone, accurately reflecting the survey figure of 68 per cent, while 15 per cent coupled vocation with financial security. Only 6 per cent added that 'it seemed the natural thing to do'. One officer saw the RUC as the answer to his quest for a career which would give him a sense of belonging in order to give him status, 'I wanted to be attached to something important – not just be an individual'.

It was perhaps unsurprising to find that for about one-quarter of those who wanted 'to serve the public by doing varied and challenging work', the RUC was not their first choice of police force. The Garda Síochána in the Republic of Ireland was preferred over the London Metropolitan Police by about three to one. A senior-ranking officer, the only one in the sample who has divorced from a Protestant partner, explained:

> I always wanted to be a police officer from early secondary school. I loved police pro-grammes on TV such as 'The Sweeney'. When I visited Dublin I'd always be found talking to a Garda. I was aware of the potential stigma of being a police officer here. I applied first to the Met and then to the Garda. I saw police work as exciting, challeng-ing and a worthy public service.

In spite of having to learn Irish to an appropriate level to enhance his chances of selection – since he had attended a state grammar school where Irish was not taught – he was not offered a place by the Garda. He did not join the Met on advice from his girlfriend's RUC officer father 'that I'd be a pariah in the Met and then there was the security thing'. He accepted an offer from the RUC unenthusiastically, 'I was worried going down the road to Enniskillen [location of the training centre] but it would have been weak to back down'.

This officer, largely a chameleon, was aware that his cultural heritage would be a burden to him joining the RUC and anticipated hostility from future colleagues. He would have preferred to realise his ambition in a less challenging professional and social context. His decision was opposed by his Nationalist father because he was worried for his son's safety, but also opposed it on cultural grounds – to the extent that by threatening to join Sinn Féin he thought he might dissuade his son or lessen his chances of being accepted. He declined an offer from the Met, fearing a hostile reception from English officers threatened by IRA atrocities on the mainland.

Three other officers who favoured the Garda also found their inadequate knowledge of the Irish language to be an impediment, or they were offered a place in the RUC first. Two officers emphasised their first preference for the RUC by describing the difficulties which they were determined to overcome. An officer from west Belfast who joined in the mid-1990s told me:

> I had to make five attempts before I made the grade – three years after I'd been accepted by the Hong Kong police at inspector level . . . I wanted excitement, to catch criminals, but most of all to help the people of Northern Ireland.

An officer doing specialised detective work deliberately tested his vocation in another way. Born in a Unionist town, where business brought his family into regular contact with local police, he was 30 years old when his application was successful, after three attempts. Some years earlier, he withdrew his first application because his mother cried when asked to sign his papers. Lest a girlfriend who was a police officer should influence him unduly, he waited for a year after the relationship ended before he applied again. His caution had an adverse effect on his fitness levels.

> When I reached the training centre I felt like a Clydesdale horse . . . I was determined to get through, because I believed I had something to offer. I wanted to make the world a better place. I put the effort in. Reward is not necessarily monetary. Giving service is a reward.

Having tested the strength of his vocation, he showed a single-minded determination to achieve his aim through ongoing commitment already of twenty years' duration. Catholic applicants appeared to be successful on their first attempt. Only two officers mentioned having been turned down on physical fitness grounds.

About two out of three officers I interviewed had, similar to the detective quoted above, been employed in one or two civilian jobs before joining or, less likely, had been in the armed services. Those who went into civilian jobs had suppressed an early urge to apply, but because of personal reservations, family opposition or peer pressure had pursued other paths. A non-practising Catholic officer, born in a Nationalist provincial town and now engaged in training, was representative in stating 'I wanted to be a police officer as a teenager, but peer pressure put it out of my mind'. He spent thirteen years in England, but returned in the mid-1990s to follow his instinct after the IRA ceasefire, 'but it took till now [eight years later] for my police income to catch up with my civilian salary'. Only five officers said they joined mainly for financial security, including one who had experienced redundancy, one who was threatened by it and one who had chosen work which he found unrewarding. A significant point is made here. The experience of working in civilian jobs enabled them to mature before joining the RUC, to experience life outside their immediate home areas and schools and break free of constraints imposed by their tight Catholic family or neighbourhood.

It should be remembered that these officers all joined from 1970 onwards. The province was gripped by violent civil unrest and Lords Hunt, Cameron and Scarman had all reported separately between 1969 and 1972, finding the RUC wanting in its ability to cope with the results of IRA infiltration into the civil rights movement. The British government's response from then on, in the glare of world publicity, was often inept, only exacerbating the situation, but specific events in the political arena were cited by 12 per cent of interviewees as having prompted them to consider the RUC as a career opportunity, for altruistic reasons.

Three of the longest-serving officers explained their reasoning in words such as 'The Hunt Report [1970] made me think that people like me should join'. For one officer, the hunger strikes (1981) and accompanying death toll of civilian and security forces were the trigger, while for two others, encouragement and approval offered by the Catholic Bishop (later Cardinal) Cathal Daly was a spur. On more than one occasion speaking to the media, he endorsed increased Catholic membership of the RUC, for example, 'If we are to have an acceptable police force, the religious balance within that police force must reflect the balance within the community as a whole' (*Irish Times*, 23 August 1989). Bishop Daly was responding to a recruitment drive for increased Catholic membership initiated by the chief constable of the time, Sir Hugh Annesley. One ponders: if strong support for Catholic recruitment had been voiced by senior Catholic clergy and accompanied by consistent denouncement of the IRA, would a controversial quota system have been a necessary recommendation by Patten?

I am persuaded that while the intrinsic features of police work attracted these officers, they were very conscious of the RUC's negative image in the Catholic community and some attempted to achieve their objective in a preferred location outside Northern Ireland. About three times as many, however, did not report thoughts of serving as police officers outside Northern Ireland, but wanted to join locally, very conscious of the disadvantages – some of them long term – which would accrue from family, peers or community. The mild political views which an overwhelming majority professed to hold may have unconsciously facilitated their paths.

Political views of serving Catholic officers

It was important to seek respondents' political views since Northern Irish Catholics have largely aspired to the reunification of the island by peaceful means – in direct conflict with the Unionist aspiration and the political purpose carried out by the RUC. Reference has already been made to cleavages within the Catholic bloc and comparison drawn between Catholics in general and Catholics who became police officers, in terms of their political aspirations. Since Catholic officers came from 'mildly Nationalist' backgrounds in the main, I wanted to find out what their views were, after an average of seventeen years' service in the RUC when paramilitary policing was the norm. In this section I shall consider how they categorised themselves and explained their views.

The political profile of the fifty interviewees showed that 64 per cent described themselves as being either neutral or non-voters (including two officers whose names were not on the register of voters). This figure matched 66 per cent registered by survey respondents. Of the remainder of interviewees, 16 per cent were broadly Nationalist, 6 per cent were Alliance voters and one individual was 'unionist'. The remainder in equal measure either voted in accordance with the personal views and personality of the candidate, or voiced a totally negative view of politicians. While refinements in voting patterns came through more clearly in the interviews, the most striking finding was the passive attitude which prevailed in both survey and interview findings. Interviewees tended to focus more on Northern Ireland's likely political future than on aspiring to specific outcomes, beyond generally voiced agreement that they wanted a peaceful society which would facilitate community policing.

It seemed that no political party could be assured of consistent support from any of these fifty interviewees. The single officer who declared himself 'unionist' insisted that the word was written in lower case and explained his stance thus, expressing a general indifference to outcome but concern about process:

> Of course the police is an arm of the state. It wasn't our fault that the Unionists claimed us as theirs. I was always unionist with a small 'u'. I couldn't vote now. I'd prefer to maintain the Union, though it's inevitable that there will be a united Ireland. I've no difficulty with that in principle. I'm concerned about how we're going to get there.

His final sentence seemed to indicate a fear that Protestant opposition to reunification would mean that civil unrest would continue, the problem being Loyalist paramilitaries' violent opposition.

The passive attitude which prevailed was well conveyed by an ex-SDLP supporter who admitted to having 'licked stamps for my mum who was a member'. He declared himself not to be a 'party animal' but, 'I am willing to go along with a majority decision, for example, joint sovereignty with the Republic of Ireland. I'm a democrat. Let the majority decide'. A Dublin-born graduate was much more concise: 'The future position of Northern Ireland is not important. I'm a cultural Catholic, but it doesn't matter'.

Two other officers born outside of Northern Ireland veered closer to despair than indifference, seeing society in the province as being incapable of change. Their words suggested that religion and politics were hopelessly and inextricably linked. The young female commented 'The Prods [Protestants] are desperate to hang onto the past; for the other crowd, the police will never do enough'. A much older male declared regretfully 'I hate the religious and political prejudice in Northern Ireland society. There will never be anything other than a tribal system, because parents pass on their prejudices on both sides'.

Membership of the EC was mentioned by about 20 per cent, though there was division between those in favour and those against. Negative responses were far fewer in number and were reflected by the sentiment 'We must retain UK autonomy. Our natural allies are the USA and the Republic of Ireland. We mustn't get swallowed up in Europe'. These words reflecting minority opinion may be contrasted with those which envisaged the path ahead leading to Europe, 'I'm neutral about reunification. It's inevitable by 2050 in a European Community context'. A non-voter in a Unionist town saw his experience in the RUC as a symbol of peaceful political co-existence. He said 'I regard myself as Irish rather than British and I've enjoyed a happy marriage of the British and the Irish in the RUC. But our future lies in the United States of Europe'.

A majority of the one-third who commented on Sinn Féin sounded like typical Catholics in that they saw potential for a positive contribution by that party to political progress. One representative of this view, a junior officer with short service, who spent most of his working life in social services abroad felt 'Sinn Féin has a big part to play to get peace. They could reduce a lot of the tensions, give support from hardline areas. They should come on the Policing Board'. The opinion that Sinn Féin would and should join the Policing Board in the short term was widely voiced. A declared SDLP voter identified Gerry Adams as 'a man of vision. He realised in the late 1970s/early 1980s that the gun was not getting them anywhere, that they had to try a new track'. Absence of emotion in remarks made about alternative political futures unified most of the responses, which simply sought an eventual outcome which evolved smoothly and without further civil strife.

However, 10 per cent spoke with emotion in their criticism of Sinn Féin. A long-serving officer who had been in Derry on Bloody Sunday said 'Sinn Féin are criminals. A terrorist is a criminal by another name. Drugs, protection rackets, fake goods . . . They're not freedom fighters'. A female officer aged 30-plus from a strongly Republican town, whose family had suffered at the hands of the RUC and the British Army, had nonetheless turned away in disillusionment from the cause which Sinn Féin espoused. She recounted her story thus:

> I don't think politically now, though I was a Sinn Féin voter till my mid-20s. The border will go, but I won't rejoice. The Irish government and the British government don't want us. I have Irish nationality, but my brother in Dublin assures me that the people in the south are not interested in us. I don't vote. I'm disillusioned by politicians generally.

The 12 per cent who said that they voted for the candidate rather than the party implied willingness to cross the sectarian divide in doing so. One, more than two-thirds way through his service, said: 'It depends on the candidate. Most likely I'd vote Alliance. It's the only non-sectarian party. It suits me. I'm cynical about the Unionist split'. A more senior officer with similar service explained 'I vote for the person, rather than the party – UU [Ulster Unionist] or SDLP. Alliance has too many gin-and-tonic, golf-club types'. The final very small group were totally negative about politicians and the political process. They were represented by a short summary of his view given by a junior officer in mid-career, 'I don't vote. No politicians are worth a vote. I don't trust them. They're out for what they can get and they thrive on the tribal system'.

Comments made by serving Catholic police officers on the political future of Northern Ireland tended overwhelmingly to reflect indifference or negativity to the political process and lack of faith in our politicians. If one considers that police reform is dependent on community-wide consent to the legitimacy of the PSNI, driven by political and social change, then the views of these Catholic police officers did not hold out optimistic prospects. Their declared lack of interest in politics prompted one to extend into the political domain Sir John Hermon's often-quoted statement that in Northern Ireland there are three religious groups – Protestants, Catholics and police officers. Perhaps there are also Unionists, Nationalists and police officers. Such categorisation would seem to suggest that these Catholic officers, on the evidence which I have presented, were comfortable in detaching themselves from their cultural background in terms of political identity.

Education: Catholic officers' experiences and thoughts

Education and the Patten recommendations were the topics which the fifty Catholic officers seemed to find most engaging and on which they were willing to speak at some length, often with obvious feeling. The Catholic Church in Northern Ireland has always ensured that separate primary and secondary-level schooling was available to Catholic children since the establishment of the state, by virtue of an agreement made with the Unionist founding fathers. Both clergy and parents have looked upon Catholic schools as a crucially important vehicle via which the Catholic faith was transmitted to future generations. It follows that the Catholic education of children who chose to become police officers must have been, after Church and family, the strongest influence on their formation. This section examines the experiences and judgements which Catholic officers aired about Catholic education. Most significant, perhaps, even among those who had no personal regrets to register, was the strong support voiced for integrated schooling as a strategy for social change and, indirectly, for increased access so that children from both major communities might be recruited into the PSNI.

About 40 per cent of Catholic officers reported that their children went to Catholic primary schools, compared with 32 per cent in the survey. This contrasted with over 90 per cent of interviewed officers who did so. The remainder were fairly evenly divided between integrated and state primary or preparatory schools, though a slightly higher percentage opted for integrated than was the case in the survey. Of those who had children of secondary age, about one-third attended integrated colleges, compared with a noticeably lower figure of 14 per cent in the survey. About 30 per cent of interviewees' children attended Catholic schools (mainly grammar), a higher figure than 21 per cent found in the survey. The remaining 30–40 per cent went to state grammar schools, a slightly lower figure than for survey respondents. Interviewees, therefore, favoured integrated or Catholic education somewhat more than survey respondents. Officers, all male, who had regrettable experiences at Catholic grammar schools were more likely to send their children to leading state grammar schools than to integrated colleges. Nearly 60 per cent had non-Catholic spouses whose influence may not have left these Catholics officers complete freedom in choosing their children's schools.

No critical comments were made of the quality of Catholic primary education. Remarks on personal experiences of Catholic secondary education, whether laudatory or critical, showed how much their attitudes had been influenced by lay staff, though priests came in for most frequent mention. Nuns, though referred to by only 10 per cent, received more compliments than did priests, who were mentioned by about 20 per cent. A young female officer, largely chameleon but partly flaunter, who had received promotion and was from a convent grammar school in a Republican town said:

> The nuns gave us a good academic education, but more importantly, they gave us values for life, such as truth and justice, which apply in any job. They were very cross-community. There was nothing political about them.

Another convent-schooled female officer, a chameleon, reinforced approval of nuns as educators, contrasting them with priests. Approaching retirement, she explained how nuns had welcomed her into their schools to advise pupils about personal protection because:

> They felt I had something of benefit to offer the girls. Nuns put a mantle of protection around children – in contrast to priests. Parish priests didn't buy into non-controversial stuff such as dealing with strangers, or incest. The nuns cottoned on to the value of what I was doing for the girls' protection and passed on the news to other convent schools that gave me access . . . I felt personally let down by priests.

This officer made oblique reference to the difficulty of police officers receiving access to some Catholic schools and the subsequent absence of Catholic police officers as role models in Republican-controlled areas – as well as the obvious contribution they could make to the personal and social education curriculum.

Eighteen per cent of male officers who attended Catholic grammar schools made mixed comment. A lack of political neutrality on the part of some priests and some lay staff in the most frequently mentioned grammar school presented some officers with problems when they were pupils. Over half of the boys who were the sons of police officers had religious/political difficulties during their school careers. The most critical account was provided by a mid-rank, mid-career officer who recounted the story of himself and his classmate – a professional prominent in public life, both police officers' sons – of life at this Belfast school. He said:

> The priests were very anti-British and they brought it into the classroom. There was a debate in religion class about two girls who lured soldiers into a trap and they were killed by the IRA. It was justified as fighting for their cause [a united Ireland] . . . Mass was said for innocent Catholics killed in explosions. There was none for soldiers and police officers. I'd have favoured all victims. Earlier, my father had a confrontation with Father --- [name of priest, then President of the school] who had a problem with police children. Anyhow, my classmate and I protested to the headmaster that police who were blown up were not prayed for . . . I'm glad we did it, but it got us nowhere.

This insensitive, seemingly politically motivated treatment coloured the narrator's attitude towards parts of the curriculum and beyond:

> This kind of thing made me hostile to the Irish language and dancing. It wasn't of any practical use to me . . . School should help children to get jobs . . . I swore that no child of mine would ever go to a Catholic school and I kept my promise . . . The whole thing made me doubt my faith and now I'm an agnostic.

The narrative of the deserter above exemplified the difficult experiences which some Catholic officers' children had to endure because their parents, traditional Catholics, felt that the best spiritual formation would be provided in Catholic schools. The absence of political congruence was, however, ignored or political neutrality was assumed by the parents – at their children's expense. The authorities in this school, and perhaps repeated in others, appear to have made no attempt to satisfy pupils' raw sensitivities at a time of great fear and tension in the community. Such omission obviously had a powerful influence on this individual's turning away from his family faith, from the Gaelic culture which was part of his legacy and from choosing Catholic education for his children. In his last words on this topic he attempted to rationalise his agnosticism:

> I'm very critical of the Catholic Church on social issues. The emphasis is all on dogma and ritual. No God with compassion would allow all the evils we have in the world, the suffering we've experienced.

Another Catholic grammar school mentioned by name and also in Belfast generally received very positive comment in terms of ethos and curriculum. However, some of the pupils presented problems to one officer's son. It was the socially mixed catchment area from which the school drew its pupils that he disliked. In his mid-30s and already at middle rank, after early and remarkably high achievement in police examinations, this officer, who dropped out of university after a term, explained:

Some boys became terrorists or barmen. Those were the low achievers: some because they had a political agenda, not an academic one. Some were bullies and thugs ... Your upbringing is everything. Survival depended on your strength of character ... I went elsewhere to do A-levels, to Methody [Methodist College in the Queen's University area, attended by a sizeable proportion of Catholic pupils.]

He seemed to prefer a school attracting solidly middle-class pupils to one which, typical of Catholic schools, crossed the social class divide. How far this deserter's perceived need to leave his Catholic grammar school caused him to detach himself from his family Church as well is impossible to judge, but he, too, identified himself as agnostic.

A slightly younger, more junior officer, part flaunter, part chameleon, who attended the same east Belfast school as the one previously quoted spoke very positively about the school's ambience and made no complaints about fellow pupils. He proudly reported that:

Large numbers of former pupils joined the RUC. The year after me, seven joined. It was a school where political aspirations were deliberately played down. It probably had the effect of making me naive, yet more open-minded. It made me an Alliance voter. Alliance has no sectarian base ... The [Catholic] recruiting sergeant was excellent. It just showed that Catholic boys needed a role model.

It emerged that a very senior officer whom I interviewed later was the recruiting sergeant mentioned in the quotation above. He stressed the central importance, in his opinion – and demonstrated by his measurable success – of Catholic officers gaining access to potential Catholic recruits in order to achieve a more culturally representative police service.

A large majority, about 70 per cent, chose to comment on types of schools rather than on their personal experiences. Fewer than 10 per cent objected to church schools per se, but those who did, tended to do so in strong terms. An officer in his 50s, a deserter, born in the Republic of Ireland, describing himself as 'Christian' insisted:

No Church should have anything to do with education. For example, in Germany there aren't any Catholic schools ... Children on both sides carry their parents' prejudices. I hate this about Northern Irish society.

He seemed to imply that if there were Catholic schools in the province, any others would be Protestant, perhaps advocating state integrated schools as a solution. Though a regularly practising Catholic chameleon, a detective felt:

The Catholic Church has far too much influence on education. Religion and education should be separate. Integrated schools are the way forward ... The divide is perpetrated and perpetuated by both religions. When Catholic police officers are cut off from their school friends, it has significant repercussions at first.

This officer pointed out one of the difficulties which Catholics experienced when they joined the police. If they attended Catholic schools, they often found that their peers from school were hostile to their choice of career and they were less likely than non-Catholics to find friends applying to join at the same time. So they felt isolated and exposed. This isolation was likely to become for most a permanent situation, since they were obliged, for security reasons, to live in non-Catholic areas. My survey showed this situation to be true of nearly 60 per cent, with 15 per cent nil responses, even though more than 90 per cent of the general population live in areas which are homogeneous in ethno-religious composition (Ellison and Smyth, 2000: 160).

An officer with relatively short service, but lengthy work experience abroad outside policing attributed a political motive to Catholic education. He advised:

> Keep religion separate from education. Segregated education is a power thing. Muslim, Protestant and Catholic should be integrated in an ideal society. You keep up your faith through the church. Certainly, integrated education would help to bring people together here.

Rather than try to satisfy all religions within integrated educational provision, he seemed to advocate that the churches should be faith educators and that integrated schools should concentrate their curriculum on secular disciplines, on citizenship and social integration.

Whatever their thoughts on Catholic education, over 90 per cent of the interviewees endorsed integrated education as a strategy for making our society less divided, more cohesive. Even those who praised Catholic education for giving 'values for life' or who wanted choice for parents – 'Don't close all Catholic schools' – advocated integrated education on social and political grounds. An English-born chameleon explained: 'Integrated education can only assist Northern Ireland as a whole. This is not like England where people mix outside of school. If it was done by the Assembly, cross party, it would sell better'.

This officer obviously favoured a fundamental policy change by the Local Assembly recognising the segregated nature of social life. This change would imply the introduction of integrated education to replace voluntary and controlled schools, replacing the system which obtained whereby a sufficient number of parents had to apply for funding to start an integrated school in a specific area.

A need for integrated schools as an antidote to family bigotry was seen by a middle-ranking officer in a Unionist coastal town. He contended:

> Integrated education is essential if there is going to be any kind of reconciliation in this country. Wee Johnny from the Shankill, wee Seamus from the Falls both support Manchester United . . . Bigotry is taught at home. A counterbalance is needed in school. The two traditions are not from separate planets.

A plea was made here to follow children's natural inclination to socialise and integrate around a common interest, focusing on what united them rather than inserting an obstacle to bring division.

Although integrated education was widely endorsed in principle, 14 per cent had reservations about educational standards in some integrated schools. An officer, who had sent all four of his children to an integrated primary school regretted that 'The integrated college did not get good reports, so they went to Catholic secondary schools where standards were high'. Another, who felt that the aspiration was not matched by reality, generalised thus: 'Integrated schools are a great idea but they're not academically good enough'. Segregated housing, common in the province, provided a difficulty referred to by an officer stationed in east Belfast, 'School catchment areas in Northern Ireland tend to have a distinct cultural–religious profile. So children from the minority group will, inevitably, feel intimidated even in an integrated school'.

From the views they expressed to me I concluded that these Catholic officers had given some thought to possibilities for change in Northern Ireland and strategies which might bring more fluidity in relationships between the two major communities. I was surprised by the central role which they accorded education as an agent of social and possibly political change. If one accepts that family, Church and school are the three most important elements in Catholic formation, then it must be noted that this generation of Catholics officers have departed radically from the practice of their parents in significant ways. As indicated earlier, fewer than one-third of their children attended Catholic secondary schools, in contrast to themselves where the fraction was just over three-quarters. This figure, added to the figure of half with non-Catholic spouses, in a sample where 84 per cent were male, hinted strongly that the influence of Catholic mothers and of Catholic schooling had waned in relation to the current generation of Catholic children whose parents are Catholics.

This sample of Catholic officers seemed to agree on two points:

1. education could be instrumental in bringing about an increased measure of social integration in Northern Ireland;
2. Catholic children could be taught to develop an understanding of what the police do for the common good if Catholic officers were given access to Catholic schools. The children could recognise them as role models, contributing to the development of policing as partnership with the community – a step in the direction of policing by consent.

The prescription for social progress, using education, as spelled out by these officers, seemed to advocate a weakening of Catholic identity as the price to be paid. Their relatively weak levels of religious observance and general lack of interest and confidence in politics and politicians suggested they were atypical of the cultural community from which they came. By their comments on education they seemed to advocate a further weakening of the cultural cluster – religion, politics and schooling – which give Catholics their distinct identity. One wondered if a majority of them were, in effect, recommending that the Catholic community became, as a majority of these officers had become, chameleons, to make their contribution to social and political change. They emerged as having very weak Catholic identity measured by conventional criteria, not representative of the general Catholic community, and yet they were cultural Catholics. They differed from retired officers who were very strong in practising their religion, on marrying and remaining with Catholic partners and on sending their children to Catholic schools. However, within the predominantly Protestant RUC they were perceived to represent the Catholic, even sometimes Republican, community. To their working lives in that context I turn next.

2   Working lives as Catholic police

Part 2 deals with how these officers coped, carrying out their duties in a predominantly Protestant workplace, since the outbreak of community violence. To their non-Catholic colleagues they represented the Catholic community which included members of the IRA. On the other hand, they represented the 'enemy' to many Catholics, particularly because the RUC earned a reputation for partisan policing by repressing the freedom of Catholics, for example, in order to allow Loyalist marches through Nationalist areas. Part 2 will refer to (a) the culture of the RUC and friction in day-to-day relationships while on duty with non-Catholic colleagues; and (b) the Catholic officers' relationship with the Catholic Church and with the Catholic community during a period when atrocities were carried out daily by the IRA.

Sectarianism in training

I asked the interviewees: 'Did you, during your training in the RUC, feel that being a Catholic made life more difficult for you than for others?

Their period in training was for Catholic officers generally a baptism of fire. I found that their responses to the sectarianism they found there largely determined their strategy for coping – as flaunter, chameleon, deserter or victim – in their careers afterwards. For officers with twenty or more years' service, if their period in the depot had not been particularly memorable because of excessive sectarianism demonstrated by the staff or by fellow trainees, they tended to make general statements and to move on to the post-training era if they were chameleons or deserters. Remarks such as 'Yes, there was anti-Catholic hostility, but I just got on with it. I knew I wouldn't be with the guys for long' or 'I know some Catholics had a hard time, but I managed OK' reflected the passive attitude of approximately 40 per cent, explained, perhaps, by the passage of time and a desire to think positively about reforms.

For some Catholic officers who, coming from Nationalist backgrounds, had to offend family and friends by joining the RUC, as well as for those from predominantly Protestant or mixed towns, their training period in the depot brought unpleasant experiences. More than 20 per cent overall had negative experiences of surprise and disappointment. They were drawn very largely from the predominantly

Nationalist areas, though one in four was from a Unionist area. An officer with more than ten years' experience, encouraged to join the RUC regular force both by his mother and his part-time reserve colleagues for security and comradeship, and who had 'received a hard time' from police in his Catholic neighbourhood explained. He recalled an experience from the first few days of his training:

> I was in the Garnerville complex, in the TV room. There was 106 in the squad. The whole place erupted when an IRA atrocity was shown on the News. 'Fenian bastards!' the shout went up. I thought, 'God, should I be here? . . . I had to be very wary about religion, about saying 'aitch' and 'haitch' [referring to the different ways in which Catholics and Protestants are alleged to pronounce the letter 'h'].

He felt that people associated him with the perpetrators because the squad identified all Catholics with the IRA by using the pejorative term 'Fenian'. Doubting the wisdom of being there, perhaps only momentarily, he resolved not to reveal his cultural identity in order to protect himself from verbal abuse from then on.

A senior officer referred to earlier, for whom the RUC was his third choice of police force but whose career progression was very successful, conveyed his initial impressions and described his experiences of harassment in training as well as his response:

> I got culture shock when I joined the RUC. My first impression was of the military environment, the short haircut, polishing our boots to a mirror-like finish, the picture of the Queen, the Union flag. I thought 'I don't belong here' . . . The least subtle incidents happened in my days at the training centre. I shared a twin dormitory with an extreme Protestant who went on and on about my cultural background. Finally, I put him against a wall and told him what I would do to him if he didn't stop. He desisted . . . Training probably ameliorated extreme views or they were less likely to express their views openly. This one was overt. Other things happened such as not being included in the group on a night out, things said behind your back. My roommate told Protestants 'Don't touch that fellow [his surname]. He's a Fenian'. Catholics identified one another to one another.

Although this officer had already recalled his unease while travelling to the depot, the reasons for his concern were clearly well founded. This passage identified a number of significant problems including his lack of familiarity with Unionist culture, Loyalist and military. His feeling of alienation was aggravated by the sectarian behaviour of his intolerant Protestant roommate, who spread information about this Catholic officer's cultural identity in order to strengthen opposition. It would seem that he was not alone in experiencing this type of hostility, since he reported fellow Catholics as trying to establish solidarity with one another, because the term 'Fenian' denoted that they were perceived to be both Catholic and Republican. He may have decided that in order to survive he had to become a chameleon – even in his private life. He had divorced from a 'born-again' Christian and his children had not been confirmed, even though he had given an undertaking at the time of his marriage to his Catholic clergy that any children would be brought up Catholic. He appeared to regret that in his laxity he had let his children down and could henceforth do little to make amends.

While the difficulties he described came from the cop culture, in his opinion it reflected, though in an extreme form, the official culture in the early 1980s, which he described as 'Unionist and Protestant. They were worried about Nationalist spies. It wasn't pervasive, but not unusual'. This officer learned from a very early stage that he would tread a challenging path in trying to manage his cultural Catholicism as an RUC officer. Wherever possible, he modified discomfort and was quick to add that after twenty years change had arrived, 'We took the oath of allegiance together in a group. I mumbled a distorted version . . . But the PSNI is an organisation on the move'. His career since training has shown that he was comfortable and effective with a chameleon image. A constable with similar length of service stated:

> In my first week I was asked 'Why did you not join the Garda [Síochána]?' I replied 'I can't speak Irish. Why did *you* not join the Met?' . . . The complaints mechanism was harped on in the depot. It was a logical approach.

Four other officers commented on being made aware of the complaints system on their first day in the depot. This might be read to mean that at the top of the RUC this Hunt recommendation was official policy, but there was an unspoken assumption that it might need to be invoked by Catholic officers who would be the subject of sectarian treatment. A female officer, with very short experience in the RUC before the PSNI was established, demonstrated in her testimony that, after almost twenty years, a similar question implying assumed loyalty by Catholics to the Republic was still current: 'Why didn't you join the bloody Guards [Garda Síochána] then? . . . I got a hard time at Garnerville. There was bullying, but the trainers noticed . . . I was naive, perhaps'. This officer, who had joined in order to change the organisation from within rather than criticise from outside, flaunted her cultural background, as opposed to concealing it as others did in order to make the road easier for themselves.

The complaints system could be seen as that part of official policy and practice which would protect Catholic officers, as well as others, from sectarianism and bullying. However, verbal insults appeared to be the most frequently mentioned abuse. Three officers commented on official policy as being facilitative of attendance at Mass, while recruits were in training as well as during their service years, when one hour away from duty was allowed for worship. The longest serving of the three officers, with close on thirty years' service, explained that, while in training, 'On church holidays of obligation [feast days, not Sundays] I went to evening Mass. I was told "Go, and I hope your God helps you to pass your exams." There was no malice, just encouragement'. One who was already a deserter found that his preference not to attend Mass on Sunday worked against him at interview. Also a long-serving member, he recorded his experience of unexpected intolerance of his apathy towards religious observance:

> I was asked at the Interview Board about going to church on Sunday. [His name and place of origin would have made his cultural Catholicism obvious.] I said I didn't go. I was turned down and spent three years in the reserve, because the president of the board was a fundamentalist type.

Of British Army stock and from the Republic of Ireland, this officer throughout his interview with me showed that after almost one-quarter century of service he could not empathise with Northern Irish social divisions and religious and political intransigence. If he had been a local recruit, it is likely that he would not have given a truthful answer in the instance cited. Conformity to prescribed orthodoxy was the official policy, though its translation into the unofficial culture was, it seemed, less than effective.

The common response for recruits from Nationalist areas was to deal in a robust fashion with sectarianism. However, there was one who could only be classified as a victim, because he did not seem to have had any personal resources on which to draw in tackling sectarian treatment. A male officer brought up in a Nationalist town, indifferent to party politics and after nearly twenty years in the RUC very disillusioned, spoke of sectarianism during his training period:

> It was sectarian. I was called a Taig [pejorative term for Catholic]. I had my rosary beads smashed. I was laughed at for blessing myself passing a Catholic church. In the depot the boys wore Rangers and Linfield tops for PE [football teams noted for their sectarian following.] I got the label of being a paranoid Catholic. It went round like bush telegraph. There was no point in reporting this sort of behaviour.

This officer's inability to cope and his unfortunate revelation of his vulnerability were obviously exploited by sectarian colleagues who held him up to ridicule and in the process insulted mainly his religion, which was an important part of his culture. His last sentence implied that reporting this objectionable behaviour would not, in his opinion, bring a satisfactory outcome; perhaps he felt that the situation would be exacerbated.

Three officers from Unionist towns reported that they too had been surprised and disappointed by the sectarianism which they found during training. From towns such as Larne, Carrickfergus or Bangor, they had managed their minority identity successfully, attending Catholic schools but having friends from both main traditions who were cross-community minded, as they were. One explained, typically:

> My mates and I got on famously going to soccer matches, looking for the biggest bonfires on the Eleventh Night [eve of Orangeman's Day], getting on together in the Scouts. It was a shock when I went to the training centre and, before they sussed me out to see what I was really like, I had a religious and political label stuck on me.

The behaviour of the Protestant recruits towards him was, regrettably, typical of the often unfounded assumptions which some Northern Irish people tend to make about others of whom they know nothing, but whose names frequently indicate cultural background.

For some, the problems did not stop with training. Four officers reported that problems which arose during training were not resolved when they were posted to stations. One senior officer with almost thirty-five years' service asked himself at the beginning of his training: 'How long will they stand me? . . . I had a difficult two or three years, then a sense of vocation developed'. A sense of vocation seemed to prove the salvation for those whose earliest days in policing were unpleasant. The female officer quoted earlier who flaunted, perhaps unwittingly, her Republican background and had her name in Irish on her credit cards and chequebook reported:

> In my first posting I was told 'Your reputation preceded you . . . When there was an all-Ireland final I had a county flag on my car. I got a call from my inspector telling me to take it down. I suppose it was all about a neutral environment. I wonder, though, if it had been a Manchester United flag . . . But I have no regrets. I found my vocation.

She had already shown herself to be a flaunter and continued to parade her Republican background by identifying with Gaelic football and celebrating her county's success in reaching the final stage of an all-Ireland wide competition.

However diverse the individual experiences and perceptions of this sample of Catholic officers, it would seem that the unofficial culture in the training centre reflected Protestant hostility towards Catholics in wider Northern Irish society. It must come as no surprise that there was strong evidence of continuity of culture as those men and women lived out their careers as serving officers.

It might be argued that their experiences of sectarianism at the training centre were likely to influence strongly the persona which they strove to put on when they were sent to their stations and to live in the community as career police officers. Whether shocked by what they found in training because it contrasted with their lives in Unionist towns before they joined, or because they expected not to find evidence of strong sectarianism there, the chameleon or deserter images might understandably have attracted them. A strong self-preservation instinct would counsel against presenting a flaunter image which would make them targets for sectarian abuse. One assumes that a victim is unable to unwilling (or both) to counter such hostility. It seems inevitable that the net result for a majority of Catholic police officers was deliberately to denude their cultural identity.

Sectarianism at work

Two out of every three Catholic officers who completed the survey, which preceded interviews by several months, disagreed with the suggestion that the RUC was sectarian. Yet every one of the fifty in the subset of interviewees made some negative comment, either explicitly or implicitly, on this topic – almost always matched by a rationalisation which excused sectarian behaviour. Only five officers considered themselves victims with no effective redress. Almost 90 per cent identified banter as being the vehicle for sectarian comment. Rather than condemn sectarianism as being unacceptable, these Catholic officers recounted occasions when they were the recipients but offered a variety of excuses as selected extracts below show.

Ten per cent referred to MSU [Mobile Support Unit] vehicles as being the most likely location for verbal abuse on religious grounds, since the ratio of Catholic: non-Catholic was very frequently 1:14. (Full capacity was for fourteen passengers and a driver.) However, one from this group explained:

> The general attitude to Catholics in the MSU was sectarian in [names of two Unionist towns]. I had sectarian experiences, without doubt. They tried to wind me up personally. I suppose they had very good reasons. Attempts had been made on their lives by Republicans.

This officer's irrational justification would appear to have been based on the perception that Republicans were drawn from the cultural Catholic community, therefore it was reasonable for his non-Catholic colleagues to see him as being one of the lumpen Catholic community. His acceptance of such behaviour from a supposedly neutral, professional, impartial force in the 1980s seemed defeatist, or self-deluding. Another officer, with one promotion to his credit, also blamed IRA atrocities and the stress levels experienced by police officers:

> Religious differences are treated in a humorous way. There's no real bite or bitterness. It's often triggered by bereavement, when a relative is killed by the IRA. An apology would follow. Nobody's a personal target ... Remember, we're the most highly stressed group in our society, according to psychologists. Not like Army personnel. They have less continuous pressure, only three months at a time. For police it's thirty years.

Approximately 20 per cent of respondents acknowledged that they had experienced sectarianism from a small minority of colleagues, but they did not have to deal with it personally. Instead, their Protestant colleagues who, it was said, overwhelmingly disapproved, dealt with such deviant behaviour. One example was an officer, a chameleon, with long experience and at middle rank who gave an informative longitudinal summary of his experiences of sectarianism, indicating reform in the application of police policy between the 1970s and the 1990s. Citing the earlier incident, he explained:

> When I was stationed at [name of politically mixed town] the sergeant, who was a Protestant from the Republic, made my life an absolute hell. Dirty duty, snide remarks. Others were embarrassed, but I got no support from them ... Now that sergeant would be dismissed immediately.

A second incident in his life brought a very different response from colleagues:

> I was the driver. We were on duty, passing the Mater Hospital [originally a Catholic-managed hospital, now in the National Health Service] and I was the only Catholic in

the group. A colleague said 'That's where the wee Fenian bastards are born'. I stopped the van and laid into him. The whole unit supported me. They pulled me off him in case I did him serious injury. But they told him that if he reported the incident, they would testify he attacked me first . . . He didn't report it.

Clearly, he alluded to a change over time in the official attitude towards unacceptable sectarian behaviour. In his earlier days, he and his unsupportive but allegedly sympathetic non-Catholic colleagues had no effective redress, but the newer official culture, he claimed, would result in serious disciplinary action today. The second incident cited showed that individual bigots could still cause mischief twenty years later. By this stage, however, in the RUC's history, silent sympathy had been replaced by active, physical support, albeit with a collective promise to deal with the culprit using deviant methods.

Another officer of similar middle rank, a deserter, a university drop-out, but much younger than that quoted immediately above, told a story which showed his superior to have invoked the official disciplinary route and his colleagues to have distanced themselves from the wrongdoer, though this time not engaging in deviant behaviour. He described an incident when, as a very young sergeant attempting to brief his team in a less boring, less conventional way than his colleagues, he was interrupted by a fellow sergeant who burst into the room shouting 'You're nothing but a "popehead"'. In response he said: 'The offender was vilified by the rest of the unit. I made a notebook entry, but I didn't take it further, though my superior officer invited me to do so'.

In spite of the incident described above, this officer who was enjoying rapid career progression insisted 'I've not suffered for being a Catholic. The political label is where the problem arises in relation to Protestant colleagues'. He refined his description of sectarianism as being 'light' or 'heavy'. 'Light' sectarianism he exemplified as simply an attempt to confirm tribal membership, such as when he was asked 'Are you a Fenian, then?'. He added 'The guy laughed. He probably didn't have a bad bone in his body'. 'Heavy' sectarianism he explained as that felt by 'others [who] have deeper feelings but don't say anything. The people who keep things to themselves'. He seemed not to object to non-Catholic officers who, typical of Northern Irish people generally, try to find out the community background of a new colleague or acquaintance in order to put on a convenient label of identity conferred by a cluster of crude, unfounded assumptions. As a deserter, he felt prompted to play down the breadth and depth of sectarianism he witnessed, so that he could take comfort in the solidarity of the police community.

Even a graduate Catholic officer with less than ten years' service, born and brought up outside Northern Ireland, spoke as if he expected sectarian insults and did not take exception, since they came from misguided individuals. His story sounded familiarly passive, though he expressed positive comment on the official culture:

I've not been badly treated by the organisation. Once a colleague said to me: 'All Fenians are bastards'. Others dealt with him. He apologised three weeks later . . . When I was 'acting up', one took umbrage and told me that I was looking after my own [fellow Catholic officers]. He was a divisive individual. Disowned by his colleagues. People offered statements. The peer group dealt with it and supported me.

Catholic officers by a very large majority appeared to cope easily with hostile behaviour from non-Catholic colleagues on the many occasions when it was witnessed by a group who hastened to isolate the deviant and try to make amends to the offended party. One wondered if sometimes a misinterpretation was made of the significance of this apparent unity of action by the majority group. The members of that group might genuinely have felt that they did not want to be identified with such deviant behaviour since it was contrary to the official rules, or contrary to their personal code of decency. It is conceivable, though, that some may have felt obliged to object precisely because they shared the deviant's sectarian view, but felt they had been betrayed by hearing it said aloud. Anyhow, if a complaint had been lodged they would have been obliged to give witness statements.

About one-third of interviewees in the serving-officers category explained sectarianism away as a form of banter, while almost as many blamed the victim's personality as making him or her to be a deserving target. One explained:

The banter is not serious but we have a weird sense of humour. When we went out to an attempted suicide and found a man disembowelling himself, the word went round that there would be a barbeque later . . . You'd hear as many Paisley jokes as Pope jokes. You give as good as you get. It's all 'even Stephen'.

Three officers referred to large companies they had worked in before joining the RUC and explained that banter was normal in them. One junior-rank officer aged over 40 put his view thus:

In everyday working with colleagues, there's no derogatory remarks. Banter is normal in any big organisation. It was, in [name of company]. The banter is about sport and religion. It's all good natured . . . It's not PC any more . . .

This officer regretted, as did more than two-thirds of those who mentioned banter, the recent insistence on political correctness from the top of the RUC, later the PSNI. Strict observance of this rule was tending to spoil their fun. Four admitted that it still continued, though officers were more circumspect as to who heard – generally trusted peers in small numbers. A former merchant seaman stated 'Our differences, our idiosyncrasies, are picked on. It's the same if you have a long nose or big feet. There's no malicious intent'. A female officer, another drop-out from university, was one of the 10 per cent who reported no negative experiences on grounds of religious identity. She felt that if it happened, it was the officer's own fault, because he or she invited it. She was a deserter who offered no solace to colleagues who were victims, as her words showed:

I have never seen a Catholic officer being harassed, even in [a Nationalist city]. Maybe, back in the 1970s, but not in my time [the 1990s]. If you have 'I'm a Catholic officer' written across your forehead and you're prickly to boot, well . . . It's your personality. You invite it, if it happens. It's the same if you're fat, black, Catholic, have a big nose.

Having heard these various excuses, one was left wondering why sectarianism used against them was not condemned by these 90 per cent of Catholic officers who admitted it happened. Would such an admission prevent them from dealing with it intellectually? Was an officer more comfortable if such negative behaviour – which attacked one's identity – could be downgraded from being morally unacceptable, to being on the same level as a remark which made fun of a distinguishing aspect of personal appearance?

Instead of taking exception, these officers offered three reasons:

1. It was prompted by external circumstances outside the control of the offender who was giving vent to emotion while under great pressure – but Catholic officers were unprotected from threats to their lives or from bereavements caused by IRA or Loyalist atrocities as were non-Catholic colleagues.
2. Sectarian banter was a normal part of everyday life at work, a form of easing for people doing a stressful job. Normal people, they argued, were not hurt by it, because a strange sense of humour, sometimes black, was shared by those engaging in it.
3. Hyper-sensitive Catholic officers were very unfortunate in that their personalities and inability to cope drew justifiable attention to this weakness and they responded as victims.

I have considered day-to-day interaction by Catholic officers with non-Catholic colleagues from across functions. Next I shall examine relations with specific groups of colleagues.

Special Branch

Allegations of ill-treatment, torture and collusion with Protestant para-militaries formed a central plank in the IRA's unrelenting campaign to demonise the RUC in the eyes of the Catholic community over a thirty-year period. It was unsurprising, therefore, that nearly 40 per cent of the interview sample made reference to Special Branch as being perceived negatively by Catholics in the community. Comment in favour, some with caveats, outweighed criticism by almost 2:1. Those who had not worked in Special Branch were numerically much stronger than those who had, by a ratio of 3:2. One former Special Branch officer dismissed criticism thus: 'There were rumour mongers in the community. In my experience there was no bad treatment in cells'. This statement must be questioned and read as a wish rather than a description of what happened. A female colleague at mid-rank and about ten years younger than the officer just quoted had strong negative views:

I was a sergeant in SB. Collusion was quite possible. One Catholic in SB had to be taken off the street because he harassed Catholics. They would sacrifice their colleague for the sake of an old tout . . . Overall the situation has improved because the whole security thing is more relaxed.

Reference to collusion between Special Branch and Protestant paramilitaries was made by four officers (8 per cent). While two admitted that it possibly took place, two colleagues seemed more confident that it did. One junior-rank officer approaching retirement, partly flaunter, partly victim declared:

Definitely there was collusion. There are those who have blood on their hands. SB are like the Masons. They're a secret organisation. Evidence was withheld from the Stevens Enquiry team. It was burnt, disappeared.

This officer acknowledged a need for Special Branch, known by that or another name, 'Intelligence still needs to be gathered. Sinn Féin are still at it'. Another junior officer, serving in a hard-line Unionist area, made specific reference to the murder of a Catholic solicitor by Loyalist paramilitaries. There was widespread belief among Catholic public opinion that Special Branch had colluded in the crime. Unsure of the truth in this instance, the interviewee made an assertive generalisation:

In the case of Finucane [a Catholic solicitor assassinated in his own home], it was possible that there was collusion. But there wasn't as much as suggested. If you were a hard-line Unionist [member of Special Branch] you might tell a Loyalist paramilitary: 'x is heavy into Republicanism. I thought you might like to know'.

Possibly by blaming Special Branch for deviant behaviour, some officers protected themselves from confronting the RUC's unpopularity. Some, however, were willing to engage with what they perceived to be a moral dilemma. An ex-soldier, born in England, gave his opinion very succinctly, 'There was mischief on both sides, some state sponsored'. One chameleon, born in a 'garrison' town and who had left the RUC to join an English police force, returning after four years, articulated at some length the moral issues surrounding intelligence-gathering and the dilemma which Special Branch officers faced. Not forgetting the important role which this specialist unit played in protecting the lives of police officers against threats from the IRA, this seasoned officer explained:

SB were vital colleagues. They saved lives. On many occasions they took measures. Otherwise we'd have been in great danger . . . There were very big moral decisions to be made in the big picture. You have to deal with very deceitful, terrorism-related people. To gain their trust you have to immerse yourself in their world. How far do you go? When do you stop? If information was revealed, someone was killed. More judgements had to be made about informants . . . Whose lives are more valuable? . . . The vast majority tried their best.

Among the Catholic community the activities of Special Branch, especially their treatment of detainees and allegations of collusion made by outside police forces (for example Stalker, 1988), presented one of the greatest obstacles towards acceptance of the RUC. On balance the Catholic officers, though they resented Special Branch being a secretive 'force within a force', empathised with their colleagues carrying out a distasteful job. On the whole, it was felt that most Special Branch officers tried to do their job honourably, though a small errant minority 'were a law unto themselves' who provided the IRA with fodder for their relentless campaign to discredit the entire RUC. Comment from an informed outsider reinforces the view of a majority of Catholic officers on Special Branch. SDLP politician Dr Joe Hendron, with direct knowledge of prisoners' ill-treatment, expressed his view thus: 'The majority of the police were doing a good job under difficult and dangerous circumstances. What was going on in Castlereagh [an RUC holding centre] was actually undermining them' (Ryder, 2000: 190). The publicity and reputation which resulted from IRA diligence in this regard affected the image of all RUC officers, whatever their function. The consensus seemed to be from those who chose to comment on Special Branch that characteristic solidarity within police forces won, over Catholic police identifying with the Catholic community in being outraged by evidence and negative rumours about some Special Branch members.

Masonic and Orange Order influence

From discussing Special Branch colleagues and their negative public reputation, I now turn to the influence of Loyal orders within the RUC culture and the adverse effects which it had on the working life of Catholic officers. Both the Masonic and Orange Orders were mentioned as being divisive influences within the RUC since 1970 by currently serving Catholic officers, providing continuity with RIC tolerance of membership of Free Masonry, though not of a political party (Fennell, 2003: 69). Retired officers had raised similar objections, but the percentages in the retired category were significantly higher than in the currently serving category. The figure of 80 per cent of retired compared with 40 per cent of serving who criticised the Masonic Order's continued infiltration of the RUC membership was matched by a similar reduction in the case of the Orange Order.

The story told by a junior-ranking officer with almost twenty years of service exemplified continuity of experience between his father's generation and his in the adverse effect which the Masonic Order visited upon their career progression. He spoke with audible bitterness of his father's treatment:

> My father was a Catholic sergeant in the RUC. He was transferred to a small town in [name of county]. He was told that he was not acceptable as the station sergeant, but he would be OK in a larger town nearby. They moved him. He was left in no doubt that local Masonic influence had been exercised against him . . . There have been occasions when I, too, have been a victim [of the Masons] within the police service. Cloak-and-dagger stuff. Certain moves have been blocked. These sorts of organisations within the higher ranks look after themselves, like getting out to quieter country locations,

vacancies not advertised. To get out of the cauldron that was [name of strong DUP town] would have been my wish, but it didn't happen for a long time.

This grandson, son and nephew of Catholic police officers in Northern Ireland was very clear in his comment on the requirement by the PSNI that officers who are members of Loyal orders should be obliged to register their membership:

> Registering membership will not do any good. You cannot be an unbiased member of the PSNI if you are a member of one of these. Police officers should not be allowed to belong. Too many conflicts of loyalty crop up. Just look at Drumcree.

The confrontation between Orangemen and the RUC at Drumcree in 1996 was viewed by commentators as a crucial event which broke the tradition of unqualified support for the RUC from the Protestant population. A ruling was made by the Parades Commission that an Orange procession should not be allowed to pass through a predominantly Nationalist area and a lengthy stand-off ensued between the security forces and the Orangemen whose numbers were hugely enhanced by brethren bussed from all over the province. Reference was made to this watershed event by almost one-third of the Catholic serving officers. It was an event to whose significance I shall return later.

Only four serving Catholic officers declared that they had been invited to join the Masonic Order and only one admitted to having accepted. There was one, seemingly not invited, who was able to offer a family member's inside knowledge of potential benefit accruing to being a Mason. The product of a cross-community marriage, whose father was an Orangeman, a junior officer volunteered advice given to him by his Orangeman/Mason uncle, 'Favours are given to those at Masonic meetings. It would help you to get promotion'.

One of the officers who declined to join described the Masonic Order as 'a secretive organisation whose members look after each other in the PSNI'. His reason, though briefly explained, suggested that there was continuity of influence from the days of the RUC into the supposedly reformed PSNI, transmitted by some personnel who transferred directly. Another declined for a very different reason, 'They're a fab organisation for their charity work, but I just don't have the time to devote to it'.

A victim, the disaffected daughter of a Catholic officer, who had about ten years' service, described the Loyal orders as 'forces within a force'. She, together with four other officers, expressed resentment at the cross-rank solidarity which Masonic membership created, revealing a division within the Protestant membership of the PSNI in their attitude to the Masons. She referred to having observed: 'I saw members of the reserve mixing with superintendents, on first-name terms. There was a "club" which included DUP politicians and solicitors . . . Protestant officers hate the Masons'.

Her remarks queried any claim that the RUC as an organisation might make to neutrality and professionalism. Her final remark I understood to mean that the camaraderie which membership of the Masonic Order seemed to create for some was atypical of a rank-conscious militaristic organisation and was resented by a majority of Protestant officers who were, with a vast majority of Catholics, outside this mutually supportive group.

Mention has already been made of the Drumcree stand-off between the RUC and thousands of defiant Orangemen in 1996. The 34 per cent of Catholic officers who commented on this test of loyalty presented to RUC personnel found that their Protestant colleagues were divided in their response. Six Catholic officers provided evidence that Protestant colleagues supported the Orangemen, either in principle by their comments such as 'They have a civil right to march where they like', or by their partisan behaviour at the site of the encounter explained – at least in part, according to commentators – by the presence among the mob of RUC officers' close relatives. A female Catholic officer spoke of 'staunch Orange Order members who went on sick leave to attend Drumcree. Some used violence against fellow officers'. Nine, in contrast, commented on 'Protestant colleagues [who] went out there and did their duty impartially, as we're all expected to do'.

The Drumcree experience provoked a clear division within Protestant officer numbers and tested their loyalty, which was either to the cultural community from which they sprang, or to the force of which they were members. It showed up those who identified with traditional division and the dual model of policing – liberal for Protestants and colonial for Catholics – or those who were part of a new, impartial, professional service envisaged by Hunt and chief constables in the quarter-century between 1970 and 1996.

Five Catholic officers (10 per cent) faced difficulties from some Protestant colleagues who annually displayed their partisanship with the Orange Order. One explained his dilemma thus:

> When I was on parade duty one 12th of July in [name of Unionist town], one of the Lambeg drummers was a colleague from my station. If he had become disorderly, what would I have been expected to do?

Even though a Protestant colleague on duty on the same occasion would have faced the same problem, a Catholic officer applying the law fairly might have been perceived to have done so on sectarian grounds. A female officer with less than ten years' service asked rhetorically 'How can you police an Orange Parade in unbiased fashion if you are a member of the Orange Order? A police officer should always remain remote and neutral'.

The time span covered by general comments as well as by reference to specific events such as Drumcree left one in no doubt that, in the closing years of the RUC, active membership of Loyalist organisations continued to have a fragmenting effect on the RUC as a body. One officer working in a liberal Unionist town voiced the sentiments of three Catholic officers who saw Drumcree as heralding positive change at least for some RUC Orangemen. He said:

Drumcree was a turning point for Protestant colleagues. They supported law and order. They were prepared to stand up against violent behaviour. They didn't go to any Orange Order meetings after that. Membership had changed, they said. Drumcree attracted the wrong sort of supporters. They were the 'rent-a-crowd' type.

The strength of the Loyal orders' influence within the later years of the RUC and the earliest years of the PSNI cannot be assessed solely from the relatively modest number of Catholic officers who chose to comment on either the Masonic or Orange Orders. Under the terms of the Police (NI) Act 2000, every police officer is obliged to notify the chief constable as to whether or not they belong to any organisation 'which may be regarded as affecting an officer's ability to discharge their duties effectively or impartially' (Police Service of Northern Ireland, 2006: 10). When the registration process was completed in March 2006, 8,240 officers out of a total of 8,956 (91.32 per cent) declared themselves not to be members of any Notifiable Organisation. Grand Lodge of Freemasons and the Orange Order were among the organisations (all Loyalist) which were specified. Over 5 per cent acknowledged being Masons and under 2 per cent being in the Orange Order. There were nil returns for equivalent organisations in the Catholic community – the AOH and the Knights of Columbanus. No Catholic officer appeared to risk damaging his neutral image by joining either group. It would appear, then, that numbers in anti-Catholic organisations are relatively small, though it is impossible to measure their ongoing influence. The Internal Investigation Branch and the Police Ombudsman are there to protect against partisan behaviour which might result from membership.

Army support

Apart from difficulties arising from the behaviour of non-Catholic RUC colleagues and the perceived influence of the Masonic and Orange Orders, working with security forces was also cited as being difficult by 32 per cent of Catholic serving officers. The Army was in charge of security only during the first seven years of the Troubles, after which a policy of Ulsterisation reversed their relative positions and the RUC came back into control. However, after thirty-five years of active military presence in the province, the PSNI still works in partnership, though the numbers and visibility of Army personnel have been reduced drastically since the Belfast Agreement in 1998.

The main criticisms made were that regiments from outside Northern Ireland were ill-trained for service here and insensitive to the local culture; members of the locally recruited UDR and their successors in the Royal Irish Regiment (RIR) were unprofessional and sectarian when working in Republican areas. One officer with lengthy service in border areas explained:

> On the border the Army were the problem – as well as the IRA. The searches in particular. They weren't diplomatic, acted like bulls in a china shop. They had no finesse, made no effort at public relations. They were insulting to people . . . They're from the

outside. They're trained for war. They're not suited to civilian-type jobs. Farmers in south Armagh would have spoken to police when they were out of the public eye. They wouldn't have spoken to the Army. The Garda [Síochána] would not speak if the Army were listening, even though we had plenty of cross-border cooperation on bombs, for example.

Soldiers' lack of suitable training and their insensitivity in dealing with the local community presented this interviewee with multiple difficulties in trying to gather intelligence and to enjoy a cooperative relationship with a neighbouring police force, whose support was invaluable in dealing with IRA atrocities and fleeing perpetrators. It is conceivable too that the storyteller sensed what he had in common with a vast majority of south Armagh farmers and the Garda – cultural Catholicism.

Another experienced officer, though not in border areas, reinforced the point about unsuitable training for work with the RUC, though he indicated that a need for improvement had been identified:

> Soldiers are not police officers. Armies fight. Their basic training before they came to Northern Ireland was not enough. Now they're trained in Kent or in Germany by the PSNI for two weeks. Legislation and other aspects of our culture are covered.

A full-time reservist pointed to the importance of Army behaviour in determining the quality of relationship between the police and the local community and how various regiments could tip the balance:

> By the mid-1990s there was good rapport between the police and the local community [in west Belfast]. The [name of Scottish regiment] who shared our police station were good lads. Then the Paras [Parachute Regiment] came. Goodwill was destroyed within 24 hours. There was all this bravado. They made a point of returning to barracks through Andytown [Andersonstown, a Republican stronghold]. It was a defiant, triumphalist gesture of self-indulgence.

While some Catholic officers, 8 per cent, reported positively on working with English and Scottish Army personnel, it was the UDR and the RIR who received consistent criticism. A twice-promoted young female graduate officer, a deserter, stated:

> I worked with the military police in [name of town]. The English Army were fine. The UDR from Fermanagh tried to make everything difficult for me because I'm a woman. The English Army worked hard. I was very uncomfortable with the UDR at road blocks. They were unprofessional and provocative towards the public.

This officer found that her gender tested the UDR's male chauvinism while, at the same time, she found they compared very unfavourably with English soldiers in the way they carried out their duties.

A relatively junior officer with long police experience modified his approval of Army personnel in general, particularly in border regions, by remarking that 'some individuals let themselves and their regiments down'. He was unequivocal in his criticism of the UDR:

> There was a UDR problem. They should have been disbanded earlier. The UDR was a very bigoted group and they were left unchallenged, though senior police officers were very uncomfortable about them. They were OK in Bangor, but not in west Belfast.

Speaking of the RIR in very recent years, a middle-aged officer with long work experience outside policing was very specific about the cause and location of sectarianism in that regiment:

> There's more bigotry from the RIR Reserve than from full-time soldiers. Some were in the UDA [a Loyalist paramilitary organisation] or other terrorist organisations before they joined. They were accepted for political reasons. The bigotry wasn't always direct, but it was there – 'How did Linfield do last night?' [Linfield is perceived to have an entirely Loyalist fan base].

The RIR Reserve were recruited in Northern Ireland only, so the obvious point made was that its members represented the worst elements of Protestant sectarianism, some even having perpetrated violence against the Catholic population.

A full-time RUC Catholic reservist who had served for several years in border stations found nothing praiseworthy about the RIR members that he encountered:

> I was concerned about the RIR. Their recruiting base was the less intelligent ex-UDR. The idea of a neutral working environment passed over their heads. They put up [Union] flags and pornographic material in bedrooms, even though there was a female cleaner.

The experiences which I have reported above and opinions expressed showed that these Catholic serving officers accepted that Army support for the RUC was necessary in order to contain the security situation in the province. Soldiers' suitability, however, was questionable. The adverse comments made on locally recruited Reserve personnel were consistent with the generally held views of the Catholic community over this period and before, while their predecessors, the 'B' Specials, patrolled particularly along the border with the Irish Republic. In Chapter 3 reference was made to supportive evidence provided by retired Catholic officers on harassment of the Catholic population by part-time soldiers. Negative reports were sufficiently plentiful to suggest that the more bigoted elements within the Army personnel, recruited locally, caused offence to Catholic police. Sectarian treatment of the Catholic public gave the security forces – including the RUC – a sectarian image, which made the job of Catholic police officers significantly more difficult and supplemented the difficulties which they experienced from some of their equally sectarian RUC colleagues.

The British government brought in the Army to help control the street violence which the RUC could not contain in 1969, particularly the threat posed by Loyalist violence to Catholic life and property. The mindset at Westminster was still neo-colonial, even the thinking behind the Hunt reforms. It is clear that the late twentieth-century equivalent of sending in gunboats to quell civil unrest brought problems for the RUC. The Army personnel were untrained to deal with the situation, making the years when the Army were in control extremely challenging for local police. In addition, Catholic RUC officers' negative experience and perceptions of the locally recruited UDR coincided with those of the Catholic community in general.

My evidence showed that Catholic police officers suffered more than their Protestant counterparts during the violent years of the Troubles. The effects of 'internal' factors, including Protestant Unionist ambience, sectarian or insensitive treatment by some colleagues of various ranks targeted at their cultural background and the influence of Loyal orders, were aggravated by the effects of 'external' factors. Although originating in the Catholic community, they were seen by many Catholics as 'traitors' who chose to join an organisation which colluded with other security forces in policing Catholics, but not Protestants, according to an oppressive neo-colonial model. Even relations with their church and co-religionists caused Catholic officers problems.

Relations with the Catholic Church and the Catholic community

The question posed was:

> As a Catholic police officer, what kind of relations did you have with the Catholic Church and community while the RUC was policing the 'Troubles'?

The fifty Catholic interviewees made comments on the Catholic Church which might be divided into two broad categories:

1. perceptions of the Catholic Church as an organisation; and
2. experiences of interfacing with individual Catholic clergy.

Virtually all of the police officers made adverse comment on the Catholic Church as a potentially influential organisation that failed to give a lead in denouncing terrorism and supporting the police in their work. This consensus view suggested that they all felt affiliated to a church which had 'let them down' in public. Their strong cultural Catholicism, demonstrated by their responses to the question above, contrasted with their relatively weak belief in God and church attendance as compared to Catholics in general. My survey showed 72 per cent of Catholic officers to be believers compared with 85 per cent of Catholics in general. Nearly six out of ten attended Mass no more than twice per year, including one-quarter who never attended. Comparable figures for the Catholic population in general were 18 per cent and 8 per cent respectively. A critical attitude towards the Catholic Church was shared across the typology spectrum, although one might have expected harsher criticism from deserters in justification of their departure from active membership within the Catholic community.

An experienced senior officer, generally balanced in his comments, was very forthcoming about what he expected:

> I would appreciate more support from the Catholic Church. As a moral body at times they took a political line rather than a moral one. They needed to say that for a society to run in an orderly manner, it needs a police force. Individual clergy came forward; the organisation did not. We need less of the politics and more of the leadership. I'm very happy about Father Faul [an outspoken commentator on police behaviour especially in Nationalist areas.] He was a gentleman to police. He was critical of anyone doing wrong. He was fair.

It was very common for these officers to comment favourably on individual priests, as the senior officer quoted above did, while they found the church hierarchy wanting in carrying out its perceived role in supporting the police. About one-quarter of the group, while criticising the Church for lack of leadership, modified the strength of their initial comments. They suggested that the church's image was compromised by its duty to give the last rites and Christian burials to all its members, including paramilitaries. Absence of visibility by clergy at times of crisis was a criticism levelled by two officers, though with qualification: 'Priests are nowhere to be seen when there's trouble such as rioting. They could have voiced greater condemnation – though they're in a very difficult position'.

Three officers considered the personality of individual leaders of the Catholic Church in Northern Ireland to be a significant factor directly related to the strength of influence which they wielded. They voiced their admiration for Cardinal William Conway who, they said, after the Hunt Report was published in 1970, encouraged Catholics to join the RUC. They judged that he was unrivalled by his comparatively supine successors. 'He was an influential figure, who felt a duty towards us', said one. He might have been sensitive to the hunger which Catholic police felt for support from their church, especially during a period when their greatest threat came from IRA members of their own cultural community.

Five officers clearly expected the Catholic Church to disassociate itself from the political aspect of traditional Northern Irish Catholicism and to say so unequivocally. Freshly aware of the George Cross award to the RUC, they spoke with some bitterness of the absence of visible recognition by their church for the sacrifices they had made in 'trying to hold the line between order and anarchy', when more than three hundred colleagues lost their lives and thousands were injured. They wanted their church to sympathise publicly and to pay tribute to their memory. One, born in England, summed up their displeasure, making a comparison between the response of the Catholic Church in England and by its equivalent in Northern Ireland:

> There's RUC medals all over Westminster Cathedral. Where are they in Northern Ireland? The Catholic Church is too black and white. It should try a few shades of grey. Why should Catholics who join the police and the Army be written off?

His words emphasised the additional burden shouldered by local Catholic police, as compared to their English counterparts for whom religious and political identities are discretely separate.

Just over one-half of the group commented on personal encounters with individual clergy and their attitudes, either in the course of their police work on in their private lives, particularly at times of rites of passage – births, marriages and deaths. One assertive female graduate, a deserter of just over 30 years old and already at middle rank, speaking of her service in a Catholic city, gave a typically balanced picture of priests' attitudes, portraying them as being helpful on some issues and unhelpful on others:

> Catholic clergy in [name of city] helped criminals get to the border. Yet, the same men were very helpful to the police in the case of sudden deaths. Their motto seemed to be: This is the House of God; we accept all people . . . They should have stayed out of it [the civil conflict] . . . Bloody Sunday – Why was Father Daly there? He knew that his flock were.

The reference here is to Father Edward Daly whose image is well known from film footage shot on Bloody Sunday. He can be seen waving a white handkerchief as dead and wounded civilians are carried out of the crowd. This officer seemed to want the opposite of the majority, in that she would have preferred priests to have detached themselves entirely from what was going on in society, rather than try to guide, if not lead.

Encounters with individual clergy suggested that priests were diverse and individualistic in their attitudes to police, making generalisation impossible. One officer, the son of an RUC father, who had not enjoyed his schooling at a Christian Brothers school, found that the priest who baptised his eldest child described the officer and his wife as 'Castle Catholics' (pro-British). Others found cooperation from Catholic clergy in unexpected places. In a small border village, for example, one officer found 'The Army was bombarded by shots from a [Catholic] school building. There was no animosity from the clergy when I went to investigate the matter'. In another Republican-dominated town, the parish priest was described by a regularly practising Catholic officer, constructively critical of the Catholic Church generally, as being 'wonderful. There was a 500-lb bomb planted in a van. Father [name of priest] warned me to stay away. He heard things on the grapevine'.

It was noticeable that the interviewees spoke most critically of the Catholic Church in centres of greatest civil conflict, such as certain parts of Belfast, Derry or in the border areas. The police were likely to confront most violence and hostility in these areas, so it might follow that they would have been grateful to have received more support from their church. Their comments on the actions of individual clergy tended – as did their thoughts on the church's disappointing display of leadership – to be balanced by being both critical and appreciative of the problems clergy faced. One explained:

I had difficulty with priests from Republican backgrounds. I acknowledge that they have a right to their political opinions, as we all have, but they should have been less willing to give Christian burials to murderers. It almost seemed like encouragement ... They were not all like that, by any means. I know they were between a rock and a hard place. But I did have a problem with the administration. It didn't affect my faith, though.

Earlier I stated that in Unionist or mixed towns, police were much more likely to get access to Catholic schools for community relations work than in areas where the IRA could instil fear into those who might be seen to support the police. Similar contrast could be drawn in the case of Catholic priests, as it was with Catholic school principals. One must draw the conclusion that priests' attitudes and behaviour were conditioned by at least two important factors – their political outlook, together with inclination to behave in a way which was acceptable to a majority of their flock. In towns such as Larne and Bangor priests' flexibility was surprising, as the story of one chameleon officer illustrated:

My brother was invited to join the Masons. He was starting a catering business in [name of Unionist town]. He always asked the priest for advice about big things in his life. I was amazed. Do you know what this priest said? 'You'll need all the help you can get when you're starting a business. Go ahead and accept that invitation. It won't bother me'.

The Catholic Church, as an organisation, appeared to Catholic police officers as unsupportive. Neutrality, or general statements about the need for an impartial police service in Northern Ireland, did not satisfy them. Individual priests were as individualistic as Catholic police officers, it would appear, but there was no evidence to suggest that if the political leaders of their flocks 'permitted' Catholics to join the PSNI, the priests would refrain from supporting applicants in trying to make the PSNI representative of the Catholic community.

Direct relations with the Catholic community might be considered of greater significance than with either the Catholic Church or individual clergy. The attitude of Catholics towards the RUC had been influenced largely by the way they were treated during the years after 1969. The RUC's inadequacy in dealing with civil unrest, and with Republican suspects, coloured the force's image strongly.

Response to my survey question which asked how fairly police officers in Northern Ireland treat civilians from the two main traditions showed a significant difference between the perceptions of the Catholic community and those of Catholic officers. Twice as many Catholic police said that both traditions were treated equally as did members of the Catholic public. This discrepancy in perception, together with the admission that at the time they joined over one-half faced opposition from family, peers and/or neighbours, suggested that hostility from the Catholic population might have been an ongoing source of discomfort for them.

Some of the interviewees seemed keen to counter the traditional Unionist explanation for low Catholic representation – ostracism by elements in their own community or fear of the IRA. Just under 40 per cent of the sample spoke positively about relations with the Catholic community, though with some modifications. Nearly 25 per cent had served for long periods in areas dominated by the IRA. Two areas, in particular, received surprisingly favourable mention. These were west Belfast and south Armagh. Of those who championed the people of west Belfast, under one-half had originated in that area. One reservist, a flaunter, born in a Unionist town and who had opted to serve long-term policing west Belfast youth, praised the local community in these terms:

> I work here because I love these people. They're incredibly resilient. The attitude of west Belfast is changing. Totally different from fifteen years ago. They're civil if approached properly. Older people, in particular, have a positive attitude. Teenagers are different. They need to be brought to another place.

He went on to explain how improvements could be effected. He blamed insensitivity on the part of his colleagues and inappropriate allocation of resources for aggravating poor relations with Falls Road youth. He recommended training in interpersonal skills for his colleagues and more Catholic officers on patrols. He considered insensitivity on the part of colleagues who 'got the PR wrong' to be a problem of crucial importance. In order to illustrate this point he recounted an occasion when a Protestant colleague reacted inappropriately and misrepresented the Falls community by putting in a false report. He explained:

> I was in an MSU patrol up the Falls Road with fourteen Protestant colleagues. A 7-year-old started to throw stones at the vehicle. This guy shouted: 'You Fenian bastard!' and drove towards him to frighten him. I asked this guy 'Why do you work in this station if you hate the people so much?' . . . He wrote a report saying that he had come under sustained attack. A 7-year-old against a 10 ton vehicle. The problem is sectarian background and lack of knowledge of human nature.

He recommended cooperation between properly trained police who wanted to serve in west Belfast or similar areas and Catholic school principals who, he felt, could influence change in pupils' attitudes, though the two constituencies would have to establish mutual respect.

Two other officers, without citing specific incidents in the same area, concurred in praising the Falls community as being 'decent, good people who need a decent, good police force'. Ten per cent of the total group, while trying to be positive, presented mixed pictures of west Belfast people, such as the story of one with considerable experience of beat and patrol work: 'The PSNI could make a difference if we could make people forget about the past. In west Belfast there's some who'll never respect me. Others do and more will, if they're treated properly'.

He expressed frustration, however, at how some members of his community there, who might not support the police, use them in order to get a double pay-out in one day of their DHSS benefits:

Twenty to thirty of them present themselves at police stations every day, claiming to have lost their payments or been robbed . . . The police have to record alleged assaults and they receive compensation.

In spite of understandable provocation from people of whom some were perceived to lie, this officer objected to the attitude of 'a small minority of police officers who are very sarcastic to the public in general. They have a gung-ho attitude'.

The most common type of response from Catholic police working in Republican areas, including west Belfast, was to find individual members of the community unpredictable. This explanation may have been a means of downplaying the hostility displayed by the community towards the police. A long-serving officer made this point in this way:

You're either met with total hatred or they invite you in for food . . . I was trying to help a badly injured pedestrian who'd been knocked down by a car. A friend of hers, a nurse, forbade me to touch her because I was police. She died . . . I got the same sort of treatment from paramedics. They wouldn't treat injured police. An ambulance driver would say 'Wait for the next one'.

He spoke, however, of positive change in attitude towards joining the police:

Some from Lenadoon go to the Met and some from west Belfast, from Ardoyne, are passionate to join the PSNI. There's more punishments beatings now than in 1990–95. It's a deterrent. But three lads I know joined lately. They wouldn't have joined ten years ago . . . Of course, the Catholics we get are the more liberal Catholics. We don't get recruits from a Sinn Féin background.

This officer viewed the general attitude of the community in west Belfast to be a barometer indicating likely level of support for police in the near future. The split in attitudes which he found seemed to suggest that without political change only 'a certain type of Catholic' would join, as in the past. A rather jaundiced view was expressed by a young officer, speaking for three others, who did not feel moved to try to improve relations with the community there, because 'Friends from west Belfast who joined were ostracised by friends. Why should we court these people to get their approval?'.

Officers who had served in south Armagh, another major Republican stronghold, spoke positively of support for the RUC from the Nationalist community. Only one had spent part of his childhood there; he was a police officer's son. His father had been a victim of Masonic influence in another station. Speaking of life in a border village, he said:

I attended primary school in [name of village]. The people were warm and friendly and very supportive towards the RUC. They helped where they could, often by passing on information, my father told me later. Yet the Official IRA was active at the time.

Another officer who had served in South Armagh concurred, 'Although they were often very scared, many gave intelligence information'. He advised that willingness should be nurtured in such areas in order to increase cooperation. He regretted that some of his colleagues focused on short-term personal rewards rather than on longer-term, widerspread cooperation, which would be a prerequisite to policing by consent. His solution was expressed as:

> Build up trust. That's the sort of policing I want to see. Rapport. Not being heavy-handed. Go with the flow. Some officers cannot talk to people. Getting notches on their belt is all they're concerned about.

A long-serving, avuncular officer had been stationed in a town very near to south Armagh in the 1970s. He joined in the chorus of praise for the Catholic community there who, under a heavy IRA yoke, 'passed on information about IRA plans that were overheard, or they reported on strange behaviour or movement of vehicles'. He quoted an example to illustrate that the community responded in accordance with the way they were treated by police:

> I had to arrest three brothers who had smashed a bar. They were very violent and tested my patience to the limit. They were brought to court and sent to prison. They thanked me for the respectful way I had treated them. They told me 'We need police like you in [name of town]. Others would have hit you with torches'.

About one-quarter of the fifty interviewees spoke with unrelieved negativity about the Catholic community, especially about absence or uncertainty of support from them – the prime criterion on which their judgement was based. An extreme view was expressed by a relatively young and rapidly progressing female who served in a Catholic city in the 1990s. She found hostility from the citizenry in general and coupled this experience with her strong view of the fickleness of support from both communities when she helped to police Drumcree in 1996:

> In [name of city] both communities hated the police. Throwing stones. Calling 'black bastards'. There was no cooperation from the community – not even from Protestants … The ambivalence of Protestants was shown clearly. Stoning police during Drumcree and offering them chips when they were attacked by Nationalists.

The fickle nature of support from the public was made with particular reference to the Catholic community by an officer who had very little experience at first-hand of policing flashpoint areas:

> People only want you for what you can do for them. The Catholic community could be very selective about when to support and when to withdraw consent on particular issues. Drumcree in 1996 was one of the key occasions.

Two officers had criticism for the Catholic middle class in particular who were more likely, as SDLP voters, to support policing in the community, as opposed to paramilitary policing. One dismissed them simply: 'We got no more support from the professional middle class than from the Republicans'. Another senior officer offered uncertain support as a reason for 50 per cent of Catholic officers having non-Catholic partners:

> When I was stationed in [name of a politically mixed town] I knocked around with Catholic girls from a middle-class background [similar to his own], but sustaining relationships can be very difficult, sometimes just impossible, because you can't be sure of [the political views of] their friends.

The constant fear which must have haunted Catholic police, even more than others, about their safety, though rarely mentioned at interview, was articulated by the officer quoted immediately above: 'The IRA would see a Catholic officer as a "better" target than a Protestant one'. This statement was borne out by IRA assassinations of Catholics, targeted precisely because they appeared by their choice of occupation to support the British administration. These perceived supporters included members of the legal profession and of the security services, who were more vulnerable if they lived in Catholic areas.

In towns where the IRA had a dominant controlling influence on the community there seemed to be additional attempts made to render the daily duties of police more arduous even than they might have been in mixed or Unionist areas. Four officers told graphic stories of calculated acts of humiliation to which they were subjected – beyond name calling and stone throwing. Two of these officers felt that they had been singled out because they were Catholics. One such story, from an officer who had a name which clearly revealed his cultural background, went as follows:

> I had buckets of urine thrown over me and many a time I was spat upon. The worst of all was an incident when a colleague was very badly injured in a bomb attack on the street. While I was attending to my dying mate – and he did die – Catholics from the pub across the street threw bricks at us . . .

He asked the same rhetorical question as three others did about Republicans: 'How can we give respect to these people?'.

Those officers who had personal, harrowing or bitter tales to tell about Republican hostility were more than matched numerically by colleagues who made positive comment on the Catholic Nationalist community and held out hope for improvement in support levels from that quarter. Unsurprisingly, they tended to be flaunters or chameleons. One such could look objectively at his role and at the attitude of some colleagues:

> I'm purely a civilian who's wearing a uniform. There's plenty of broad-minded people [Catholic police officers] who feel that they could make a change. Others feel hard done by. Some of us keep on trying for acceptance. I'm sure that can happen – but what about Sinn Féin?

In this short extract an important point is touched upon. Catholic police who in carrying out their daily duties try to win acceptance, consent and support from the Catholic community are hampered in their efforts by political stalemate in the Assembly. The officers can derive some hope, though, from the attitudes of Catholics in the 18–29 age group and those of 46 and above. In 2001 (NILT) more than one in three stated that they would encourage a close friend to join the police while only one-quarter would discourage a potential recruit. These figures may have reflected optimism associated with the Belfast Agreement expressed in plans for police reform. They suggested that the attitude of Catholics in the general recruitment age group and those of their parents gave cause for hope to Catholic officers striving to win support from their co-religionists.

The influence and acquired power of Republican activists and Sinn Féin politicians were commented on by about three-quarters of the sample, also on Sinn Féin's carefully orchestrated campaigns to control the minds of the Catholic population. The power of the Sinn Féin public-relations machine – and the comparative failure of the RUC's equivalent – came in for comment by about twenty officers. One officer with fewer than ten years' experience explained:

> All Catholics don't want to blow up police officers. But from pressure within their own community, people believed rumour-mongers, especially about what was supposed to go on in cells. Sinn Féin had a fabulous PR machine. We just didn't sell ourselves. The media feeds on bad comment … Policing in the community is the only way to counteract this. It has to start with the individual officer building up trust, for the community can differentiate between the individual and the organisation. But you've got to work at it and it's going to take time.

The consistent campaign conducted against the RUC by the IRA, coupled with powerful indoctrination of their members, was exemplified by a female officer, largely chameleon but with a flaunter element, who was approaching retirement on medical grounds. She gave a fascinating insight into how she negotiated her way through challenging situations involving IRA suspects in a number of functional areas, but especially when she served in the CID. Yet she could accord the organisation respect.

While at school in a Republican town she had joined other girls in writing on a pavement 'God save the Queen when I get my hands on her'. She added 'It was just fun, no malice intended'. When questioning girls and women from Cumann na mBan [the female branch of the IRA] she appeared to treat them with compassion, even though they despised her for the job she was doing. She told of how she assisted a teenager fill in a form lodging a complaint against her, in accordance with IRA rules which demanded that their members had to sustain an injury while in police custody. The girl had deliberately banged her head against the sharp corner of a metal cabinet so that she would have a bleeding wound.

This officer excused the suspect by seeing her as a victim, 'It was "hip" to be involved in the IRA at that stage'. Yet the provocation which the officer had to endure seemed unbearable. She continued:

A police father and daughter had been murdered by the IRA in [name of city]. The suspect tried repeatedly to goad me into hitting her. She kept on, giving me a graphic description of how the young woman slowly bled to death . . . It was so unbearable to listen to. It tried my patience to the limit.

The difficulties which the IRA presented to this female officer approaching 50 years old spread into her private life. When she was in a maternity hospital giving birth to her son she realised that she was sharing a floor with the local leader of Cumann na mBan. She arranged to have her child 'rescued' through a bathroom window by a police officer who took him to her home in an unmarked car – 'I was more fearful for my son than for myself'. The narrative continued:

When I met the woman out shopping later she said: 'How's the baby?' It was surreal. Different life experiences but with one in common. Neither of us wanted to be seen talking to the other. She paid me a compliment, though. 'At least you were a civilised bastard', she said. She was referring to the time when I had questioned her as a teen-ager. She'd shot a soldier. I'm glad I was able to interrogate her for murder but still relate to her as a human being. That's what we should all be able to do.

In spite of her experience of Republican atrocities and of dealing with those alleged to have carried them out, she understood their point of view, which she explained:

The British were on their territory. People like Dominic McGlinchy [a well-known Republican activist] had commitment. That must be understood. They gave their lives too. It was like the French Resistance against the Germans in World War II.

The officer I have just quoted at some length was the only one who tried ver-bally to empathise with the IRA cause. Her testimony, I believe, raises the ques-tion about whether the PSNI should take special steps to recruit from Republican communities while not accepting ex-activists, in order to make it representative of all shades of Catholic community opinion. In addition, this female officer's story prompts a thought about the effect which higher Catholic female representation might have on relations with the public and possible improvement of the police image in Republican communities. Would the 'softer' skills generally attributed to females allow them to engage with individuals, rather than with 'police property' or 'the enemy'? Would this approach help to re-establish trust with members of the Catholic community who have supported Republicanism in the past – as a step towards partnership and policing by consent?

Of pieces of research carried out prior to my interviews, the two most directly relevant were my own survey which preceded the collection of qualitative data being discussed; the other was a small internal survey carried out by Maguire (1994). A number of the topics from my survey were revisited in order to pursue some of the issues in greater depth and possible only by qualitative method. I have found no contradictions between the three sets of data. There were close matches in the profiles (and data) of my larger survey group (138) and of the self-selecting interviewees (50). I concluded that those who volunteered to be interviewed were keen to reinforce their views by further elucidation in order: (a) to protect the reputation of the RUC sullied by IRA propaganda and accusation of collusion with Loyalist paramilitaries; or (b) in order to reduce the weight of quantitative evidence which might portray an exaggerated picture of sectarianism within the RUC; or (c) to register clearly their strong disapproval of the scope of the Patten reforms in relation to the manner and the pace at which they had been implemented (very recent to the time of the survey, 2002–3). I believe the interviewees, in some cases at least, more likely from the higher ranks, were conscious of the bias which can accompany survey reports and wished to avoid this possibility by taking up an invitation to meet me and to 'put the record straight'.

Irrespective of the unequal individual cost to Catholic officers in pursuing careers in the RUC averaging seventeen years, they felt that there were corresponding rewards. 'Costs' which they identified were:

- hostility from family and peers when they joined;
- isolation from the Catholic community and, in some cases, from their families;
- living in predominantly Protestant 'safe' areas;
- sectarianism visited upon them by some colleagues;
- ongoing fear for their personal safety and that of their children;
- lack of recognition by the Catholic community for the sacrifices made and service given throughout a sustained period of civil unrest; and
- absence of public support from the Catholic Church.

The clearest message which came through from the interviews about 'rewards' was that these PSNI officers who had recently transferred from the RUC, valued solidarity with colleagues as their most important reward. This finding resonated with views of the retired group. The body language, the positive tone of voice and often the graphic choice of verbal language in which they conveyed their thoughts suggested strongly that an intense feeling of solidarity was the greatest cause of joy in their professional lives. As already explained, a vast majority who acknowledged that, in the unofficial culture, sectarianism was rife, were willing to excuse it in return for acceptance as full members of the police 'family'.

One full-time reservist with seventeen years' service summed up his thoughts thus: 'Once you join the police you become a member of the "family". You share a lot of your life with colleagues'. A detective with more than twenty-five years' service and with close family links to the old IRA agreed: 'We belong to the police family. Yes, we close ranks against citizens. What we have in common causes solidarity'. Although all of the interviewees still serving, save this officer and one other, attributed the solidarity largely to protection against shared physical danger, he downplayed this simple explanation by adding: 'There are much more dangerous occupations – like being a miner' – even though he was shot in a border town at the height of the Troubles.

An inspector, a flaunter well past mid-career, elaborated:

> Religion meant nothing when we were in a tight corner. It was 'Can you really rely on
> him?' We're all facing the same danger. What we stand for brings us together. A stone
> or a bottle from whatever source has the same consequences . . . Being open about
> religion paid dividends. People look up to Catholics because they know what they've
> been through.

Sixteen per cent of the sample, exemplified by a middle-aged reservist with relatively short service, stressed the inevitability of solidarity in operational policing, 'If
you're trapped for twelve hours in the car together, you have to learn to support one
another'. A very senior officer, while focusing momentarily on 'the pride of facing
and coping with danger' hinted that solidarity may be conditional on prevailing
circumstances. He added: 'But the solidarity has been diluted because there's less
danger now'. While he showed sensitivity to the changing scenario in Northern
Ireland, particularly to the cessation of violence at that time, a junior officer, representing about 20 per cent of the group, perceived solidarity from a more personal
and emotional angle. Still in the first half of his service years, he explained:

> Comradeship is a great reward. I was the only Catholic in 20–30. I got a life threat from
> the Provisional IRA in [a strongly Republican town]. That established trust. [He had
> earlier been treated with suspicion by non-Catholic colleagues]. I got on with them all.
> They still ask after me.

He pointed to an unusual benefit of being a target. Hostility from the IRA to
Catholic police brought him a form of compensation – trust from non-Catholic
colleagues.

It was as if Catholics in the police service exchanged the cement of shared community background for an equally durable commonality which crossed the traditional Unionist/Nationalist divide. This commonality was likely to be enhanced
in the future for two reasons. With parity of esteem for both major communities
having been embedded in the Belfast Agreement, Catholic officers' detailed knowledge of their culture is welcomed in diversity training programmes for all officers
in order to equip them to function in an increasingly multicultural society. Second,
the Patten reforms ensured that the police were no longer 'our police' in the minds
of Protestants. The liberal model principle of neutrality means that there is a new
unified service containing Catholic and Protestant officers who single-mindedly
pursue civilians who break the law from across the community.

Solidarity, though universally within my sample the most treasured reward from
their service, was not the only source of pleasure which they derived. Fourteen per
cent reaped satisfaction from the dramatic side of policing, for example, 'I enjoy
catching criminals', 'I love to nobble drug dealers', 'I just love the adrenalin rush
I get when we're speeding to a serious incident'. This low figure surprised me and
conflicted with sociological literature. Manning identifies the 'threat-danger-hero'

syndrome (1977: 302) as a widespread phenomenon in police officers' perceptions of their routine work. Reiner describes it as 'old-fashioned machismo' (1985: 99–100), also finding it a common feature as do Brewer and Magee (1991: 66–70) in their ethnographic study of policemen and women in Easton. In contrast, about 60 per cent indicated that the rewards they experienced were very similar to their reasons for joining, for example, 'providing a service', 'bringing people to a better place', 'doing my bit for the community', 'trying to bring peace to this wee country of ours'. Eight per cent valued the approval and respect they gained from colleagues for being professional police officers, one explaining: 'I have been trusted with many sensitive investigations. The reputation I have earned among my colleagues for being a good police officer is the reward I value'.

A young female officer, from a Republican town and in a cross-community marriage, enthused endorsing the idea – expressed by more than three-quarters – that policing is a vocation:

> I love to get up in the morning, come to work and do what I do. I can empower people who are victims. It's good PR for the police. I work a lot with Catholics and I find them more open to change than Protestants.

Apart from her enthusiasm and sense of worth arising out of her caring work, her final remark quietly pointed to the progress which she as an individual felt she could make in encouraging mainly female victims from the Catholic community to be more positively disposed to the police – an important small step towards gaining widespread acceptance.

Just over one-quarter of the sample made reference to ways in which their Catholicism had been facilitated or they, as Catholics, had felt support from their seniors in the course of their careers. Reference has already been made to general permission to attend Mass while in training and while serving in police stations. Another reference was to the provision of armed protection at family funerals in Republican areas, to officers who requested it. Earlier in this chapter I have alluded to an example of protection by 'rescue' for a baby born to a police officer who found herself sharing a hospital maternity unit with a senior member of Cumann na mBan.

One female officer, going back to the late 1970s, explained how her inspector protected her from possible embarrassment when Reverend Ian Paisley visited her station. Her Christian name immediately identified her as Catholic, so the inspector, anticipating sectarian comment from the visitor, advised her '[Christian name], I've decided to call you Elizabeth, just for today'. Incidentally, this officer had also been ostracised by her family when she applied to join. The recruiting sergeant who faced hostility from the applicant's father on visiting their home, simply said as she left 'Your daughter is an adult. She has a right to make her own decisions. You have no right to stop her'. This declaration of support was enough to encourage this officer to continue with her application. Being a chameleon type, this woman accepted her inspector's behaviour as protection against likely embarrassment, but one could interpret suppression of her cultural identity as sectarian. The action taken was intended, however kindly, to give an impression that she was Protestant.

The rewards were many which Catholic officers valued in return for the difficulties which they faced, internal and external to their organisation. One could not, I suggest, come to any conclusion other than that they were consolation prizes, rather than providing balance between costs and rewards.

Conclusion

In this section I shall examine the rich store of data which I gained from interviewing fifty volunteers who had earlier completed my survey. I shall briefly summarise the findings and reflect on what they mean for the main questions underlying my research which are: (a) to establish the reasons for low Catholic representation in policing Northern Ireland; and (b) to ascertain the likely success of the PSNI becoming numerically representative of the Catholic community.

Data in Part 1 showed Catholic officers to be atypical of Catholics in their attitudes and behaviour, though they were born of Catholic parents and received normal Catholic religious upbringing and schooling, with a small percentage of exceptions in the case of schooling. The generational differences in attitudes to worship, choice of partners and selection of schools for their children were very marked and indicated that these officers' Catholic identity was much weaker than that of their parents, but also weaker than Catholics in general. Surprisingly, their political attitudes, they claimed in the main, to be similar to those of their immediate family, favouring neutrality or mild Nationalism. Within their extended families, though, there was considerable dissonance and consequent hostility or isolation.

Though about one-half of their immediate families were relaxed about the officers' choice of career on political grounds, fear for their safety was an important concern and indeed continued to be a cause of concern to the officers, for good reason, throughout their careers. Alienation from school friends and neighbours for those brought up in Catholic areas was equally long term in its effects. Catholic officers moved out of their traditional mindset. Half of the officers – born in Catholic or mixed areas – had to move away physically to live in predominantly Protestant 'safe' areas.

Seventy per cent said they crossed their social Rubicon to join for vocational reasons, feeling moved to contribute to social and political progress. They were spurred on either by high-profile events, including atrocities, exhortation by the Catholic Primate or a general wish to do worthwhile public service as police officers. A surprisingly small minority were attracted primarily by the machismo dimension. The strength of their cultural background created tension for some on joining, though for a quarter the RUC was not their first choice. The Garda Síochána was three times as popular as the Met, showing their (however mild) Nationalist instinct, as well as their awareness of the RUC's negative image in the Catholic community. However, for three-quarters, service in their native, familiar Northern Ireland was their considered preference.

They showed a thoughtful attitude towards social change here. Comments indicated their sensitivity to the need for a favourable social context as a necessary parallel with the political change promised by the Belfast Agreement. Their emphasis on the importance of education in this regard was marked by their strong support for integrated schools and their constructive ideas for curriculum reform designed to open children's minds to world cultures and religions. Most particularly, they saw integrated education as serving to weaken community divisions and to inculcate in children from their earliest years respect for commonality rather than hostility towards difference. The anti-police ambience felt in some Catholic grammar schools for boys was criticised especially by the sons of Catholic officers who suffered discomfort, though Catholic education per se was considered to be of high academic quality and strong on character formation.

The more liberal interpretations which interviewees gave to expression of Catholic identity served to weaken it in a large majority of cases. In order to understand the various ways in which respondents managed their Catholic identity in society and at work, I designed a typology which, in broad terms, categorised them according to the more dominant features of their behaviour informed by their perceptions, experiences, best interests and judgement. These categories I named flaunters, deserters, chameleons and victims, and I provided vignettes to exemplify them. This typology helped to explain how the RUC was able to retain Catholics in its membership. (It would have been interesting to have compared retention and attrition rates of Catholics in the RUC and to search for trends over time. Sufficiently detailed information had not been recorded, however, on reasons for leaving, or the cultural background of those who left.)

Part 2 dealt with the working lives of Catholic officers. Deterrents from joining, present in their private lives, were aggravated by difficulties internal to the RUC and externally in the Catholic population whom they served and from whom they had sprung. The widespread presence of sectarianism emerged as incontestable, all fifty respondents making corroborating comment. Sectarian banter became much less acceptable in the later years than it had been in the 1970s and 1980s. Protestant colleagues who disapproved in the later period actively challenged sectarianism against Catholics. Senior officers had become more vigilant in applying consistent professional standards of neutrality and Catholics were more likely to have had recourse to the official complaints system, with an expectation that they would be fairly treated. How Catholics coped with sectarianism was determined by their position on the typology spectrum. Flaunters typically tended to meet aggressive or hurtful language with its match; deserters blamed Catholic officers themselves for being hypersensitive or played down its significance; chameleons exercised a strong self preservation instinct by keeping a low profile, rationalising or challenging it assertively; victims felt hurt but helpless.

For many, sectarianism started in training and continued when they were posted to stations where they felt they were perceived to be part of the Republican enemy 'camp', even though two chief constables strove to make the RUC neutral, professional, impartial. Political correctness which prohibited sectarian banter was explained as a form of easing which officers identified as being offensive or benign.

Other sources of bigotry or discomfort were reported to be the Loyal orders, Special Branch and the British Army, particularly the locally recruited UDR which was replaced by the equally unacceptable RIR Reserve. The insidious influence of the Masonic Order and, to a lesser extent, of the Orange Order, provided continuity with evidence from the retired officers, though it seemed that Masonic policy had changed and invitations to join were issued to 'loyal' Catholic officers.

Lack of appropriate training and insensitivity to the social and political situation by British regiments stationed in Northern Ireland caused a significant problem for Catholic police in the eyes of the Catholic community. Neo-colonial-style behaviour in searching homes of Catholics and roughly handling residents provided very effective propaganda for Republicans. Even more contentious was the negative reputation of Special Branch. This secretive unit was seen as 'a necessary evil' by about 30 per cent of the Catholic officers or condemned out of hand by half as many. Some acknowledged the likelihood of individual Special Branch officers colluding with Loyalist paramilitaries in facilitating or condoning the murder of Catholics reported to be active Republicans.

Against a background of military might and counter-insurgency policing, it would surprise no one that Catholic police, unsupported at least and more likely despised by the Nationalist population, were seen by Catholics as cogs in a machine which was trying to suppress their legitimate demands for equality in civil rights. There must have been a strong temptation to become deserters and be totally assimilated into the RUC, but the strength of their cultural identity is demonstrated by two out of three becoming chameleons, while only 14 per cent emerged as deserters.

Sharp criticism was levelled at the Catholic Church as an organisation from which they expected support and sympathy in the form of 'more leadership and less politics'. Hunger generated bitterness in some cases, though about one-quarter acknowledged a dilemma faced by priests having to offer Requiem Mass for terrorists in accordance with unjudgemental church rules. The experiences of individual Catholic officers testified to fragmentation among lower Catholic clergy in their attitudes to them. The data overall suggested that neutrality on the part of the church or its priests was not considered acceptable, nor even calls for impartial policing. Possible intimidation by the IRA was, however, cited as a mitigating factor.

Support from the Nationalist community was acknowledged, even in areas such as west Belfast and south Armagh, which were saturated by IRA dogma and control. Though they were constantly haunted by fear of death or serious injury, none gave graphic descriptions of attempts on their lives. Those who suffered repeated personal humiliation by Republicans tended to acquiesce in victim status, though not always. Some were prompted to comment on the unacceptable behaviour of some officers who invited hostility by their insensitive policing of Catholic areas, not interested in improving relations but centred on short-term gain leading to promotion.

One-fifth voiced unrelieved negativity about the absence or uncertainty of Catholic community support which was advanced as the reason for half of Catholic officers having non-Catholic partners. Three-quarters blamed Republicans and the Sinn Féin Party for the temerity of potential recruits who wanted to join from areas of west Belfast such as Lenadoon. A tiny percentage were willing to engage in 'oppositional discourse', for example one woman empathised with, though she did not approve of, the IRA perspective. She had plenty of experience in dealing with Cumann na mBan members while serving in the CID.

In identifying police solidarity as being by far the greatest unanticipated reward reaped from pursuing a career in the RUC, respondents shared this phenomenon with police across the world. However, in a sample who largely joined for vocational reasons, it was clear that their cultural identity was sacrificed to this commonality, which successfully challenged the traditional Unionist–Nationalist divide.

5

More of the same? PSNI trainees

Introduction

In Chapter 3 and Chapter 4, I presented and analysed data from retired and from serving officers who transferred from the RUC to the PSNI. In Chapter 5 I focus on qualitative data produced by a snowball sample of ten Catholic recruits who joined the PSNI in the first two years of its existence. Ongoing themes from the previous chapters shape the structure, though the new officers' relative lack of experience precluded direct comparisons with their predecessors in some instances. However, this vacuum was filled by fresh thinking which they offered in terms of their hopes and aspirations for a new era in policing, informed by the philosophy and practice recommended by the Patten Commission.

The aims of Chapter 5 are to identify ways in which the PSNI appears to differ from the RUC – according to Catholic officers' perceptions – and the promise held out for a future partnership of policing with the Catholic community. Even though Catholic membership of the PSNI has grown from 7–8 per cent at its formation to more than 27 per cent at August 2009 as a result of 50:50 recruitment, management of Catholic identity within a service predominantly Protestant is still an issue worthy of attention.

I shall present and discuss data from ten officers recruited in the very early stages of the PSNI's history on their biographies and socio-political backgrounds pre-service; their lives as PSNI trainees and their personal and professional aspirations.

1   Biographical and socio-political backgrounds

First, I shall provide a summary profile of the sample. The average age of the group was 28 years and the age range was from 22 to 32 years. Although they were all within two years of recruitment into the PSNI, they included three subsets: (a) one trainee within the first phase of training which would last twenty-one weeks; (b) two trainees on supervised practice which would last ten weeks; (c) seven trainees who had been allocated to their first stations and were working under careful guidance from experienced officers until they completed a total of two years in the PSNI. Six were male and four were female. One held a higher degree; two a primary degree; two had sub-degree qualifications; three had completed A-levels and two had GCSE or equivalent qualifications. Four were in stable relationships/married; one was engaged to be married and five were without long-term partners.

Four interviewees said they were regularly practising Catholics; three practised rarely, and three did not practise but were not members of any other church or faith group. Seven declared that they had no political affiliation; two were likely to vote for the Alliance Party and/or the Women's Coalition (which wound down officially in 2006 after a ten-year lifespan as a second non-sectarian party) and one identified himself as a moderate Nationalist. Seven members of the group had been born in Northern Ireland, two in the Republic of Ireland and one in England.

Nine out of ten had two Catholic parents and one had a Protestant mother and Catholic father. The partners of all four in stable relationships were Protestant; a fifth, a trainee, had a Catholic fiancée. All ten in the group had been previously employed, eight in the UK or Republic of Ireland in public or private sectors and two in the USA, while one had served in the British Army, one had done vacation jobs and another had completed one stage in an apprenticeship.

All the members of the group were born in the first decade after the Troubles began, so they had no experience of pre-1969 'normal' policing in Northern Ireland if they were born here. Those born outside the province had family connections with it, or in the case of the English-born ex-soldier, had served here with a British regiment. None claimed to have a family member of any generation in the RUC or the PSNI. Three, however, had relations in the British Army or Merchant Navy currently and one of those had two grandfathers who had served in both World Wars, though she had an uncle in the IRA and living in the south of Ireland. The father of one female officer had occupied a senior security post in Northern Ireland, outside of policing and the Army. Her sister currently held a junior position in the same service. Three trainees were born in predominantly Protestant areas of a city or a provincial town and four in predominantly Catholic areas of Northern Ireland.

One of those Catholic areas, west Belfast, is generally perceived to be the most Republican-dominated in the province. It followed that the two male trainees brought up there had personal and lengthy experience of violence in the streets, house searches, consistent attempts by the IRA to recruit 16-year-old boys and girls into their ranks. They also had mothers with Republican sympathies and one had a father who had been detained on a prison ship in Belfast Lough during the Second World War for being a member of the IRA. In contrast, a graduate from a Nationalist city with a strong Republican element had a father who, as an independent councillor, served as deputy mayor on the city council. His mother had no interest in politics. The trainee had eschewed Gaelic games in his Catholic grammar school and put his sports energy into becoming the school's golf champion, as well as playing rugby. Although totalling only ten, this sample of Catholic trainees reflected a very broad range of backgrounds, experiences and views which I shall try to reflect in the data which follow.

Cultural Catholics – religion, education, politics

In the summary profile I stated that 95 per cent of the ten trainees' parents were Catholic. All of the group had attended Catholic primary and second-level schools, except the female who was the product of a 'mixed' marriage and who had favoured her Protestant mother by choosing two state schools because she wanted continuity of friendship with peers. Nine out of ten, therefore, reflected in their upbringing close similarity to the wider Catholic community – Catholic parents, Catholic schools and a wide political spectrum, the only other being the one female referred to above who did not attend church, but saw her father attending Mass and her brothers going to a Catholic primary school and an integrated secondary school. It was surprising that she was the first in the group just out of training the previous week to volunteer to be interviewed, choosing to give herself a Catholic identity, favouring her father. Married in a registry office, she reflected on her culturally indeterminate childhood: 'It would have been good to believe in anything'. I noted that a second person from this subgroup, on his first day out of police college, who volunteered for interview, was the ex-soldier who was confident and clear in acknowledging his identity. The remaining seven, in their second year since they began their traineeship reflected confidence, probably borne out of the training they had received and the affirmation which their clarity of vision provided for them individually by their choice of career.

All ten held liberal views (i.e. not in accordance with the official teaching of the Catholic Church) on moral questions such as abortion, distancing themselves with such statements as: 'It's a medical decision', or 'Sometimes it's a necessary evil'. There was, in contrast, wide diversity in terms of religious practice and relations with the Catholic Church. Of the four who said they worshipped regularly, two pointedly referred to their religion being 'a very private matter' or 'my faith is a very private thing'. One was the ex-soldier with English-born parents, though with Irish ancestry on his father's side. The other was the councillor's son from a Nationalist city. They appeared to have decided that being a 'flaunter' was unlikely to pay dividends in the PSNI, or that in social interaction outside their job – for example in mixing with members of the RIR or among the golf fraternity – discretion was required in order to avoid possible danger or embarrassment. Already, they showed themselves to be 'chameleons'.

The two officers from the most staunchly Catholic area of Belfast were among those who had ceased to attend Mass, but not because they were in the police. 'I stopped going when there was no priest available to give my father the last rites', said one. The other had ceased to practise before going to live in the USA, where he said he 'did a lot of growing up'. Married to a Protestant, living in a Unionist town and identifying with Hermon's notion of 'a third religion' (not Catholic, not Protestant, but a police officer), this self-styled 'Westie' explained:

> I have no conflict between being a Catholic and a police officer. I'm a police officer who happens to come from a Catholic background. I've a Methodist wife and a son

at a Protestant school; I was married in a Church of England in Cyprus. I'm a cultural Catholic.

The strength of residual cultural Catholicism when asked about religious observance, was expressed as 'No, but . . .', meaning that they did not attend Mass regularly, but they still considered themselves Catholics. Although they had both distanced themselves by ceasing to attend Mass and by having non-Catholic partners, they could not be described as 'deserters'. A third 'No, but . . .', a female, expressed her difficulty: 'Some priests preach politics. I cannot accept religion and politics being mixed'. The range of views on religious practice was perhaps aptly expressed by the opposing stances adopted by a non-practising graduate from the Republic of Ireland on the one hand, who said that he would not have any of his children baptised, to that of a female from a northern provincial town, with a Protestant partner, who said that she would baptise – secretly if need be – any child she might have.

After religion and family, the next most important pillar of cultural Catholicism might be seen as education. Although, as indicated earlier, nine out of ten interviewees were educated in Catholic schools, three in the Republic of Ireland – including the ex-soldier, whose parents' marriage broke up and he moved from England with his father – from all there was solid support voiced in favour of integrated education as being a necessary prerequisite to social change, though Catholic education was widely praised for its perceived strengths. The 'Westie' who described himself as a 'lazy student', managing to pass only one A-level subject, praised his Catholic education for 'providing discipline and stretching'. However, with a child at a state primary school in a Unionist town, he felt 'There shouldn't be 100 per cent Catholic maintained schools because segregation is our problem'. He seemed to suggest that if children were educated together the level of interest in education generally would rise – in addition to promoting integration rather than segregation.

A female, the head of a one-parent family with a child at a Catholic primary school, who praised her own Catholic education for having 'given her a conscience', wanted her child to attend an integrated secondary school which offered Irish on the curriculum, since she considered the Irish language to be part of her cultural heritage and quite separate from Catholic education. Another female regretted that she had been too old to benefit from integrated schooling in her area, though she felt that her convent schools had done her proud. Her mother had, however, been instrumental in starting an integrated school in their town later. A second officer brought up in west Belfast (not 'Westie') supported integrated education, but also believed that separate Catholic schools should stay. Choice ought to be available.

A male trainee brought up in the Republic pursued undergraduate studies in Northern Ireland and intermitted indefinitely from higher-degree study so as not to miss his offer, when the PSNI refused to defer a place for him. With success in inspector-level examinations already achieved as he progressed on a high-potential development scheme, he was loud in his praise of the academic education given in his schools run by Christian Brothers, but described the personal development aspect of the curriculum to have been disappointing, 'Civics taught by people who had been institutionalised for thirty years'. In contrast, a female from across the Irish border, having failed her leaving certificate, went back to school, completing at nineteen and a half years old.

An indication of change in the curriculum of a popular Catholic grammar school was revealed by remarks from a graduate. This school had been criticised by a retired officer whose son had suffered there. Having received abuse on and off the pitch because his father was in the RUC, the son had refused to play Gaelic games. The trainee remarked, as already mentioned, that he had chosen to play rugby rather than Gaelic games and had been golf champion. This increased variety in sports available surely indicated movement in the direction of a cross-community curriculum practised by a school which had a reputation – as had other grammar schools which were also, in part, seminaries – for propagating Gaelic culture. Another indication of change on a small scale was given by a trainee from west Belfast who revealed that police officers had been admitted to his primary school to give lessons in road safety. This was a practice which, during the Troubles, had been likely only in Catholic schools situated in Unionist towns. In strongly Republican areas, head teachers would not have risked incurring the wrath of the IRA and Sinn Féin by admitting members of the RUC. Clear cultural identity showed signs of greater fluidity in religious and educational terms. Trainees' views on the political future of Northern Ireland and on their political identity provided a varied range, too.

Seven out of the sample of ten had labelled themselves neutral in terms of political affiliation, claiming not to have voted in the previous election, one suggesting that police should not be allowed to vote. All were in favour of Northern Ireland remaining an entity within the UK – though two felt that Direct Rule might be the best form of governance through 'the foreseeable future'. Two said outright that they did not want reunification and qualified their statements. The ex-soldier believed that 'any attempt to remove partition would bring civil war'. A female from a security family, while declaring herself to be Irish, wanted sharing of cultures to develop in Northern Ireland. 'The 12th of July is mine too', she said. Describing her approach as 'pragmatic' she explained: 'The south abandoned us', referring to perceived neglect by the Republic of Ireland's government of beleaguered Northern Catholics when the civil unrest broke out in 1969 and they were at the mercy of marauding Loyalist paramilitaries, until the arrival of the British Army. She criticised Assembly members for neglecting domestic issues and, while wishing to have the British national anthem dropped, she approved of the royal family as a tourist attraction.

Indifference on the part of the southern government was reinforced by a trainee from there who assured me 'Northern Ireland should remain part of the UK for its own sake. The south of Ireland people don't care one way or the other'. A colleague from a Republican area in Northern Ireland who described himself as 'a moderate Nationalist' spelled out his views:

> The Good Friday Agreement was of monumental importance. Northern Ireland can run itself without help from outside. I am optimistic about the future, if we would just listen to one another. Facts are used by politicians for their own purposes. Northern Ireland should remain part of the UK. Unification would not help. Northern Ireland is a big sore thumb to both Ireland and England.

This explanation of a moderate Nationalist's perception seemed to have moved very far from what it might have been a generation ago – closer to a definition of 'a moderate Ulster Nationalist' (someone whose allegiance is to Northern Ireland and its people, not Britain and not the Republic.) Cultural Catholicism expressed in terms of political aspirations might be seen as being a fluid term, as in the cases of religious practice or preferences in education provision. The ex-soldier believed that the greatest problem facing Northern Ireland was its economic dependence on Britain. A female from the Republic used other graphic metaphors to describe the province: 'A thorn in the side of Britain. A nightmare. I don't think that the Irish government wants Northern Ireland. On its own, it's not economically viable'.

The importance of Sinn Féin in the political future of Northern Ireland was raised by a majority of the group. The 'Westie' admitted that at a future election he would consider voting Sinn Féin, explaining:

> Sinn Féin have political savvy. The SDLP opened doors for them. Sinn Féin hit the ground running. They're committed. Protestants will vote for them in future. They ran a professional campaign. They had good PR compared with the PSNI.

He had been a strong Republican in his teenage years. A certain admiration for their professionalism as a political party seemed to have been rekindled. In contrast, a female officer with strong Republican links in her extended family said that she would not open her door to Sinn Féin councillors. Her younger sister, she added, though keen to join the PSNI was still intimidated by Sinn Féin's refusal to take places on the Policing Board, thereby feeling without 'permission' for her to apply.

The significance of Sinn Féin on the Policing Board was stressed by a large majority with reference to Catholic recruitment. None was more emphatic than the southern Irish graduate whose prediction the passage of time has shown to be over-optimistic. He said:

> But Sinn Féin on the Policing Board is hugely important to recruitment. The floodgates will open for people from middle-class Nationalist backgrounds. That will happen within a year or two.

Although membership of a newly constituted Policing Board was announced in 2009 with Sinn Féin representatives and increases in Catholic recruitment have been very favourable, it is impossible to measure the impact which Sinn Féin support for the PSNI has had in terms of recruitment figures.

Previous employment

The views which the ten trainees expressed about the political future of the province were perhaps influenced by the varied work experience they had gained before joining the PSNI. Of the ten interviewees, six had worked outside Northern Ireland and outside of policing, before starting on a police career. This variety in their experiences probably assisted their transition from the narrow cultural Catholicism of Northern Ireland. The newest entrant worked locally with an engineering firm and on a provincial newspaper, while a female with just five months in training, had managed a health and leisure club after graduating from a local university. It was interesting to learn that she had given up her place at a Scottish university after one week there, suffering from homesickness. Yet, she had in the meantime matured to a point where she contemplated that after some years in the PSNI, preferably in a specialist CID unit, she would like to serve in the Australian police. An ex-civil servant, who had occupied a post servicing the RUC before joining the PSNI, was provided with personal reminiscence of life in the Australian police service by his father.

The two trainees from the Republic of Ireland had different educational opportunities which influenced the types of work they did. The male was an only child and the female was from a large family and a broken home. The male, a graduate, had done vacation jobs typical of students, in labouring and the postal service, while the female, as I mentioned earlier, had left school with no qualifications but had returned to complete her leaving certificate in due course. This level of success enabled her to be selected as an apprentice (the only female in a total of 200) in a typically male occupational culture, but this choice proved unrewarding. She was then disappointed to be rejected by the Irish Army on medical grounds. It was only after jobs in food retail, catering and security work that she found her niche, prompted by a PSNI recruitment advertisement.

Two other trainees, a female and the youngest in the group, and 'Westie', had their life experience enhanced by living in the USA for two and three years respectively. The female had worked for an airline and had been a nanny, while the male did bar work among a rich mixture of nationalities. This broadening cultural experience provided him with plentiful supplies of food for thought which informed his judgement of Northern Ireland when he returned to manage a branch of a clothing chain. The ex-soldier had been stationed abroad and in England, as well as having had tours of duty in the province immediately preceding his application to join the PSNI – prompted by his admiration of the RUC when he worked alongside them.

What was striking about this small snowball sample was the wider life experiences which they had, compared with previous generations of police officers in the RUC, especially the retirees. They seemed empowered to welcome change rather than to struggle against it, both inside and outside policing. As representatives of the Catholic community they appeared willing and able to accept reality and the possible, rather than focusing on long-term idealistic outcomes. Adaptation to new social and political developments in the interests of lasting peace seemed to dominate their agenda.

Typology

In Chapter 4, I showed that Catholic police used a variety of means to manage their identity, explained by the use of vignettes illustrating 'flaunter', 'chameleon', 'deserter' and 'victim' types. Among the ten trainees I found eight (80 per cent) to have predominantly 'chameleon' profiles, none with strong flaunter characteristics, one deserter and one victim. (Compared with serving officers these figures showed an increase in chameleons and a decrease in flaunters and in deserters.) Below I present a trainee 'chameleon' as Vignette E, which illustrates the fluidity and potential for change of Catholic identity. The subject of Vignette E named himself 'Westie'.

Vignette E came from a lower middle-class family in west Belfast and was baptised on Bloody Sunday, 1971. His father was a strong constitutional Nationalist and his mother was less opinioned but with a romantic view of patriotism and with passive Republican sympathies. He came in the middle of eight children who attended Catholic schools, but he was a lazy grammar school pupil, achieving only one A-level. Although Gaelic sports were compulsory and he had to study the Irish language until fifth year, he participated in football and swimming outside of school.

He was brought up at the epicentre of inter-communal violence where he saw the fathers of neighbouring children being 'lifted' by the police and Army. As a teenager he became very Republican in his views, shouted support for the IRA in public and bought their newspaper. Yet, at the same time he had a wish to become a police officer, largely fed by American television programmes.

> I met the first Protestants in my life at sixteen or seventeen. They didn't have horns. I soon realised that paramilitaries kept up and controlled divisions – ethnic cleansing, ghetto mentality. We thought that Protestants had everything, but we're just different sides of the same coin.

Accepting as fact that division in Northern Irish society was aggravated by vested interests and after three years working in the USA he returned and in time implemented his own cross-community identity. He married a local non-Catholic in a Church of England abroad, had their child baptised (with his priest's permission) in the Church of Ireland. He sent him to a state primary school and set up home in a Unionist town when he joined the PSNI.

On deciding to apply, his SDLP father approved, saying 'It's a job for life unless you mess it up', though he experienced ongoing opposition from siblings. 'Three brothers still don't speak to me. We had a one-day truce at my brother's wedding in Donegal.' Friends who learned later of his career choice said 'You sold out'.

Having distanced himself from his cultural background in a number of ways, he declared himself to be a member of the 'third religion'. He admitted, though a former altar boy, that he had ceased practising Catholicism, except socially, before going to the USA. He used his cultural Catholicism as a PSNI trainee to establish rapport with Gaelic sports enthusiasts in the community he served. He explained what the PSNI signified for him in these words: 'We recognise that we don't represent both sides of the community. I have to be a model of what I represent. I can't change the past, only do what I'm doing'.

Although this trainee would appear to have some characteristics of a deserter, his subjective identity as a cultural Catholic seemed to be intact and he firmly felt that he represented his community in the PSNI. Furthermore, he saw it an important part of his work to assist fellow Catholics to identify with him and with the PSNI in order to establish trust and partnership, necessary conditions governing policing by consent. His profile demonstrated, significantly, that the recruitment base had widened to include Catholic police from Republican backgrounds. It was interesting, therefore, to find out the motivation of the trainees for joining and their hopes for the future.

2   Motivations, expectations and reality

Reasons for joining

One of the political developments which the trainees responded to was the Belfast Agreement; one of the outcomes was *A New Beginning: Policing in Northern Ireland*, popularly known as the Patten Report. How far the recommendations made by the Patten Commission provided a stimulus for applicants to join the PSNI I shall consider in the case of this snowball sample. The reasons given by the group for joining fell into predictable categories, though a call to action in a worthwhile cause was a reason shared by all. Reiner (1992: 11) draws attention to a sense of mission commonly felt in police culture which elevates policing above being a job and makes it a purposeful life. Five agreed with Reiner, but said that in addition the PSNI appealed as a good career with prospects, though two others made clear that they weren't 'in it only for the money'. Three admitted that they were influenced by the glamour of excitement, risk and fast police cars depicted in the media. Reiner (1992: 11) also finds the 'machismo dimension' a common feature across all police, 'a game of wits and skills', rarely experienced in the course of an officer's normal routine day. Individual accounts provided varied and informative insights into the thought processes of those who, stimulated by a widely diffused advertising campaign conducted by the PSNI and intended to attract substantially larger numbers from the Catholic community, found a personal call.

Recruits applying from Unionist areas did not have to sacrifice the friendship of peers when they joined, because they had been brought up to mix with the majority community. They socialised and participated in sport with members of the armed forces, so there was continuity in their lives if they joined another branch of the security services. For interviewees from strongly Nationalist and Republican areas, the decision to apply required more in-depth personal reflection. A fine balance had to be struck between career motivation and negative contextual factors associated with family, or community, or both.

Asked if they would have joined the RUC in the event of its still being in existence, seven said that they would, while three had reservations as the following quotations show. A graduate from a Nationalist city explained his reasoning:

A police officer in Northern Ireland? It didn't happen overnight, but I knew I wanted to be one for a long time. As a youngster I was heavily into Sherlock Holmes, not so much television programmes. There were no police officers in our family and I didn't have any bad experiences involving treatment by police . . . The idea of becoming a police officer seemed to come up from my subconscious . . . The name change from RUC met my conscience halfway. I could not have joined if it had still been called the RUC. I couldn't have gone against the Nationalist judgement . . . No, I didn't see the RUC as the armed wing of the Unionist Party, but it was too much of a grey area. It had a blotted copybook . . . But I grabbed it with both hands.

This trainee conveyed clearly his battle with his conscience in trying to reconcile his own career preference while respecting the legitimate reservations of his community about the RUC image and legacy. Indeed he had applied to an English police force at the same time, but when he was offered a place in the PSNI he explained: 'I crossed the Rubicon. You cross the Rubicon if you join the police from my area'. He was fortunate, though, in having strong parental support. Of his father's attitude he said: 'Dad was 100 per cent behind me. He's a pragmatist. He said: "If you can make society better, then embrace the challenge with open arms"'.

In contrast, the 'Westie' had a father with Republican sympathies as a young man and a mother who prayed he would leave the police college. He was obviously still under family pressure not to join, even though he had already embarked on training. He exemplified the survey finding that family opposition to joining may continue for an uncertain period. As a child, the trainee was allowed to watch the American detective show *Starsky and Hutch* on television as a treat after he had his bath. This experience gave him a desire to be a police officer in New York, where he lived for three years, but settled for bar work instead. In his early childhood he had dressed in an RUC uniform which had been discovered by a playmate in a neighbour's attic. Describing his early life in west Belfast he explained:

> Bomb scares were the main problem. Members of the IRA were 'lifted' [by British soldiers] at the bottom of our street. We were surrounded by corrugated iron barriers. We believed about the Army: 'They're bad boys who'd take your Daddy away'. We watched foot patrols. We threw stones at the police. We had more trouble from 'the Brits' [soldiers], though. Very few police there. We talked to the soldiers: 'Give us a gun, chum'. They'd let us look down their guns . . . I became very Republican in my teenage years. I bought *Republican News*. Played rebel music like 'Boolavogue' [name of a Republican song]. Shouted 'Up the Provies' [Provisional IRA]. But I realised I was more SDLP. I thought 'I'm not 100 per cent behind it, am I? . . . I probably wouldn't have joined if it was still the RUC. The word 'service' appealed to me. Such a fundamental change said to me: 'We recognise that we don't represent both sides of the community'.

The lengthy passage just quoted indicated how far this trainee had to travel in his thinking – a path which typically other Catholic applicants from west Belfast would have to tread before arriving at the police college. It also measured the strength of pull which even the name 'PSNI' – but also its whole significance – could exercise in attracting applicants from this and similar areas.

Two trainees had joined because they had worked as civilians in close proximity to the RUC and admired that force's professionalism – one for two years while serving in the Army, while a second was from west Belfast. His mother had been knocked down by an Army Saracen in 1971 while she was pregnant, but this experience did not prevent him from saying of the RUC, 'I found they were ordinary human beings', though he added: 'The "B" Specials were the police force for the Unionist population'. After eleven years as a civil servant, procuring supplies for the RUC, he said 'I would have joined the RUC if it had gone through transition' – meaning that a change in name was not important to him, but other reforms would have been necessary to make him join. A female from the Republic, perhaps because, as she explained, her parents had little understanding of Northern politics, admitted: 'I don't know if I'd have joined if it was still the RUC. My friends [on the northern side of the border] were hostile to the police per se. There was an underlying atmosphere'. Another female, coincidentally from the town to which the previous speaker referred, who did not experience any family hostility, said: 'If I'd had family opposition, I'd have joined anyhow'.

All of the ten saw in joining the PSNI an opportunity to make the Belfast Agreement work in policing terms for the whole community and three said that already they felt they could recommend it to friends. Three saw themselves cast in a role where they had to neutralise the negative behaviour of politicians, whom they blamed for keeping Northern Irish society divided because it was in their interests to do so; yet people continued to elect them, knowing what their views were. One summed up his views on this subject:

> There has been tragedy in Northern Ireland for both sides. We must get on with applying justice in our dealings. And we cannot trust politicians. People are strange: think of that free vote when the people chose Barabbas over Jesus.

He pointed to the unfortunately potent influence which intransigent politicians exercise over the voting patterns of the Northern Irish electorate and the lack of rational issue-based judgement shown by voters, who cannot break out of the traditional confrontational mindset. The trainees had invested their futures in the PSNI, sometimes at great cost. It was likely, then, that they held views on what the returns might be.

Aspirations and rewards

Aspirations might be seen as reflecting a combination of the ideal and the real in the careers they anticipated. They focused on two aspects, not mutually exclusive: (a) career progression and functional specialisms; and (b) principles and practice of public service.

Five out of ten mentioned ranks they aspired to, the two least experienced and youngest aiming modestly at sergeant level. One had already completed the inspector's examinations and a fourth, a female, aspired to achieve inspector level. In company with another female she considered options. One of them would prefer 'a sideways move' into a crime specialism, while the other wanted a position of 'either high status or caring' without any specific level of rank in mind.

There was wide diversity in functional preferences expressed, which sometimes related to their reasons for joining. Two males favoured community policing, one, the 'Westie', because he had discovered it to be 'his forte'. Perhaps his background of having been brought up in difficult circumstances in west Belfast had heightened his awareness of a need for legitimacy and for partnership in policing. He explained: 'If you don't mix, you further myths. We're different sides of the same coin' (meaning Catholics and Protestants). The ex-soldier favoured community policing because 'I want to work for the community rather than make somebody rich'. Two females envisaged themselves as dramatic heroines in the drugs squad, while only one female included the traditional niche for female officers among her preferences – caring. The majority preference might indicate the presence of 'new woman' who thought of the PSNI as providing a unisex career, attending pub brawls, riots, drug swoops, rather than serving in relatively 'safe' locations such as offices dealing with administration, or interviewing battered wives or abused children.

Altruism as dedication to public service was expressed by all ten trainees in realistically modest terms. The 'Westie' encapsulated the thinking of the group saying 'I want to make a difference, but I'll not change the world. I want to be a part of history'. Although some had been attracted at an early age to policing as it was portrayed in fiction, even those in the first few months of training focused on anticipated daily reality and the way they intended to carry out their mission. The single mother found a harmonious convergence between meeting parental need in supporting her child and contributing to the public good: 'I need to do something with my life; I'm making a difference', she said, inspired by her father whom she greatly admired and who had also tried to do so in a security post. The male still at training stage one signed up to the predictable idealistic code that he 'will be fair and unbiased in carrying out my duties'. The more reflective, for example the former civil servant, found in his career choice 'a challenge following the Belfast Agreement to make a more normal policing situation'.

The trainees' aspirations were closely linked to the rewards which they reaped. In the darkest times of the RUC it seemed that solidarity, the traditional cement of police culture, was the only reward which police reaped in combat against paramilitary threats. The new PSNI personnel had stories with different emphases to share. Only three mentioned solidarity, suggesting, perhaps, that its importance was felt less in the new dispensation. One of those, a female, chose the word 'camaraderie' explaining a fine point:

There's tremendous camaraderie, the result of humorous banter . . . It's not true friendship, though. It's total trust. We all know that a malicious accusation would be dealt with.

One of the two trainees from west Belfast, however, spoke of solidarity in the RUC sense, 'You look after each other rather than the public. Police are piggy in the middle'. Four, including the three least experienced, spoke in general terms of their job offering variety and challenge, which they welcomed. Four mentioned the PSNI as providing an interesting and demanding career; for one it was a vocation. A female contrasted despairingly the security and challenge which policing offered, with the alternative for her – 'a single parent on benefits'. Three found that their interests in sport were catered for, either in meeting the physical challenge of the training curriculum, or as a leisure pursuit. As well as benefiting personally from sport, two mentioned it as a means to an end. For one it meant encouraging better community relations by organising cross-country rambles for school children, while for the ex-soldier schooled in the Republic he could continue to support Gaelic games and play on a PSNI team.

Four out of ten trainees used the words 'love' and 'happy' in relation to their work, though two regretted that they were prevented from saying so openly, precisely because they were police. A female from the Republic explained:

I'm extremely happy and proud of what I've become. Yet I can't shout it from the roof tops. In the South, if you graduate from Templemore [police college] you get your picture in the newspapers. You're made a fuss of in your local area. That doesn't happen here. It has to be kept secret.

The law graduate declared:

I'm a very happy constable in the PSNI. I come into work and I love it every day. I'm lucky I've found the career that's right for me. This is the career for me. I won't change to anything else . . . It's not about financial security. If I'd stayed with the firm I was working in, I'd be earning £16,000 more a year than I am now.

The fast-track graduate from the Republic was even more extreme in expressing his pleasure. 'I love everything about it', he said, adding 'I would recommend the PSNI to anyone who wanted to join. Intelligence is a lot better now. There's less risk', referring to an enduring deterrent. The former civil servant contrasted his positive attitude which he shared with colleagues, with reservations he had to begin with:

I've settled in it as a career. I want to get up in the morning and go to work. Everyone in my station feels that way. I feared a 'them-and-us' situation. RUC versus PSNI. Instead of 'Are they going to fall flat on their faces?' we got 'Are you OK, cub?'. It's challenging, but not as frightening as at first.

The joys of being a trainee PSNI officer did not come without cost, though. The price paid seemed to centre around personal safety, social isolation or the post-Patten emphasis on officer accountability and transparency. Personal safety was an issue referred to by eight out of ten trainees. Most were exercised by the risk of death or serious injury, though they were divided on whether they carried their personal weapons at all times, as advised. One said 'I keep my personal weapon with me. I live in a dodgy area' (a mixed estate in a Unionist town with a serious drug problem). The ex-civil servant from a Republican city, however, seemed to adopt a contradictory approach, explaining: 'I'm careful about what I do, where I go. I've been fourteen years in my house in a Protestant area. I only talk to family and friends about work, but I leave my weapon at work'.

A female from the Republic admitted that her mood dictated whether she carried her weapon or not. A bigger problem, for her, which she shared with five other trainees, was 'feeling a bit apart as a police officer'. A trainee from a Nationalist city illustrated how personal physical risk and the effects of social isolation went hand in hand. He explained:

> If the security issue was removed, life would be even better. I can't go home at the moment. I'm under a death threat since September. I was spotted at home and got a threat through the post. My family come to visit me now, not the other way round. I'm not that important, though, that I'd carry a personal weapon around with me when I'm off duty. If there was a wedding or a funeral in my family in [name of city], I'd probably go home for it. I'd have to think about having protection. It would depend on the security situation at the time, I suppose.

This latter trainee's testimony summed up a consensus attitude of the group very well, in that pragmatism reigned, while they refused to be denied freedom of choice in dealing with threatening situations. Individuals had unique combinations of difficulties, some blaming aspects of the Patten reforms. The trainee still in phase one of training expressed fear of how the stress on accountability might affect him personally, if he made an unintentional mistake and was held to account without any support from the PSNI establishment. This view must be read in a context of inexperience which 'makes everything look very frightening at this stage'.

Downsizing presented the 'victim' female with an ongoing source of discomfort:

> I have a fear of not having experienced support in a difficult situation. We've got only 10 per cent experienced colleagues and 90 per cent inexperienced. There's the shift work, too, and stress and the 'pig' stigma with friends.

Still suffering ostracism by her Catholic friends, she seemed to pay a higher price than others to achieve her reward of variety and challenge. She was the youngest in the group and lacked the self-confidence of the others, who were nearly all chameleons. She had also been accepted on her second application because her fitness levels were deemed to be below par when she first applied.

Another female, very positive about her choice of career and its rewards, had multiple concerns though. A major source was part of the apparatus of accountability. She felt threatened by the confidential telephone which officers were invited to use in order to report colleagues for breaking rules of political correctness or human rights legislation. This lack of trust by her employer, as she saw it, was aggravated by the perception that 'the police takes over your whole life', to the extent that her mother had to take the responsibility for her child during out-of-school hours, in order to fit in with her duty schedules. She added: 'When a Catholic joins it's a sacrifice. In my case history repeated itself. It happened to my father, too'. Her siblings continued to show hostility to her for joining the police, repeating the long-term, unresolved difficulty which her father experienced from his strongly Republican family when he joined a security service. He progressed to a high-profile position which did not ease his burden.

Trainees' perceptions of the Catholic community

For many Catholic officers the Unionist image which blighted the RUC was a constant in their lives. I asked the Catholic trainees, therefore, about their perceptions of the Catholic community they served or were likely to serve in the near future.

Those who had not yet served in stations outside Belfast, being still in their first or second phase of training, tended to have formed vague impressions of the public from the mythology current in police culture. Though not necessarily without foundation, it was provided largely by officers who had transferred from the RUC and were in tutor posts. For example, the trainee with the shortest service said: 'I believe Newry is not a very pleasant place. They have an attitude towards police'. He came from a Unionist town where his family home had been attacked by Loyalist paramilitaries only two years before he joined. The ex-soldier, in contrast, viewed Northern Irish society from a distant vantage point, born in England of English Catholic parents but schooled in the Republic. On only his first day out of police college he drew upon his experience of Army service, during which he found 'Family values are the same on both sides [of the community]. People welcomed you into their homes'.

Trainees of local origin tended to look on the negative side, finding attitude change in society as either very slow or unlikely. For example: 'There'll always be people who'll keep it [division] going. Maybe in ten years' time . . ..'. A female with about one year of service cited the ambivalence of the Garvaghy Road residents in their attitude and behaviour towards the police at Drumcree as a warning against making unfounded assumptions about support from the community. It seemed to her to depend on the situation and which 'side' of the community the police seemed to favour at a particular point in time: 'One minute they're offering you tea and a bun. The next they're trying to knock your head in'. Neutrality was a concept which the public at large, particularly in situations which generated heightened emotional response, did not appreciate. She took a view that there were enduring problems for the police in any multicultural society (which she saw Northern Ireland to be approaching). The public would never say of the police 'Well done'.

This same female trainee with multiple disadvantage – including ongoing hostility to her career choice within her extended family, being a lone parent whose own parents separated when she and her siblings were adults – made two recommendations for change in relations with the [Catholic] community. She felt that partnership would be promoted by police working in teams with the social services in order to solve social problems which lead to criminality or to help rehabilitate those who have broken the law. Her other remark, which was generally endorsed by her colleagues, referred to the positive effect which would result from Sinn Féin taking their places on the Policing Board, 'allowing not only increased recruitment of Catholics, but also potentially a greater measure of support for the PSNI from the Catholic community'. She was one of two who spoke most positively of the support given by Sinn Féin councillors to improving social and economic conditions. In her case she admired how they use their political weight to enhance special educational provision in her home area.

A striking aspect of the comment from the trainees was their propensity to refer to 'the public' or 'the community', knowing the tribal division. One can only surmise that this approach, inculcated in training, was intended to ensure that all citizens are treated in a neutral and equal way. They used terms such as 'Treat people fairly' and 'Accept people for what they are' as well as the more negative 'You'll never get everybody to accept the police'.

Two trainees, a male and a female, both from Republican areas used their Irish Catholic backgrounds as a lever to initiate dialogue with Nationalist communities in their respective areas. The male from Northern Ireland with just one year's experience in a Unionist town with a hinterland of Republican villages courageously used his knowledge of Gaelic games in trying 'to open things up'. When on duty in those areas he let his cultural background and sporting interests be known, in order to develop dialogue and acceptance of police. He pointed to the difficulty of his project by quoting a Catholic school principal who, having listened, said 'That's all very fine. But sure you're on *their* [British government's] side'. He reported, too, that Loyalists whom he encountered playing rugby tended to think that all police were Protestant and taunted him with 'Yis are afraid of the Fenians'. His female counterpart demonstrated her shared identity with Catholic children when doing duty in a Nationalist area of a predominantly Unionist town by writing and pronouncing all their names for them in Irish. She used her good standard of Irish learned at school in the Republic to establish rapport as a community police officer and to begin to break down barriers between the police and the community they served.

Lack of experience hampered the trainees' ability to make meaningful comment on interacting with the Catholic community, particularly since they had very restricted opportunity to deal with the public on an individual basis. While they were trainees even in the third phase – attached to stations across Northern Ireland – they worked in teams under the supervision of experienced officers whose judgement was likely to prevail in making decisions. They did, of course, share the experiences and perceptions of the Nationalist community towards police before they joined, so it should not have been difficult to empathise with Catholics from the two major categories. One category, Republican sympathisers, refused to give support to the PSNI because Sinn Féin refrained; whereas the other group, Nationalists, saw in the PSNI a new policing service supported by the Nationalist SDLP.

Conclusion

My snowball sample of ten trainees in the PSNI obviously differed from the two other groups because they had no experience of working in the RUC and all of them had fewer than two years' experience in the PSNI. Nevertheless they had responded to a call from a new PSNI, an innovation which followed from the Belfast Agreement and, more specifically, from the Patten Report.

Their biographical profiles clearly showed change in the backgrounds of Catholic police in Northern Ireland. Though strong in Catholic identity in terms of parentage and schooling, there was increasing deviation from norms of Catholic conformity in terms of religious observance, endogenous partnership and political views. The average age of the six males and four females was 28 years and they all have varied work experience, eight in the UK or Republic of Ireland and two in the USA. The oldest was born in 1970, so they had no experience of life in Northern Ireland before the Troubles. None was the child of police parents, though three had relations in the British armed services. Interestingly, two of the males had been brought up in Republican areas of west Belfast, yet they had deviated from the cultural norms significantly. Although a small sample, they represented a whole spectrum of family backgrounds, experiences and attitudes. Neutral in their political affiliation – even those from Republican neighbourhoods – four out of five in stable or prospectively stable relationships had non-Catholic partners.

A comparison between the numbers of serving Catholic police officers and trainees who fell into the four categories of my typology was instructive, as Table 2 in Appendix 1 shows. In the trainee group there were no flaunters provoked by a Unionist culture; there was a slight reduction in the size of the deserter group; there was one victim and the chameleon group had increased from 66 per cent to 80 per cent. In percentage terms the differences between categories are not enormous, though an increase in 'chameleons' and decrease in 'flaunters' is clear.

Although there were other chameleons in the group, I chose the subject of Vignette E to show that cultural Catholicism is a relatively fast changing concept. If one were, for example, to compare this trainee with Vignette A in Chapter 4, one could see major differences in aspects of religious identity in practice. Vignette A, just over twenty years senior to Vignette E and brought up in the same Republican area, had gone to the same Catholic grammar school and he, too, had spent some years outside Northern Ireland. The older man deviated from the 'Catholic cluster' norm in his attitude to the Masonic Order but his fidelity to the basic features of traditional Catholic identity were much more marked. The younger man used a selected aspect of his Catholic identity – interest in Gaelic games – primarily in an instrumental way to gain support for the PSNI and to assist in making it numerically representative of the Catholic community, as an alternative strategy to 50:50 recruitment which he deemed 'a necessary evil'. A noticeable feature of the data was the relatively greater ease with which the trainees were able to manage their identity within a police service still culturally unbalanced. A combination of confidence and a positive internal work environment appeared to explain this ease.

Part 2 examined trainees' motivation for joining and their aspirations within the PSNI, against a social and political background of uncertain support from the Catholic community and a negative historical legacy from the RUC. All ten trainees claimed to have chosen the PSNI as a career out of a sense of mission (some at financial cost). They saw an opportunity to do something worthwhile with their lives, in working to translate the ideals of the Belfast Agreement into reality. Half of the group also saw it as a career with prospects and three were attracted by the 'machismo dimension' fed by media presentation. The energetic advertising campaign conducted during the early days of the PSNI worked as a clarion call, not least to the two trainees from the Republic.

From their aspirations it seemed that they had optimistic plans for their career progression with only one adopting a wait-and-see attitude towards his accelerated academic success being translated into promotion. Tempered altruism promised intrinsic rewards which appeared to be of much greater importance to them than financial gain and no one complained about salary levels. In common with police around the world, as well as with their predecessors in the RUC, camaraderie was a prized reward, as was humorous banter which they felt would be kept under control by the parity of esteem which the Patten principles demanded. Already they were exercised by the tension between being Catholics and police officers, not least in the thought most had given to carrying personal weapons in particular neighbourhoods or on certain occasions. They realised that risk of death or injury and social isolation would remain challenges on the path ahead.

Bearing in mind the historical difficulties which the Catholic community had in relating to the RUC, the trainees' perceptions of that community were important to explore in the light of Patten's emphasis on establishing consent and compliance. The impressions they had formed were gleaned from their trainers, from a small number of experienced officers, including mentors, or from their memories as civilian members of the Catholic community. Especially those brought up in Northern Ireland were not optimistic about sudden attitude change towards police and realised that views were often conditional on policing decisions made at high-profile events.

They agreed that in any society police face enduring problems, but they were ready to make suggestions as to how relations with the Catholic community might be developed. The Irish language and Gaelic games were vehicles already being employed, while partnership with other service providers and especially Sinn Féin support for the Policing Board were seen as means to increase the speed of progress.

I return to the Patten theme in Chapter 6.

6

The verdict on Patten

Patten and the PSNI

In this chapter I shall present some of the differences and similarities between and within the experienced serving PSNI and the trainee groups on selected Patten recommendations and their implementation. The question is posed as to whether the classic features of that model, namely representativeness, policing by consent, impartiality, professionalism, transparency and accountability, can be achieved by the PSNI in a context of an uncertain political future.

The fifty serving Catholic officers were well positioned to comment since they had lived and policed through the transition from the RUC into and since the establishment of the PSNI in November 2001. They appraised in turn:

1. the process by which the Patten recommendations were implemented;
2. key recommendations identified as being the change in name, uniform and regalia; accountability; 50:50 recruitment; and
3. perceived changes still required to achieve a police service which meets the liberal model criteria for the first time in Northern Ireland's history.

Their perceptions will be interwoven with trainees' ideas and experiences, of necessity much more limited in scope without a comparable backdrop of service in the RUC.

The trainees experienced Patten recommendations in action and they spoke about topics on which they felt best equipped. These included their perceptions of how their training programme seemed to fit the post-Patten demands, their views on the potential of the Patten vision, together with understanding of the PSNI culture.

It was very noticeable that the more senior the serving PSNI officers, the more likely they were to view police reform in a strategic and balanced way. They were much more likely to stress the positive potential for change which Patten heralded than the junior officers who focused on the personal pain which they had suffered in the process of change. An officer at command level, a discreet flaunter with some chameleon qualities and likely to be promoted again, summed up what Patten was about. Drawing attention to the direct link between the Belfast Agreement and police reform he summarised the situation as he saw it:

The Belfast Agreement was the first opportunity for Catholics in Northern Ireland to become part of the state on a basis of consent and agreement. There was cultural dominance by Unionism, Protestantism . . . [Patten] is about power-sharing in policing. Fifty:fifty recruitment was a bitter pill for some to swallow, but it was the only way to address the cultural imbalance, to put equity into this arm of government. Confident, competent people are in the ascendancy in the PSNI. Policing structures are there.

He went on to highlight the feeble response of the RUC to a need for reform, which justified the British government's intervention:

The social contract theory was redrawn. This was imposed. Ronnie Flanagan looked at the RUC which was out of date and out of step with British policing and said 'We have to think differently. We've not gone there because of the Troubles'. Patten said 'Thanks, Ronnie. You've identified the changes that are needed, but we have to be more fundamental. You let us down once too often, boys. 1996 [Drumcree] was one mistake too far. Forgiveness was withdrawn by the Catholic middle class, Nationalist and Republican. We need to challenge the whole thing'. The police leadership saw nothing wrong at that time. We took the shit for seven or eight days. Then we changed and changed for good. The police leadership had buckled under political pressure from Unionism.

This officer's perceptive and succinct analysis acknowledged that internally generated reform was not enough and that urgent, coercive change was necessary in the absence of policing with consent from the Catholic community. His thorough approval of the philosophy and practices advocated by Patten was atypical of comment offered by a majority of his Catholic colleagues. The 26 per cent of senior and middle ranks seemed more capable than their juniors of taking a strategic view and seeing police reform as good news which they endorsed with enthusiasm. The junior ranks tended to praise the efforts of Ronnie Flanagan, their last chief constable in the RUC who seemed to symbolise for them all that was good about that force. This finding contradicted the usual suspicion in which junior ranks hold the 'bosses'. A Belfast man who had risen through the ranks, he appeared to be trusted across ranks.

I hasten to add that there was fragmentation within these two rank-based groups. For example, one middle-ranking deserter, though a stalwart supporter of the RUC, spoke for himself and less than one in three of the lower ranks by declaring that:

The heart and soul of the organisation has not changed. It is still about providing a police service. We have the same people, the same processes, the same structures. There was no practical reason for the change. It gives no assistance in doing our job.

He did not seem to grasp the fundamentally changed political context of policing and did not welcome the notion of irreversible change. Similarly, nearly 50 per cent of the junior ranks, while praising Ronnie Flanagan for his efforts to be fair and to welcome Catholics into the force, saw Hugh Orde, his successor, as the man for the time. One officer explained:

The RUC needed change. Although he was a good CC, according to Ronnie we could do no wrong. Hugh Orde is different. He says 'We do get things wrong. We could have done it better'.

A junior officer with one promotion and lengthy experience spoke for 26 per cent who believed that necessary reform would not come from inside the RUC. He said 'Patten was definitely needed. Reform needed an outside driver. They would have just sat on it. "If it's not broken, don't mend it" would have been the attitude'. My survey findings showed that whatever their length of service a clear majority agreed that there had been too much change, though almost a quarter of experienced Catholic officers felt there had been 'about the right amount'.

Even among those who welcomed Patten enthusiastically or acknowledged a need for reform, there was widespread criticism of the way the changes were implemented. 'Too much, too quickly' was a commonly expressed sentiment. The demise of the RUC was interpreted to have been deemed urgently necessary by the British government in the wake of the Belfast Agreement, to reflect the new power-sharing political arrangement. The criticism levelled was at the absence of sensitivity shown towards a force of men and women who had done their best according to their lights. Twenty-two per cent of officers used the word 'hurt' to describe either their own feelings or those expressed by colleagues.

Almost one-third spoke of the powerlessness of their position, their lack of autonomy when the PSNI was announced. One female officer summed up her feelings, 'The RUC had been found guilty – that seemed to be the impression. It was like a wake. There was a deep sense of betrayal at 9 November 2001' (the date when the changeover from the RUC to the PSNI took place). Frustration was expressed by a male colleague, 'We are pawns. We can blister and boil, but the government controls. They hold the reins.' Sensitivity to the demise of the RUC and its replacement by the PSNI caused 10 per cent to focus on one comparatively trivial feature of the handover. 'It was a bit rich', said one, 'having Hugh Orde signing certificates for officers retiring from the RUC, when he'd never served an hour in the force'. Catholic officers appeared to have been affected as strongly as any might have been, irrespective of their religious affiliation. Perhaps this commonality in response can be explained by the strength of police solidarity to which reference has already been made.

Of the 20 per cent of serving Catholic officers interviewed with fewer than 10 years' service, more than half, somewhat surprisingly, expressed loyalty to the RUC by stressing reforms that had been introduced before Patten and his team deliberated. One such, engaged in community policing in a country town assured me that 'Reforms were coming in before Patten. Human rights, equal opportunities – these aspects were there already'. However, two females contested this assertion. They accused both the RUC and Patten of having ignored their particular needs for crèche facilities or nursery vouchers. While they were keen to carry out exactly the same duties as male officers, including riot control and attendance at bar brawls, one pointed to ongoing male chauvinism in official policy, asking rhetorically 'When I was the only female in a party lying in a field for thirteen hours, where was I supposed to go to the toilet? What about personal hygiene? Nobody gives that a thought'. One wondered if the points raised by these two women might be of wider significance, by adversely affecting the recruitment of females who might consider the equal opportunities programme to be under-developed.

Over 80 per cent referred to the complex network of political relationships and sensitive interests which had to be served if the Patten recommendations were to extend and support the philosophy and promise held out by the Belfast Agreement. Only one said that he was impressed by the thoroughness of the consultation process, while three grumbled about perceived lack of genuine interest in police officers' views shown by Commission members. Almost 40 per cent saw the Patten reforms as the implementation of a sudden root-and-branch government policy for change in policing, one officer suggesting that both Flanagan's and Patten's recommendations were produced at the behest of government:

> Flanagan's reforms stemmed from political interference. He was told what to do. Patten did not come up with all those changes. He, in turn, was told what to do. Too much, too quickly has left the police in the mess we're in.

These officers' comments suggested mixed reaction to the sudden arrival of police reform imposed from without, adding credence to the belief shared by RUC retired and RUC/PSNI still serving that in Northern Ireland, policing is 'a political football'. However, a vast majority indicated their acceptance that root-and-branch reform was necessary in order to satisfy all the interests reflected by the power-sharing executive which gave politicians representing the Catholic community – both Nationalist and Republican – unprecedented parity with Unionists in the government of the province. A minority wanted to recognise reforming efforts that had been made internally prior to Patten. One of the most positive messages was the enthusiasm, or at least positive acceptance, registered by senior and middle ranks in particular. Lack of sensitivity in the way the reforms were introduced, particularly lack of recognition for service and sacrifice, seemed to be sustainable objections, though perhaps inevitable.

Patten and training

Changes of priorities and indeed of values in the policing service reflected in the training programme brought strong comments from the trainees. The various backgrounds from which they came, the life experiences they had in Northern Ireland and outside and the level of formal education which they had attained before joining influenced their views of the training provided in three phases. The first phase of twenty-one weeks was spent at the police college. A very recently recruited young man gave an account of his initial impressions. He commented, as others did, on

(a) the curriculum; (b) the trainers; and (c) his personal response to the training experience. He felt that the curriculum was right for males but very challenging for females in the level of physical fitness required. This observation raises the vexed question of how far equal (opportunity) means similar at a time when further developments are taking place to encourage women to specialise in greater numbers in traditional male areas such as riot control and weapon use. (In August 2009, more than 24 per cent of PSNI officers were women.) He considered role-plays were useful techniques for reinforcing and applying new knowledge and he enjoyed the homework set, which encouraged them to reflect on their life maps. Overall he thought there was a great deal to learn in the time allocated. Though he found the ambience militaristic, he described the trainers as being 'laid back'. He was confident that his Catholic school had developed his communication skills to a standard where he felt comfortable in contributing to discussion assertively.

A male and a female on their first day out of police college had greater experience on which to base judgements. The ex-Army trainee felt he was at an advantage over his colleagues in weapons expertise, though he felt that he 'was looked down upon by graduates', providing a weak whiff of anti-intellectualism said to characterise police culture (Brewer and Magee, 1991: 236). Whether this reflected a slight inferiority complex or an 'us and them' attitude I could not judge. Within the curriculum he believed that there was too much emphasis on what he described as 'watch your back'. A female graduate deserter and exact contemporary of his, who had enjoyed the physical education curriculum enormously, found the 'booby traps' lecture on the first day to have been rather insensitive, but justified in making officers' safety a priority. It contributed to the culture shock which she experienced in relation to the entire regime which she found to be very militaristic, reflected in the absence of civilian tutors. The PSNI admits that the civilianisation programme recommended by Patten has not progressed to a level projected. She also voiced detailed criticism of the curriculum content, teaching methods and standards of presentation.

Overall, while there was fairly balanced comment on the training programme and the atmosphere in which it was taught, individuals differed in their judgement which tended to depend upon their expectations and the backgrounds from which they came. For example, a female looking back from the third phase of training, found that by expecting the worst she could report that the regime in police college became better as time passed. Expecting 'boot camp', she found it less militaristic than that. Considering it 'the best training in the world' she admitted that much psychological stress resulted from 'being stripped down and built up again'. She suggested that greater emphasis should have been placed on 'people service' rather than on meeting targets, though the two aims are not mutually exclusive.

A graduate with professional training predictably found the sub-degree level course to be intellectually undemanding, objecting to the emphasis placed on information-giving at the expense of discussion. In contrast, a female from the Republic of Ireland knew what to expect – that it would be academically challenging for her, especially in learning law – but she welcomed the physically demanding aspects, enjoying the sport and being pushed beyond her comfort level. She also enjoyed being 'a foreign novelty' who could be completely open in her views, not constrained by the tribal division in Northern Ireland. One can easily accept that a problem arises in trying to pitch the curriculum to suit all in such a diverse group of students.

The seasoned civil servant in the group found that his views on training moved from negative to positive as he progressed through the phases. Of police college he said: 'They treated us like children for the first two weeks. There was too much emphasis on human rights'. He objected specifically to the emphasis which, he felt, favoured the public rather than the police. Generally he disagreed with the strong insistence on political correctness, though he found the second stage, lasting ten weeks, to be 'fantastic'. He approved strongly of the third and final stage of the two-year training programme, when they were closely supervised as they worked in teams on operational policing. He liked particularly how trust and confidence within groups was built up. His words gave a distinct impression that trainees were taken through gradual steps designed to progress them from dependence to independence, with appropriate support mechanisms to suit the stage they had reached.

Two other trainees were able to focus on their training as a prerequisite to meeting policing needs in the future and the demands of the public and of legislation. One, for example, found phase two of the programme 'a breath of fresh air'. Not knowing what to expect, he found the regime militaristic, though he thoroughly agreed with an emphasis on discipline in policing and on tuition in human rights law and application of it, in order to meet current demands in public scrutiny. Another concurred, explaining that the broad purpose of the training was:

> to try to get you ready for the future. This included getting used to and practising political correctness . . . There was a lot of box-ticking and 120 reports over twenty-one weeks but it made you reflective and that was good.

In a statement of mixed comment on her experience of training so far, the only one in the group who approximated to being a 'victim' revealed perhaps unwittingly what her main concern had been on joining. Brought up on a mixed housing estate in a country town, she said of the training environment: 'There was no sectarianism. Religion was not an issue'. This was a very important point not made by others who appeared to take neutrality for granted. She did, however, have criticism to make which identified her areas of discomfort, rather than an attempt to evaluate objectively. These criticisms included overzealous application of political correctness:

> It's all far too PC [politically correct]. Everything has to be neutral. Clean walls, and all that. They took down a photograph of the Queen making a presentation to a police victim that had his legs blown off. Objections were raised. It was just too neutral. The picture was put back up . . . You're afraid of what you might say. You're stifled and stressed.

She explained that the picture was restored to its original position by popular request from the mixed group who pointed out that it justifiably honoured an RUC officer and was not intended as a Unionist symbol. She also objected to the boarding school-type rule of curfew at 11.30 p.m., signing out and in, having to be in their bedrooms by midnight – and the bar being open only two evenings per week. On a more positive note she approved of role-play as a learning device and found the trainers in conflict resolution to be 'fluffy bunnies', implying that their style was not directive and they were not passing on 'hard' information but focusing on attitude change. She made a useful recommendation though in remarking: 'For me, there was a big gap in the training. There was no one to mentor me. There was a gap between book knowledge and reality'. The comment she made which, if significant, had serious implications was: 'People are political, so police are. Twenty weeks' training did nothing for some on the course. Some people just shut down and some move on'.

From the data provided by the group of ten it seemed that the training programme became more acceptable to the trainees as they progressed through the three phases. The comments revealed understandable ignorance which they shared at the beginning, though a persuasive large majority seemed to have enough confidence to ensure an open-mindedness which allowed them to make balanced judgements. The content of the programme must, inevitably since Patten, have provided for operational policing skills underpinned by the principles of neutrality and equality expressed in the form of human rights application and political correctness. The implications seemed to have been quite well understood by these trainees and they were not only very largely in favour in theory, but also in how they were applied in practice in relation to themselves.

One important impression which emerged was that the PSNI training staff were striving bravely to meet the demands made upon them by Patten, but had not yet quite made a satisfactory transition from the previous regime. Successful curriculum development requires time to achieve with regular evaluation and subsequent modification. At the period these interviews were carried out the PSNI was barely two years old. Training staff from the RUC days were providing continuity while having to absorb the implications of new legislation. By fundamentally changing the philosophical basis and restructuring the curriculum content within a very short time-frame, trainers were expected to turn out police officers who personalised the liberal model in what they represented and who they represented. A tall order indeed. Although seven of the ten trainees had worked in police stations for only twelve to eighteen months, their impressions of life in the PSNI outside the police college were worthy of capture. Was there a discernible PSNI culture already established across a sample of police stations which reflected Patten thinking?

PSNI culture
While, as discussed earlier, a minority of the trainees could not or would not have joined if the RUC had been retained, they were conscious of ex-RUC personnel

working with them and training them in the stations. All of the group had some knowledge of the RUC's reputation among the Nationalist community. It was important, therefore, to hear how they dealt with the negative aspects of the RUC's reputation, while rejoicing in being part of the PSNI, which was still in its pioneering days.

The newest trainee and the ex-soldier were positively disposed towards the RUC. In the first case because he had kept himself updated on the satisfactory experience in training of friends who joined before him; in the latter case because he had admired the RUC while he served alongside them in the province. He explained:

> I served in Northern Ireland from 1999–2001. I saw them police Drumcree very fairly to both sides of the community. It was a difficult job. I saw police on helicopter television carrying out crowd control. Bricks and spades being thrown at them. I felt powerless. I felt 'I must do this', but I didn't think I had what it took.

The graduate from a Nationalist city had been 'rescued' by RUC officers from an illegal taxi when, as a teenager, he was on his way to a golf competition. The officers drove him in a police car so that he would not be late. All three trainees above demonstrated that personal experience of a sample of police officers at work can have a very powerful effect in determining an attitude to police in general – whether the experience was positive or negative. This trainee, to whom I referred last was, however, hesitant to comment on specific aspects of the negative legacy. Wishing not to speculate, he said: 'I cannot comment on the legacy of misdemeanours. It's nothing to do with me. I'm not interested in CID or Special Branch'.

Of the remaining seven interviewees, five adopted a general attitude of forgetting the past while acknowledging, as one expressed it:

> There will be scandals in the PSNI as there were in the RUC. Don't stereotype the police. Jesus chose twelve apostles . . . I've not experienced any kind of misbehaviour by police – brutality, verbal abuse. There's been a lot of brain-washing by the media.

The reference to Jesus and the apostles was intended to convey that however carefully police officers are selected, a minority will fall short of required moral standards. Reference to misrepresentation by the media was also made by two other trainees, though one believed that collusion was a possibility:

> There will always be corrupt police officers in every police force in the world. I disapprove of corruption. I don't know if corrupt people in the RUC were protected, or not.

The ex-civil servant who would highly recommend the PSNI as a career because 'I love everything about it', acknowledged the possibility of a murky past, while being hopeful for the future:

> What happened in the 1970s and 1980s you hope is not happening now. It's embarrassing for the RUC, but not for the PSNI. From a human rights perspective, the RUC was not so well informed. Systems are in place now which will prevent similar happenings in the future.

The 'Westie' had the last word in realistically acknowledging the association in Catholic minds of past violence against their community and possible Special Branch collusion with Loyalist perpetrators. He had been a classmate of a murdered Catholic solicitor's son and had visited the victim's family home after the atrocity where he saw the bullet marks. Yet his philosophy was:

I cannot change the past, only do what I'm doing. Don't keep harping back. It changes nothing. We're at a watershed. Don't forget the past but leave it behind.

His words – an exhortation not to make capital out of past misdemeanours in order to feed mythology – belied the popular image of west Belfast Catholics. While some of the trainees acknowledged that 'The RUC had blotted their copybook', these PSNI members could afford to be generous because they were not under a shadow. Preference not to comment on or to disown the past showed confidence in a present and a future that were different. Since the PSNI was a new entity, they felt no obligation to apologise or accept even partial ownership of deviance by rogue elements.

Perhaps their positive outlook allowed them to think sympathetically of their colleagues who had transferred from the RUC. The trainees' comments reflected both appreciation and pity towards ex-RUC who had to accept such enormous change as Patten demanded within a very short time-frame. The brevity of their time in policing of necessity meant that the interviewees based their comments on police culture on social interaction with relatively restricted numbers of personnel. However, accepting this limitation on generalisation, the general picture which their remarks conveyed indicated that sweeping change had taken place. One detected little in the way of reservation about disadvantage accruing from their community background.

Females, in particular, felt sorry for 'these ordinary human beings' from the RUC, though they voiced appreciation too. One – from Belfast – had positive memories of RUC officers going into her (state) schools and organising sporting activities for the pupils. She said 'Old officers leaving is a great loss to us. Golden handshakes were a mixed blessing'. Another female – from a 'mixed' estate – expressed her views generously:

I've heard horror stories about the RUC. A lot of it was Republican bigotry. It's sad for the RUC who built up what we've inherited. They're doing everything they can for us, coming through. We're favoured. It's as if someone has died. They kept photos of their squads up.

A graduate from a mildly Nationalist background, chosen to represent the PSNI on a European television network, praised 'the most non-political environment possible', while a colleague declared: 'The organisation is trying to be fair, as balanced as possible'. Two females commented on the absence of sectarianism, one stating 'There is no sectarianism. Religion is not an issue'. A colleague from the Republic of Ireland was comfortable in stating: 'The three religions idea sums it up'.

A large majority of both retired and serving officers had acknowledged the

presence of sectarian banter in the police culture, while offering a variety of explanations. Eight out of ten trainees commented on the welcome presence of banter;
the remaining two did not refer to it. The male fast-track trainee from the Republic
stated: 'The sectarian banter is not offensive', while a female from Northern Ireland
declared: 'The religious banter is excellent'. The law graduate nuanced his comments:

> There's no sectarianism. You can differentiate between banter and venom . . . If I had
> a problem, I'd pursue it. Political correctness has to be put in perspective. This has all
> been far better than I expected.

Political correctness was found to be irksome, as it had been to the ex-RUC
officers. One described it as being 'restricting', while another rejoiced that 'PC-ness
is all very fine, but I'm glad that sometimes it breaks down'. Even a trainee from a
strongly Republican area who feared a 'them and us' division between the ex-RUC
personnel and those who were recruited directly into the PSNI found his reservations to be without foundation. On the contrary, he found the more experienced
officers to be very supportive towards the newcomers. Although he had not experienced any examples in practice, he confidently hypothesised that discriminative or
racist abuse would be dealt with 'in a flash'. The trainees' attitudes to banter and to
political correctness exemplify Fielding's suggestion (1988) that recruits tend to be
selective in identifying with those aspects of the sub-culture which they find acceptable, challenging the widely held notion that police subculture is an undifferentiated
whole. Furthermore, their attitudes may support the division of the subculture into
canteen culture and operational culture (Shearing and Ericson, 1991) – one being
the private social arena, the other where professionally trained police officers visibly
serve a demanding public, to whom they are accountable at various levels. There
may be little or no consistency in these discrete areas of behaviour.

Two from the group commented on one of the structural aspects which Catholic
RUC, particularly the retired officers, had found problematic. While they agreed
that they felt indifferent to the notion of Masonic Order members signing a register,
acknowledging membership, one went further. The graduate from the Republic,
although he was in the first PSNI cohort and had, therefore, little experiential
evidence, speculated that he would not dismiss membership of the Orders – particularly the Masons – as being insignificant. He voiced his reservations about the
potential importance in selection for promotion of 'a wink and a nod, or a phone
call by one Order member to another, asking "What can you do for our friend?"'.
As someone on the fast track for promotion, he probably would be able to test out
his theory before long in the transitional culture of the PSNI, since he had already
successfully completed examinations for inspector rank.

Image, accountability and Catholic representation

In order to focus the discussion, I invited views on three specific key recommendations which resonated with some of the sustained objections of the Catholic

community against the RUC. I refer to Britishness visible in uniform, name and regalia; lack of accountability to the community they served and of transparency and absence of policing by consent as reflected in low Catholic representation. Implementation of the Patten recommendations to meet these objections would obviously go a considerable distance to embedding the liberal model in Northern Ireland's police service.

Comments on the name change and image fell broadly into three categories – those indignantly critical of the betrayal of fallen comrades who served in the RUC and the forgotten 'noble history' of the force; those who felt insulted by the inferior quality or unsuitability of the replacement uniform and regalia; those who pondered the significance of the changes and what had prompted them. While some interviewees made knee-jerk reactions which suggested still smarting sores caused by personal disappointment, or rejection, or both, some of the same officers could combine emotional responses with reflective acceptance of change, as being a worthwhile investment for the future of the PSNI.

Officers from police families seemed to have great difficulty in accepting the name change. One officer enjoying early success at middle rank, with a brother in Special Branch, was clear in his view: 'It was an absolute disgrace. Just appeasement of Sinn Féin. My grandfather, my uncle, my dad all served in the RIC or the RUC. My heritage was suddenly done away with'. Allegations of government appease-ment of Sinn Féin were not restricted to officers from police families. Almost 50 per cent shared this feeling, explaining that this 'capitulation' to Sinn Féin caused much hurt, though about 30 per cent admitted that 'Catholics did not like "Royal" and "Ulster" in the name. But Sinn Féin wanted the change. That's where the hurt lay'. A very senior officer, enthusiastic about the future of policing, suggested that the combination of harp and crown had been misinterpreted and that the change was painful:

It was very difficult. There was a grieving process. The harp and crown were not a symbol of Loyalism, but a crude attempt to deal with different cultures. We were rub-bished by the change of name.

Twenty-two per cent referred with pride to the 'noble history' of the RUC. A sea-soned inspector explained:

They attempted to destroy the premier police service in the world. Our superiority over the Met and other English forces was well recognised. When we went to confer-ences they were jealous of the quality and style of our uniform. The RUC was a force in the UK and in the world. It had a noble history. Symbols were changed out of spite. The elegance has gone from the uniform; with it, authority and respect.

Enforced change of name and uniform was resented across all ranks and age groups, but those with longest service seemed to have a nostalgic attachment to the past. While criticism was widespread of the quality and appearance of the new uniform and crest, four younger officers acknowledged that the uniform needed to be updated for practical reasons 'to become parallel with other forces'. One reservist remarked that: 'Tunics don't lend themselves to jumping into armoured cars. Tunics are for standing in'.

The poor quality of the new uniform received as much criticism as the change per se, various pieces being referred to as 'rubbish', 'crap' – except the boots, which received general approval. Seven officers took offence at the new design on the grounds that the wearer could be confused with a worker doing an unskilled job, including a postman or a cinema attendant, while the PSNI 'strove, as had the RUC', said one, 'to become more and more professional in the way they carried out their work'. Fourteen per cent of the sample, in contrast to a larger group who stressed the symbolic nature of uniform, commented on the superficiality of appearance, stressing that if the changes in image were to enhance the chances of wider acceptance, it was a price worth paying. One argued: 'Just because you change a badge, a name, a uniform, you don't change what's behind it'. The officer who featured as Vignette C, a deserter, spoke for more than three-quarters of the sample who, initial response to one side, gave an impression that in the medium term and beyond:

> We must keep our ethical framework. We are all public servants. If we put that within our psyche and keep it there, these changes shouldn't matter. History and symbolism can look after themselves.

I was left with a distinct impression that if these physical alterations were to create an image of the PSNI which made the service acceptable across the board, the Catholic officers were very willing to make the sacrifice or pay the price, depending on the depth of feeling of the individual. However, there was strong nagging resentment that the changes could be interpreted as appeasement of their long-term enemies – Republican activists. Whatever their judgements about change in name and appearance, it was clear that the approach to their introduction was felt to have been coercive rather than persuasive.

In contrast, the trainees did not take the decision to join lightly and doing so implied acceptance of the new image. As I indicated earlier only two trainees voiced reservations about joining if the name had not changed from RUC. One would not have joined because to do so would have been 'counter to the Nationalist judgement' and the other trainee would have had a problem because in his native Republican area the RUC's activities were reflected in the word 'force'. The change to 'service' echoed what he wanted the PSNI to provide for the people there.

Generally there was indifference to the name change and the visible aspects of change. No one referred to emblems and only one to uniform. One female went so far as to say: 'They should have kept the name. It was sad for the RUC'. She would have joined even if the name had not changed. The ex-soldier, one of seven who had no problem with the name 'RUC', said: 'The name change was unimportant. A peeler is a peeler', while a colleague added: 'If there was a name change again, it wouldn't matter a wrinkle to me', perhaps missing the significance on this occasion. One supported the view of some serving officers that 'the new uniform is not professional in appearance or quality'. Females in particular, while feeling indifferent to the name change, regretted it only on behalf of the serving ex-RUC. One from the Republic sympathised: 'The majority have got over it. It's the end of an era. For the good guys it was sad. They lost husbands, wives, parents, mates. The RUC was their life'. She, together with the male Southerner did not seem to be burdened by personal bad experience of the RUC and was attracted to the PSNI for intrinsic reasons, irrespective of the RUC's history and reputation. This observation raised a question about 50:50 representation and the thought that Catholics recruited from outside Northern Ireland could contribute numerically to this statistical requirement. They would not be representative of the Northern Irish community, however, but of the universal Catholic Church, which varies in local presentation according to social, political and economic factors. It was probably unsurprising that having no sense of loss, but only of gain from the changes in name and regalia, the trainees had little to say on the subject.

There was clear indication that serving officers were keen to leave irreversible changes such as badge and uniform in the past and to move on to talk about other reforms which impinged more forcefully on their relations with the Catholic community and which held out hope for winning a higher level of consent from that quarter.

Response to Patten's main recommendations

Patten rightly addressed public accountability by the police in Northern Ireland as a justifiable key demand. One significant feature of Patten's solution was the appointment of the first policing Ombudsman in the United Kingdom. Seventy-six per cent gave her appointment unqualified approval, though two officers felt that the wife of an SDLP councillor, however suitable her credentials, was an unfortunate choice, leaving decisions made by her Office more liable to receive unjustified DUP criticism. A middle-ranking female officer with about ten years' experience expressed the consensus thus 'I'm happy that the Ombudsman's Office should be totally independent. If you're doing your job properly, why should it bother you? It probably keeps the public happy too. Win–win'. A colleague saw accountability as part of a reciprocal agreement: 'The public pay you, therefore, accountability is right. Help from the public is required in return'. A seasoned officer from outside the province went further by saying: 'The Ombudsman is a good thing. The best thing to come out of Patten. Investigations are clear, open, honest. Ombudsman staff do not treat police officers as criminals'.

The acid test of the way they are treated was perhaps best provided by the experiences of two officers against whom complaints had been made. A junior-ranking female graduate explained, 'I was on the receiving end after a charge of common assault was brought against me. I was questioned for an hour and a half. No further action was taken. That was fair enough'. She hastened to add, however, a downside to the provision of an Ombudsman's office:

> There's panic over human error now. Malicious complaints make people feel important and make us feel rubbish. Unfounded complaints are a good source of propaganda, of course.

Here she plausibly pointed out that Sinn Féin, still unrepresented on the Policing Board at the time of interview, could cause negative propaganda for the PSNI by drawing attention to the numbers of complaints made against it – however flimsy the bases for individual cases, or the outcomes.

A second officer, this time a young male detective, with an allegation against him still standing, preferred the post-Patten arrangement to internal investigations conducted by the RUC which he described as 'a tissue of lies'. However, he pointed to another negative aspect: 'I was abandoned by the PSNI. There's no legal aid for police officers. I'd have to pay for my own solicitor'. This lack of support from the PSNI for its officers seemed surprising, as though an opportunity was being missed to improve the image of the police by demonstrating the authorities' faith in their officers' integrity and observance of the law in dealing with the public.

Only 12 per cent of the sample felt that the public interest was being served at the expense of police officers. One rehearsed an incident when a chief superintendent visiting a riot site reminded participants of their rights, inviting them to make complaints if they felt they had been harshly dealt with by the officers who quelled the riot. The authorities' apparent fear of people power and corresponding insecurity visited upon rank and file members was a point brought up by victims in my typology. The female subject of Vignette D explained the implications, as she saw them, arising from the new emphasis on accountability:

> We've swung too much in the other direction. You have to watch your every move. There's someone waiting to pounce. A 19-year-old police officer's son complained about me recently. We're always watching our backs. There's less solidarity now. The job is traumatic since Patten.

She seemed to suggest that the protective cover provided by RUC internal investigations and solidarity with colleagues were preferable to the new accountability and transparency emanating from Patten. Ironically, in one important respect at least, she felt her life was less traumatic during the years of police deaths and maiming, than during the ensuing period of relative peace.

As I indicated earlier, Vignette D reflected the view of only a tiny minority of the interviewees. I was surprised, therefore, to hear an experienced sergeant say of others in general that 'the Ombudsman's appointment is seen by most police officers as a negative change, because they're still in the RUC mindset'. This statement led me to wonder if Catholic police officers welcomed Patten more than their non-Catholic colleagues, reflecting the Catholic community's general positive view of the Belfast Agreement and of Patten. Even so, there were some who saw Patten's recommendations as no more than a beginning to solving the broad problem of non-engagement by Catholics with the RUC. Identification of Catholic officers with co-religionists on accountability seemed a promising development.

The role of the Ombudsman's Office was not the only new feature to be mentioned which was designed to establish visible accountability. There was similar strong support from 30 per cent for the Policing Board and for District Policing Partnerships (DPPs), in principle, though the strength was modified by caveats attached by more than half. (The Policing Board and the DPPs were the fora established to make police accountable at central and local levels to elected politicians and non-politically aligned members of the public. Meetings are advertised and open to the public.) The main criticism levelled was that both fora were dominated by politicians who had not, as compared to the police, 'moved on'. The officer depicted as Vignette B, the flaunter, expressed this view succinctly but somewhat caricatured: 'In spite of the good intention, the Policing Board is just an Alex Attwood [SDLP] versus Sammy Wilson [DUP] contest', implying that politicians simply use the Board's meetings to engage in party political verbal abuse. A more common response, by a ratio of 2:1, however, was voiced by an officer referred to earlier who had, at the height of the Troubles in the 1980s joined an English police force but returned to the RUC four years later. Of the Policing Board and its chair he said: 'We give full support to Des Rea and what he stands for. It's genuine and not a political stunt'. Predictably, the most frequently voiced reservation about the Policing Board was with reference to Sinn Féin representation, the most serious result from their absence at that time being lack of encouragement to some potential Catholic applicants to the PSNI.

On this subject of accountability and transparency there was a tendency for senior officers to have, in the main, thought more about the potential influence on change which the Policing Board and the DPPs could have. A large majority of the lower ranks who commented tended to focus on the Ombudsman's Office because, presumably, they might be personally accountable to answer to a charge brought against their behaviour. The role and activities of the Policing Board and the DPPs were of greater interest to those operating at a strategic level who were able to put their own interpretation on the broader front of policing with the community, of which accountability is a part.

A very successful senior chameleon enthused about the new openness in policing and saw it operating at three levels:

It's been a great triumph for the Policing Board to get agreement from politicians on important issues. I'm a big fan of DPPs. They're not mature enough to be effective yet. Accountability brings transparency and puts local politicians in their place. They're given the facts . . . It's energising to invite people into my station to show them what policing is about. It's not just a game and it's fraught with risks. Local politicians are still playing politics . . . The mindset of officers had not changed since the early 1980s [when he joined] until Patten. Some are still hard to convince. In some ways account-ability has gone far enough, but I'm accountable mainly to myself.

This officer's contribution highlighted the fact that new structures can only facilitate change which must happen in the minds of people. He regretted that both politicians and some police officers were having difficulty in 'moving on' in order that our community could realise the potential benefits accruing from structural changes. He used his own experience of a case study where he grasped the idea of transparency and implemented it at station level, in order to establish rapport with Republicans in a predominantly Republican town. His own interpretation of com-munity policing, implemented before 2002, happily coincided with Patten's recom-mendation and led to signs of positive change:

> I got a public handshake from the Sinn Féin chair of the council whose brother was a hunger striker. He said 'No doubt we'll do business again'. He was referring to negotia-tions which opened up a 'no go' area to the PSNI. It was a reward for the pain.

His story suggested that if widely copied, new attitudes could be encouraged in the Republican community where the people had ceased to acknowledge that the police writ ran in their neighbourhoods. His story also underlined the crucial role playing by local politicians in promoting policing by consent and the importance of innovation and calculated risk taken by inspired senior police officers who, in some areas, need to be Catholic to succeed. (This officer was a 'deserter' though his name suggested strongly that he was a cultural Catholic.)

Proof of opposition to this type of innovation and associated risk was provided by an experienced, though junior-ranking, officer who commented on similar practice by his senior officer, this time in a Unionist town:

> I take great exception to having paramilitaries coming into our station for tea and sticky buns. They're a security risk, for one thing. It's wrong too. Deals are done. 'If you leave us alone on Bonfire Night [eve of 12 July], we'll not break Catholics' windows.'

When asked about Patten's emphasis on accountability and transparency, train-ees were much more vocal than on visible changes in image. Comments were divided between accountability in principle and personal reactions to its applica-tion, though the latter received most coverage. The ex-soldier and serious reader of Irish history agreed with accountability in principle but disagreed with Patten's interpretation of it. A minority of one, he stated:

> The police should not be brought through the courts. An internal enquiry should be held. Each case should be treated on its merits. We need a Special Branch to know what terrorists are doing. They should not be accountable to the public.

His remarks suggested that he had not thought through the implications of accountability in practice and the unsatisfactory reputation which internal enquiries had earned both in the RUC and the Army. It appeared that his socialisation in Army discipline and lack of transparency proved to be transferable into the PSNI.

A female, who consistently wanted to put the past behind, doubted that there was a great need for onerous structures to ensure accountability and transparency since all police were well versed in human rights legislation. A negative feature, she found, (noted earlier in discussion of police culture) was the encouragement given by present arrangements to the use of the confidential telephone and 'touting on colleagues'. While admitting that deviant police should feel the full rigour of the law, she saw the Ombudsman's Office as being administratively inefficient.

The ex-civil servant concurred with colleagues who stated that: 'The full rigour of the law should be applied to bad cops'. However, he bemoaned the emphasis placed on investigating the behaviour of police officers as opposed to the public, for example, by the use of digitally enhanced videos. He found an unfortunate pairing of high expectations from the public with the complaints which they generated, leaving the police with no support from compliant higher ranks. He was unequivocal in his belief that: 'The police should always have been transparent', adding though, 'It is an operational necessity to have Special Branch and some degree of unaccountability'.

The least experienced of the trainees, only weeks in police college, had already absorbed the anxiety felt by some PSNI officers and presumably conveyed by the emphasis on human rights legislation within the training programme. He found Patten's demand for transparency to be threatening to him personally. He explained that in many situations police officers have to make a decision in a split second 'but the system will treat him harshly and it'll all be magnified. It's frightening at this stage to think of "the goldfish bowl" syndrome'. While agreeing in principle with the idea of accountability, three trainees did not wish to engage on discussing its application. Two simply observed 'There will always be corrupt police in every police force in the world' and 'There will always be criticism of the police' as justification for accountability. A third trainee would not comment on the pretext 'I'm not senior enough to comment on accountability or transparency'.

A female from a county town balanced her support for accountability by reiterating a complaint made more mildly by others that 'The Ombudsman's Office is very harsh. Even if false allegations are made against you, she'll go through you for a short cut. There's not enough human rights for us'. She also bemoaned the enduring effect which one deviant act by a small number of police can have across national frontiers, citing the Rodney King case in the USA, where a group of white officers were caught on video camera beating an Afro-American man mercilessly. 'We'll never hear the end of it', she said. A graduate from the Republic resented 'having more resources spent on investigating us, rather than on investigating others'. One of the trainees from west Belfast supported the Patten innovation on the grounds that:

> If you've nothing to hide, what's the problem? I'm in favour of complete transparency within reason. Even SB should be accountable. It's a force within a service. The Sneakie Beakies have a culture of secrecy. You don't know what they're doing. There are those who don't toe the party line.

Perhaps the latter words were spoken by a trainee influenced by the reputation which Special Branch had earned in his native Republican area and reinforced by his acceptance of experienced colleagues' views of working alongside that specialist unit in the RUC during the difficult years of the Troubles.

In general, it seemed that the trainees would have needed more experience of practical policing before making informed judgements about the Patten demand for accountability to the public in order to win legitimacy and partnership. They were aware of the discipline which it imposed on their behaviour and which was more likely to cause division than solidarity. Their utterances suggested fear of its personal implications for them when they came out of training and had to take decisions as professional police officers.

The subject of my research being Catholic participation in the policing of Northern Ireland, I sought the views of this sample of Catholic officers on one of the most crucial and highly controversial provisions of Patten. This recommendation constituted a bold step – that the PSNI should engage an external agency to select police officer recruits on a 50:50 Catholic: non-Catholic basis, in order to enhance substantially the proportion of Catholics in the PSNI from a baseline of 7–8 per cent. It was argued that a service which was numerically representative of the population was a prerequisite to achieving consent and compliance. Over 80 per cent of serving officers agreed that the idea was good in principle, as an outworking of the power-sharing spirit enshrined in the Belfast Agreement, though difficulties in achieving the objective were identified. The weight of opinion of the remaining minority objected to the discriminatory nature of the new arrangement. A mid-ranking officer who, though an unusual 'deserter' in that he had joined a Protestant church, voiced his strong feelings in this way:

> It's unfair, admittedly discriminatory. It's intended to redress a blatant imbalance, but that blatant imbalance was not the fault of the organisation, although it gets blamed for it. Rejectees are demoralised. What is the point of having human rights and equal opportunities legislation if it's flouted?

The three objections summarised implicitly in this quotation – discrimination in legislation, recruitment always having been open to Catholics in the RUC, rejected Protestant applicants feeling bitter and alienated because they did not have Catholic 'partners' in the cohort – were the most commonly expressed criticisms of the 50:50 policy, though there were variations on those themes. Some seeing the policy as discriminatory also found it embarrassing in that the Catholic community had consistently complained about being discriminated against and they, Catholic police, were guilty by association with this new reverse version. Four officers feared that in time it might be thought that Catholics with lower standards were allowed in, in order to meet the target numbers. One young constable confessed: 'I'm worried about the type of recruit that might get in. If one was bigoted or stupid, I'd be seen as a member of the same "club"'.

A graduate colleague, born in the Republic of Ireland, was more forthright:

> I'm against it [50:50]. I'm here because of my abilities. It might be demeaning in years to come. If you're in the pool, selection should be merit based. I agree with Cardinal Conway's philosophy that a police officer's religion doesn't matter. What matters is that we act fairly.

The implications of how the selection system worked were criticised by 12 per cent, even by 8 per cent who agreed with the policy in principle. Specific points raised included the length of time that applicants were kept on a waiting list before they were given a definite offer. Equally, they found it an inefficient system which required applicants to fill in forms, sit examinations and tests three or four times even though they met the requirements on their first occasion, because unequal numbers of Catholics and non-Catholics had qualified for one cohort. Said one: 'The stress and pressure of the waiting time are unnecessary. Think of Catholics who have told some of their family who might not be in favour of it, anyhow. "Rejected?" – "I told you so!"'.

It was, however, more usual for Catholic officers to quote actual cases of Protestant candidates rejected than the hypothetical situation alluded to in the last quotation. In particular they sympathised with unsuccessful full-time Protestant Reservists anticipating disbandment in 2005–6, whom they considered worthy, since these Reservists were heavily relied upon in some areas where large numbers of regular officers retired in 2002–3. By 2009 numbers of full-time reserves (FTRs) had decreased gradually but strong political pressure is still being put on the British government not to abolish them completely.

Five of the interviewees questioned the wisdom of precise numerical representation per se, contending that it would most likely not be achieved because the political context was not conducive. One serving in a northern Unionist town explained:

> As an idea it's commendable, but we're in a political vacuum. Why not 60:40? Young people who would have joined the RUC anyhow are joining now. Middle-class Catholics are coming in. Just more from the same backgrounds. We'll always get people from Coleraine and Ballymoney, but what about Twinbrook and Crossmaglen? [strongly Republican areas].

The second more important point made here about the areas from which recruits were likely to come was a recurring theme which brought conflicting views. By a ratio of more than 2:1 the interviewees perceived a decision by Sinn Féin to take up places on the Policing Board would give a green light to men and women in Republican areas to join. They felt that the interest was already there, but 'permission' was required in order to protect themselves and their families. Strabane and Lenadoon in west Belfast were mentioned by officers who said they had relations there very keen to join 'but not while their families would suffer'. While positive signs of increased recruitment from Republican areas were assured by just over one-half of the interviewees, a slightly lower fraction felt that the PSNI would continue to depend upon 'the sort of Catholics that always joined'. A small minority of less than 10 per cent seemed, without saying so specifically, to hope that this restricted recruitment base would continue in a self-selecting way, as they feared the implications of ex-Republicans being admitted. The same sort of reservation was voiced by 12 per cent about increasing numbers of civilians being employed by the PSNI on the grounds that the IRA were still engaged in intelligence-gathering and they feared security leaks, either voluntary or under duress, by people from Republican areas. It did not seem to occur to them that similar objections could be raised in relation to police and civilians from Loyalist paramilitary areas. The traditional anti-Republican RIC and RUC mindset, though not strong, was still traceable and provided enduring evidence of the strength of police solidarity.

An interesting point was made by two officers – one born in England, another born in a northern port town and from a seafaring family. The latter expressed his point strongly, 'Catholic recruits have to be Northern Irish by birth and upbringing. If they have an English accent or come from an Army background, they're no better than Unionists'. They both said that birth and upbringing in the province were prerequisites to understanding the public which the police had to serve, but that a perceived Nationalist background, whether pale or deep green was necessary in order to have credibility with the Catholic community. Ironically, perceived political affiliation seemed more important than shared religious community background, according to this tiny minority of two, who may simply have felt outsiders from both Northern Irish communities.

'It's a worthwhile goal, but you don't get it in any country', was a remark made by an officer who supported the 50:50 principle, but considered it to have many attendant problems. He summed up the general attitude of the interviewees – since even those who opposed it did so on grounds of the embarrassment it caused, that it implied positive discrimination or that it was impractical. None questioned that it was a commendable attempt to establish power-sharing reflected in policing.

The third and final of the Patten recommendations affected the trainees directly in the sense that they were all recruited in accordance with a 50:50 Catholic:non-Catholic policy to make the PSNI representative of the total population in the foreseeable future. Comments on this most controversial recommendation covered a wide range from 'an excellent idea which isn't working' to 'a necessary evil'. A comfortable majority had said that they would have joined even if the name had not changed from RUC to PSNI. A similar weight of majority found fault with the 50:50 scheme. Their reservations centred on two features – reverse discrimination and poor timing.

The graduate from the Republic who described the policy as 'an excellent idea which isn't working' went on to explain:

> Catholics are warned not to join by Sinn Féin. The time is not ripe. People are afraid of retaliation. Sinn Féin coming on the Policing Board is hugely important in one to two years time. The floodgates will open for Catholics from middle-class Nationalist backgrounds.

A male from a northern Republican area agreed that the innovation was politically inopportune and so obstacles to recruitment remained, requiring determination to overcome them. 'Individuals need to be strong enough to join', he said. The importance of Sinn Féin being on the Policing Board was stressed by a large majority with reference to Catholic recruitment, which showed a constant awareness that there was still strong pressure on Catholics not to join.

Five interviewees found the 50:50 policy to discriminate against Protestants. A female indignantly explained her objections:

> I'm tired of Catholics and the 'poor me' syndrome. It's not justified any more. I find 50:50 embarrassing. It's reverse discrimination. It's reinforcing division which we're trying to get rid of in a polarised society. We live in a multicultural society now. I didn't join to increase the numbers. I can't accept religion and policing being mixed in this way.

Dissatisfaction with police reform for having gone too far was not, however, shared by the Catholic community. A total of 77 per cent in 2003 said either that it had 'not gone far enough' or was 'about right' (NILT, 2004). My survey results showed corresponding figures of 29 per cent of respondents with five years' service or fewer and 35 per cent if they had longer experience. The figures just quoted for serving officers referred to implementation of the Patten proposals in general. However, I conclude that if 50 per cent of trainees objected to the key recommendation, for 50: 50 recruitment, their loyalty to co-religionists is suspect, that they are keen to forget past debts to the Catholic community, in order to make a fresh beginning, favouring recruitment on merit, irrespective of cultural background.

The idea of accepting people on grounds of religious affiliation was widely frowned upon, even though the trainees knew full well that successful applicants had to meet at least minimum standards over a range of criteria before being selected, whatever their community background. They could not argue that 50:50 policy properly implemented by an external agency would reduce standards, but it did make it possible for strong Protestant candidates to be rejected or to have to reapply if numbers of Catholic applicants were low. Four trainees expressed regret that 'long-serving and competent' members of the FTR were being rejected (partly because they were overwhelmingly Protestant in numbers). Not only was it embarrassing but also it was 'alienating people and breeding distrust'. They feared that a sectarian split between Catholics in the PSNI and still serving FTRs awaiting redundancy might occur, through no fault on the part of either.

There was complete agreement that selection should be on merit, irrespective of religion. It should be 'the best person for the job', according to the least experienced trainee who questioned if the policy was human rights compliant. A graduate disapproved of community background being mentioned on the application form, expressing discomfort at the combination of apparent discrimination and apparent fairness which a 50:50 policy reflected. A related point made by two interviewees stressed a shortage of recruits from ethnic minorities and a need for an energetic targeted recruitment campaign to attract them. One of the females noted that out of 300–400 people at the training centre there was one Chinese woman representing all the ethnic minorities in Northern Ireland.

Only two interviewees gave their views on the perceived eligibility of ex-prisoners becoming police officers. One from the Republic was adamant that ex-prisoners should not be admitted:

> Ex-prisoners as police officers? They had no respect for the law then, why should they have it now? The public would have no confidence in our impartiality if we had ex-prisoners on board.

In contrast, a female of local origin raised no objection and justified her stance:

> Sinn Féin was let down by the British government over decommissioning. That's why we have to wait for Sinn Féin to come on the Policing Board. Then we'd get an influx from places such as Twinbrook [in west Belfast]. Ex-prisoners? OK. If they shot a police officer twenty years ago? Well, the same sort are already in government.

Fear of death or serious injury to themselves and fear of retaliation against their families, already discussed, emerged clearly as perceived deterrents to the potential success of the 50:50 policy, though as indicated above, they tended to focus on less obvious features of it. One from a Republican area saw some Catholics coming in from his neighbourhood 'but not quickly enough'. He placed the blame for needing such a policy squarely on Republican paramilitaries, though his 'Nationalist friends saw it as a new, fresh start'. An additional deterrent was a fear of Loyalist opposition to police in general. From a group of ten friends who applied at the same time, only he was selected. This poor strike rate would suggest that his status as a civil servant compensated for Republican geographical place of origin in winning security clearance and that, in the first few months of PSNI, applicants' postcodes might have affected their chances of initial selection.

Change still needed

The serving officers were very clear that there were further downsides to the Patten reforms which, in their opinions, centred around management of the PSNI as an organisation and the effects of downsizing on service levels. Little, if any, thought appeared to have been given by the government's architects of reform to the likely response from officers who had been plucked from the RUC and, literally overnight, been thrust into a new organisation intended to bring liberal policing to Northern Ireland for the first time in its history. Demands from the public in keeping with their new expectations regarding service in the form of response to calls, accountability and transparency were the most commonly felt reasons for complaint from officers. An experienced junior officer in a northern coastal town explained:

> There should be accountability, but not number crunching. Figures can be played around with. A murder enquiry and common assaults are all assaults. Three hundred cannabis users and one heroin dealer – are they comparable?

He gave examples of a widely voiced criticism that practices from the business world were imported wholesale into an occupation where the product is service and cannot be measured simply by numerical targets. A young female deserter at mid-rank, though with fewer than ten years' service, complained:

> The job is not what it used to be. I've never been more stressed than since the PSNI started. We're just hung out to dry by the authorities, even though the superintendents are not available to advise. They're remote, three floors up, writing reports. But then, so am I. Here writing a report, while my team are out on the street.

The core problem touched on by officers quoted above is the tension between accountability to the government and the public via the NIO, the Policing Board and the DPPs, and autonomy for the PSNI in deciding on purely professional policing matters. Quantitative data can be communicated and presented in easily digestible form to non-specialists, whereas professional judgements made in trying circumstances leave greater room for interpretation with political bias. Decentralisation and accountability – though positive features of the liberal model – do not come without cost in a divided society.

The decision by the Patten Commission to encourage officers with service in the RUC to take enhanced pensions was very widely criticised by about 80 per cent of the sample. Only a small minority saw it 'a timely opportunity to get rid of the dinosaurs'. Many quoted evidence of the devastating effects on staffing levels of Patten's aim to rid the PSNI of officers who had joined before 1995. 'In my current station', said one mid-ranking chameleon, 'forty-three per cent went in eighteen months. It was politically driven, too', implying that this encouragement to retire was another example of appeasement favouring Sinn Féin, who wanted all traces of the RUC to be removed as soon as possible.

Reduction in numbers of the total service to 7,500, partly by gradually disbanding the FTR, was seen as a rash, bad judgement. It put the PSNI in an impossible position, in that the public expectations of this new, trumpeted crack force could not possibly be met, especially in the area of community policing which was likely to be a strategy for achieving policing by consent. According to one disgruntled ex-Army interviewee, 'It's all about finance. We can't plan for eventualities. When I go to the DPP meetings, I tell no lies about what the police can offer – none of the boss's fairy stories'. Another officer explained that in his opinion morale was low among front-line officers because response times were not good enough to satisfy the public and again accountability 'steals' personnel. He named a county in which there were six response officers and fifty working in offices. 'Nobody believes in the police any more. They can't do their job', he added.

The most senior Catholic officer I interviewed, an ex-choirboy and ex-altar boy whose father encouraged him to join, expressed a timely view of management which seemed not to be shared by others of similar rank. Focusing on officers' need to be appreciated after all the change, his opinion was:

> We're now in this different place. Our management skills should show appreciation of what our people have been through. Let's be good to them. Let them feel good about themselves. But the wider organisation is not switched on to this need. We must engage with our officers and they'll engage with the people. It would be an investment.

The effects of poor management and sudden, extreme downsizing suggested that not enough emphasis, if any, had been placed on the change process itself, though the reforms appeared to have been thoroughly researched and then comprehensively included all the main characteristics of the liberal model. It seems reasonable to assume that maximum change will take place within the PSNI only when officers have inspiring leaders; competent, confident managers; and the motivation and energies of all have been harnessed towards achieving agreed aims and objectives. According to the officers in my sample, progress had been made undoubtedly, but it fell far short of achieving what one seasoned officer described as 'a vision that will take twenty years'. His timescale was rather longer than those of the ten officers who suggested that between five and ten years would pass before the PSNI dream would become a reality.

I pondered the impact of the possible restrictions which the shortcomings discussed above might have on Catholic recruitment. I have come to the view that however aggrieved the officers felt about the seemingly insensitive way the reforms had been introduced, in time the difficulties would be seen as mere teething problems which would be forgotten – as one officer said: 'Police officers gripe and whine – but they get on with the work'.

Conclusion

The general reaction from the fifty respondents who had served in the RUC and transferred into the PSNI to Patten's radical reform proposals was positive, though there was a variety of caveats. They saw reform as necessary in order to realise the potential implied in the power-sharing Belfast Agreement. Divisions in opinion were sometimes seen between senior and junior ranks, or between chameleons and flaunters as opposed to deserters and victims. The more mature and/or more senior in rank made a balanced judgement, approving the strategic approach and comprehensive policy and structures provided by Patten. Seniors tended to be involved in applying the policy and appreciated fully the potential for positive change which it provided.

Of the 20 per cent of lower rank and those with fewer than ten years' service, more than half had restricted 'vision' and tended to apply a test of personal comfort in making their comments. The complexity of the political interests to be satisfied was generally recognised but a sizeable minority focused on the hurt they felt when the RUC name and image were suddenly removed. Deserters chose to praise the 'old values' of the RUC and the contribution to reform of the last chief constable and his senior team, the credit for which, they alleged, went to Patten. Seniors, though they paid due tribute to Sir Ronnie Flanagan's efforts, recognised them as not going far enough.

An interesting point emerged in terms of the typology. Even among the deserters there was marked enthusiasm for the changes which had been introduced. They saw in the PSNI, perhaps, whether established as a sop to Republicans or not, a huge opportunity to win the gradual consent of the Catholic population. One sensed they felt that the vehicle had arrived on which they would travel back from the wilderness of alienation to re-engage their own community. There was in contrast quite widespread criticism of how admittedly good ideas had been hastily introduced and, to a lesser extent, of how they worked in practice against officers' interests.

Accountability to the Policing Board, the Ombudsman's Office and DPPs was seen by some as acceptable and reasonable 'if you've nothing to hide'. There was criticism of strong political representation on the Policing Board and the DPPBs. The first incumbent in the role of Ombudsman was found more acceptable as time passed, particularly as she demonstrated fairness in judgement. There were plentiful objections to the manner and speed with which PSNI structures were set up and experienced officers paid off, in a process deemed to be coercive, rather than persuasive in the way it was introduced. Many of the objections raised were to be expected while the reforms were initially bedding down (at the time when the interviews were conducted) but the general welcome accorded the principles of accountability and transparency was encouraging. One plausible objection to the application of modern management principles in an organisation where the product was service seemed sustainable. For example, the effects of downsizing, an aspect of efficiency, and target setting, places undue emphasis, it was felt, on measurable outcomes and report writing. Most important for promoted but inexperienced sergeants and inspectors, superintendents were not available to guide and advise because they were occupied by administrative tasks demanded by accountability. A very important and undesirable effect of downsizing was that inevitably poor response rates would feed criticism that the service was not effective and unworthy of support. Policing by consent would not be helped by unmet public expectations from the Catholic community. Most of the problems raised by downsizing were likely to be shared with non-Catholic colleagues.

The introduction of a 50:50 recruitment policy was of great significance to Catholics and to Catholic police. Whereas some non-Catholics, for example Unionist politicians, saw the innovation as contrary to equal opportunities legislation, the Catholic population saw it as a rightful attempt to redress the balance. A difficulty unresolved at the time of interview was Sinn Féin's refusal to be represented on the Policing Board because the policing function had not been devolved to the Assembly. Seen by Patten as a prerequisite to consent and compliance by Catholics, 80 per cent of the interviewees were enthusiastic about the new basis for recruitment. However, they found personal embarrassment in its apparently discriminatory provision. Preference was for selection on merit, which is built into the system but concern was expressed at the possibility or even perception of lower-quality Catholics being admitted. Significantly, over half felt sure that Republicans would join if 'allowed' to by Sinn Féin, while slightly fewer thought that Catholic officers would continue to come from predominantly Unionist towns. Importantly, as a group these respondents were optimistic that the PSNI would become a representative service, but estimates about the time it would take for Patten's dream to become reality ranged between five and twenty years.

Were the optimistic judgements of this larger sample corroborated by the views of ten trainees whose only policing experience had been in the PSNI and who, when they joined, realised they were choosing an organisation intended to be an example of the liberal model in action in a divided society? In general, their attitude was one of open-mindedness towards the negative aspects of the RUC's reputation. There was admiration for the RUC because they had satisfactory encounters with police while they were civilians or, in one case, as a soldier serving in Northern Ireland. Others were dismissive, suggesting that there will always be some rogue officers, that the media distorted the RUC's image, or simply that they were not in the RUC and couldn't comment. Their focus was on the future and their positive attitude allowed them to speak generously of their colleagues who had transferred from the RUC. They appreciated the guidance they, as trainees, were being given by those who had not been offered or who had not accepted early retirement payments. Comparison with the sectarian culture of previous years brought positive comment on absence of religious bigotry and a large majority welcomed good-humoured banter but not political correctness, which they found restrictive. Only one remained wary of the influence which Loyal orders might wield in selection for promotion; a large majority were indifferent towards registration of membership of the Masonic, Orange or any other of the orders.

The generally positive reports given of the PSNI culture were not repeated in the respondents' views on training. Mixed comment was not surprising since their backgrounds were so varied and the college curriculum was, of necessity, tightly packed within a twenty-one-week period. Comment suggested that the programme was designed with the Patten principles in mind. Human rights obviously permeated all aspects of the curriculum, and the teaching and learning were organised in accordance with best educational practice. Although much information had to be presented and assimilated, there was considerable emphasis on role-play, discussion and opportunities for reflection and personal engagement provided by the materials used and exercises set.

Objections of various kinds were inevitably raised to some aspects, including a militaristic ambience, too much emphasis on human rights legislation and its application, curriculum content and standards of presentation, and absence of mentors and of civilian trainers – which seemed a reasonable criticism. Those who had left the police college thoroughly enjoyed the supervised operational policing, seeing it as striking a satisfactory balance with 'book knowledge'. Some of the criticisms of the college programme seemed idiosyncratic and typical of students in general. Overall, it appeared to be a thoughtful response to Patten's demands and a reasonably balanced approach to preparing the trainees for their careers.

Of the three main Patten recommendations on which I invited comment, the change in name and symbols drew least response. Seven out of ten had no difficulty with the name 'RUC', while the only remark made about the new uniform was its allegedly unprofessional appearance. Sympathy, however, was offered in generous measure to the serving ex-RUC, focused on the deaths and injuries which members had sustained and their sense of loss and lack of appreciation.

In contrast, trainee respondents were very vocal on the principle of accountability, but more so on its application. One extreme view was given by the ex-soldier whose military training he did not appear to have shed, favouring internal enquiries to deviant police being brought through the courts. General approval of accountability was voiced in that it was felt all should be amenable to the law, though allowances were made for Special Branch, seen as requiring a form of accountability outside the mainstream. A number feared that the emphasis on accountability could work against them personally, by encouraging malicious use of the confidential telephone by colleagues. It was felt that the cards were stacked against police officers in that their human rights were less protected than those of criminals. High public expectations would generate complaints against police and the Ombudsman's Office was seen as a threat. In developing these attitudes they were possibly influenced by ex-RUC personnel.

It was noteworthy on the subject of accountability but also in relation to the Patten package in general, that the strong chameleons from Nationalist and, even more so, from Republican areas adopted an approving, pioneering stance. They seemed to have great belief that the PSNI would work for them and for enthusiastic, honourable police officers who 'had nothing to hide'. Those from Unionist areas were more likely to assess accountability in accordance with how it might affect them personally.

On the third and final, though very significant, of Patten's recommendations, 50:50 recruitment, there was a wide range of comment. It obviously impacted on all of them, since that system of selection had applied in their case. Criticism was made on two grounds – reverse discrimination and inauspicious timing, which obstructed success. There was widespread disapproval of selection by religious affiliation, ignoring the system which covers a range of criteria. Some feared it would lower standards, while there was loud regret expressed that it worked against the selection of the mainly Protestant FTRs, for whom redundancy was planned in tranches by 2008. There was a suggestion that community background should not appear as a question on the application form and there was a difference of opinion on whether or not ex-prisoners should be admitted. Objections on principle aside, it was felt that the failure by government to win Sinn Féin's agreement to serve in support of the PSNI was the biggest obstacle to much larger numbers of Catholics applying to join. Once that problem had been overcome, it was thought that the potential for increase was enormous and, according to the two trainees from west Belfast, as well as others from Republican areas, applications would flood in. They did not appear to anticipate any significant threat from dissident Republicans.

The lasting impression left by data from the trainees was one of excitement and promise. They had thought deeply about the step they had taken and felt that they were pursuing a worthy career in which they would serve the whole community. Their lives before joining showed them to be flexible and open-minded to new experiences and challenges. The PSNI seemed to have the potential and an appetite for incorporating all that is best in modern liberal policing. The prospect of increased representation from Republican areas heralded the arrival of myriad variations on the 'cultural Catholic' theme, testifying to identity being a fluid and changing concept.

7

Looking back and looking forward

Introduction

In Chapters 2–6 I have presented data from: (a) a survey of 300 Catholic officers serving in the PSNI and qualitative data from (b) a snowball sample of ten retired RUC officers; (c) a self-selecting sample of fifty serving officers who transferred from the RUC to the PSNI and who completed the survey; and (d) a snowball sample of ten PSNI trainees. My aim was to elicit from their experiences, opinions and perspectives, collectively stretching back over nearly sixty years, data on (a) their biographical backgrounds as cultural Catholics in Northern Ireland who chose policing as a career and the strategies which they used in order to manage their dual identity in a non-Catholic work environment (b) the main factors internal and external to policing which have historically prevented numerical representation by Catholics in the RUC and (c) the Patten reforms as a radical attempt to establish a culturally representative service for the first time in the province, thereby testing the viability of a liberal model working across a divided society.

In this conclusion I shall summarise the findings from my semi-longitudinal study which bear directly on my research questions tracing respondents' subjective realities across time in changing social and political conditions. I shall, too, in reflexive mode consider, with the illuminating benefits of hindsight, the comparative strengths and shortcomings of my research, tentatively estimating its residual worth. Third, I shall attempt to speculate on the likelihood of further progress towards replacement of a neo-colonial model of policing Catholics by a liberal one and by identifying outstanding inhibiting factors. Finally I shall briefly consider the exportability or otherwise of the Patten model for police reform.

Data findings

What kind of Catholics were they?

Catholic police officers were (and still tend to be) the children of traditional Catholic parents who brought them up to be devout Catholics and who sent them to Catholic schools. A change was discernible over time, though, in a number of ways, in keeping with changes in wider society. Retired officers had married and remained with Catholic wives; about half of serving officers had non-Catholic wives/partners, with a small number in second relationships; recruits in stable relationships were with non-Catholic partners and three had parents whose marriages had broken down. It should be noted that in the Catholic community, respondents to NILT surveys have shown a constant figure of about 80 per cent saying that they would not mind a close relative marrying someone of a different religion (Lennon, 2004: 3). This finding suggests therefore that the high percentage of Catholic police officers with non-Catholic partners should not be presented with a problem on that account from their families, in a large majority of cases.

Political affiliation being one of the strong cultural identifiers in Northern Ireland, one of the ways in which Catholic police differed from their co-religionists (according to my survey results) was the declared political affiliation of their families. They emerged as being moderately or mildly Nationalist. A contrast was struck, however, with the recruits of whom two came from strong Republican family backgrounds. A striking feature of the recruits' profile was the speed at which those from west Belfast, for example, accepted the declared traditional police culture in political outlook by adopting a neutral stance, even cynicism towards politics and politicians. Unlike most older officers, though, a minority could openly declare an identification with Republicans, acknowledging Sinn Féin councillors as formidable pressure groups targeting solutions to community problems. This declaration would not have been possible years ago, as their loyalty to the RUC would have been in grave doubt. This identification with Sinn Féin is a measure of change within the police, that such would be considered acceptable.

The increased professionalisation of policing was reflected in the officers' and trainees' level of formal education. The younger the officers, the more likely they were to have benefited from education beyond the statutory school-leaving age, particularly from university education. None of the retired officers had third-level education, but 40 per cent of serving officers interviewed held primary or Master's degrees and 50 per cent of trainees had successfully completed third-level courses. One of the most striking findings was the united support from all samples for integrated education, even though a vast majority were too old to have benefited from it themselves. Even the retired officers, arguably more likely to hold traditional views, enthusiastically endorsed the notion of children from all traditions being educated together. They saw in integrated education a powerful force for social change and a strategy whereby cultural division could be inhibited, at least. However, this preference did not imply widespread criticism of Catholic education. Quite the contrary, it was praised for its academic rigour, though aspects of the Gaelic culture which some schools promulgated presented problems for a minority of officers and their children.

Accompanied by this groundswell of support for integrated education was an unmistakeable message coming from the high numbers of their children who attended non-Catholic maintained schools, making them quite different from other

Catholics. This phenomenon seemed to make two points: first, the decision might have been influenced by the large number of serving officers with non-Catholic partners and second, the officers lowered their children's profile and gave them predictably more comfortable daily lives than they might have endured in some Catholic schools. Their police parents' occupation might have provoked hostility from fellow pupils or from adults in the area.

Keeping a low profile and consequently protecting personal safety motivated not only choice of schools but also choice of family residence. Catholic police lived in mainly Protestant and mainly middle-class areas, a preference based partly on advice from Special Branch. So, in a province where education has historically been segregated, Catholic police stood out as a subgroup acting contrary to most Catholic and Protestant parents in supporting integrated education where possible and contrary to most Catholic parents in sending their children in some instances to state schools. They also chose to live outside Catholic areas.

The most fundamental aspect of Catholic identity, participation in collective Catholic worship, was a practice on which Catholic police over a sixty-year period of service showed themselves to have changed drastically. From retired officers who were regular worshippers there was a huge drop in Catholic religious practice by serving respondents and by the subset of interview volunteers. Of the ten trainees, four said they practised regularly, though of those two stressed that their religion was a private matter. The others tended to combine indifference to worship with selecting a non-Catholic partner. The officers and trainees showed themselves to be heterogeneous in origins, attitudes and behaviour, the latter provoked by stimuli in their work environment which required responses.

I must conclude that as generations of Catholics joining the police have succeeded one another, their Catholic identity as traditionally interpreted has weakened markedly. Within the wider Catholic community in Northern Ireland there have been similar liberalising trends, especially in relation to religiosity and choice of schooling, but the pace of change would seem to be faster in the case of Catholic police. Particularly, the trainees gave a distinct impression that their Catholic identity was ascribed at birth, but that it was a fluid, changing concept which, in its practical manifestation, was contingent upon circumstances. One must, however, be wary of unqualified generalisation of findings which are limited in this instance by the size and non-random nature of the sample.

Managing Catholic identity

Their work and community environments inevitably had a strong influence on the quality of these officers' lives. Obviously, the retired officers with an average service record of thirty years and the serving with an average of seventeen years had a wealth of experience from which they could support and illustrate their views. In contrast, of the trainees only seven had any practical experience of interacting with fellow officers other than trainers, and they had very limited exposure in the community either. Nevertheless, the trainees were clearly influenced by the police culture as mediated by their internal contacts and by their own life experiences – for example, being brought up in Republican areas, being in contact with police before joining, or having gained work experience in civilian or Army jobs inside Northern Ireland or outside.

Probably the most interesting bodies of data which emerged from this piece of research reflected the interaction of political and social context with policing and the effects of police reform on Catholic officers and trainees. Police officers are products of the communities from which they come and are likely to reflect their dominant values. The internal culture was identified by survey respondents as predominantly 'British', 'welcoming to Roman Catholics' and 'neutral', the official culture being less alien to Catholic officers than the unofficial culture. Testimonies by the Catholic police I surveyed and interviewed left no doubt, however, that RUC culture included a number of features which created serious difficulties for them. In spite of reluctance to acknowledge its presence by a large minority of the survey respondents, sectarianism emerged on closer inspection to be a significant feature of the canteen culture, though it was also present, particularly in the pre-1969 era, in the official culture.

Structural difficulties identified include the undue and potent influence which the Masonic Order and to a lesser extent the Orange Order had on officers' promotion prospects and on their duty rosters. This abuse resulted from RUC identification with a Protestant Unionist state. Membership of both these organisations, especially by senior officers, signified this identification. Data from the trainees, however, indicated that these orders were of only marginal interest and no longer a conspicuous feature of the PSNI landscape. A register of Notifiable Organisations has, however, been collated in order to enhance transparency, particularly since police membership of the Masonic and Orange Orders has long been a cause of discomfort to the Catholic community. Membership has been perceived as being in conflict with the rhetoric of neutrality and impartiality claimed by the RUC.

The ever-present possibility of sectarianism being visited upon Catholics provided a wealth of data showing how they managed their cultural identity in the RUC. Various explanations or excuses were used to explain away or reduce the importance of sectarianism, some officers turning a negative aspect into a positive feature by suggesting that banter of this nature was a form of 'easing' that was welcome. Even the trainees joined this chorus in opposing the strong emphasis which human rights legislation and ethos placed on political correctness in their day-to-day interaction with colleagues.

Support for the regular RUC from the 'B' Specials before 1970 and from the RUC Reserve and Army personnel since then aggravated the difficulties which Catholic police faced. Sectarian attitudes towards the Nationalist community by the 'B' Specials and predominantly Protestant RUC Reservists, especially in border areas, together with widely publicised insensitive behaviour by soldiers in Nationalist and Republican areas, darkened the image of Catholic officers by association in the eyes of their co-religionists, who did not differentiate between subsets of the security forces. The officers' response was to stress the support which they said the RUC received in the form of cooperation and low-level intelligence-gathering, particularly in Republican-controlled areas. Most were convinced that the Catholic population wanted to support them, but that fear of the IRA or misleading Sinn Féin anti-police propaganda alienated them from their community. The trainees did not share these experiences and saw their Reservist colleagues in a positive light, regarding them as supportive to beginners. They had sympathy for them as twice victims of Patten's recommendations, namely to downsize the Service and to recruit on a 50:50 basis. Adverse circumstances entirely outside their control clearly reinforced for retired and serving officers a sense of isolation from their own community far beyond the 'normal' sense of isolation shared by all police (Cain, 1973; Waddington, 1999). Trainees sensed both types of isolation – from civilians generally and from the Catholic community also – even those in the early weeks of their training.

There was general disapproval, indeed disappointment, expressed by a large majority of all categories of interviewees at the painful lack of support which they experienced from the Catholic Church hierarchy. One cannot judge if withdrawal from the Church led to criticism of it, but the data would suggest otherwise. Even the most faithfully traditional strong Catholic officers, retired and serving, were able to judge the Catholic Church as an organisation wanting in support for them. Notable exceptions were seen to have been Cardinal Conway, Bishop Filbin and Father Faul. There was consensual acknowledgement that bishops and parish clergy were obliged during the Troubles, as at any other time, to offer unjudgemental solace to the bereaved and to carry out funeral rites for both victims and perpetrators of violence. However, heavy criticism was voiced at the absence, with few exceptions, of proactive and vocal condemnation of terrorist activity rather than resounding silence, whether the reason was fear of repercussions from the IRA, from elements within their flocks, or tacit empathy. There was fairly balanced evidence showing that individual clergy gave either support on the one hand, or implied or voiced criticism of Catholic police on the other. They viewed the officers at one end of the spectrum as Catholics trying to do an unenviable job, or at the other extreme they perceived them as representatives of an illegitimate British presence causing suffering to fellow Catholics. Catholic clergy were represented as carrying out a pastoral role in the lives of their parishioners rather than acting as community leaders. This approach allowed them to avoid coming into direct conflict with Sinn Féin and the influence which it exercised over their flocks. This perceived abdication of responsibility as leaders did not raise Catholic officers' hopes that their clergy would encourage Catholics to join the PSNI while Sinn Féin remained outside the Policing Board. Encouraging signs of fruitful cooperation between police, clergy and community in dealing with crime are increasing.

An example is included later when I discuss a variety of initiatives which have been taking place in community policing.

The unsympathetic attitude of clergy was graphically detailed by some officers who bitterly described how their children were ostracised in some of the leading seminary schools, often on sports fields, because their fathers were police. On occasions, the direct sources of hostility were fellow pupils from Republican families who projected their spleen sometimes in anonymous ways. The trainees had no such harrowing tales to tell, because none had police fathers or mothers.

Interviewees tended to hold strong views about their relations with the lay Catholic community, often insisting that the police had a great deal of silent support from people too scared of the IRA to show it overtly. Those who served in Republican areas, especially along the border, spoke of the good relations they enjoyed with the locals, who shared intelligence when they dared with the RUC, though not with the Army. Reference was also made to the victimhood of Catholics living in Republican areas such as west Belfast, who were not only a prey to IRA intimidation, but also to sectarian Protestant police who demonised even young children and made no effort to gain respect or support from 'decent' Catholics. The fickle and unpredictable nature of Catholic community support was often attributable to contrasting policing tactics during quiet and violent periods when the style alternated between 'ordinary' and paramilitary.

In spite of some political progress, Catholic police and trainees were mindful of ongoing threats to their personal security from armed dissident members of the IRA, although decommissioning by the Provisional IRA has since been recorded (IMC Report, April 2006). This threat had caused continuing widespread fear among retired and serving officers about attending Mass in churches where they might be recognised, or in socialising in unfamiliar company or surroundings. In spite, however, of weekly briefings on the security situation, individual trainees made their own choices about carrying personal weapons on all or only on selected occasions when off duty. The trainees were fearful of death or injury caused by dissident Republicans, but defiance was part of the response made by some who, nevertheless, needed to manage ongoing threat.

Joining and remaining

Catholics were a very small minority of the RUC since a marked decline in the 1920s and this situation was still true at the inception of the PSNI. It was central to my piece of research to find out the reasons for these unlikely men and women deciding to join and make careers in policing. Identification of the types who succeeded might help in a search for more. Their reasons for joining and remaining were worthy of investigation at interview, since my survey had indicated that substantial hostility from family and peers had been obstacles.

It was a persistent feature of serving officers and trainees that, even in the case of those who had immediate family support for joining, there was an element of anti-police feeling within their extended families, from relatives with Republican sympathies. Although some respondents to the survey were reluctant to detail the seriousness or the duration of the opposition, the interview data demonstrated that family and peer opposition, sometimes taking the form of lasting alienation, might in less determined breasts have dissuaded them from joining. Saddened, but determined to resist pressure to leave, they were obliged to stay away from family social events, though some accepted police protection to attend parents' or siblings' funerals. Some did not tell their family where they were stationed, but met on 'safe ground'. To this opposition in principle must be added, of course, more widely felt concern for the officers' and for their families' personal safety. Officers serving after 1969 in particular had to keep a low profile, yet be vigilant about car and household security and make careful judgements about when and where they should carry personal weapons. Their children had to be briefed about answering telephones, doorbells and, in many cases, they attended non-Catholic schools where they were less likely to receive attention on account of their police parentage. The officers were vulnerable while discharging their daily duties, or while socialising, being staked out as 'traitors' by the IRA. While family opposition and vulnerability to physical threat are likely to have reduced since the Belfast Agreement, these disincentives to joining are still real for PSNI officers and trainees. The murder of Constable Stephen Carroll in Craigavon in March 2009, while responding to a call for help from a householder, is a cold reminder of a continuing threat.

The main reason given for joining has not changed since the retired officers' time. Catholic officers and trainees said that they grasped, in effect, an opportunity to give paid public service. Career progression was of lesser importance to a majority of the older officers than to the trainees, who felt that they were in a new policing context since the Patten changes, which would facilitate their potential contribution to bringing peace. Data suggested that those who achieved promotion would be even better positioned to determine the nature and scope of innovative contributions, since the arrival of the PSNI. Opportunities had been opened up among serving officers for mid and senior ranks of cultural Catholic officers to identify creatively, yet apply judiciously, new strategies to win respect, enlist support and begin to police in partnership with those of the Catholic community who were keen to exercise the public responsibilities which parity of esteem had brought.

In spite of the formidable discouraging features to which the trainees were alerted during their initial weeks in police college – and of the challenging hostile context in which policing had to be carried out – Catholics in the service spoke persuasively of the personal rewards which their work brought. Most important, and consistent with internal police research, the camaraderie which they enjoyed seemed to dwarf in significance the social isolation typical of police which characterised their lives. This isolation was and still is much more marked than in any comparable liberal democracy.

Response to Patten

History, unfavourable internal conditions and external factors of a political and social nature conspired to keep the number of Catholic police at a minimal level, relative to the proportion of Catholics in the population. This poor level of representation was identified by the architects of the Belfast Agreement and acknowledged by the Patten Commission as a seminal issue to be addressed in their Report. The Patten recommendations, translated into legal terms by the Police Act 2000 brought radical and controversial change in policing philosophy, structures and practice. Changes in name and symbols, in accountability and in community representation were the three aspects of Patten's liberal model on which I focused in my research. Was Patten 'good news' for Catholic police and those who might aspire to join? Responding to this question retired officers could view Patten in their capacity as interested civilians. They were obviously at an advantage, though, in having had lengthy work experience in the RUC which they could use as a knowledge base against which they could test the recommendations. Serving officers enjoyed an advantage in that they had pre- and post-experience of radical change. Trainees had inside knowledge of the PSNI only, though they had useful comparative material on which to draw, as 'children of the Troubles' and members of the Catholic community policed by a predominantly Protestant RUC. A minority of the trainees from outside the province had watched media portrayal of the RUC public order policing, while one had an additional perspective as an ex-soldier who had served alongside.

Survey respondents had approved of Patten in principle but objected overall to the introduction of change being 'too much, too fast'. It was inevitable that perceived resistance to change within the RUC ensured that the British government chose the 'decree approach' (Greiner, 1965) or 'coercive change' (Bennis, 1966) as mechanisms, rather than attempting negotiated change. Imposed change in any organisation brings criticism of aspects of the change – often as they are perceived to disadvantage individuals – even though staff agree with the broad principles. Serving officers or recently retired from senior ranks contested the authorship of the reforms and gave credit to the last Chief Constable, Sir Ronnie Flanagan. There was general agreement that the Catholic community's consent to policing could be won only if the service was perceived to be neutral, depoliticised and representative of the whole community.

Complaints were voiced on each of the three main recommendations. The name 'RUC' was one of the greatest disadvantages which burdened the force in the eyes of Catholics and if cross-community progress were to be made, a new service had to replace a dishonoured force. There was marked difference in attitude to the change of name and insignia between the hurt expressed by many serving officers and the response voiced by trainees, whose regret was focused on that hurt felt by their supportive colleagues who were inducting and mentoring them in their early weeks and months in the PSNI. Some officers, who had served in the RUC, accepted the need for a change in name and symbols to make it acceptable to Catholics. However, they were hurt because the change implied that the RUC was dysfunctional and unappreciated, in spite of the hundreds killed and thousands injured during the Troubles. Human rights legislation came in for strong criticism from serving officers and trainees. In its application it was seen to favour civilians over police officers. Internal contradiction in their attitudes to accountability was shared by the two groups. They agreed in principle that police should be accountable for their actions but mixed comment was made about the role of the Ombudsman in their lives. There was strong minority support that some aspects of policing, especially intelligence-gathering, should not be accessible to public scrutiny. In regretting the passing of autonomy and self-regulation they showed solidarity with police in general, but it was noteworthy that some of the trainees showed themselves to have been quickly socialised and sharing a typical police mindset of 'them and us'.

The 50:50 recruitment policy was seen, as Patten intended, as a means of redressing the balance in community representation. However, trainees in particular saw drawbacks. These critics expressed a preference for recruitment on merit, irrespective of community background. Some saw it as a form of reverse discrimination, a source of embarrassment when Protestant friends were rejected. There was concern, too, that the policy would send out an untruthful message that Catholics with lower entry standards would be accepted to make up quotas.

The essential difference highlighted by data from the trainees, as compared with data from serving officers, lay in the ordinariness of the complaints they made against treatment by the authorities and of isolation from the people they served. There were no complaints as in earlier times of offensive sectarianism shown by non-Catholic colleagues or by training staff. Even if latent sectarianism remained, the official culture demanded that it was not given overt expression. Catholic trainees showed undoubted confidence in the effectiveness of the complaints system, should they need to invoke it. The confidence was demonstrated in their approval of balanced, good-humoured sectarian banter rather than political correctness which prohibited it.

The general attitude of trainees conveyed optimism, satisfaction and belief that they had chosen a rewarding though challenging career in which they would make a valuable contribution to public life as competent, professional, fair and cross-community police officers. Thirty per cent of the trainee sample were born outside Northern Ireland, which showed the effectiveness of PSNI recruitment advertising in Britain and the Republic. This broader recruitment base increased the heterogeneity of the mixture. In addition, recruits reflected social changes in their attitudes. They left a distinct impression that they were in control of their lives, usually quite highly educated and able to choose from a variety of possible careers available to them. They also spoke of the positive and welcoming culture of the PSNI with its emphasis on diversity and tolerance, while they made perfectly clear that if conditions were less favourable, they would resign. The formation in recent times of associations for women police and for gay and lesbian police illustrates this trend towards liberalisation.

It was hoped that their experience cautiously reported back to selected members of their community would encourage like-minded Catholics to join, though Sinn Féin's lack of support would continue to delay such potential progress. By maintaining this stance, Sinn Féin emerged as having a very powerful influence on the level of support coming from some elements within the Catholic community and, therefore, on the numbers of Catholics offering themselves as applicants. In the meantime, the trainees were conscious of sharing the Patten dream of a new future in policing a new Northern Ireland. They were, perhaps, more realistic than Patten in recognising that it could not be achieved within a short time because the success of a liberal model of policing is premised on assumptions about social and political context which are at a considerable distance from being met.

Reflection on research methodology

Before I draw back from my data and try to estimate their significance in the broader context of social and political Northern Ireland, I must look critically at the research methodology process in order to establish their value. On the positive side I gained privileged access to a highly sensitive organisation to research a category of people never studied before. My data were limited, however, by contextual factors influenced directly by the 'hidden' identity of my respondents – Catholics in a predominantly Protestant organisation who did not want to draw attention to their cultural identity. A response rate of 46 per cent to my survey was disappointing, as was the number of nil responses. Some of those questions enquired about their rank, the level and duration of opposition from family and peers to their choice of career and the level of hostility which they endured from sectarian colleagues. Reluctance to participate seemed to stem from fear of identification and unwillingness to break a code of secrecy, a strong feature in the image-conscious police culture which seeks to present a united, positive front. Understandably, there may also have been resistance to rehearsing the pain or embarrassment which their choice of career brought them. Easy identification of these issues by the survey analysis achieved exactly what the entire survey was intended to achieve. That purpose was to highlight areas to be pursued at interview.

On the other hand, a 46 per cent response rate should be applauded, as internal survey rates in the RUC had brought response rates of 25–30 per cent, according to my liaison officer who facilitated delivery of the questionnaire. The respondents were self-selecting as with all surveys and the percentage who chose to write open comment indicated a promising level of interest, borne out by volunteering to be interviewed. I have no idea of the identities of non-respondents or how, or if, they differed from respondents. It would have been very satisfying to have found a sample of people who had served in the RUC but had resigned, either voluntarily or otherwise and their reasons for doing so. However, their testimonies may have been contaminated by bitterness and alienation. The people I surveyed became volunteers when they responded and agreed to an interview, but I might have found instead sycophantic parrots of the official discourse, which would have provided a less interesting, less varied and less believable story. Some, particularly senior officers, who resented Patten's perceived lack of appreciation of the RUC's achievements appeared defensive about accusation of collusion with Loyalist paramilitaries by rogue elements, or the activities of Special Branch. There were no blatant propagandists, only those who positioned themselves within a turbulent era of policing and reflected a shared mindset.

Heartened by the discovery that there was a sample of sufficient size willing to proceed, I was not irreparably daunted by having to abandon the idea to hold focus groups or to tape interviews. Determination and resilience brought a solution to the latter problem which simply required creation of a private system of shorthand, which caught the spirit of the interaction and of relevant data, and facilitated recording of exact quotations. Looking back, I think that even contemplating the use of focus groups was a naive notion prompted by planning an ideal triangularised research design, rather than a realistic appraisal of the constraints operating in the PSNI – an organisation sensitive both internally and externally. The officers could be sure that the compromise arrangement precluded the possibility of anyone deliberately, or by default, obtaining a record of their voices discussing their private and professional lives and using such information mischievously. Even though I could not build up rapport leading to trust as strongly as in an ethnographic study in the field, this sample gave me permission to make notes as fully as I wished and they did not ask to see them or to have them read back.

I was not able to find large samples of retired officers or of new recruits for different reasons. The retired had 'disappeared' into civilian seclusion and it would have taken an impractical investment of time to prize out more. On advice, I submitted a brief article for publication in an internal newspaper circulated to retired officers, appealing to those from the Catholic community to volunteer for interview. The article did not appear. I suspect it was the victim of an editorial power struggle. I settled for ten retired officers whose service stretched over a sixty-year period. I decided that when I had reached a similar number of trainees, a satisfactory 'before and after' balance had been reached to provide historical continuity and to complement the major sample of fifty who could provide experience of serving in both the RUC and the PSNI. The retired may from a temporal distance have viewed their years in the RUC through slightly rose-tinted spectacles, but I found a willingness to engage dynamically in discussion and to position their stories in political and social context. Deeply held views were spoken by them in strong, even acerbic terms. The advantage derived from including the PSNI trainees was their inability to speak from experience about serving in the RUC, so they brought a freshness of approach and novelty of perception to the data which made distinctly different contributions to answering the research questions.

Finally, the overview which I take of this piece of research shows it to have been a worthwhile small-scale project investigating a sensitive topic in a sensitive context, which constitutes a minor, though significant, contribution to police research. Reflexivity has been exercised throughout the process trying to ensure that the data is trustworthy. I concur with the conclusion arrived at by Brewer (2000: 142) commenting on his ethnographic study of the RUC:

> that tenacity, toughness and single-mindedness are important when undertaking sensitive research – so is the possession of a certain balance and pragmatism that helps researchers avoid over-reaction to specific problems at the time; the travails can be worth it in the end.

The future of Patten and the PSNI

Moving my focus firmly from the past to the present, and especially the future, I shall cautiously speculate on the chances of Patten's dream coming through in the uncertain context of Northern Ireland.

Progress and problems

A necessary precondition for making judgements about the future of the PSNI is to survey its achievements in its short life, in spite of an uncertain and unpromising political context. It can be clearly seen that the PSNI is implementing 'policing with the community' in a variety of ways which include projects specifically targeted at Nationalist areas where joint efforts are being made involving police and locals to solve long-standing problems of mutual concern, but which could not have been tackled until street violence subsided. One such collaborative effort is 'Operation Clean Up' in west Belfast. It includes representatives from the NIO, the PSNI, the Fire and Rescue Service and the Vehicle Licensing department. It is a long-term partnership initiative to reduce car theft, domestic burglary, robberies and vehicle arson. In the 2005 Community Policing Awards staged in the USA, 'Operation Clean Up' won the runner-up prize. Judges praised the PSNI campaign for 'the meaningful change that can occur when law enforcement officials and their communities are empowered to utilise all available resources for crime prevention' (Magill, 2006). Most significantly, arguing for further development of such collaboration, a local Catholic parish priest commented: 'Among other things, it has helped people in the area to see, at first hand, the positive effects of policing in response to community needs' (Magill, 2006: 4).

Recommendation by Patten (16.10) that police recruits should be educated in part on university premises alongside civilians has been further developed in the form of a specially designed postgraduate qualification for all detectives, achieved by study at Queen's University, in *Law, Policing, the Investigation of Serious Crime and Work-based Learning*. Importantly, representatives from gay, lesbian and ethnic minority communities make input, since homophobic and racist crime receives special attention. The two initiatives to which I have referred are a small sample which supports the contention that the PSNI is acting to work in partnership with all the people they serve. The knowledge and skills acquired during the long years of civil strife in Northern Ireland are appreciated in trouble spots abroad facing similar difficulties. For example, a PSNI chief superintendent was appointed head of the European Union Peace Mission to the Palestine Authority, continuing work which he had done earlier in Gaza and in the West Bank.

However, at mid-2009, a political storm blew up when it was revealed that Libya had received assistance from senior PSNI officers while the Lockerbie bomber was in prison and later released on health grounds. Whereas a generally positive spin can be put on the PSNI's legacy from the Troubles in its application abroad, a negative legacy inhibits the pace of progress which it can achieve at home. I refer to the annual ritualistic displays of division in our society. For example, during the annual marching season the Unionist and Nationalist communities, especially in flash-point areas, clash in exercising their perceived territorial imperatives. Nationalists try to restrict the routes used by the 'outsiders' to pass through their areas, while Orangeman proffer a civil rights argument as defence. In recent years Orange Order marches in west Belfast celebrating the Protestant King William's victory over the Catholic King James at the Battle of the Boyne in 1690 have attracted most media attention. Republicans express their triumphs and their sacrifices on anniversaries of the Easter Rising against British rule in Ireland, 1916; internment of Republican activists, 9 August 1969 or the death in prison of the first hunger striker, Bobby Sands, protesting against withdrawal of political status from Republican prisoners, May 1981. Old sores are reopened by celebration and by condemnation of foolish decisions taken by the British government against their community. On such occasions historic prejudices and unwillingness to accord mutual parity of esteem are visibly demonstrated, often in violent fashion. The PSNI is, therefore, inevitably involved in public order policing, often using technology and tactics reminiscent of paramilitary policing. Their often split-second operational decisions can unfortunately provide long-term rhetorical resources for more extreme politicians on both sides. Problems arising from the presence of violent supporters and the inability of the Parades Commission to make legal determinations on supporters mean that the police cannot win.

Many months spent in building up community relations in an area can be dashed in minutes providing, for example in west Belfast, fuel for negative propaganda. The chief constable illustrated (*Irish News*, 24 August 2004) a consistent policy of Sinn Féin to undermine the PSNI 'playing us as the old RUC' (even though Sinn Féin have taken their places on the Policing Board, their councillors are vigilant in monitoring the behaviour of police at riot schemes, frequently accusing the PSNI of being heavy-handed).

Demands by the Catholic community on the PSNI, supported by Sinn Féin since they joined the Policing Board in 2007, to bring more criminals to justice are also thwarted by sporadic violence of dissident Republicans who generally call themselves the Continuity IRA or the Real IRA. They seek to continue the armed struggle against British presence in Northern Ireland, using familiar means – shooting police and soldiers, orchestrating shows of armed strength at funerals and road roundabouts, and placing real and hoax bombs at carefully selected locations such as railway lines. Realising but regretting the problems faced by some Catholic would-be supporters of the PSNI in helping to produce evidence to bring criminals to court, Sir Hugh Orde acknowledged:

> Fear is the key. It's how you break the cycle. Communities and police together can beat it. They can beat it tomorrow. We need communities to work with us and to be vocal, to stand up – which is a big ask.

Although the name changed from RUC to PSNI, the current service cannot shed the historical link with its predecessor whose record of misdemeanours is ever present. Twice postponed, publication of the Report of the Saville Enquiry into the Bloody Sunday events is expected in the spring of 2010, eleven years after it began. Accusations of RUC collusion with Loyalist paramilitaries are legion, not least in the findings of Sir John Stevens, and among the 1,800 'cold cases' (unsolved murders) currently being investigated by a special corps of officers to bring 'closure' for victims' families. It would seem that whatever the level of effort made by the PSNI to meet the demands of the Patten Report, translated in modified form into legislation, the RUC legacy burdens the service like an albatross.

The Belfast Agreement was welcomed by many with optimism, fired by belief that rapprochement was possible after nearly thirty years of strife and Direct Rule since 1972. However, the implications of the compromises necessary in order to translate promise into reality may not have been anticipated. Initial euphoria for the new beginning presided over by Tony Blair and Bertie Aherne dissipated as local signatories and their voters came to terms with the implications of what they had done. Old enmities re-emerged as traditional intransigence, particularly by the largest parties.

The fact remains that differential constitutional allegiances in communities have proved to be a huge obstacle for the PSNI in realising Patten's ambition for embedding a liberal model of policing in Northern Ireland. The Independent Commission began its work within two months of the Belfast Agreement being signed. The excellent blueprint which it provided might be seen with hindsight as an ideal to be aspired to, but whose realisation was and is contingent upon political and social conditions which do not and may not exist within a lifetime. Patten's potential success has been hampered, as was Hunt's thirty years earlier when he, too, tried to introduce a liberal model in an inimical environment. The fate of the PSNI is inextricably linked with the outcome of current political activity whereby, on the British government's insistence, political parties have been forced to try again to make the

Assembly work. A deadline – 24 November 2006 – came and went ignoring a threat that, if devolution was not in working form, all members' salaries and allowances would be discontinued without payments of compensation. Further negotiation brought the return of a devolved Assembly in May 2007.

The inadequacy of applying security measures to solve a constitutional problem was demonstrated by British government policy for most of the Troubles period (Ellison and Smyth, 2000). Internal tension between the interests of conflicting groups continue to make difficulties for the PSNI. The threat of international terrorism is used to justify security being entirely in the hands of British intelligence, while 'normalisation' continues apace by the gradual removal of Army look-out posts and reduction in the numbers of soldiers stationed in Northern Ireland to 'peacetime garrison' proportions. While progress in 'normalisation' measures is a positive development for the PSNI trying to move away from paramilitary to solely community policing, a fundamental requirement of the liberal model – legitimacy – continues to elude the PSNI.

Contradictory narratives of the past from the two divided communities present the police in two conflicting lights as being 'our police' or 'their police'. Survey data discussed earlier showed cleavage within the Catholic community in attitudes to the police over time and between age groups. Research shows that both Catholics and Protestants differentiate between how they perceive the PSNI treat their community in the local area, as opposed to their behaviour across Northern Ireland as a whole. In surveys carried out by the Policing Board (NIPB, 2004–2005: Omnibus Survey, tables 3 and 4) an interesting trend can be detected. Between 2003 and 2005 there was a rise in the percentage of Catholics who felt that the police treated both Catholic and Protestant communities equally. For their immediate area, the figure rose from 58 to 63 per cent. Across Northern Ireland the equivalent figures for the period were 50 per cent rising to 55 per cent. It would seem that Catholics can locally approve of community policing, but the institution can appear in a slightly less positive light because of its provenance. (This resonates with my data from officers who served in border areas.) The wider political context has, as I have indicated, imposed constraints at operational level.

A further feature of the liberal model, where the organisation and the public interface, is in recruitment to the PSNI. Progress towards achieving a representative service in numerical terms has not been disappointing. There is no evidence available, however, about the political backgrounds or postcodes from which trainees have been recruited. The PSNI figures show that by late 2009, approximately 28 per cent of their full-time police personnel were cultural Catholics, compared with 8 per cent at January 2001. The figures for Catholic female strength have increased over the same period to 6 per cent from 1 per cent. Overall female strength was 20 per cent, having risen from 12 per cent. The effects of increased female participation is difficult to predict, though it is likely to increase significantly. Australian research reports present contrasting evidence. On the one hand Prenzler (1997) contends that female recruits are generally less authoritarian and ethnocentric than males, while Chan (1997) concludes that female recruits are no less likely than male counterparts to embrace the orthodox police culture.

Although the numbers of ethnic minorities are small but growing, Patten was clear that they should be recruited to the PSNI. In March 2005 'Campaign 9' was launched to address disadvantage to those for whom English is not their first language, as this difficulty was the main reason for being rejected by the PSNI. A spelling and grammar section at the written test stage has been removed in order to facilitate selection. Increased recruitment from Catholics, women and ethnic minorities (who are categorised as Catholic or non-Catholic) promises change in the make-up and culture of the PSNI.

A flavour of the new type of PSNI personnel was provided by my snowball sample of trainees, who included some born outside of Northern Ireland and some from Republican areas. Unlike retired and some serving ex-RUC they have optimism, confidence and good education which shows them eminently employable and deliberately choosing the PSNI as a career. They have entered a reformed culture where senior officers, many of them Catholic, have bought in wholeheartedly to the new political dispensation expressed in policing terms. The trainees have everything to gain from leaving the past behind and rather than harking back vengefully to inequalities (which they experienced socially but not as police officers) they vent their spleen on Sinn Féin for not moving on at a speed parallel to the PSNI. One wonders how they might respond now – when Sinn Féin has taken positive steps to support the PSNI.

Sociological theory

The trainees have been in the PSNI for a very short time. Their chances of sustaining their autonomy and individuality need to be tested against the potent conservative forces of traditional police culture. In order to carry out that task I must briefly survey the large body of sociological research on this topic. Police culture has been a popular subject of research mainly (though not exclusively) in liberal democracies since the 1960s. Findings and insights fall into two distinct categories: those which stress the unchanging, homogeneous nature of police culture and those which acknowledge increasing heterogeneity in personnel, potential for change and strategies for achieving it. One definition of police subculture is 'accepted practices, rules and principles of conduct that are situationally applied and generalised rationales and beliefs' (Manning, 1989: 360).

Banton (1964) and Skolnick (1966) carried out pioneering work in Britain and the US respectively. They identified danger and authority as being the main elements which constitute the police officers' world, making suspicion, internal solidarity, conservatism and social isolation the core referents. Together, these features generate constant tensions in officers' professional lives. In the 1970s research focused on the interaction between the police and the public (Bittner, 1970; Butler and Cochrane, 1977; Reiner, 1978) and the tensions between being feared and being the admired citizen, the personification of law and order. Reiner (1992) characterised the police officer as the heroic figure on a mission, the 'thin blue line' protecting society from anarchy. The 'machismo syndrome' explained the exaggerated tales of courage in the face of danger as well as emphasising moral superiority over certain types of citizens, which are said to abound in 'canteen culture'.

Inevitably, by the 1990s, however, homogeneity of police culture was questioned or rebuffed by a large body of research. Hierarchical divisions had been identified, for example 'management cops' and 'street cops' (Holdaway, 1983; Punch, 1983; Reuss-Ianni, 1983) or a threefold division of command, middle management and lower ranks (Chan, 1997: 66). Fielding (1995) and Holdaway (1996) found differences on functional and gender bases. Of particular interest has been evidence of the strength of cultural resistance to change which questions compelling material on the capacity of police culture to change. At this confluence my data are addressed because I found that the trainee group brought fresh and varied perspectives that fitted an organisation which had changed unrecognisably in ethos, philosophy, systems and practices. Yet there inevitably remained in the PSNI a corps of influential senior officers as well as rank and file who still valued the legacy of the RUC in which they had been proud to serve. The trainees respected their views and were mindful of the experience and expertise on which the beginners depended. If the 'old' culture proved to be more durable than the 'new', would this strength inhibit real as opposed to cosmetic change? Instead of striking out as self-selecting agents of change, would these cultural Catholic officers simply be absorbed and socialised into the 'third religion' mindset?

Chan (1997) developed the discourse and drawing upon Bourdieu's concepts of habitus and field she criticised the way in which police culture has been conceptualised. Two new ideas to which she drew attention were: a need to place police culture within its organisational, social, political, legal context and not isolated from it; and importantly a notion that police officers rather than being 'cultural dopes' (Garfinkel, 1967) are active agents within a police culture. However, she concludes that no identifiable link between either field or habitus with police practice can be claimed. This unpredictability is evidenced by findings (Foster, 1989) which show the introduction of community-focused policing to succeed in one police station and to fail in another, both in inner-city locations. Reiner (1997) is led to conclude that management philosophy and practice are potent determinants of how basic features of police work are implemented. He is supported by Sackmann (1991) and by Chan (1997) who identify axiomatic knowledge as being the most important type of cultural knowledge. Axiomatic knowledge is the preserve of top management. In the case of the PSNI the top team and district commanders have been carefully selected as 'Patten people' to drive through reform. Senior officers who could not embrace such radical change resigned.

The prospect of change becoming embedded in the fabric of the PSNI seems rosy when one looks at the Patten package holistically. An international team informed by best practice designed a blueprint to make the PSNI a model for other countries to ape. Loopholes such as the discretionary power of individual officers to interpret the law were closed as far as humanly possible by a system which monitors the behaviour of officers via the Ombudsman's Office, an internal complaints system, technology for record keeping and the confidential telephone, all founded on human rights legislation. However, police retain autonomy which can be exercised in positive, rewarding ways by showing initiative in carrying out community policing. Such space for individual innovation was used by some of my respondents – a district commander negotiated successfully with Sinn Féin in order to open up a 'no go' area and two trainees used their knowledge of the Irish language and of Gaelic games respectively to open up dialogue in areas hitherto hostile to police.

A fine balance must be struck between systems which monitor the application of values, philosophy, law and style by PSNI officers and the retention of enough 'political space' (McConville *et al.*, 1991: 212) to make micro-level progress towards partnership policing. If consensual agreement on acceptance of axiomatic knowledge as reflecting a shared vision is not achieved, then that familiar resistance to change will occur. Brogden *et al.* (1988) comment appositely on this point. They identify rule tightening and informal cultural change as being two distinctive approaches to police reform. Patten took cognisance of both, I suggest. The first I have referred to already in the case of the PSNI and the second is likely to be achieved by greater variety in personnel, resulting from new recruitment methods and targets. The report made clear that the aim was to recruit not just cultural Catholics 'of a certain kind', as happened in the past, but from Catholics who, though from Republican and Nationalist backgrounds, see in the PSNI a new beginning worthy of their support. Whether this extension of franchise should include ex-prisoners is, as my data indicated, contested within the PSNI, as well as in the wider social and political community. The fact remains that the Patten recommendation, now enshrined in legislation, is demonstrably changing the informal culture by the different variables which are being brought together for common cause.

Contemporary sociology explains culture as 'a tool kit' (Swidler, 1986), 'frames' (Gamson, 1992) or as 'multiple, fractured and contingent' (Sewell, 1992:16). They all agree that human actors draw upon culture as from a store cupboard of resources which enable them to form views, make decisions, actively responding to situations in the light of past insights and experiences. Although many of these resources may be contradictory, they equip the active agent to deal with the challenges which present themselves. A primary dynamic to facilitate selection from the store cupboard of resources had not been identified, however, until Herbert (1998) voiced his main concern with the lack of precision from which this 'new cultural sociology' suffered, but especially its concern with cognitive dimensions at the expense of the normative. Building on the term 'normative order' which Parsons (1937), explained as meaning 'to capture the importance of internalised values for structuring individual behaviour', Herbert (1998: 34) favours the 'internal' view of culture which stresses the influential role of values in determining action consciously or unconsciously. He claims that the six normative orders: law, bureaucratic control, adventure/machismo, safety, competence and morality both assist and burden police officers, since they may on occasion be internally inconsistent. Reform, he argues, is premised upon redefining police work so that there is a fine balance between the normative orders in order to facilitate positive police-community relations. Herbert's contribution to the debate is to import values to add to 'the complexity of culture and the activity of agents who deploy cultural resources in a set of structured improvisations' (Herbert, 1998: 364).

Identity crisis?

The early monochromatic view of police culture has given way largely to a very complex kaleidoscope where the collective no longer takes precedence over the individual as a focus of attention. The construct of identity which has been a central theme running through my data analysis, which I mined in order to find out how cultural Catholics managed their identity in a predominantly Protestant culture. Culture and identity meet in trying to explain what I found.

A brief overview of the development of social identity theory, selected in accordance with its relevance to my research seems appropriate at this point. I shall draw upon two main sources in seeing the story unfold in a way which I consider beneficial to my purpose (Dillon, 1999; Jenkins, 2004). Going back about a century, identity was squarely in the preserve of social anthropology; identity has now become of pressing interest to the broad family of social scientists, including sociologists. Contemporary focus is on twin aspects: the fundamental unchanging aspects of selfhood and the modern and postmodern emphasis on changing identity which is fragmented and which is contingent upon location in time and space.

An early contribution to the development of identity theory was made by Mead, who isolated two aspects of the 'self', the 'I' and the 'me'. He explains: 'The self is essentially a social process going on with these two distinguishable phases' (1934: 178). The 'I' he explains as the immediate unrehearsed, creative response of one to others which is important for four reasons: it is a key source of novelty in the social process; the 'I' is the site of our most important values; the 'I' is the realisation of self; the 'I' allows us to develop a definite personality. Mead concludes that in modern societies the 'I' is dominant, contrasting with the 'me' who is the conventional creature of habit. He defines social control as being the dominance of 'me' over 'I' and is premised on the crucial assumption that humans can think.

Jenkins (2004: 17), acknowledging the work of Goffman and Giddens, suggests that 'the world as constructed and experienced by humans can best be understood as three distinct orders': the individual order, or 'what-goes-on-in-their-heads'; the interaction order, or 'what-goes-on-between-people'; the institutional order, or 'the established-ways-of-doing-things'. Our identity, then, is established by the iterative relationship between how we see ourselves and how others see us. Other ways of expressing this duality are self-image and public image; whereas some identities are primary – for example gender, ethnicity – others are acquired, for example occupation, rank. Barth (1969) warns that significant others must validate an individual's claim to an identity before it is 'taken on'. Negotiation takes place at boundaries between internal identification and external classification by others. Barth further distinguishes between nominal and virtual identity. Nominal identity is a label which is shared with others, but which may be interpreted in different types of behaviour – for example, Catholic. Jenkins (2004: 77) explains virtual identification as 'what a nominal identification means experientially and practically over time, to its bearer'. He draws attention to the importance of the difference between the two types of identification for four reasons:

- the difference that a name or label makes in the life of an individual;
- dissonance between a label and its consequences may inhibit 'substantial internalisation';
- the nominal may result in 'a plurality of virtualities', depending upon place and time;
- the unique features of the individual need to be separated out from the generalised features of the collective (bestowed, for example, in an organisation) because 'some part of the virtual is always individually idiosyncratic' (Jenkins, 2004: 77).

In addition, he raises an important related issue: whether identity (individual and collective) is more or less important than individual and collective self-interest in determining human behaviour. In developing an answer he draws upon Weber's 'iron cage' and Giddens' 'reflexive self-identification' but leaves one with a persuasive argument that identity and interest are in practice not discrete concepts (except perhaps for analysis):

> What I want is in some sense shaped by my sense of who I am. On the other hand, in clarifying my interests I may sometimes begin to redefine my sense of self. (Goldstein and Rayner, 1994: 367–8)

In an effort to bring together the significance of identity and of police culture in the lives of the samples I studied, I developed a typology using four metaphors – 'flaunters', 'chameleons', 'deserters' and 'victims' in order to depict with broad strokes the profiles of Catholic officers as they accomplished their police work. In the serving and trainee groups I found 66 per cent and 80 per cent respectively to be 'chameleons' rather than traditional Catholics in the Northern Irish mould. Institutionally marginalised, a majority ignored one or more of the conventional practices, for example, of marrying Catholic partners in Catholic churches, having their children educated in Catholic schools, living in Catholic neighbourhoods and socialising with their Catholic families and friends. Many chose to flout all or some of these conventions, yet only a minute number had either joined or attended services in non-Catholic churches.

My use of the 'chameleon' was intended to indicate that while remaining, in essence, a chameleon, this animal could vary its appearance so that it blended with its environment, in order not to be detected by predators. Protection in the case of the human species might be from risks physical, as well as psychic, such as emotional hurt or embarrassment. The Catholic officers' popular choice of resorting to 'the third religion' as a label for identity seemed to me a human solution to a problem shared with the animal. Further delving was required, though, in the application of the metaphor to humans. Not only did they acquire an ability to pass in various social and duty contexts with colleagues from the majority community, they had to justify their behaviour to themselves, and satisfy their consciences. This normative/cognitive mechanism had to be exercised over a working lifetime by many, for example, in the canteen, watching IRA atrocities on television in a station, taking coercive action against Catholics whose cause might have appeared legitimate to them.

The apparent inconsistency or unpredictability of 'chameleon' officers exemplified in serving and trainee vignettes had considerable light thrown on it by the notion of fragmented identity, particularly in the work of Dillon (1999). She considers Catholic identity in a way which is pertinent to Catholic officers in Northern Ireland. She studied progressive or 'pro-change' Catholics in the USA who could manage to sustain their Catholic identity while flouting traditional rules and hierarchical guidance on matters of faith or morals. They did not deny their cultural origins, and did not convert to other faiths. Dillon (1999: 254) explains: 'Religious identity for pro-change Catholics is an achieved identity, but the achievement involves creating new identities and practices within Catholicism'. Dillon argues persuasively that rather than exemplifying selective 'cafeteria style' Catholicism, they reflect a long-established tradition of institutional transformation which she claims is closer to the truth than 'the constant tradition' (Dillon, 1999: 252). She couples her explanation with the idea, currently widely accepted, that identity is never fixed:

> Cultural identity is a matter of becoming as well as of being. It belongs to the future as well as to the past . . . Cultural identities come from somewhere, have histories. But, like everything which is historical, they undergo constant transformation. (Hall, 1992: 225)

Dillon's exposition of cultural identity alongside Jenkins' longitudinal treatment of social identity together suggest that change over time is not restricted to the individual but can apply to a collective as well. My vignettes outlined in Chapters 4 and 5 are intended to exemplify 'chameleons' from among serving officers and trainees respectively. As well as being portraits of individuals from the largest category of the typology, they represent different generations of collectivities.

The demands of police work, the transition from family support to social isolation and the impact of political instability on the management of change in the PSNI, conspire to draw Catholic officers away from the 'constant' version of their cultural identity, especially when Jenkins' link between identity and interests are considered. I suggest that their identity is in a constant state of becoming. Two related questions I would raise in relation to my respondents. One, I believe that some are at the point they have reached on their journey for reasons of convenience rather than conviction. For example, the senior officer who attended a Protestant church so as to remain on amicable terms with his wife's family, or those who sent their children to state schools because their Catholic identity – a potential source of problems for the children or their parents – could be conveniently 'hidden' (reminiscent of Jenkins' comments quoted earlier on interest and identity). The other point I would simply flag, as I am not in a position to support it with evidence, is the possibility, perhaps likelihood, that if social and political circumstances changed, these officers would retrace their steps, positioning themselves closer to the 'constant' category of Catholics. Indeed, retirement might be the rite of passage which could facilitate it, when they would cease to have an identity provocative to Republican Catholics. One might speculate that since Sinn Féin has found it advantageous to support the PSNI as a representative police service, the profile of the 'chameleon' may become less varied and complex, depicting the features of police officers generally, without the additional elements which characterise only those in this divided society.

What contribution do my data make to how sociology understands identity? They serve to exemplify current postmodern thinking. I find that the most strongly represented category from my typology, chameleons, is my metaphorical explanation for multiple identity. The term 'chameleon' encapsulates in Mead's dichotomy the dominance of 'I' over 'me'. My respondents are examples who show unchanging aspects of selfhood as cultural Catholics and fragmented identity contingent on time and place. My three samples show increasingly powerful dominance of 'I' over 'me' and the trainees show the postmodern victory of 'I'. Even admirers of Sinn Féin were willing to admit their psychic affiliation or empathy, something which would have been unheard of in the RUC days.

The short history of the PSNI places an emphasis on two of Jenkins' 'distinct orders' – the individual and interaction orders, rendering the institutional order relatively weaker in weighting, because at the time I conducted the interviews there was little in the way of 'the-established-ways-of-doing-things' within the nascent PSNI. With Barth's nominal and virtual identity in mind, my data exemplify very strongly virtual identity, explaining the chameleon qualities and their application in practice. A 'plurality of virtualities' succinctly expresses the unpredictable variety of behaviours to which respondents' subjective experiences testify. Jenkins' emphasis on self-interest is eminently plausible in explaining the course which virtual realities take over time which are unpredictable and contingent upon contextual factors. Joining the Masonic Order or marrying in a Presbyterian Church and sending children to non-Catholic schools might be cited as relevant examples generated by my data.

The work of Dillon enables me to tighten the focus on my sample of Catholics who joined the RUC and/or the PSNI. She provides a historical and philosophical explanation, even justification in a universal context where my respondents fit. According to traditional church views they would be classified as deviant Catholics. My data support her thesis that there are ways of living out ones Catholicism with integrity and justification which do not deserve the dismissive title 'cafeteria-style Catholics'. This pejorative term suggests a group devoid of an ontological framework for their behaviour which is apparently inconsistent with official church teaching. It is exciting for me to find that my data support Jenkins' and Dillon's discourse expressed by Hall. I refer to the contention that cultural identities 'undergo constant transformation' and that this developmental renewal can apply to collectivities as well as to individuals. I hope that Catholic officers' self-interest will converge with those of Catholics in the community. If that happens I optimistically consider it likely, rather than possible, that the PSNI will win consent from the Catholic community.

Hope springs eternal?

At this stage it is appropriate to return to the key research question which asked if a liberal model of policing is viable in Northern Ireland. In Chapter 6 and earlier in this conclusion I drew attention to huge measures of reform which have been achieved, or are ongoing in the PSNI. The most fundamental feature of the liberal model, legitimacy, continues to elude the service. The more I try to find a clear answer to my key question, the more questions arise. The meaning of words such as 'peace' and 'stability' are invested with complexity which was not apparent earlier. For example, when is peace accomplished? Does 'peace' mean absence of community conflict in street riot terms or, at the other end of the spectrum, will it be accomplished only when the Assembly is working as other Western democracies do?

Policing and criminal justice were such highly contentious matters that they could not be devolved with other functions under the Belfast Agreement in 1998, but were shelved until such time as approval by the parties could be reached. It was on the understanding that devolution would take place – thereby making the justice system more accountable – that Sinn Féin agreed to work towards acceptance of the PSNI. Their acceptance came gradually from political prisoners were released until by 2007 Sinn Féin members had taken their places on the Policing Board and DPPs. However, Sinn Féin, expressing deep frustration at the protracted nature of talks, warned that if agreement on a date for devolution had not happened by Christmas 2009, a 'full blown crisis' would occur in the Assembly. This remark contrasts strongly with Martin McGuinness' confident and tempered remark at the Labour Party Conference (29 September 2009): 'We are very close to agreement and people must remain patient'.

The First Minister, Peter Robinson, while favouring devolution (though without full support from all party colleagues) made transfer of powers conditional on 'timing and community confidence'. Over several months very successful negotiations were held in Belfast, London and New York between the two leaders (separately and together) with the British prime minister, resulting in a generous financial package of £1 billion being allocated which would include provision for a shortfall in pensions funding and compensation to officers suffering from hearing loss sustained in the course of duty.

The DUP's wish to drag out negotiations as long as possible to achieve terms most favourable to their party and their supporters seemed in part to demonstrate their unwillingness to accede to Sinn Féin's demand, but may also have been influenced strongly by the prospect of a general election in May 2010. It is important to remember that the DUP did not sign up to the Belfast Agreement, thereby failing to embrace power-sharing as a way forward. They would not accept the notion of ex-IRA members becoming Members of the Local Assembly (MLAs). The triumph of the DUP in the elections to Stormont demonstrated that their rejection of power-sharing was robustly supported in the constituencies. Dr Paisley's decision to share power with Martin McGuinness, representing the old enemy, when the Assembly was re-established in 2007, left many grass-roots supporters amazed, betrayed, some angry and unforgiving because they viewed their ageing 'Ulster says no' stalwart as having been tempted by the bait of personal aggrandisement and the prospect of being first minister before he retired. Some might see this as an inaccurate interpretation of a road-to-Damascus experience.

Independent MEP Jim Allister, ex-DUP member who had written the party manifesto came to the rescue of alienated members in the 2008 elections to the European Parliament. Although he lost his seat, he polled over 60,000 votes, thereby sending shock waves through the DUP, engendering fears of future general and Assembly election results. The formation of Allister's Traditional Ulster Voice (TUV) is one example of political fragmentation in Northern Ireland, which may have the effect of breaking up historical power blocks based on ethno-religious identity. One cannot ignore the possibility in the foreseeable future of Sinn Féin votes outnumbering those for the DUP, making Sinn Féin the largest party in Stormont. 'Would the Unionists find common ground on which to unite again and what might the implications be?' one might ask. New political alliances and pacts inevitably address the concepts of changing identity which I have already discussed. Alienated Unionists would argue that the British government 'bowed the knee' to pressure from Republican demands in order to achieve peace in Northern Ireland. Unquestioned loyalty to Britain and the British government has been replaced by resistance in the breasts of, for example, members of the TUV. In recent years an alternative identity has been gaining popularity; a replacement for British or Loyalist, is Ulster-Scots. Conscious of their ethnic roots in Scotland and irritated by the status accorded the Irish language and culture by the Belfast Agreement, resulting in support for education through that medium, an alternative Unionist identity project was born. Explained as a dialect spoken in North Antrim mixed with elements of Lowland Scots dialect of English it is a focus for disillusioned Unionists who wish to reinvent themselves. The 'language' is of course, part of an entire package of elements which constitute a cultural identity.

Ramsay (2009), a former senior Stormont civil servant and Eurocrat, argues that the Ulster Scots identity would fit well within a European Union context. He believes that by taking on this new identity its adherents would receive international recognition. In a belief that the Unionist community must acquire a pro-Union identity he states:

> the most important aspect of the development of the Ulster Scots identity is that it would take [Unionism] out of the internationally damaging context of religious division, into one which is not only understandable, but is even fashionably in harmony with the zeitgeist of today's European Union. (Ramsay, 2009: 320)

All Republicans and most Nationalists seem to be comfortable in their Irish identity, though welcome blurring is shown in the growing numbers of people who describe themselves as Northern Irish. Such an identity does not have provenance and would have to invent new symbols to express it and to unify its adherents. The PSNI has succeeded in meeting a similar challenge.

Viewed in the round, the Northern Ireland Executive has not worked as it was intended and its credibility and durability have to be questioned. I conveyed in previous chapters Catholic police officers' pessimistic views of political progress and of the immaturity, indeed inability of local politicians to work together in a consociational dispensation. There is an iterative relationship between politicians and the people who support them, so it is not surprising that (reflecting the police officers' predictions) the ability of the public to move on in their attitudes has, in general, been disappointingly slow.

There are plenty of items on the agenda which could fall victim to traditional tribal divisions. I include here the impasse reached over selection in education, the results of the latest Saville Enquiry into events on Bloody Sunday, the Review of Public Administration and rationalisation within local government, as well as changes in electoral boundaries already feared by the DUP to herald the 'greening' of Belfast (that the province's capital city would have a majority of Catholic citizens).

In fairness to the public, some of the problems inhibiting progress in the peace process are shared by communities throughout the developed world and by events which were not anticipated. Human rights legislation was firmly at the top of the agenda in many countries in 1998 and provided a philosophical justification for the entire Patten blueprint for the PSNI. However, when the Twin Towers in Manhattan were attacked and terrorism became the focus of international attention, security became the urgent concern. The 'war' on international terrorism had begun in earnest and one might argue that dealing with her recent violent past became even more difficult for many families in Northern Ireland who could identify emotionally with the horrific images from Ground Zero.

One of the most enduring obstacles toward social and political progress has been and continues to be lack of agreement on defining a victim. At one level it is easy: the widow of a police officer killed by the IRA or the children of a Catholic civilian with no paramilitary involvement, who was targeted and killed by Loyalists simply because of their cultural background. The issue of compensation for victims when the term is interpreted more widely is highly contentious. A detailed enquiry by a team led by the former Archbishop Robin Eames of the Church of Ireland and the former Deputy Chair of the Policing Board, Denis Bradley was published in early 2009. It brought the issue sharply into the foreground. One pertinent and controversial question which it provoked was: should the families of IRA members who were killed or injured on active service be treated as victims? An answer is sought as the devolution of justice emerges in practical form.

The division which has been a historical feature of Northern Irish society remains, in spite of some evidence of fluidity in identity and fragmentation within cultural groups (which I have discussed at length in relation to Catholic police officers). These phenomena may be added to creeping secularism, substantial reduction in church attendance figures and a strong trend towards people identifying themselves as being neither Catholic nor Protestant. Increasing secularism is thought to have brought a rejection of traditional values, replaced by convincing evidence of greed and egocentricity. Over the past year in Britain greed has been well exposed by the public scandals involving irresponsible risk-taking by bankers and of politicians claiming expenses to a level which ignored the traditional values of honesty and integrity. Stormont politicians were not excepted, although abuse of the rules was less widespread and less extreme than in Westminster. The media identified, though, politicians who employed several members of their family in running their constituency offices, while some, in addition, 'double jobbed' by holding seats in both Houses, reaping the obvious benefits from two salaries and two sets of expenses claims. (The DUP founder, Dr Paisley had 'triple jobbed' when a member in Stormont, Westminster and Brussels for some years.) Both problems are being taken care of by the British government in terms of tighter guidelines for expenses claims and a smack on the wrist for Stormont politicians who favoured 2015 as the year when 'double jobbing' would end. It is much more likely to happen in 2011.

The problem of victimhood and finding a strategy to deal with the psychic legacy of violent death and serious injury needs to be confronted across the globe, not just in Northern Ireland. It might be argued that peacebuilding is a much more complex process than politicians and diplomats have hitherto understood at macro level or even that psychologists and psychotherapists have grasped at the level of individuals affected by communal conflict. A seminal figure in the field of conflict resolution, John Paul Lederach (1997: 106) writing on the subject of sustainable reconciliation in divided societies suggests that 'the major components of a peacebuilding paradigm – structure, process, reconciliation and resources – need mechanisms that link and coordinate the various facets that each component represents'. In practical terms this close relationship requires identifying and establishing better links between various initiatives in order to strengthen and maximise the level of success attainable.

Lederach argues that the challenge is to maintain that reconciliation, which is a process of relationship building, as a central and permanent component of dealing with conflict and restructuring divided societies at every stage of peace building. Lederach provides conceptual models for deeper analysis into the cause of conflict and also for potential solutions. Exposition and analysis of Lederach's ideas are outside the scope of this book. Suffice to say that Northern Ireland, in company with trouble spots emerging from violent conflict throughout the world, provides numerous examples of organisations and groups attempting to make progress in peacebuilding, especially in trying to deal with the past, as its wounds are a potent source of continuing division if left to fester. These agencies appear, however, to lack the coordination of which Lederach writes, in spite of being relatively well resourced.

For a number of reasons, politicians and the general public in Northern Ireland tend to 'drag their past behind them' as one retired officer expressed the people's tenacious grip on history interpreted in a selective way. While wishing to forget negative aspects of their legacy and to deal with the present, PSNI officers are still dogged by the more inglorious and regrettable episodes from the past such as the Omagh bombing, the murder of Robert Hamill, allegations of collusion by Special Branch with Loyalist paramilitaries. The officers I interviewed did not presuppose that the new political arrangements would provide a smooth road ahead. Years of political intransigence have demonstrated the accuracy of their pessimistic predictions in regard to social and political change. Nor did they believe that the hearts and minds of the communities would feel or think in transformed ways so that they would immediately hail the Patten blueprint as the solution to the province's policing problems. They were enthusiastic about their new future as police officers and could see that the Patten philosophy, principles and structures were likely to bring positive changes if they worked very hard at policing with the communities, especially by engaging with and winning the support of the Catholic community.

PSNI command demonstrated ongoing seriousness of intent in making the service of world standard by producing a thought-provoking document. The content of the Report recorded less progress than one might have hoped. Commissioned by the first Chief Constable, Sir Hugh Orde who stepped down at 31 August 2009, giving way to his successor, Mr Matt Baggott from the Leicestershire Constabulary, the report, which I understand to be based on academic research, public confidence and satisfaction surveys and internal stakeholder interviews was leaked and reported by BBC Northern Ireland's home affairs correspondent (26 August

2009). Described by him as 'a withering critique of the state of policing in Northern Ireland', he highlighted some very fundamental weaknesses in policing provision over seven years after the PSNI was set up, as perceived by command level officers directed to draw up a three- to five-year strategic vision.

Using unambiguous language and clarity of expression appropriate to the restricted readership intended by its authors, the text rebukes the service on a number of criteria. Among the more damning admissions is the news that 61 per cent of police officer time is spent in stations on administrative tasks; 'there is little evidence of the PSNI having an over-arching crime prevention strategy (detection rate of 2.64 per cent being the lowest in the UK); there is not 'an effective 24-hour policing service' because a 9–5 culture has developed in the organisation, even though evidence suggests that visible police presence is in greater demand from the public between 6 and 10 p.m.

Sir Hugh Orde advised, however, to 'read it in the round' stressing substantial increase in clear-up levels of reported crime by 23 per cent. An Ulster Unionist Party (UUP) representative on the Policing Board, Basil McCrea, offered a plausible defence suggesting 'this is not really a critique of the police but the environment we put the police into'. He went on to explain that if the police must operate in a compliance culture, society and the oversight bodies must be challenged, not just the police. It is clear from the limited knowledge which can be derived from a summary version of this leaked document that the PSNI is a learning organisation which is holding up a mirror to itself and acknowledging the presence of curable warts. Serious tensions obviously exist between meeting the Patten demands for accountability and effective policing with the community. This tension is exacerbated by resistance on the part of some officers to adapt to change. Perhaps a 9–5 administrative culture feels safer than having to confront evening displays of rioting which include discharge of weapons in public places.

Micro-level progress towards partnership policing is promised, giving individual police officers greater autonomy and empowerment. In company with their counterparts in England and Wales PSNI officers will be allowed to issue fixed-penalty notices imposing fines of £40-£80 for minor crimes such as antisocial behaviour – which might go some distance towards satisfying public demand to force miscreants to pay for their negative endeavours. It would appear from limited revelation of the document's content that the authors are not putting blame outside their organisation for disappointing results from their seven years' performance under review. Even a superficial analysis must, however, lead one to conclude that Patten's stringent demands coupled with tardy political and social progress in Northern Ireland have conspired to put a brake on what the PSNI can achieve. An additional negative determinant is clearly internal sluggishness in achieving required culture change.

Leaving internal problems aside let us return to the challenging context in which the PSNI operates. One problem which the Catholic PSNI officers did not appear to anticipate in their earlier years was the re-emergence of dissident Republican groups who refuse to accept the terms of the Belfast Agreement, or who perceive partnership politics not to be working in their interests. New Year resolutions announced at the beginning of 2010 leave no one in doubt about their intentions. There would appear to be unity of purpose linking the Real IRA (RIRA), the Continuity IRA (CIRA), Eirigi, Republican Sinn Féin and the Thirty-Two County Sovereignty Movement to name those with highest profiles. The murders of two soldiers at Massereene Barracks, Antrim and of a police officer in Craigavon in March 2009 clearly indicated the level of threat which exists to security forces. Lacking the resources and the grass-roots support which the IRA enjoyed during the Troubles, these dissident groups are actively campaigning and planning strategy to counter progress made in community relations. Their existence testifies to the fact that Northern Ireland, in spite of the peace process, is still and will continue to be for a small minority with violence in their plans, a contested political entity. They obviously present great difficulties for both Sinn Féin and for the PSNI. Sinn Féin, realising that a military victory against the British security forces was not possible, settled for a draw. The party is engaging fully with the institutions and giving the PSNI full support.

The dilemma for the PSNI lies in the tension between the human rights philosophy which underpins their thinking and their actions when they have to deal with dissident violence. The protection of life and property is their essential role, but their application of human rights legislation can, on occasions, make them appear weak or incompetent. A question asked by some commentators is: 'Does the PSNI have the technical skill to defeat the dissidents?'. Naturally, the official answer from the PSNI is affirmative. The incompetence of dissident activists in causing disruption to normal life (such as planting bombs which do not go off) has been demonstrated on many reported occasions. While their power base at the moment appears to be relatively weak, it is difficult to speculate if membership of one of these groups would appeal to numbers of ex-Provisional IRA activists who disagreed with a ceasefire and decommissioning of weapons and who would bring their skills in support of continuing the armed campaign. If the dissidents can muster strength, it could have an adverse effect on PSNI engagement with elements in the Catholic community whose hostility to police has gradually waned. One politician has explained this improvement as 'no go' areas changing into 'slow go' areas, but there is no guarantee that such progress will continue.

Events attributed to dissident groups in recent months have demonstrated the tension between partnership policing and counter-insurgency. One such recent occasion exemplifies the problem. A patrol at Meigh in south Armagh encountered armed and masked men stopping motorists at a roundabout. Instead of engaging them it was reported that the officers sent for reinforcements, but the entire convoy of police cars withdrew from the scene without interrupting the dissident show of strength. Was the PSNI action motivated by caution, lest engagement might result in death or injuries to innocent civilians, or were they incapable of dealing with the situation because they were technically unskilled? I don't know the answer. Some or all of these dissident groups have clearly made police officers legitimate targets of assassination, especially those officers who are cultural Catholics. Responsibility for the death of Stephen Carroll in Craigavon was claimed by the CIRA. British intelligence thwarted the efforts of dissidents in Garrison, County Fermanagh who targeted a young Catholic officer on a visit to the village in late 2009. There have also been examples of bombs being placed under officers' cars. The threat from Republican Sinn Féin is that, 'British rule in Ireland will be met with resistance' while Eirigi, an organisation that targets Catholic youth promise 'uncompromising active resistance'. The political ambition of the Thirty-Two County Sovereignty Movement, intent on continuing the revolutionary Irish Republican tradition is expressed thus: 'Democracy can only be returned to the Irish people when their national sovereignty is recognised'. These statements were contained in New Year messages from the leadership of the various dissident groups (*Irish News*, 4 January 2010).

While the size of their combined threats may not be significant, indeed minute compared to the might of the pre-Agreement Provisional IRA, Catholic police officers have good reason to be fearful for their lives and even the most optimistic joining the PSNI may after a time doubt the wisdom of choosing this career and resign. Such a development would obviously erode the progress made in recruiting Catholics, by lowering the numbers of applicants as well as forcing resignations. Indeed the trend in attrition dates has been upward since 2006. It would also seriously inhibit culture change within the PSNI and progress in partnership policing with the whole community.

What has been learned?

I doubt that Northern Ireland is in a position – nor is it likely to be for years to come – to advise other deeply divided societies on how to undertake reform, except perhaps on pitfalls to avoid, since the peace project is still 'business in progress'. It appears to me that the British and Irish governments for their own obvious reasons and under pressure from the US had to use their concerted diplomatic strength to bring power-sharing government to Northern Ireland. (The importance of inward investment cannot be underestimated as a motivating factor.) The public wanted peace and prosperity so a deal was forged with parties unprepared for government after Direct Rule lasting a quarter century. Almost twelve years after the Belfast Agreement, some commentators express the traditional divisions by renaming 'shared power' as 'shared out power'. The promise of parity of esteem for all citizens inevitably meant that both communities, often encouraged by their party leaders, saw each change as either a victory or a defeat for their tradition, the DUP being particularly attracted to the term 'concessions to Sinn Féin IRA'. Members of the DUP have consistently found difficulty in sitting down to do business with Sinn Féin, the second largest party and their partner in government. Sinn Féin members, who include some former IRA activists, now peace-seeking 'children' of the IRA, regretful though unapologetic for past paramilitary activities of that organisation, are grasping the opportunity presented to progress their agenda for a non-sectarian peaceful future and a long-term ambition for reunification of the island of Ireland. Serving police officers, particularly those I interviewed while still trainees, were very optimistic that Sinn Féin, once it joined the Policing Board, would support the PSNI publicly and encourage the Republican community to gather and pass on evidence to solve crime and even to join the PSNI. Energetic support for the police has come from the Sinn Féin leadership, even though some DUP members on the Policing Board might say that there is not unanimity among serving Sinn Féin representatives.

Against a background of progress towards and of regression from reaching the ultimate goal of embedding a liberal model of policing in Northern Ireland, one is minded to reflect on the process so far, looking for lessons in what might best be summed up as a cautionary tale:

1. Signatories to the Belfast Agreement did not necessarily promise to do any-thing beyond trying to work within an unfamiliar consociational framework. This measure of success was achieved as an acceptable balance between ben-efits and losses, as each Party perceived them.

   The Party members probably could not even conceive of the difficulties which they would experience in trying to share power in government, while retaining the support of their grass roots. It is hardly surprising, then, that the experiment has proven to be disappointing to the architects of the Agreement, particularly in the snail's pace at which progress has been made. One wonders if the protagonists might have benefited from monitoring informed by experi-ence of consociational government in other divided societies.

2. Policy makers of police reform were hampered by new political arrangements already in place. While the logic of such is easily understood, Patten and his col-leagues were, inevitably, given a political brief and their freedom was curtailed by terms already 'won' during the political negotiations. I refer, for example, to the disbandment of the FTR within a given timeframe and huge financial incentives to retire being made available to experienced, often very senior RUC officers, because Sinn Féin saw the RUC as the old, rotten regime, sectarian and guilty of collusion with Loyalist paramilitaries. These two issues have, more than a decade later, continued to cause problems for the PSNI. My interview-ees spotted these problems, while realising that such a price had to be paid for a 'fresh start'.

3. Patten, while making 50:50 recruitment of officers a fundamental feature of his policing model, ignored the cultural composition of civilians in servicing the police. Predominantly non-Catholic, their continuing presence in such numbers has modified the effect which this further change in the internal culture might have made. (At 1 August 2009 the figures for police officers perceived to

be cultural Protestants was 70.35 per cent and for cultural Catholics was 27.31 per cent. For civilian staff the figures were 78.66 per cent and 17.71 per cent respectively.)

4. The implementation model was one of coercive change which ignored the feelings and the attitudes of the RUC officers who transferred into the PSNI. The lack of appreciation and extreme hurt felt by many was shared empathically even by my sample of trainee officers. Changes in symbols, name and uniform were seen by many as an attempt to obliterate the RUC from history, together with the huge sacrifices which they had made especially during the Troubles. The importance of all of this to officers with service was underestimated, creating an obstacle to progress.

5. Patten might have assuaged pain if he had acknowledged that serving officers had experience and opinions which ought to have been considered more seriously. My respondents felt that their unique perspective was ignored effectively during the consultation process while the Patten team chose public focus groups as the sources of evidence to inform their recommendations; merely going through the motions while consulting officers – or so it appeared to them.

6. Patten ignored a three-stage change model which has been in favour since the 1960s (Bennis *et al.*, 1964) and which it might have been wise to consider. The stages are named as 'unfreeze, change and refreeze'. A very important stage precedes the introduction of change when personnel who will be affected are brought into the decision-making process and 'buy in' to a need for change and the direction which it will take. Implications of proposed change for individuals are given due consideration so as to avoid sharp reactions from employees whose work practices, conditions and environment may be altered drastically. 'Refreeze' refers to the new regime bedding down and requiring sensitive monitoring of implementation together with united effort on the part of all with appropriate support, especially for those experiencing greatest difficulties in adjusting or coping. Lack of consultation, speed of implementing drastic change in ethos, philosophy, structures and practices put enormous pressure on senior staff who were unavailable to their juniors. The superintendants were upstairs writing reports to meet transparency and accountability needs, while middle and lower ranks did not have the advice and support which they needed and deserved.

7. An outside driver for change was required, because Sir Ronnie Flanagan and his team tended in their internal review to concentrate on greater technical efficiency and measurable targets for success, ignoring that the RUC was part of the political problem afflicting Northern Ireland and if success was going to be achieved, policing had to be a large part of the solution. Instead of consistently denying that some officers engaged in deviant behaviour, they should, years earlier have carried out investigations into such allegations, particularly

about collusion with paramilitaries. This omission they have recently rectified by setting up a unit to investigate this problem.

8. The PSNI might be well advised to engage in or sponsor academic research at regular stages in the PSNI's evolution. It would be beneficial to capture and explain difficulties and achievements both internal to the organisation as a whole and to its various groups of personnel, as well as focusing on its interaction with political, social and economic dimensions of the communities which it serves. Snapshots and longitudinal studies should both be considered for the complementary benefits which would accrue.

9. Some officers in my sample questioned the wisdom of allocating ten places on the Policing Board to politicians and nine to independent members. The Policing Board is a very important body which, with the Ombudsman's Office is the watchdog protecting transparency and accountability in the public interest. It is perhaps unfortunate that the dominance of politicians on the Policing Board has seen much disagreement, haggling and time-wasting while the party representatives have used the meetings as an extension of daily conflict in Stormont. One wonders if membership by independents had been dominant would more progress have been made faster.

10. Police form a very interesting as well as indispensible group in any society, because they are drawn from it, yet as my samples have shown – partially out of necessity and partially out of choice – they can isolate and insulate themselves in order to observe the motivations and behaviour of their fellows who are civilians. The officers I surveyed and interviewed had considered the political and social issues confronting Northern Ireland and their responses to my probing proved to be very accurate predictors of the slow progress which change would make and of the inhibiting factors. The wealth of data which they accumulate in their daily interaction with the public might profitably be sought more widely by other professional groups and agencies engaged in serving society.

Determined to forge ahead and to play a leading role in creating a just and equal society, they fell short (as I have reported earlier) of fully embracing change inside their own organisation, at least in its first seven years. However, as we progress through the second decade of the twenty-first century, one may feel confident that their command-level officers have learned from this first phase of Patten in practice. Sir Hugh Orde in his response to the leaked report reminded critics that, in spite of shortcomings, the PSNI had made enormous progress against a 'unique background' – a claim which one would find difficult to challenge.

End piece

I have discussed in some detail above the political and social landscape within which the PSNI operates. The volume of space devoted to these contextual elements testifies to their enormous significance in the lives of PSNI officers and on the constraints which they impose on the organisation's progress. The passage of time has not brought any reduction in indirect pressure from traditional sources. By mid-January 2010 public interest in politics was hugely heightened by a series of events – some shocking, some tragic, some both – which had taken place over a couple of weeks. The first minister and his wife – a 'triple-jobbing' DUP politician – seen as a devout Christian couple found themselves at the centre of a scandal that provoked a political crisis. This, in turn, rocked with unprecedented intensity public confidence in political institutions and in the integrity of politicians who present themselves as occupying the high moral ground.

Iris Robinson, exposed as a grandmother who at the age of 59 in 2008 conducted an illicit sexual relationship with a 19-year-old man for whom she obtained £50,000 from property developers to set him up in business, attempted to commit suicide when she learned that within a few days her behaviour would be the subject of a television documentary. It is alleged that she promoted the young man's cause so that his application was duly accepted to rent a property from Castlereagh Borough Council where she was a long-standing councillor and mayor three times. In spite of codes of conduct governing her role in Castlereagh, Stormont and Westminster she failed to declare an interest. Even though he advised her to repay the money to the developers her husband suffered collateral damage because he admitted that he gradually became aware of his wife's wrongdoings in private and public life.

Three months later, while his wife was still a hospitalised psychiatric patient, the spotlight was back on the couple's financial dealings. Questions were raised about the circumstances surrounding their purchase from and sale to developers of a strip of land alongside their garden for a sum of £5. The matter is in the hands of their lawyers while a plausible explanation is awaited.

Sinn Féin is seen by some commentators to be well positioned against a weakened DUP Party whose support base is seriously threatened. However, Gerry Adams' authority within his party may be less solid since his knowledge of his brother's alleged sexual abuse of his daughter has come to public attention. Adams arguably faces somewhat weaker political challenges, though pictorial evidence of him canvassing for his brother's election as a local councillor, after he had learned of his immoral behaviour still remains to be explained. The significance of personal difficulties which the two leaders face and which might impinge strongly on political progress was tested on the electorate in the run-up to the May 2010 elections.

Wishing to increase their representation and their influence at Westminster and having only one sitting MP, Lady Sylvia Hermon whose loyalty was growing increasingly doubtful, the UUP formed an electoral pact with the Conservative Party at a time when the latter was comfortably positioned in the polls ahead of Labour. Agreed candidates will contest all eighteen seats. Catholic candidates are said to have withdrawn, however, when it was rumoured that the UUP might link up with the DUP in certain constituencies to maximise representation by a Unionist 'family' having reached a point of temporary pragmatic reconciliation.

Nominations show that such a pact was made in Fermanagh and South Tyrone where an agreed candidate will stand in an attempt to unseat the Sinn Féin Minister for Agriculture, Michelle Gildernew. Wider water appears to separate SDLP from Sinn Féin. An overture by Gerry Adams to the new SDLP leader, Margaret Ritchie, was immediately rejected without discussion. A surprisingly generous act followed: Sinn Féin's candidate in strongly middle-class south Belfast, Alex Maskey, withdrew in order to enhance the chances of SDLP's sitting MP, Dr Alasdair McDonnell being returned. A less generous interpretation of Sinn Féin's motivation might be that the decision freed up party workers to concentrate on north Belfast. Pre-election manoeuvres by the parties in order to achieve best possible results may result in some tactical voting complicated by the likelihood of a hung parliament at Westminster.

At the same time as the political bombshell regarding the Robinson couple dropped, a 33-year-old police officer was critically wounded by a bomb attached to the underside of his car which exploded as he drove to work. Subsequently he had to have a leg amputated. His very personal tragedy is shared by the PSNI as a progressive organisation. Peadar Heffron is the personification of transformed policing in Northern Ireland. Culturally Catholic with ten years of loyal and energetic service, a fluent speaker of the Irish language and an accomplished sportsman, he was captain of the PSNI Gaelic football team, a highly respected member of his local Randalstown Rugby Club and a soccer player. He obviously crossed the community divide with ease and exemplified growing cultural diversity within the PSNI.

No dissident group claimed responsibility but there was speculation in the media and by the police that this atrocity may have triggered a sectarian bomb attack on a community centre in the same town less than a week later. On that evening the local Gaelic football team was engaged in indoor training. One fears that in addition to Republican dissidents there may have emerged Loyalist dissidents too, since the Ulster Defence Association (UDA), the last large, very influential Loyalist association announced that their weapons had been put beyond use and witnessed by Lord Eames and Sir George Quigley, a local businessman. If, days later, there was a sectarian attack on Catholic sportsmen, one has to wonder if sustained Republican dissident acts are likely to prompt tit-for-tat activity by Loyalist dissidents opposed to the peace process, who would argue that there has been no peace dividend for Protestants living in deprived areas.

Is devolution the solution?

In the ongoing, complex, evolving unpredictable saga of Northern Ireland, the PSNI is hampered but not prevented from making the progress that Patten hoped for. Therein lies hope. On 12 April 2010 the much trumpeted devolution of policing and justice to the Northern Ireland Assembly became a credible reality when

David Ford, leader of the Alliance Party, which includes Catholics, Protestants and others, and agreed choice of the two largest parties was selected as Justice Minister. According to the rules he had to have cross-party support. Policing had been largely devolved as more of Patten's recommendations were implemented – with the very notable exception that the chief constable, the Policing Board and the Ombudsman were still answerable to the Secretary of State. Devolution means that the Stormont minister for justice replaces the Secretary of State in this regard and takes on greater responsibility than his predecessors did before Direct Rule. Among the main provisions, the courts and the judiciary, hitherto the responsibility of the Lord Chancellor, transfer to the minister. The court service comes under the department of justice headed by a chief executive. Responsibility for right of appeal from Northern Irish courts to the House of Lords (and the UK Supreme Court when established) and legal aid for such appeals will become the minister's remit. An agreement between the Northern Ireland judiciary and the Northern Ireland executive is also a necessary element. In addition, north-south cooperation, already established, guarantees cooperation on criminal justice matters between the jurisdictions. Matters related to policing and justice were termed 'reserved'. There will remain 'excepted' matters pertaining to national security and extradition which will become the responsibility of the security service. The minister has responsibility for appointing independent Policing Board members and relations between the minister, the Board and the Assembly's Policing Committee were determined before devolution.

Premised on human rights and a shared future for all the people in the province, new structures and processes are intended to build on significant changes achieved over the previous decade. Increased confidence in the fairness and effectiveness of the criminal justice system and its agencies will be crucial in winning acceptance by all sections of the community. Areas identified by the minister's Alliance Party (2010) as being due for reform include avoidable delay in bringing young offenders to court; identifying reasons for antisocial behaviour and for offending; paying greater attention to rehabilitation and to the mental health and personality problems of offenders. He favours greater police visibility and rationalisation of DPPs and Community Safety Partnerships; large-scale reform of the prison service to cover governance and accountability and review of the Prison Ombudsman's brief; revision of sports law and spectator control; a victims' code of practice for victims and witnesses; sentencing guidelines – which would be welcomed by a public seeking fairer and more consistent sentences.

Historical enquiries, 'peace walls', public display of flags and hate crime will all receive attention if the minister's ambitious plans for reform are shared and he receives approval across the executive. A number of the issues referred to above have been contentious in the past, have divided the communities and have influenced heavily whether support for law and order was given or withheld. If a justice system gradually evolves which satisfies a vast majority that the law is fair and is being administered in an even-handed way, the PSNI can only benefit in ways which would make policing by consent a genuine possibility in the medium-term future.

Undoubtedly the greatest challenge to the smooth functioning of policing and justice is the upsurge of sustained, well targeted and increasingly successful violent activity by dissident Republicans. Although until recently they have been dismissed by many as being few in number, unskilled technically, lacking community support and likely to cause only minor disruption, the RIRA and the CIRA (some ex-Provisional IRA) are said to have joined forces to share knowledge and expertise and to cooperate in wreaking havoc. Car bombs placed at the Policing Board Headquarters in Belfast, the Court House in Newry, Palace Barracks in Holywood where the Northern Ireland branch of MI5 is housed and two such bombs within one week positioned outside the police station in the border village of Newtownhamilton testify – by their choice of targets – to their diligent intent and symbolic opposition to devolution. The level of threat from these groups is now at its highest since just before the Belfast Agreement was signed.

Although cooperation between the PSNI and the Garda Síochána is not in question, the inadequacy of intelligence-gathering and the relatively slow response rate of the PSNI on some occasions are the issues to be addressed. In the politically sensitive area of south Armagh where Newtownhamilton is located the apparently tardy response of the PSNI put the safety of the community in jeopardy. Indeed two civilians were injured in the second incident and it was officers from the local fire and rescue service who were first on the scene to deal with the emergency, almost an hour, it is reported, ahead of the police. The anger and frustration of the villagers was voiced by the local Presbyterian minister who said that the residents of the village felt 'abandoned' by the PSNI (Nolan Show, BBC NI, 23 April 2010). The judgement and motivation must be called into question at command level – central and local since, even on the evening of the second attack, the station was unstaffed.

The recurring problem in the history of policing in Northern Ireland surfaces once more: violence and counter-insurgency take precedence over community policing, threatening progress towards policing by consent. The problem raises questions to be faced: does the PSNI have the will, the technical skills and resources and the necessary support from MI5 and from the public to overcome the dissident threat? If a political solution were needed to bring an end to Provo violence and win Sinn Féin support for the institutions, what else can be done, now and in the future to persuade dissidents to lay down their weapons and their explosive devices? Perhaps the British and Irish governments working together can provide a satisfactory solution.

It is only in peaceful, stable societies, according to the liberal model, that police can be accorded legitimacy because law-abiding citizens must agree on how police use their power and who the police are. While political and social cleavages in our society continue then, in my opinion, there cannot be full police reform because there is not full peace. The police will not enjoy consent, and try as they might, there will be no widespread partnership, until that real full peace has been achieved. Unfortunately for the PSNI, legitimacy has to be given voluntarily. The PSNI cannot afford to rest on its laurels but must adapt to a changing context and its changing demands. When Northern Ireland's politicians eventually resolve their difficulties there ought to be a police service second to none, able to add legitimacy to all the other features of the liberal model which have been embedded in its philosophy and practice since it began. A numerically representative police service will not of itself invest its members with recognition by the whole culturally Catholic community that officers have a right to police by consent. After further stages in incremental change have been achieved – brought about by the devolution of policing and justice largely – legitimacy is the Holy Grail to be sought.

Appendix 1 Questionnaire and quantitative analysis: tables

Questionnaire

(You are asked to give some basic information about yourself and your immediate family)

Q1   In what year were you born? ☐

Q2   Are you: male ☐   female ☐

Q3   Where were you born?
Northern Ireland	☐
Republic of Ireland	☐
England	☐
Scotland	☐
Wales	☐
Other	☐ Please specify ....

Q4   Are you **now**:
Married	☐
Living as married	☐
Single (never married)	☐
Divorced	☐
Separated	☐ } **Go to Q6**
Widowed	☐

Q5 (a)   Which of the following statements is true of your partner/spouse?
Working full-time	☐
Working part-time	☐
Not working (seeking work)	☐
Retired	☐
In full-time education	☐
Looking after the home	☐
Other	☐ Please specify ....

Q5 (b)   What is her/his job title?
         (*e.g. Vice Principal of a secondary school*)
         Please specify ....

Q5 (c)   Is she/he:
         Roman Catholic   ❑
         Protestant   ❑
         Other   ❑   Please specify ....
         No religion   ❑
         Don't know   ❑

Q6 (a)   (i) Have you ever had children?   Yes ❑   (ii) How many? ❑
                                           No   ❑   **Go to Q7 (a)**

Q6 (b)   Have/do your children attend/ed primary school in Northern Ireland?
         Yes   ❑
         No   ❑   **Go to Q6 (d)**
         Don't know   ❑

Q6 (c)   Were/are the pupils:
         Exclusively Roman Catholic   ❑
         Exclusively Protestant   ❑
         Some Roman Catholic, some Protestant   ❑
         Officially integrated   ❑
         Don't know   ❑

Q6 (d)   Have/do your children attend/ed secondary school in Northern Ireland?
         Yes   ❑
         No   ❑   **Go to Q7 (a)**
         Don't know   ❑

Q6 (e)   Were/are the pupils:
         Exclusively Roman Catholic   ❑
         Exclusively Protestant   ❑
         Some Roman Catholic, some Protestant   ❑
         Officially integrated   ❑
         Don't know   ❑

Q7 (a)   Are the heads of households where you live mainly security personnel?
         Yes   ❑
         No   ❑
         Don't know   ❑

Q7 (b) How would you describe the social profile of your neighbourhood?

Mostly middle class ☐
Mostly working class ☐
Well balanced in class terms ☐
Not sure ☐

Q7 (c) Indicate the proportion of your neighbours you estimate to be Roman Catholic:

All ☐
Most ☐
Fewer than half ☐
Very few ☐
Probably none ☐
Not sure ☐

Q8 (a) Did you attend primary school in Northern Ireland?

Yes ☐
No ☐ **Go to Q8 (c)**

Q8 (b) At your primary school were the pupils:

Exclusively Roman Catholic ☐
Exclusively Protestant ☐
Some Roman Catholic, some Protestant ☐
Officially integrated ☐
Don't know ☐

Q8 (c) Did you attend secondary school in Northern Ireland?

Yes ☐
No ☐ **Go to Q9**

Q8 (d) At your secondary school were the pupils:

Exclusively Roman Catholic ☐
Exclusively Protestant ☐
Some Roman Catholic, some Protestant ☐
Officially integrated ☐
Don't know ☐

Q8 (e) While you were at school, did you learn the Irish language?

Yes ☐
No ☐
Don't know ☐

Q8 (f) Did you learn Gaelic games?

Yes ☐
No ☐
Don't know ☐

Q8 (g) As far as you know, did police officers visit from time to time any of the schools you attended?
Yes ❑
No ❑
Don't know ❑ } **Go to Q9**

Q8 (h) In what capacity did they visit?
To teach road safety ❑
To arrange sports fixtures ❑
To improve community relations ❑
Other ❑ Please specify...

Q9 What is your highest educational qualification?
(i) Primary degree or higher ❑
(ii) BTEC (Higher), BEC (Higher), TEC (Higher, HNC, HND) ❑
(iii) GCE A-Level (including NVQ Level 3) ❑
(iv) BTEC (National), TEC (National), BEC (National), ONC, OND ❑
(v) GCSE (including NVG Level 2, GCE O-Level (including CSE Grade 1), Senior Certificate, BTEC (General), BEC (General) ❑
(vi) No formal qualification ❑
(vii) Other, please specify....................................... ❑

Q10 (a) Have you been in paid employment **outside of police forces** since you completed your full-time education?
Yes ❑
No ❑ **Go to Q11 (a)**

Q10 (b) For how long were you in other paid employment?
Less than 2 years ❑
3–5 years ❑
6–10 years ❑
More than 10 years ❑

Section 2

(This section deals with your police career)

Q11 (a) Are you a currently serving police officer?
Yes ❑ **Go to Q11 (c)**
No ❑

Q11 (b) Are you a retired police officer?
Yes ❑
No ❑

Q11 (c)   How long have you served in RUC/PSNI in complete years?

[ ]   Years

Q11 (d)   What rank do you currently hold/did you hold on retirement from RUC/PSNI?
Please specify..

Q11 (e)   Have you served in a police force outside Northern Ireland?
Yes ❏   Where? Please specify..
No ❏   **Go to Q11 (g)**

Q11 (f)   For how long did you serve in a police force outside Northern Ireland?
Less than 2 years ❏
3–5 years ❏
6–10 years ❏
More than 10 years ❏

Q11 (g)   In what branch of police work in Northern Ireland have you served longest?
(*e.g. traffic, special branch*)
Please specify..

Q11 (h)   In what type of geographical location have you spent **most** of your service as a
police officer? (Please tick **one** box only)
City in Northern Ireland ❏
Town in Northern Ireland ❏
Border area in Northern Ireland ❏
Other rural area in Northern Ireland ❏
Outside of Northern Ireland ❏

Q11 (i)   Approximately how many police officers are/were employed there at any one
time during your service?
1–5 ❏   6–10 ❏   11–20 ❏   21–50 ❏   More than 50 ❏

Q12 (a)   When you joined RUC/PSNI did you experience opposition?
Yes ❏
No ❏   **Go to Q12 (e)**

Q12 (b)   Where did the opposition come from?
(i)   Family ❏   (ii)   Peer group ❏   (iii)   Neighbours ❏
(iv)   Friends of your family ❏
(v)   Other ❏   Please specify..

Q12 (c)   Was the opposition at that time:
Very mild ❏
Mild ❏
Strong ❏
Very strong ❏
Not sure ❏

Q12 (d) How long did the opposition last? Please indicate:

Did it end after a short period?	❏ Yes	❏ No	
Has it weakened but remained as time passed?	❏ Yes	❏ No	
Is it still a big problem?	❏ Yes	❏ No	

Q12 (e) Have you had to position yourself apart from the Roman Catholic community in Northern Ireland since you joined RUC/PSNI?

Yes   ❏
No   ❏   **Go to Q12 (g)**

Q12 (f) By how much have you had to position yourself apart?

Very little   ❏
To some extent   ❏
To a large extent   ❏
Almost totally   ❏
Totally   ❏
Don't know   ❏

Q12 (g) How would you classify the political opinions you held on joining the force?

Strongly Unionist   ❏
Mildly Unionist   ❏
Neutral   ❏
Mildly Nationalist   ❏
Strongly Nationalist   ❏
Don't know   ❏

Q12 (h) How far were your political opinions broadly shared by your close family?

Definitely not at all   ❏
To a small extent   ❏
Probably not at all   ❏
A considerable amount   ❏
Definitely a great deal   ❏

Q13 (a) Think of your reasons for choosing a police career.
Put a figure **1** in the box after your most important reason, and number the others in **descending order** of importance to you **at the time you were recruited**.
(You need not number all of them if you do not wish to)

(i)   Following family tradition   ❏
(ii)   Job security   ❏
(iii) Varied and challenging work   ❏
(iv)   Opportunities for career advancement ❏
(v)   Wish to serve the community   ❏
(vi)   Good pay   ❏
(vii) Other   ❏ Please specify.........................

Q13 (b) Think of your reasons for being in PSNI.
Put a figure **1** in the box after your most important reason, and number the others in **descending order** of importance to you **now**.
(You need not number all of them if you do not wish to)
(i) Following family tradition ❑
(ii) Job security ❑
(iii) Varied and challenging work ❑
(iv) Opportunities for career advancement ❑
(v) Wish to serve the community ❑
(vi) Good pay ❑
(vii) Other ❑ Please specify ....

Q13 (c) Suppose a friend of yours was thinking about becoming a police officer here in Northern Ireland and asked you for advice. What would you do?
Encourage ❑   Discourage ❑   Neither ❑
If depends ❑   Don't know ❑

Section 3

(Kindly provide some factual information about your parents and relatives by answering the questions which follow)

Q14 (a) Have you any relatives who are serving police officers?
Yes ❑   How many? ❑
No ❑

Q14 (b) Are any of your relatives retired members of a police force?
Yes ❑   How many? ❑
No ❑

Q14 (c) Please give details for serving or retired police relatives:

	Name of force	Length of service in years	Rank now or on leaving	Relationship to you	Gender
Family member 1					
Family member 2					
Family member 3					
Family member 4					
Family member 5					

Q14 (d) Has your father been included at 14 (c) above?
Yes ☐   **Go to Q14 (f)**
No ☐

Q14 (e) What has been your father's occupation for most of his adult life?
Please specify, giving job title or level, if appropriate
....

Q14 (f) Has your mother been included at 14 (c) above?
Yes ☐   **Go to Q14 (h)**
No ☐

Q14 (g) What has been your mother's occupation for most of her adult life?
Please tick if she was a housewife ☐
Other ☐   Please specify, giving job title or level, if appropriate
....

Q14 (h) What religion are/were your parents?
Roman Catholic ☐
Protestant ☐
Other ☐   Please specify ....
No religion ☐
Don't know ☐

Section 4

(In this section you are invited to give your views on police culture – official and unofficial)

Q15 (a) Here is a list of terms which might be used to describe the **official culture** inside the police force. Please indicate how far you agree with each of them:

	Strongly agree	Agree	Disagree	Disagree strongly	Can't choose
Anti-Nationalist					
Anti-Roman Catholic					
Unionist					
Protestant					
British					
Sectarian					
Neutral					
Welcoming to Roman Catholics					
Welcoming to Nationalists					

Q15 (b) Here is a list of terms which might be used to describe the **unofficial culture** inside the police force. Please indicate how far you agree with each of them:

	Strongly agree	Agree	Disagree	Disagree strongly	Can't choose
Anti-Nationalist					
Anti-Roman Catholic					
Unionist					
Protestant					
British					
Sectarian					
Neutral					
Welcoming to Roman Catholics					
Welcoming to Nationalists					

Q15 (c) Have you experienced any discomfort caused by Protestant colleagues on religious grounds?
Yes ❑
No ❑   **Go to Q16**

Q15 (d) What caused the discomfort?
(Please make as many ticks as apply)
Sectarian jokes   ❑
Personal insults   ❑
Verbal intimidation   ❑
Physical intimidation   ❑
Uncooperative behaviour ❑
Ostracism   ❑
Other   ❑   Please specify...

Section 5

(This section invites you to give your views on moral, religious and socio-political matters)

Q16 (a) Roman Catholics in Northern Ireland have more in common with Northern Irish Protestants than with Roman Catholics in the Republic
Agree strongly   ❑
Agree   ❑
Disagree   ❑
Disagree strongly   ❑
Don't know   ❑

Q16 (b) Northern Irish Protestants have more in common with Northern Irish Catholics than with people in Britain

Agree strongly   ❑
Agree   ❑
Disagree   ❑
Disagree strongly   ❑
Don't know   ❑

Q16 (c) Separate Protestant and Roman Catholic schools have been a major cause of division in Northern Ireland

Agree strongly   ❑
Agree   ❑
Disagree   ❑
Disagree strongly   ❑
Don't know   ❑

Q16 (d) Religion will always make a difference to the way people feel about one another in Northern Ireland

Agree strongly   ❑
Agree   ❑
Disagree   ❑
Disagree strongly   ❑
Don't know   ❑

Q17 (a) Do you think it is wrong or not wrong if a **married** person has sexual relations with someone other than his or her wife or husband?

Always wrong   ❑
Almost always wrong ❑
Wrong only sometimes ❑
Not wrong at all   ❑
Can't choose   ❑

Q17 (b) What about sexual relations between two adults of the same sex?

Always wrong   ❑
Almost always wrong ❑
Wrong only sometimes ❑
Not wrong at all   ❑
Can't choose   ❑

Q17 (c) Do you personally think it is wrong or not wrong for a woman to have an abortion?

*(Please tick **one box** in **each line**)*

		Always wrong	Almost always wrong	Wrong only some-times	Not wrong at all	Can't choose
(i)	If there is a strong chance of a serious defect in the baby					
(ii)	If the family has a very low income and cannot afford any more children					

Q18 (a) Please tick **one** box to show which statement comes closest to expressing what you believe about God.

I don't believe in God ☐

I don't know whether there is a God and I don't believe there is any way to find out ☐

I don't believe in a personal God, but I do believe in a Higher Power of some kind ☐

I find myself believing in God some of the time, but not at others ☐

While I have doubts, I feel that I do believe in God ☐

I know God really exists and I have no doubts about it ☐

Q18 (b) What religion are you now?

Roman Catholic ☐

Protestant ☐

Other ☐

No religion ☐

Don't know ☐

Q18 (c) How often do you worship at a church service?

Never ☐

Less than once a year ☐

About once or twice a year ☐

Several times a year ☐

About once a month ☐

2–3 times a month ☐

Nearly every week ☐

Q19 (a) How successful do you think the PSNI is likely to be in **recruiting Roman Catholics** over the next 5 years?

Very successful ☐

Quite successful ☐

There will be no appreciable change ☐

Quite unsuccessful ☐

Very unsuccessful ☐

Don't know ☐

Q19 (b) Which of the following statements comes closest to your view on how the **Patten recommendations** on police reform have been implemented?

Too much change has taken place ❑
Just about the right amount has taken place ❑
Not enough change has taken place ❑
Undecided ❑

Q20 (a) Do you think the long-term policy for Northern Ireland should be for it . . .

To remain part of the United Kingdom ❑
To reunify with the rest of Ireland ❑
To become an independent state ❑
Other ❑   Please specify ....
Don't know ❑

Q20 (b) Thinking back to the Belfast Agreement, would you say it has benefited some members of the community more than others? Choose from the options below:

Unionists benefited a lot more than Nationalists ❑
Unionists benefited a little more than Nationalists ❑
Nationalists benefited a lot more than Unionists ❑
Nationalists benefited a little more than Unionists ❑
Unionists and Nationalists benefited equally ❑
Neither group benefited ❑
Other ❑   Please specify ....
Don't know ❑

Q21 Consider how fairly police officers in Northern Ireland treat civilians from the two main traditions
(*Please tick **one box** only*)

Roman Catholics are treated much better ❑
Roman Catholics are treated a little better ❑
Both are treated equally ❑
Protestants are treated a little better ❑
Protestants are treated much better ❑
Don't know/ Undecided ❑

Using the space below, please feel free to comment on the Questionnaire, and/or to answer more fully any of the questions asked.

Thank you for completing the Questionnaire.

Would you like to take part in a follow-up focus-group discussion?
❏ Yes ❏ No

Quantitative analysis: tables

Table 2 Typology categories applied to serving officers and trainees

	Flaunters	Chameleons	Deserters	Victims
Officers who transferred (N=50)	10%	66%	14%	10%
Trainees in PSNI (N=10)	—	80%	10%	10%

(The statistics must be read cautiously because the sizes of the samples were so unequal.)

Religion
Respondents were asked to give their current religion, that of their partners and of their parents.

Table 3 Religion of respondents, partners and parents

Religion	Respondents (%)	Partners (%)	Father (%)	Mother (%)
Roman Catholic	76	28	92.0	98
Protestant	3	49	8.0	2
Other	4	<1		
No religion	15	3		
Don't know	2	7		
Missing	<1	12		

'Please tick a box to show which statement comes closest to expressing what you believe about God'.

Table 4 Certainty of belief in God: Catholic police officers and the general Catholic population of NI

	Catholic police (%)	Catholic population (%)[1]
I don't believe in God	11	2
I don't know whether there is a God and I don't believe there is any way to find out	7	<1
I don't believe in a personal God, but I do believe in a Higher Power of some kind	10	3

Table 4   (continued)

	Catholic police (%)	Catholic population (%)[1]
While I have doubts, I feel I do believe in God	36	25
I know God really exists and I have no doubts about it	29	58

Note: 1   NILT, 2002

'How often do you worship at a church service?'

Table 5   Patterns of church attendance comparing Catholic officers and the Catholic population

Catholic officers	%	Catholic population	%[1]
Never	24	Never	8
Less than once a year	12	Less frequently than several times a year	10
About once or twice a year	20		
Several times a year	11	Several times a year	6
About once a month	12	Once a month	6
2–3 times a month	5	2–3 times a month	11
Nearly every week	15	Once or twice a week	59

Note: 1   NILT, 2003

Education

Table 6   Types of schools attended by officers and their children

	Respondents (%)		Respondents' children (%)	
	Primary	Secondary	Primary	Secondary
Exclusively Catholic	91	78	32	21
Exclusively Protestant	<1	7	18	11
Mixed	3	11	23	32
Officially integrated	<1	1	16	14
Don't Know/Missing	4	3	11	22

'What is your highest education qualification?'

Table 7   Highest education qualifications compared

	Catholic officers (%)	Catholic population (%)[1]
Primary degrees or higher	15	11
BTEC higher or equivalent	12	4
A-levels or equivalent	18	8
BTEC national or equivalent	6	3
GCSE or equivalent	34	25
No formal qualification	11	47
Other	4	3

Note: 1   NILT, 2003

Neighbourhoods
'How would you describe the social profile of your neighbourhood?'

Table 8   Perceived social-class profiles of officers' neighbourhoods

	%
Mostly middle class	51
Mostly working class	15
Well balanced in class terms	31
Not sure/Missing	3

'Indicate the proportion of your neighbours you estimate to be Roman Catholics'.

Table 9   Percentage of Catholic officers' neighbours perceived to be Catholic

	%
All	2
Most	10
Fewer than half	28
Very few	36
Probably none	9
Not sure/Missing	15

Previous employment

'Have you been in paid employment outside of police forces since you completed your full-time education? If so, for how long were you in other paid employment?'

Table 10   Catholic officers' employment experience before joining the RUC

	%
Less than 2 years	20
3–5 years	25
6–10 years	22
More than 10 years	16
Missing	17

Rank and service

Respondents were asked to declare their current rank and their length of service in Northern Ireland.

Table 11   Catholic officers' distribution of ranks

	%
Constable	59
Sergeant	14
Inspector	7
Chief inspector	1
Superintendent or above	<1
Missing	19

Choosing a police career

Officers surveyed were asked to select in descending order of importance their reasons for joining the RUC.

Table 12   Most important reasons for officers joining the RUC

	%
Following family tradition	2
Job security	13
Varied and challenging work	38
Opportunities for career advancement	5
Wish to serve the community	25
Good pay	10
Other/Missing	7

'Would you encourage a close relative to join the police, discourage them from joining, or neither?'

Table 13   Level of encouragement from Catholics to a close relative wishing to join the police

	1999 (%)			2000 (%)			2001 (%)		
	Age 18–29	*Age 30–45*	*Age 46+*	*Age 18–29*	*Age 30–45*	*Age 46+*	*Age 18–29*	*Age 30–45*	*Age 46+*
Encourage	19	25	37	20	19	28	34	24	36
Discourage	43	38	21	34	24	20	24	38	25
Neither/it depends	36	35	38	41	51	46	35	33	35
Don't know	2	2	5	5	7	7	6	4	5

Political opinions

Respondents were asked to report their political ideology when they joined the RUC.

Table 14   Self-reported political ideology and extent to which it was shared with their family

Political ideology of officers	%	Extent it was shared with family	%
Strongly unionist	<1	Definitely not at all	3
Mildly unionist	6	To a small extent	25
Neutral	66	Probably not at all	12
Mildly Nationalist	22	A considerable amount	43
Strongly Nationalist	3	Definitely a great deal	16
Don't know/Missing	2	Don't know/Missing	<1

Opposition to joining

'When you joined the RUC did you experience opposition?'

Table 15   (a) Sources of opposition; (b) Strength of opposition

(a)	%	(b)	%
Family	23	Very mild	7
Peer group	10	Mild	17
Neighbours	1	Strong	17
Friends of family	4	Very strong	8
Family + peer group	4	Not sure	<1
Family + friends of family	3	Missing	50
Other			
Missing	55		

Police culture

'Here is a list of terms which might be used to describe the official culture inside the police force. Please indicate how far you agree with them'.

Table 16   Officers' descriptions of police cultures

Strongly agree or disagree that it is:	*Official culture (%)*	*Unofficial culture (%)*
Anti-Nationalist	28	51
Anti-Roman Catholic	9	22
Unionist	49	69
Protestant	54	70
British	73	78
Sectarian	6	21
Neutral	68	51
Welcoming to Roman Catholics	76	65
Welcoming to Nationalists	36	28

Patten Report and police reform

'Which of the following statements comes closest to your view on how the Patten recommendations on police reform have been implemented?'

Table 17   Views on Patten's recommendations related to length of service

	Five years or less (%)	*Six years or more (%)*
Too much change	60	54
About the right amount	16	23
Not enough change	13	12
Undecided	11	12

'How successful do you think the PSNI is likely to be in recruiting Roman Catholics over the next 5 years?'

Table 18   Officers' perception of PSNI success in Catholic recruitment

	%
Very successful	7
Quite successful	55
No appreciable change	17
Quite unsuccessful	9
Very unsuccessful	5
Don't know	6

Community relations and constitutional preferences

'Roman Catholics in Northern Ireland have more in common with Northern Irish Protestants than with Roman Catholics in the Republic'.

Table 19   Catholic officers' perceptions of community commonality

	Current study (%)	Mapstone's study (%)
Agree/agree strongly	55	73
Disagree/disagree strongly	25	7
Don't know	18	20
Missing	2	<1

'Do you think the long-term policy for Northern Ireland should be for it. . .?

Table 20   Respondents' constitutional preferences compared with those of NI Catholics

	Catholic police officers (%)	Catholic population (%)[1]
. . . to remain part of the UK	53	22
. . . to reunify with the rest of Ireland	15	46
. . . to become an independent state	7	9
Other	13	3
Don't know	12	20

Note: 1   NILT, 2002

'Consider how fairly police officers in Northern Ireland treat civilians from the two main traditions'.

Table 21   Police treatment of civilians: comparison

	Views of Catholic police (%)	Views of Catholics (%)	Views of Protestants (%)
Catholics treated much better	0	0	1
Catholics treated a little better	3	1	4
Both treated equally	71	36	70
Protestants treated a bit better	19	32	12
Protestants treated much better	3	19	2
It depends/don't know	4	13	11

Note: 1   NILT, 1998

Appendix 2 Interview guide

Do you think that the Belfast Agreement was good news, or bad news for the people of Northern Ireland? Why?

How far do you think it will be implemented?
What are the main difficulties ahead?

The Patten Report was a direct result of the Belfast Agreement. How do you view the changes and the way they were introduced?

How far do you think broadly based, radical change was needed? Could the RUC have coped?

I'd like, if I may, to hear your views on three of the main recommendations:

(a)   the change in name and image
(b)   the emphasis placed on public accountability and transparency
(c)   50:50 Catholic:non-Catholic recruitment.

What effect did the name change, new badge and new uniform have on you and your colleagues?

How do you feel about new structures for accountability, such as the Ombudsman's Office, the Policing Board, the DPPs?

Do you think that the Catholic population should be represented numerically in the PSNI? Leaving the numbers aside, what other criteria should be taken into account when recruiting? Should Catholics from outside Northern Ireland be eligible? Do you think ex-prisoners should be accepted, other things being equal? Why?/Why not?

Why do you think Catholics, over the years, have applied in very small numbers? What are the chances of the PSNI recruitment targets being met in the foreseeable future? What factors might inhibit success?

Why did you decide to join? What was your main reason? Was it a difficult decision? Why? What sort of work did you before?

I'd like to hear about your family background – if you don't mind telling me about such things as your parents and extended family, your childhood, including your education. Would you say that you come from a traditional Catholic family? For example, Mass and prayers, Catholic schools, Irish culture, political outlook?

Did you give anyone a problem when you said that you wanted to join the RUC? What form did it take? What have relations with your family been since you joined? Any lasting problems?

What are your memories of training in the depot? Did you get any surprises? Were they good or bad? Did you feel that being a Catholic made life more difficult for you than for others? If so, what did you do about it? If not, why not?

Let's move on to your working life as a Catholic in the RUC. Were you proud of being a member? Why? In some quarters the RUC had a bad reputation. Was that in any way justified? Have any of the reasons for it gone away? Have any remained?

What kind of relations did you, as an individual, have with the Catholic Church and with the Catholic community while the RUC was policing the Troubles? What role do you think the church played in the community? Do you think it ought to have been different in any ways? How supportive or otherwise did you find your co-religionists?

In which types of areas have you served longest, for example in a city, along the border, in a Unionist town? Do you think that where an officer has served longest and his function influence his perception of the Catholic community? Might his area of origin make a difference, too?

Do you think that the Catholic community is likely to be more supportive of the PSNI than it was of the RUC? Do you think that geography, class or political outlook will play a part? How?

Do you consider that being a police officer is a career or a vocation? How would you explain the difference? Have your reasons for being a police officer changed since you joined? If so, how?

What do you understand by the term 'cultural Catholic'? What form does your cultural Catholicism take, for example are you a regular Mass attender, do you/would you send your children to Catholic schools, do you socialise with Catholics?

My survey showed half of the officers who returned the questionnaire had non-Catholic partners, which is much higher than in the general Catholic population. How would you explain this? What effects might this 'marrying out' have for the Catholic officer and the children? Can you identify with this situation?

Tell me about how you manage being a Catholic and a police officer. Have you a strategy which works for you? What is it? Which identity is more important to you? Why?

What do you think would be the best political arrangement for Northern Ireland's future? Do you think that your political views have changed since you became a police officer? If so, how and why?

Are there any comments you'd like to make as we come to the end of our discussion, which you've not been prompted to make already?

What has it been like so far overall? How do the rewards and the sacrifices compare? What are they? Would you recommend the PSNI to a relative or friend wanting to join? On conditions?

Will the PSNI meet the demanding standards which the government and the public expect? What sort of help will they need?

SOME QUESTIONS WERE OMITTED, MODIFIED, OR REPLACED
TO SUIT THE THREE SAMPLES INTERVIEWED –
RETIRED, SERVING AND TRAINEES

Appendix 3 Confidentiality agreement and the terms and conditions of access to the RUC for research purposes

This is an agreement between **Ms Mary Gethins** (hereinafter 'Recipient') and **Corporate Development** on behalf of the Chief Constable of the Royal Ulster Constabulary (hereinafter 'Discloser') under which the Discloser may disclose and the Recipient may receive certain confidential information for the sole purpose described in Appendix 'A' (hereinafter 'Information').

Confidentiality and Commitments

1. To consult with the Discloser on the detail of the proposed research and to seek the advice of the Discloser. This will involve submitting and agreeing a full research project specification.

2. To report to the Discloser any proposal to change the scope or content of the research and to advise the Discloser on the progress of the research.

3. From the date of the disclosure, the Recipient shall maintain the information in confidence and limit the use of that information in the purpose specified in Appendix 'A'. Recipient shall use a reasonable standard of care to avoid disclosure of information.

4. (a) The Recipient shall limit internal access to such information only to individuals, who have a need to know the information for the purpose of this Agreement, and only with the prior approval of the Discloser.

   (b) Each Officer will be approached ONLY from within the organisation to ask if they are willing to partake in this research. This will ensure privacy and confidentiality whilst also allowing the research to be entirely voluntary.

5. (a) The recipient shall not copy or reproduce, in whole or in part, any information without written authorisation of the Discloser, except as is necessary to fulfil the purpose stated in Appendix 'A'.

   (b) The Recipient shall submit the text of any proposed report, thesis, or other publication in connection with the research to the Discloser, permitting the Discloser the opportunity to comment on, and seek identification of any part of the text derived from official sources. This is to enable the Discloser to ensure that nothing published would be likely to cause embarrassment, for example, by the identification of any individual or institution.

   (c) The Recipient will ensure that no publication or communication in connection with the research through any channel of publicity will take place, without the approval of the Discloser, with regard to content, format and timing of any such publication.

(d) The Recipient shall, on completion of the research, make all reasonable efforts to promptly return all tangible information and copies thereof.

Ownership and Publication of Information

1. Ownership and copyright of information supplied by the Discloser to the Recipient shall remain with the Discloser.

Storage of Information

1. The Recipient shall ensure that all information supplied by the Discloser will be stored securely when not in use, whether in paper, computer disk or any other format.

General

1. The Discloser does not guarantee that the information to be supplied to the Recipient will be accurate and complete, unless otherwise agreed upon.

2. The Discloser accepts no responsibility for any expenses, losses or action incurred or undertaken by the Recipient as a result of the receipt of the information.

3. This agreement expresses the entire agreement and understanding of the Recipient and the Discloser, with respect to the subject matter thereof and supersedes all prior oral or written agreement, commitments and understandings pertaining to the subject matter.

4. This agreement shall not be modified or changed in any manner, except in writing and signed by both the Recipient and the Discloser. This shall also apply to any waiver of this requirement.

5. I accept that failure to comply with the above conditions may influence any future applications of a similar nature.

6. I recognise that failure to comply with the terms and conditions of the Data Protection Act (1984) is a criminal offence and contravention could lead to prosecution.

7. This agreement shall be governed by the substantive laws of the United Kingdom. The courts of Northern Ireland shall have exclusive jurisdiction over any dispute arising out of or in connection with this agreement. This shall not affect, however, any mandatory exclusive jurisdiction as provided by applicable law. The Discloser may also commence any court proceedings at the general place of jurisdiction or the registered principal office of the Recipient.

Recipient

Signed _____ Date _____

Discloser (On behalf of the Chief Constable of the Royal Ulster Constabulary)

Signed _____ Date _____

Appendix 'A'

The Discloser and Recipient agree the following as information:

(Include details of the Research in this section and, if applicable, stipulate caveats or conditions applying to the use, release, or subsequent disclosure of information.)

"Information" shall mean for the purposes of this contract, information in connection with the research proposal concerning **"RECRUITMENT TO THE POLICE SERVICE OF NORTHERN IRELAND"**.

No specific caveats apply so long as there is no contravention of the Data Protection legislation.

Bibliography

Ainsworth, P.B. (1995) *Psychology and Policing in a Changing World*. Chichester: Wiley.

Alliance Party (2010) *Alliance Party Proposals for a Programme for Government for Policing and Justice* (online), 8 February 2010. Available at: http://www.allianceparty.org/pages/justice.html

Altheide, D. and Johnson, M. (1998) 'Criteria for assessing interpretive validity in qualitative research'. In: Denzin, N.K. and Lincoln, Y.S. (eds) *Collecting and Interpreting Qualitative Materials*. London; Thousand Oaks, CA: Sage.

Amnesty International (1978) *Report of an Amnesty International Mission to Northern Ireland (28 November-6 December 1977)*. London: Amnesty International, International Secretariat.

Amnesty International (1994) *Political Killings in Northern Ireland*. London: Amnesty International British Section.

Anderson, D.M. and Killingray, D. (eds) (1991) *Policing the Empire: Government, Authority and Control, 1830–1940*. Manchester: Manchester University Press.

An Phoblacht, November 1993.

Arthur, P. (1984) *Government and Politics of Northern Ireland*. 2nd edn, London: Longman.

Asmal, K. (1985) *Shoot to Kill? International Lawyers' Inquiry into the Lethal Use of Firearms by the Security Forces in Northern Ireland*. Cork: Mercier Press.

Atkinson, P. (1990) *The Ethnographic Imagination: Textual Constructions of Reality*. London: Routledge.

Aydin, A.H. (1997) *Police Organisation and Legitimacy: Case Studies of England, Wales and Turkey*. Aldershot; Brookfield, VT: Avebury.

Babbie, E.R. (1995) *The Practice of Social Research*. 7th edn, Belmont, CA: Wadsworth.

Banton, M. (1964) *The Policeman in the Community*. London: Tavistock.

Bardon, J. (1992) *A History of Ulster*. Belfast: Blackstaff Press.

Barth, F. (1969) 'Introduction'. In: Barth, F. (ed.) *Ethnic Groups and Boundaries: The Social Organization of Culture Difference*. Bergen; London: Allen & Unwin: Universitetsforlaget.

Baxter, N.S.J. (1999) 'Policing the line: the development of a theoretical model for the policing of conflict through an examination of the role of the police in the management of conflict between divided societies within the United Kingdom'. Unpublished D.Phil. thesis, University of Ulster.

Bayley, D.H. (1976) *Forces of Order: Police Behavior in Japan and the United States*. London; Berkeley, CA: University of California Press.

Bayley, D.H. (2004) *Patterns Of Policing: A Comparative International Perspective*. New Brunswick, NJ: Rutgers University Press.

Bayley, D.H. and Mendelsohn, H. (1969) *Minorities and the Police: Confrontation in America*. New York: Free Press.

Belfast Telegraph, 6 February 1985.

Bell, J. (1993) *Doing Your Research Project: A Guide for First-Time Researchers in Education and Social Science*. 2nd edn, Buckingham: Open University Press.

Bellingham, T. (2000) 'Police culture and the need for change'. *Police Journal*, 73 (1), 31–41.

Bennett, B. (1999) 'Beyond affirmative action, police response to a changing society'. *Journal of California Law Enforcement*, 33 (2), 10–14.

Bennett, H.G. (1979) *Report of the Committee of Inquiry into Police Interrogation Procedures in Northern Ireland*. London: HMSO.

Bennis, W.G. (1966) *Changing Organizations: Essays on the Development and Evolution of Human Organization*. New York: McGraw Hill.

Bennis, W.G., Benne, K.D. and Chin, R. (1964) *The Planning of Change: Reading in the Applied Behavioral Sciences*. New York: Holt, Rinehart & Winston.

Bittner, E. (1970) *The Functions of the Police in Modern Society: A Review of Background Factors, Current Practices, and Possible Role Models*. Cambridge, MA: Oelgeschlager, Gunn & Hain.

Bland, N. (1999) *Career Progression of Ethnic Minority Police Officers*. London: Home Office, Policing and Reducing Crime Unit.

Blumer, H. (1969) *Symbolic Interactionism: Perspective and Method*. Englewood Cliffs, NJ: Prentice-Hall.

Bourdieu, P. (1990) *In Other Words: Essays Towards A Reflexive Sociology*. Cambridge: Polity Press.

Boyce, D.G. (1979) '"Normal policing": public order in Northern Ireland since partition'. *Eire-Ireland*, 14, 35–72.

Boyd, A. (1969) *Holy War in Belfast*. Tralee: Anvil Books.

Boyle, K. and Hadden, T. (1994) *Northern Ireland: The Choice*. London: Penguin.

Bradley, D., Walker, N. and Wilkie, R. (1986) *Managing the Police: Law, Organisation and Democracy*. Brighton: Wheatsheaf.

Bradley, R. (1998) *Public Expectations and Perceptions of Policing*. London: Home Office, Policing and Reducing Crime Unit.

Brady, C. (1974) *Guardians of the Peace*. Dublin: Gill and Macmillan.

Braiden, C. (1994) 'Policing from the belly of the whale'. In: Macleod, R.C. and Scheiderman, D. (eds) *Police Powers in Canada: The Evaluation and Practice of Authority*. Toronto; Buffalo: Published in association with the Centre for Constitutional Studies, University of Alberta, by University of Toronto Press.

Breathnach, S. (1974) *The Irish Police: From Earliest Times to the Present Day*. Dublin: Anvil Books.

Breen, R. (1996) 'Who wants a United Ireland?'. In: Breen, R., Devine, P. and Dowds, L. (eds) *Social Attitudes in Northern Ireland*, 5th Report. Belfast: Appletree Press.

Brewer, J.D. (1988) *The Police, Public Order and the State: Policing in Great Britain, Northern Ireland, the Irish Republic, the USA, Israel, South Africa, and China*. Basingstoke: Macmillan.

Brewer, J.D. (1990) *The Royal Irish Constabulary: An Oral History*. Belfast: Institute of Irish Studies, Queen's University of Belfast.

Brewer, J.D. (1992) 'The public and the police'. In: Stringer, P. and Robinson, G. (eds) *Social Attitudes in Northern Ireland*, 2nd Report. Belfast: Blackstaff Press.

Brewer, J.D. (1993a) 'Policing in Northern Ireland'. In: Matthews, M.L., Heymann, P.B. and Mathews, A.S. (eds) *Policing the Conflict in South Africa*. Gainesville, FL: University Press of Florida.

Brewer, J.D. (1993b) 'Re-educating the South African police'. In: Matthews, M.L., Heymann, P.B. and Mathews, A.S. (eds) *Policing the Conflict in South Africa*. Gainesville, FL: University Press of Florida.

Brewer, J.D. (1993c) 'Sensitivity as a problem in field research: a study of routine policing in Northern Ireland'. In: Renzetti, C.M. and Lee, R.M. (eds) *Researching Sensitive Topics*. London; Newbury Park, CA: Sage.

Brewer, J.D. (1993d) 'Public images of the police in Northern Ireland'. *Policing and Society*, 3, 163–76.

Brewer, J.D. (1994) *Black and Blue: Policing in South Africa*. Oxford: Clarendon Press.

Brewer, J.D. (2000) *Ethnography*. Buckingham: Open University Press.

Brewer, J.D. (2002) 'Are there any Christians in Northern Ireland?' In: Gray, A.M., Lloyd, K., Devine, P., Robinson, G. and Heenan, D. (eds) *Social Attitudes in Northern Ireland*, 8th Report. London: Pluto.

Brewer, J.D. and Magee, K. (1991) *Inside the RUC: Routine Policing in a Divided Society*. Oxford: Clarendon.

Brodeur, J.-P. (ed.) (1998) *How to Recognize Good Policing: Problems and Issues*. London; Thousand Oaks, CA: Sage.

Brogden, M. (1982) *The Police: Autonomy and Consent*. London: Academic Press.

Brogden, M. (1989) 'The origins of the South African Police: institutional versus structural approaches'. In: Bennett, T.W. (ed.) *Policing and the Law*. Cape Town: Juta.

Brogden, M. (1995) 'An agenda for post-troubles policing in Northern Ireland – the South African precedent'. *Liverpool Law Review*, 17 (1), 3–27.

Brogden, M. and Shearing, C. (1993) *Policing for a New South Africa*. London: Routledge.

Brogden, M., Jefferson, T. and Walklate, S. (1988) *Introducing Policework*. London; Boston: Unwin Hyman.

Brown, L. (1977) 'Bridges over troubled waters: a perspective on policing in the black community'. In: Woodson, R.L. (ed.) *Black Perspectives on Crime and the Criminal Justice System: A Symposium*. Boston: G.K. Hall.

Bruce, S. (1986) *God Save Ulster: The Religion and Politics of Paisleyism*. Oxford: Clarendon Press.

Bruce, S. (1992) *The Red Hand: Protestant Paramilitaries in Northern Ireland*. Oxford: Oxford University Press.

Bruce, S. (1994) *The Edge of the Union: The Ulster Loyalist Political Vision*. Oxford: Oxford University Press.

Bruce, S. (1995) *Religion in Modern Britain*. Oxford; New York: Oxford University Press.

Bruce, S. and Alderdice, F. (1993) 'Religious belief and behaviour'. In: Stringer, P. and Robinson, G. (eds) *Social Attitudes in Northern Ireland*, 3rd Report. Belfast: Blackstaff Press.

Buckland, P. (1979) *The Factory of Grievances: Devolved Government in Northern Ireland, 1921–39*. Dublin: Gill and Macmillan.

Bulmer, M. (1980) 'Comment on "the ethics of covert methods"'. *British Journal of Sociology*, 31 (1), 59–65.

Bulmer, M. (ed.) (1982) *Social Research Ethics: An Examination of the Merits of Covert Participant Observation*. London: Macmillan.

Butler, A.J.P. and Cochrane, R. (1977) 'An examination of some elements of the personality of police officers and their implications'. *Journal of Police Science and Administration*, 5, 441–50.

Cain, M. (1973) *Society and the Policeman's Role*. London: Routledge & Kegan Paul.

Cain, M. (1979) 'Trends in the sociology of policework'. *International Journal of the Sociology of Law*, 7 (2), 143–67.

Cameron, J. (1969) *Disturbances in Northern Ireland: Report of the Commission Under the Chairmanship of Lord Cameron appointed by the Governor of Northern Ireland* (The Cameron Report). Belfast: HMSO.

Cameron, M. (1993) *The Women in Green: Golden Jubilee 1943–1993: A History of the Royal Ulster Constabulary's Policewomen*. Belfast: RUC Historical Society.

Cash, J.D. (1996) *Identity, Ideology and Conflict: The Structuration of Politics in Northern Ireland*. Cambridge: Cambridge University Press.

Castles, S.B., Cope, M.K. and Morrissey, M. (1988) *Mistaken Identity: Multiculturalism and the Demise of Nationalism in Australia*. Sydney: Pluto Press.

Cawthra, G. (1993) *Policing South Africa: The South African Police and the Transition from Apartheid*. London: Zed.

Chan, J.B.L. (1997) *Changing Police Culture: Policing in a Multicultural Society*. Cambridge: Cambridge University Press.

Clark, C. (1971) *Tales of the British Columbia Provincial Police*. Sidney, BC: Gray's Publishing.

Coffey, A. (1999) *The Ethnographic Self: Fieldwork and the Representation of Identity*. London; Thousand Oaks, CA: Sage.

Commission for Racial Equality (1996) *Race and Equal Opportunities in the Police Service: A Programme for Action*. London: Commission for Racial Equality.

Committee on the Administration of Justice (1996) *The Misrule of Law: A Report on the Policing of Events during the Summer of 1996 in Northern Ireland*. Belfast: Committee on the Administration of Justice.

Coulter, C. and Murray, M. (eds) (2008) *Northern Ireland after the Troubles: A Society in Transition*. Manchester: Manchester University Press.

Critchley, T.A. (1978) *A History of Police in England and Wales*. Rev. edn, London: Constable.

Cummings, L.L. and Straw, B.M. (eds) (1982) *Research in Organizational Behavior: An Annual Series of Analytical Essays and Critical Reviews*.Vol. 4 Connecticut, CO: JAI Press.

Cunneen, C. (1990) *Aboriginal-Police Relations in Redfern: With Special Reference to the 'Police Raid' of 8 February 1990*. Sydney: Human Rights and Equal Opportunity Commission.

Curtis, R. (1869) *The History of the Royal Irish Constabulary*. Dublin; London: Simpkin & Company: Moffat & Company.

Daly, C. (1989) 'Interview of Bishop Cathal Daly'. *Irish Times*, 23 August.

Dantzker, M.L. (ed.) (1997) *Contemporary Policing: Personnel, Issues and Trends*. Oxford: Butterworth-Heinemann.

Darby, J. (1976) *Conflict in Northern Ireland: The Development of a Polarised Community*. Dublin: Gill & Macmillan.

De Silva, P.L. and Munck, R. (eds) (1999) *Postmodern Insurgencies: Political Violence, Identity Formation and Peacemaking in Comparative Perspective*. Basingstoke: Macmillan.

Denzin, N.K. and Lincoln, Y.S. (eds) (1994) *Handbook of Qualitative Research*. London; Thousand Oaks, CA: Sage.

Dillon, M. (1999) *Catholic Identity: Balancing Reason, Faith and Power*. Cambridge; New York: Cambridge University Press.

Dippenaar, M. de Witt (1988) *The History of the South African Police, 1913–1988*. Silverton: Promedia Publications.

'Dissident groups warn of continued resistance in "10"'. *Irish News*, 4 January 2010, 15.

Doyle, C. (1991) *Police Recruitment from Ethnic Minorities: A Strategy*. London: Home Office.

Dunphy, D.C. and Stace, D. (1990) *Under New Management: Australian Organizations in Transition*. Sydney; New York: McGraw-Hill.

Elias, N. (1965) 'Introduction: a theoretical essay on established and outsider relations'. In: Elias, N. and Scotson, J.L. *The Established and the Outsiders: A Sociological Enquiry into Community Problems*. London: Frank Cass.

Ellison, G. (1997) 'Professionalism in the Royal Ulster Constabulary: an examination of the institutional discourse'. Unpublished D.Phil. thesis, University of Ulster.

Ellison, G. and Smyth, J. (2000) *The Crowned Harp: Policing Northern Ireland*. London: Pluto Press.

Enloe, C.H. (1980) *Ethnic Soldiers: State Security in Divided Societies*. Harmondsworth: Penguin.

Farrell, M. (1980) *Northern Ireland: The Orange State*. 2nd edn, London: Pluto Press.

Farrell, M. (1983) *Arming the Protestants: The Formation of the Ulster Special Constabulary and the Royal Ulster Constabulary, 1920–7*. Dingle: Brandon.

Fennell, D. (1989) *The Revision of Irish Nationalism*. Dublin: Open Air.

Fennell, T. (2003) *The Royal Irish Constabulary: A History and Personal Memoir*. Dublin: University College Dublin Press.

Field, S. and Southgate, P. (1982) *Public Disorder: A Review of Research and a Study in One Inner City Area*. London: HMSO.

Fielding, N. (1988) *Joining Forces: Police Training, Socialization and Occupational Competence*. London: Routledge.

Fielding, N. (1991) *The Police and Social Conflict: Rhetoric and Reality*. London: Athlone.

Fielding, N. (1994) 'Cop canteen culture'. In: Newburn, T. and Stanko, E.A. (eds) *Just Boys Doing Business? Men, Masculinities and Crime*. London: Routledge.

Fielding, N. (1995) *Community Policing*. Oxford: Clarendon Press.

Findlay, M. and Zvekić, V. (eds) (1993) *Alternative Policing Style: Cross-Cultural Perspectives*. Boston; Deventer, the Netherlands: Kluwer Law and Taxation Publishers.

Finnane, M. (1990) 'Police corruption and police reform: the Fitzgerald Inquiry in Queensland, Australia'. *Policing and Society*, 1, 159–71.

Finnane, M. (1994) *Police and Government: Histories of Policing in Australia*. Melbourne; New York: Oxford University Press.

Flick, U. (1998) *An Introduction to Qualitative Research*. London: Sage.

Forcese, D. (1992) *Policing Canadian Society*. Scarborough, Ont.: Prentice-Hall Canada.

Fosdick, R.B. (1969) *European Police Systems*. Montclair, NJ: Patterson Smith.

Foster, J. (1989) 'Two stations: an ethnographic study of policing in the inner city'. In: Downes, D.M. (ed.) *Crime and the City: Essays in Memory of John Barron Mays*. Basingstoke: Macmillan.

Froyland, I.B. and Skeffington, M. (1993) *Aboriginal and Torres Strait Islander Employment Strategy: A Five Year Plan for the Police Force of Western Australia*. Perth, WA: Centre for Police Research, Edith Cowan University.

Galtung, J. (1967) *Theory and Methods of Social Research*. Oslo; London: George Allen & Unwin: Universitetsforlaget.

Gamson, W.A. (1992) *Talking Politics*. Cambridge: Cambridge University Press.

Gardiner Committee (1975) *Report of a Committee to Consider, in the Context of Civil Liberties and Human Rights, Measures to Deal with Terrorism in Northern Ireland*. Cmnd 5847. London: HMSO.

Garfinkel, H. (1967) *Studies in Ethnomethodology*. Englewood Cliffs, NJ: Prentice-Hall.

Garrow-Green, G. (1905) *In the Royal Irish Constabulary*. London: James Blackwood.

Gaughan, J.A. (ed.) (1975) *Memoirs of Constable Jeremiah Mee*. Dublin: Anvil Books.

Giddens, A. (1979) *Central Problems in Social Theory: Action, Structure and Contradiction in Social Analysis*. London: Macmillan.

Girden, E.R. (1996) *Evaluating Research Articles: From Start to Finish*. London: Sage.

Goffman, E. (1969) *The Presentation of Self in Everyday Life*. London: Allen Lane.

Gold, R.L. (1958) 'Roles in sociological field observations'. *Social Forces*, 36 (3), 217–23.

Goldstein, J. and Rayner, J. (1994) 'The politics of identity in late modern society'. *Theory and Society*, 23 (3), 367–84.

Government of Northern Ireland (1972) *Violence and Civil Disturbance in Northern Ireland in 1969: Report of Tribunal of Inquiry* (The Scarman Report). Belfast: HSMO.

Greiner, L.E. (1965) 'Organization change and development: a study of changing values, behavior, and performance in a large industrial plant'. Unpublished Ph.D. thesis, Harvard University, Graduate School of Business Administration.

Griffin, B. (1991) 'The Irish police, 1836–1914: a social history'. Unpublished Ph.D. thesis, Loyola University of Chicago.

Griffin, B. (1997) *The Bulkies: Police and Crime in Belfast, 1800–1865*. Dublin; Portland, OR: Irish Academic Press in association with the Irish Legal History Society.

Griffiths, C. (1988) 'Native Indians and the police: the Canadian experience'. *Police Studies*, 11 (4), 155–60.

Griffiths, C.T. (1994) 'Policing Aboriginal peoples'. In: Macleod, R.C. and Scheiderman, D. (eds) *Police Powers in Canada: The Evaluation and Practice of Authority*. Toronto; Buffalo: Published in association with the Centre for Constitutional Studies, University of Alberta, by University of Toronto Press.

Guelke, A. (ed.) (1994) *New Perspectives on the Northern Ireland Conflict*. Aldershot: Avebury.

Bibliography

Guelke, A. and Wright, F. (1992) 'On a British withdrawal from Northern Ireland'. In: Stringer, P. and Robinson, G. (eds) *Social Attitudes in Northern Ireland*, 2nd Report. Belfast: Blackstaff Press.

Hahn, P.H. (1998) *Emerging Criminal Justice: Three Pillars for a Proactive Justice System*. London: Sage.

Hainsworth, P. (ed.) (1998) *Divided Society: Ethnic Minorities and Racism in Northern Ireland*. London: Pluto.

Hall, S. (1992) 'Our mongrel selves'. *New Statesman and Society*, 19 June, special supplement, 6–8.

Hammersley, M. (1990) *Reading Ethnographic Research: A Critical Guide*. London: Longman.

Hammersley, M. (1995) *The Politics of Social Research*. London: Sage.

Hammersley, M. and Atkinson, P. (1989) *Ethnography: Principles in Practice*. London: Routledge.

Harding, J. (1994) 'Policing and Aboriginal justice'. *Canadian Journal of Criminology*, 33 (3–4), 363–83.

Harkness, D.W. (1983) *Northern Ireland Since 1920*. Dublin: Helicon.

Hart, C. (1998) *Doing a Literature Review: Releasing the Social Science Research Imagination*. London: Sage.

Haysom, N. (1989) 'Policing the police: a comparative survey of police control mechanisms in the United States, South Africa and the United Kingdom'. *Acta Juridica*, 139, 150.

Heidensohn, F. (1992) *Women in Control? The Role of Women in Law Enforcement*. Oxford: Clarendon.

Herbert, S. (1998) 'Police subculture reconsidered'. *Criminology*, 36 (2), 343–69.

Herlihy, J. (1997) *The Royal Irish Constabulary: A Short History and Genealogical Guide*. Dublin: Four Courts Press.

Her Majesty's Inspectorate of Constabulary (1992) *Equal Opportunities in the Police Service: A Report of Her Majesty's Inspectorate of Constabulary*. London: Home Office.

Her Majesty's Inspectorate of Constabulary (1996) *Primary Inspection, Royal Ulster Constabulary: A Report of Her Majesty's Inspectorate of Constabulary*. London: Home Office, for the Northern Ireland Office.

Her Majesty's Inspectorate of Constabulary (1997) *Winning the Race: Policing Plural Communities: HMIC Thematic Inspection Report on Police Community and Race Relations 1996/97*. London: Home Office.

Hermon, J.C. (1997) *Holding the Line: An Autobiography*. Dublin: Gill & Macmillan.

Heskin, K. (1980) *Northern Ireland: A Psychological Analysis*. Dublin: Gill & Macmillan.

Hillyard, P. (1997) 'Policing divided societies: trends and prospects in Northern Ireland and Britain'. In: Francis, P., Davies, P. and Jupp, V. (eds) *Policing Futures: The Police, Law Enforcement and the Twenty-First Century*. Basingstoke: Macmillan.

Hillyard, P. and Tomlinson, M. (2000) 'Patterns of policing and policing Patten'. *Journal of Law and Society*, 27 (3), 394–415.

Holdaway, S. (1983) *Inside the British Police: A Force at Work*. Oxford: Blackwell.

Holdaway, S. (1991) *Recruiting a Multi-Racial Police Force: A Research Study*. London: HMSO.

Holdaway, S. (1993) *The Resignation of Black and Asian Officers from the Police Service*. London: Home Office.

Holdaway, S. (1996) *The Racialisation of British Policing*. Basingstoke: Macmillan.

Holdaway, S. and Barron, A.-M. (1997) *Resigners? The Experience of Black and Asian Police Officers*. Basingstoke: Macmillan.

Holdaway, S. and Chatterton, M.R. (eds) (1979) *The British Police*. London: Edward Arnold.

Home Office (1981) *The Brixton Disorders 10–12 April 1981: Report of an Inquiry by Lord Scarman*. London: HMSO.

Horowitz, D. (1994) *Ethnic Politics*. London: Cornell University Press.

Horrall, S.W. (1973) *The Pictorial History of the Royal Canadian Mounted Police*. Toronto; New York: McGraw-Hill Ryerson.

House of Commons (2000) *Police (Northern Ireland) Bill*.

Hughes, E.C. (1994) *On Work, Race and the Sociological Imagination*. Edited and with an introduction by Lewis A. Coser. Chicago: University of Chicago Press.

Hughes, J.A. (1990) *The Philosophy of Social Research*. 2nd edn, London: Longman.

Independent Commission on Policing for Northern Ireland (1999) *A New Beginning: Policing in Northern Ireland: the Report of the Independent Commission on Policing for Northern Ireland* (The Patten Report). Belfast: HMSO.

International Monitoring Commission (Northern Ireland) (2006) *Eighth Report of the International Monitoring Commission: presented to the Government of the United Kingdom and the Government of Ireland under Articles 4 and 7 of the International Agreement Establishing the Independent Monitoring Commission*. London: Stationery Office.

Irish News, 24 August 2004.

Jarvis, J. (1992) *Inventory of Aboriginal Policing Programs in Canada, Part 1: Aboriginal Police Officer Development and Policing*. Ottawa: Ministry of Supply and Services.

Jeffries, C.J. (1952) *The Colonial Police*. London: Max Parrish.

Jenkins, R. (2004) *Social Identity*. 2nd edn, London: Routledge.

Jobson, K.B. (1993) *First Nations Police Services: Legal Issues*. Victoria, BC: Policing in British Columbia Commission of Inquiry.

Johnson, P. (1981) *Ireland: A History From the Twelfth Century to the Present Day*. London; New York: Granada.

Kearney, V. (2009) 'Report blasts state of policing' (online). *BBC News*, 26 August (available at: http://news.bbc.co.uk/1/hi/northern_ireland/foyle_and_west/8223225.stm).

Kennedy, A. (1967) 'The RUC'. *Police Journal*, 40 (February), 53–61.

Krueger, R.A. (1994) *Focus Groups: A Practical Guide for Applied Research*. 2nd edn, Thousand Oaks, CA: Sage.

La Prairie, C. (1995) *Seen But Not Heard: Native People in the Inner City*. Ottawa: Department of Justice of Canada, Communications and Consultation Branch.

Laffan, M. (1983) *The Partition of Ireland 1911–25*. Dublin: Dublin Historical Association.

Landa, D.E. (1995) *Race Relations and Our Police: A Special Report to Parliament under Section 31 of the Ombudsman Act: January 1995*. Sydney: NSW Ombudsman.

Latham, R. (2001) *Deadly Beat: Inside the Royal Ulster Constabulary*. Edinburgh: Mainstream.

Law Society of England and Wales (1995) *Northern Ireland: An Emergency Ended? Report of the International Human Rights Working Party*. London: Law Society.

Lawyers Committee for Human Rights (1993) *Human Rights and Legal Defense in Northern Ireland: The Murder of Patrick Finucane: The Intimidation of Defense Lawyers.* New York: Lawyers Committee for Human Rights.

Lawyers Committee for Human Rights (1996) *At the Crossroads: Human Rights and the Northern Ireland Peace Process.* New York: Lawyers Committee for Human Rights.

Lederach, J.P. (1997) *Building Peace: Sustainable Reconciliation in Divided Societies.* Washington, DC: United States Institute of Peace Press.

Lee, R.M. (1995) *Dangerous Fieldwork.* London; Thousand Oaks, CA: Sage.

Lennon, B. (2004) 'Catholics in Northern Ireland: Ambivalence Rules?'. *Research Update,* 22.

Lijphart, A. (1975) 'Northern Ireland problem: cases, theories, and solutions'. *British Journal of Political Science,* 5 (1), 83–106.

Lincoln, Y.S. and Guba, E.G. (1985) *Naturalistic Inquiry.* Beverly Hills, CA: Sage.

Lofland, J. (1971) *Analysing Social Settings: A Guide to Qualitative Observation and Analysis.* Belmont, CA: Wadsworth.

McArdle, P. (1984) *The Secret War: An Account of the Sinister Activities Along the Border Involving Gardaí, RUC, British Army and the SAS.* Dublin: Mercier Press.

McCall, C. (1999) *Identity in Northern Ireland: Communities, Politics and Change.* Basingstoke: Macmillan.

McConville, M., Sanders, A. and Leng, R. (1991) *The Case for the Prosecution: Police Suspects and the Construction of Criminality.* London: Routledge.

McCullagh, H.M. (1981) 'The Royal Ulster Constabulary'. *Police Studies,* 4 (4), 3–12.

McGarry, J. (2000) 'Police reform in Northern Ireland'. *Irish Political Studies,* 15, 173–82.

McGarry, J. and O'Leary, B. (1995) *Explaining Northern Ireland: Broken Images.* Oxford: Blackwell.

McGarry, J. and O'Leary, B. (1999) *Policing Northern Ireland: Proposals for a New Start.* Belfast: Blackstaff Press.

McGinty, R. and Wilford, R. (2002) 'More knowing than knowledgeable: attitudes towards devolution'. In: Gray, A.M., Lloyd, K., Devine, P., Robinson, G. and Heenan, D. (eds) *Social Attitudes in Northern Ireland,* 8th Report. London: Pluto.

McGuigan, B.J. (1995) 'The future role of the RUC in policing the nationalist community in Northern Ireland'. Unpublished MA dissertation, University of Exeter.

McKenzie, I.K. and Gallagher, G.P. (1989) *Behind the Uniform: Policing in Britain and America.* Hemel Hempstead: Harvester Wheatsheaf.

McLysaght, E. (1950) *Irish Life in the Seventeenth Century.* 2nd edn, Cork: Cork University Press.

McNiffe, L. (1997) *A History of the Garda Síochána: A Social History of the Force 1922–52, with an Overview for the Years 1952–97.* Dublin: Wolfhound Press.

Macpherson of Cluny, Sir W. (1999) *Sir William Macpherson's Inquiry into the Matters Arising from the Death of Stephen Lawrence on 22 April 1993 to Date, in Order Particularly to Identify the Lessons to be Learned for the Investigation and Prosecution of Racially Motivated Crimes: Evidence Submitted by the Home Office to the Second Part of the Inquiry* (The Macpherson Report). London: HMSO.

Magill, M. (2006) 'A community perspective'. *Call Sign,* January, 1–4.

Maguire, B.P. (1994) 'The causes and effects of under-representation of Catholics within the Royal Ulster Constabulary'. Unpublished BA dissertation, University of Ulster at Jordanstown.

Mann, P.H. (1976) *Methods of Sociological Enquiry*. Oxford: Blackwell.

Manning, P.K. (1972) 'Observing the police: deviants, respectables and the law'. In: Douglas, J.D. (ed.) *Research on Deviance*. New York: Random House.

Manning, P.K. (1977) *Police Work: The Social Organization of Policing*. Cambridge, MA: MIT Press.

Manning, P.K. (1989) 'Occupational culture'. In: Bailey, W.G. (ed.) *The Encyclopedia of Police Science*. New York: Garland.

Mapstone, R.H. (1994) *Policing in a Divided Society: A Study of Part Time Policing in Northern Ireland*. Aldershot: Avebury.

Marenin, O. (ed.) (1996) *Policing Change, Changing Police: International Perspectives*. London; New York: Garland.

Marshall, C. and Rossman, G.B. (1995) *Designing Qualitative Research*. London; Thousand Oaks, CA: Sage.

Martin, S.E. (1980) *Breaking and Entering: Policewomen on Patrol*. Berkeley, CA: University of California Press.

Mason, J. (2002a) 'Qualitative interviews: asking, listening and interpreting'. In: May, T. (ed.) *Qualitative Research in Action*. London: Sage.

Mason, J. (2002b) *Qualitative Researching*. 2nd edn, London: Sage.

Matthews, M.L., Heymann, P.B. and Mathews, A.S. (1993) (eds) *Policing the Conflict in South Africa*. Gainesville, FL: University Press of Florida.

Mawby, R.I. (1990) *Comparative Policing Issues: The British and American System in International Perspective*. London: Unwin Hyman.

Mead, G.H. (1934) *Mind, Self and Society: From the Standpoint of a Social Behaviorist*. London; Chicago, IL: University of Chicago Press.

Mehta, V. (1993) *Policing Services for Aboriginal Peoples*. Ottawa: Ministry of Supply and Services.

Miller, W.R. (1977) *Cops and Bobbies: Police Authority in New York and London, 1830–1870*. Chicago, IL: University of Chicago Press.

Mills, C.W. (1959) *The Sociological Imagination*. New York: Oxford University Press.

Morgan, D.L. (1997) *Focus Groups as Qualitative Research*. 2nd edn, Thousand Oaks, CA: Sage.

Morrison, W.R. (1985) *Showing the Flag: The Mounted Police and Canadian Sovereignty in the North, 1894–1925*. Vancouver: University of British Columbia Press.

Moser, C. and Kalton, G. (1971) *Survey Methods in Social Investigation*. 2nd edn, Aldershot: Gower.

Mulcahy, A. (2000) 'Policing history: the official discourse and organizational memory of the Royal Ulster Constabulary'. *British Journal of Criminology*, 40 (1), 68–87.

Mulcahy, A. (2006) *Policing Northern Ireland: Conflict, Legitimacy and Reform*. Devon: Willan Publishing.

Murphy, E. and Dingwall, R. (2001) 'The ethics of ethnography'. In: Atkinson, P., Coffey, A., Delamont, S., Lofland, J. and Lofland, L.H. (eds) *Handbook of Ethnography*. London: Sage.

Murray, D. (1995) 'Culture, religion and violence in Northern Ireland'. In: Dunn, S. (ed.) *Facets of the Conflict in Northern Ireland*. New York; Basingstoke: Macmillan: St. Martin's Press.

Murray, R. (1990) *The SAS in Ireland*. Cork: Mercier Press.

Murray, R. (1998) *State Violence in Northern Ireland, 1969–1997*. Cork: Mercier Press.

Neligan, D. (1968) *The Spy in the Castle*. London: MacGibbon and Kee.

Newman, K. (1978) 'Prevention in extremis: the preventative role of the police in Northern Ireland'. In: Brown, J. (ed.) *Cranfield Papers: The Proceedings of the 1978 Cranfield Conference on the Prevention of Crime in Europe*. London: Peel Press.

Niederhoffer, A. (1969) *Behind the Shield: The Police in Urban Society*. Garden City, NY: Doubleday.

Northern Ireland Affairs Committee (1998) *Composition, Recruitment and Training of the RUC, Volume 2: Minutes of Evidence and Appendices*. London: Stationery Office.

Northern Ireland Census 2001: Key Statistics (2003) Belfast: Northern Ireland Statistics and Research Agency.

Northern Ireland Council for Integrated Education (2005) *NICIE Annual Report 2004–2005*. Belfast: NICIE.

Northern Ireland Life and Times Survey: Annual Report, 1998 onwards. Belfast: ARK.

Northern Ireland Office (1998) *The Belfast Agreement: An Agreement Reached at the Multi-Party Talks on Northern Ireland*. London: Stationery Office.

Northern Ireland Office (2005) *Devolving Policing and Justice in Northern Ireland: A Discussion Paper*. Belfast: Northern Ireland Office.

Northern Ireland Parliament (1969) *Report of the Advisory Committee on Police in Northern Ireland* (The Hunt Report). Belfast: HMSO.

Northern Ireland Policing Board (2005) *Annual Review 2004–2005*. Belfast: Northern Ireland Policing Board.

Ó Dochartaigh, N. (1997) *From Civil Rights to Armalites: Derry and the Birth of the Irish Troubles*. Cork: Cork University Press.

Oakley, R. (1996) 'Black marks'. *Police Review*, 22 March, 24–5.

O'Neill, S. and Bathgate, J.L. (1993) *Policing Strategies in Aboriginal and Non-English Speaking Background Communities: Final Report*. Winnellie, NT: Northern Territory Police.

O'Rawe, M. and Moore, L. (1997) *Human Rights on Duty: Principles for Better Policing: International Lessons for Northern Ireland*. Belfast: Committee on the Administration of Justice.

O'Sullivan, D.J. (1999) *The Irish Constabularies, 1882–1922: A Century of Policing in Ireland*. Dingle: Brandon.

Oppenheim, A.N. (1992) *Questionnaire design, interviewing and attitude measurement*. London: Pinter.

Palmer, S.H. (1988) *Police and Protest in England and Ireland, 1780–1850*. Cambridge: Cambridge University Press.

Parsons, T. (1937) *The Structure of Social Action: A Study in Social Theory with Special Reference to a Group of Recent European Writers*. New York: McGraw-Hill.

Phoenix, E. (1994) *Northern Nationalism: Nationalist Politics, Partition and the Catholic Minority in Northern Ireland 1890–1940*. Belfast: Ulster Historical Foundation.

Police Authority for Northern Ireland (1997) *Listening to the Community, Working with the RUC*. Belfast: Police Authority for Northern Ireland.

Police Service of Northern Ireland (2006) *Chief Constable's Annual Report 2005–2006*. Belfast: Police Service of Northern Ireland.

Pollak, A. (ed.) (1993) *A Citizens' Enquiry: The Opsahl Report on Northern Ireland*. Dublin: Lilliput Press.

Pope, D.W. and Weiner, N.L. (eds) (1981) *Modern Policing*. London: Croom Helm.

Prenzler, T. (1997) 'Is there a police culture?'. *Australian Journal of Public Administration*, 56 (4), 47–56.

Punch, M. (1979) *Policing the Inner City: A Study of Amsterdam's Warmoesstraat*. London: Macmillan.

Punch, M. (ed.) (1983) *Control in the Police Organization*. London; Cambridge, MA: MIT Press.

Punch, M. (1985) *Conduct Unbecoming: The Social Construction of Police Deviance and Control*. London: Tavistock.

Radford, K., Betts, J. and Ostermeyer, M. (2006) *Policing, Accountability and the Black and Minority Ethnic Communities in Northern Ireland*. Belfast: Institute for Conflict Research.

Ramsay, R. (2009) *Ringside Seats: An Insider's View of the Crisis in Northern Ireland*. Dublin; Portland, OR: Irish Academic Press.

Regan, D. (1984) 'Police status and accountability, a comparison of the British, French and West German models'. Paper presented to the European Consortium for Political Research, Salzburg, Austria, April 1984. Bergen: Chr. Michelsen Institute.

Reiner, R. (1972) 'The New York police: colonial times to 1901'. *Sociology*, 6, 155–6.

Reiner, R. (1978) *The Blue-Coated Worker: A Sociological Study of Police Unionism*. Cambridge: Cambridge University Press.

Reiner, R. (1985) *The Politics of the Police*. Brighton: Wheatsheaf Books.

Reiner, R. (1991) *Chief Constables: Bobbies, Bosses or Bureaucrats?* Oxford: Oxford University Press.

Reiner, R. (1992) *The Politics of the Police*. 2nd edn, London; New York: Harvester Wheatsheaf.

Reiner, R. (1997) 'Policing and the police'. In: Maguire, M., Morgan, R. and Reiner, R. (eds) *The Oxford Handbook of Criminology*. 2nd edn, Oxford: Oxford University Press.

Renzetti, C.M. and Lee, R.M. (1993) (eds) *Researching Sensitive Topics*. London; Newbury Park, CA: Sage.

Reuss-Ianni, E. (1983) *Two Cultures of Policing: Street Cops and Management Cops*. London; New Brunswick, NJ: Transaction Books.

Robbins, S.P. (1990) *Organization Theory: Structure, Design and Applications*. 3rd edn, London; Englewood Cliffs: Prentice-Hall.

Rokeach, M. (1960) *The Open and Closed Mind: Investigations into the Nature of Belief Systems and Personality Systems*. New York: Basic Books.

Ronalds, C., Chapman, M. and Kitchener, K. (1983) 'Policing Aborigines'. In: Findlay, M., Egger, S.J. and Sutton, J. (eds) *Issues in Criminal Justice Administration*. Sydney; Boston: Allen & Unwin.

Rose, R. (1971) *Governing Without Consensus: An Irish Perspective*. London: Faber & Faber.

Royal Canadian Mounted Police (1996) *Royal Canadian Mounted Police: Performance Report for the Period Ending March 31, 1996*. Ottawa: Government Review and Quality Services.

Royal Ulster Constabulary (1997) *Survey of Religious and Political Harassment and Discrimination in the Royal Ulster Constabulary* (online) (available at: www.serve.com/pfc/survey, accessed 23 April 2002).

Ruane, J. and Todd, J. (1996) *The Dynamics of Conflict in Northern Ireland: Power, Conflict and Emancipation*. Cambridge: Cambridge University Press.

Ryder, C. (2000) *The RUC 1922–2000: A Force Under Fire*. Rev. edn, London: Arrow.

Ryder, C. (2004) *The Fateful Split: Catholics and the Royal Ulster Constabulary*. London: Methuen.

Sackmann, S. (1991) *Cultural Knowledge in Organizations: Exploring the Collective Mind*. Newbury Park, CA: Sage.

Samuelson, L (1993) *Aboriginal Policing Issues: A Comparison of Canada and Australia*. Ottawa: Ministry of Supply and Services.

Samuelson, L. and Strelioff, B. (2001) 'Indigenized urban community policing in Canada and Australia: a comparative study of aboriginal perceptions'. *Police Practice and Research*, 2 (4) 385–419.

Schroeder, M.G. (1987) '*Ethnic minority recruiting*'. Basingstoke: Bramshill Police College (unpublished).

Seagrave, J. (1997) *Introduction to Policing in Canada*. Scarborough, Ont.: Prentice-Hall Canada.

Seagrave, J. (2001) *Introduction to Policing in Canada*. 2nd edn, Scarborough, Ont.: Prentice-Hall Canada.

Sewell, W.H. (1992) 'A theory of structure: duality, agency, and transformation'. *American Journal of Sociology*, 98 (1), 1–29.

Shea, P. (1981) *Voices and the Sound of Drums: An Irish Autobiography*. Belfast: Blackstaff.

Shearing, C.D. and Ericson, R.V. (1991) 'Culture as figurative action'. *British Journal of Sociology*, 42 (4), 481–506.

Sinclair, G. (2000) 'From Hunt to Patten: the 30 year debate on policing reform – continuity or change?' *Constabulary Gazette*, Historical Society supplement, v–viii.

Sinn Féin (1987) *Scenario for Peace*. Dublin: Sinn Féin Party.

Sinn Féin (1992) *Towards a Lasting Peace in Ireland*. Dublin: Sinn Féin Party.

Skolnick, J.H. (1966) *Justice Without Trial: Law Enforcement in Democratic Society*. New York: Wiley.

Skolnick, J.H. and Bayley, D.H. (1986) *The New Blue Line: Police Innovation in Six American Cities*. New York: Free Press.

Skolnick, J.H. and Bayley, D.H. (1988) *Community Policing: Issues and Practices Around the World*. Washington, DC: United States Department of Justice.

Skoog, D.M. (1992) 'Taking control: native self-government and native policing'. *Canadian Police College Journal*, 16 (1).

Smith, D.J. and Gray, J. (1985) *Police and People in London: The PSI Report*. Aldershot: Gower.

Smyth, J. (2002) 'Community policing and the reform of the Royal Ulster Constabulary'. *Policing: An International Journal of Police Strategies and Management*, 25 (1), 110–24.

Southgate, P. (1984) *Racism Awareness Training for the Police: Report of a Pilot Study by the Home Office*. London: Home Office.

Stalker, J. (1988) *Stalker*. London: Harrap.

Stokes, L.D. (1997) 'Minority groups in law enforcement'. In: Dantzker, M.L. (ed.) *Contemporary Policing: Personnel, Issues and Trends*. Oxford: Butterworth-Heinemann.

Stone, V. and Tuffin, R. (2000) *Attitudes of People from Minority Ethnic Communities Towards a Career in the Police Service*. London: Home Office, Policing and Reducing Crime Unit.

Strauss, E. (1951) *Irish Nationalism and British Democracy*. London: Methuen.

Swidler, A. (1986) 'Culture in action: symbols and strategies'. *American Sociological Review*, 51 (2), 273–86.

Taylor, G. (1989) *The Student's Writing Guide: For the Arts and Social Sciences*. Cambridge: Cambridge University Press.

Taylor, P. (1980) *Beating the Terrorists? Interrogation at Omagh, Gough and Castlereagh*. Harmondsworth: Penguin.

Taylor, S. (1995) *A Comparative Study of the Canadian Association of Black Law Enforcers (ABLE) and the Metropolitan Black Police Association*. Wembley: Metropolitan Police.

Tobias, J. (1975) 'The police and people in the United Kingdom'. In: Mosse, G.L. (ed.) *Police Forces in History*. London; Beverly Hills, CA: Sage.

Townshend, C. (1975) *The British Campaign in Ireland, 1919–1921: The Development of Political and Military Policies*. Oxford: Oxford University Press.

Townshend, C. (1983) *Political Violence in Ireland: Government and Resistance Since 1848*. Oxford: Clarendon Press.

Uglow, S. (1988) *Policing Liberal Society*. Oxford: Oxford University Press.

Urban, M.L. (1992) *Big Boys' Rules: The Secret Struggle Against the IRA*. London: Faber & Faber.

Van der Spuy, E. (1990) 'Political discourse and the history of the SAP'. In: Hansson, D. and van Zyl Smit, D. (eds) *Towards Justice? Crime and State Control in South Africa*. Oxford; Cape Town: Oxford University Press.

Van Eyk, M. (1993) 'The principles and problems of policing in a changing South Africa'. *Conference on Policing in a New South Africa*, University of Natal, Pietermaritzburg.

Van Maanen, J. (1981) 'The informant game: selected aspects of ethnographic research in police organizations'. *Urban Life*, 9, 469–94.

Van Maanen, J. (1988) *Tales of the Field: On Writing Ethnography*. London; Chicago, IL: University of Chicago Press.

Waddington, P.A.J. (1991) *The Strong Arm of the Law: Armed and Public Order Policing*. Oxford: Clarendon Press.

Waddington, P.A.J. (1999) *Policing Citizens: Authority and Rights*. London: UCL Press.

Walker, C. (1990) 'Police and community in Northern Ireland'. *Northern Ireland Legal Quarterly*, 40, 105–42.

Walsh, D. (1988) 'The RUC – a law unto themselves?'. In: Tomlinson, M. Varley, T. and McCullagh, C. (eds) *Whose Law and Order? Aspects of Crime and Social Control in Irish Society*. Belfast: Sociological Association of Ireland.

Weitzer, R. (1985) 'Policing a divided society: obstacles to normalisation in Northern Ireland'. *Social Problems*, 33 (1), 41–55.

Weitzer, R. (1986) 'Accountability and complaints against the police in Northern Ireland'. *Police Studies*, 9 (2), 99–109.

Weitzer, R. (1987) 'Contested order: the struggle over British security policy in Northern Ireland'. *Comparative Politics*, 19 (3), 281–98.

Weitzer, R. (1995) *Policing Under Fire: Ethnic Conflict and Police-Community Relations in Northern Ireland*. Albany, NY: State University of New York Press.

Welford, A.T., Argyle, M., Glass, O. and Morris, J.W. (eds) (1962) *Statistical Surveys*. London: Routledge.

Westley, W.A. (1970) *Violence and the Police: A Sociological Study of Law, Custom, and Morality*. Cambridge, MA: MIT Press.

Whyte, J.H. (1981) *Catholics in Western Democracies: A Study in Political Behaviour*. London: Gill & Macmillan.

Whyte, J.H. (1990) *Interpreting Northern Ireland*. Oxford: Clarendon Press.

Wiggins, W.T. (1998) 'The RUC – culture and diversity: a study of the developing organisational culture within a group of police recruits'. Unpublished M.Phil. thesis, Queen's University of Belfast.

Wilson, D., Holdaway, S. and Spencer, C. (1984) 'Black police in the UK'. *Policing*, 1 (1), 20–30.

Working Party for Northern Ireland (1976) *The Handling of Complaints Against the Police: Report of the Working Party for Northern Ireland* (the Black Committee). Belfast: HMSO.

Zelditch, M. (1962) 'Some methodological problems of field studies'. *American Journal of Sociology*, 67 (5), 566–76.

Lightning Source UK Ltd.
Milton Keynes UK
UKOW030656240313

208075UK00002B/32/P